Stealing Horses to Great Applause

The Origins of the First World War Reconsidered

Paul W. Schroeder

VERSO

London • New York

First published by Verso 2025
Collection © Paul W. Schroeder 2025
Introduction © Perry Anderson 2025

1 3 5 7 9 10 8 6 4 2

Verso
UK: 6 Meard Street, London W1F 0EG
US: 207 East 32nd Street, New York, NY 10016
versobooks.com

Verso is the imprint of New Left Books

ISBN-13: 978-1-80429-579-3
ISBN-13: 978-1-80429-580-9 (UK EBK)
ISBN-13: 978-1-80429-581-6 (US EBK)

British Library Cataloguing in Publication Data
A catalogue record for this book is available from the British Library

Library of Congress Cataloging-in-Publication Data

Names: Schroeder, Paul W., author.
Title: Stealing horses to great applause : the origins of the First World
War reconsidered / Paul W. Schroeder.
Other titles: Origins of the First World War reconsidered
Description: London ; New York : Verso, 2024. | Includes bibliographical
references and index.
Identifiers: LCCN 2024024409 (print) | LCCN 2024024410 (ebook) | ISBN
9781804295793 (hardback) | ISBN 9781804295816 (ebook)
Subjects: LCSH: World War, 1914-1918—Causes. | World War,
1914-1918—Diplomatic history.
Classification: LCC D511 .S293 2024 (print) | LCC D511 (ebook) | DDC
940.3/2—dc23/eng/20240603
LC record available at https://lccn.loc.gov/2024024409
LC ebook record available at https://lccn.loc.gov/2024024410

Typeset in Sabon by Biblichor Ltd, Scotland
Printed and bound by CPI Group (UK) Ltd, Croydon CR0 4YY

Contents

Introduction

Perry Anderson

Paul Schroeder (1927–2020) was the most powerful and original, though far from the best-known, American historian of his generation. Once described, with justice, as "probably the foremost expert on the history of international politics in the world," he had an unusual career. His master's thesis, awarded the American Historical Association's annual Beveridge Prize for the best book on American history, was published as *The Axis Alliance and Japanese-American Relations, 1941* by Cornell when he was thirty-one. Within another four years came *Metternich's Diplomacy at Its Zenith, 1820–1823*, and a decade later *Austria, Great Britain, and the Crimean War* (1972). Commissioned by Oxford University Press as a prequel to A. J. P. Taylor's *The Struggle for Mastery in Europe: 1848–1918*, the work he produced in 1994, *The Transformation of European Politics, 1763–1848*—centered on the Napoleonic wars and the peace of Vienna that followed them—was widely acknowledged as a masterpiece, establishing his reputation as a great scholar for the rest of his life. Completed when he was sixty-five, it was his last book, but not by a long way his last publication, which thereafter took the form of a prodigious series of essays—totaling about eighty in all—in historical journals of some five countries, covering an extensive range of subjects.

Outstanding in this later flow of texts was his writing on the First World War, brought together for the first time in this volume. Since the essential object of *The Transformation of European Politics* was the "Vienna system," a Concert of Powers designed to assure the continent peace and stability of a kind it had never known before, the catastrophic breakdown of peace in Europe in 1914 a century later formed a logical field of investigation to follow it. Schroeder's concern with the First World War, however, predated *Transformation* by two decades. His first essay on it, "World War I as Galloping Gertie," appeared in 1972—the same year in which his book on the Crimean War, where the Vienna system began to break apart, was published. An article on Romania's switch from the Central Powers toward the Entente in 1913–14 soon followed. So it looks as if he may have contemplated a book on the Great War at that time, before being diverted to write what became his magnum opus at the end of the nineties. Certainly he had already developed key arguments he would make about the First World War long before he published *Transformation*—perspectives he amplified and deepened from 2000 onward in the texts that comprise the bulk of this book. A recurrent feature of these, unusual in historical essays, is resort to dialogic interjection in the course of an exposition: Schroeder setting out objections—the term is frequent—to his own arguments, before proceeding to reply to them.

What sets Schroeder's writing on the First World War apart from any other account of it are three characteristics of all his work, which define his originality as a historian. The first is its longitudinal depth, extending from his own time as far back as the sixteenth century: readers of the companion volume to this collection, covering his writing on the twenty-first century and its predecessor, will find comparisons to their problems drawn with a confidence and ease all his own from the times of the Reformation, the Thirty Years War, the age of Louis XIV, the French Revolution, or the ascendancy of Bismarck.[1] The second is its latitudinal width. He was a Europeanist, but his range of reference was far from confined to the continent on which he was a specialist, his analysis of the origins of the First World War extending to Asia, Africa, and the Americas with the same fluency and precision he brought to its sources in Europe. Third, and in the eyes of fellow historians, perhaps most striking, was Schroeder's theoretical bent—a gift for both conceptual complexity and clarity rare among them, which gave him an affinity and an audience among political scientists concerned with international relations, perhaps

---

1   Paul W. Schroeder, *America's Fatal Leap, 1991–2016* (London and New York, 2025).

unique in his cohort. As another scholar in his own field—with a touch of deprecation?—once put it: his "interest in theoretical approaches and perspectives turned him into an exotic bird amongst his historical colleagues who tend, for the most part, to sport less colourful conceptual plumage."[2] Engagement with the discipline of international relations did not, however, make him any kind of foot soldier in it. He was a firm critic of the neo-realism propounded by Kenneth Waltz then dominant in America, feeling much closer to the "English school" of international relations whose leading thinkers—Herbert Butterfield, Martin Wight, Adam Watson—were all, like the philosopher Michael Oakeshott who influenced him, trained in history. The sharpness of his theoretical mind illuminated but never affected his empirical command of the past, whose accuracy of fact and detail was unfaltering. What it yielded was rather the strain of iconoclasm that marked all Schroeder's writing. He was not much given to any conventional wisdom.

From the time of his book on the Crimean War onward, the premise of Schroeder's approach to international relations was the causal primacy of the system they comprised over the units of which they were composed. To understand the history of European politics, the first essential was to grasp the general pattern of the interrelations among the major powers of the continent, rather than to focus attention on the particular character of its different states, or the bilateral or other dealings between them. The eighteenth century had seen the passing of religious wars in Europe, but no general peace had ensued. Power-political wars remained a normal condition of international life, military competition between states for territory or wealth a regular feature of the time, culminating in the Seven Years War and the Partitions of Poland. The French Revolution, a unit-level event, marked no significant change in the pattern, other than intensifying it with the arrival of the *levée en masse*, and escalating its destructiveness with Napoleon's conquests. In and through the emperor's

---

2   T. G. Otte, "Paul W. Schroeder and the Nineteenth-Century International System, or Viewing the World from the Windows of the Ballhausplatz," in *H-Diplo/ISSF Forum* 28 (2021) on "The Importance of Paul Schroeder's Scholarship to the Fields of International Relations and Diplomatic History," 31.

eventual defeat, however, a novel system was created at the Congress of Vienna, founded on an agreement between the victor states of Russia, Austria, Prussia, and Britain that the ruinous conflicts of the recent past be banished henceforth from Europe by common acceptance of rules for preserving the peace and stability of the continent and institutional coordination between them—a union of powers that France, its monarchy restored, was invited to join. This was the change that produced the Concert of Europe, regularly invoked in subsequent years as the guarantor of continuing peace and control of sedition (when it arose) across the continent. Coordination by the Pentarchy spelt commonality, but not parity: hegemony within it was shared by Russia and England, Europe's leading powers respectively on land and sea. Such was the baseline of Schroeder's understanding of the politics of the old world in the nineteenth century. It was a starting point that set him apart from all other historians of the First World War.

Schroeder's essay on its origins, "World War I as Galloping Gertie," was certainly noticed when it appeared in America, featuring in not a few bibliographies of writings of the conflict thereafter, without being ever seriously discussed. Written some thirty years later, his subsequent three essays were largely ignored. One of the reasons for this, no doubt, was that each was written for a collection edited by others, two of which were not—as his essays were—specifically about the Great War at all, rather dealing with more general topics.[3] In the most considerable current account of the historiography of the conflict, by Annika Mombauer, 300 pages in length and listing close to 1,000 contributions to it, Schroeder receives a single sentence.[4] His trio of later texts on the First World War clustered closely enough chronologically

---

3   "Embedded Counterfactuals" was commissioned by Geoffrey Parker for a volume entitled *Unmaking the West*, whose publisher rejected it, and then decanted into *Systems, Stability and Statecraft*, a collection of Schroeder's own essays edited by David Wetzel, Robert Jervis, and Jack Levy; "International Politics, Peace and War" was commissioned by Tim Blanning for the collection *The Nineteenth Century*; "Stealing Horses to Great Applause" by Holger Afflerbach and David Stevenson for their collection *An Improbable War?* For particulars, see "Sources," p. 356 of this volume.

4   Annika Mombauer, *The Causes of the First World War: The Long Blame Game* (London and New York, 2024), 280–1.

to resist any straightforward reconstruction of their sequence, since there might be a substantial gap between composition and publication. The first was certainly "International Politics," which must have been written by 1998 or so; "Counterfactuals," the second, was at any rate drafted by 2000; the third, "Stealing Horses," by 2004, since it was delivered as a paper in Atlanta that year. Of these, "International Politics" is both the longest and the least known, and the only text by Schroeder to cover the whole period from 1815 to 1914, including especially the era of Bismarck and what followed it, in a continuous narrative. It is with its account of these years that his analysis of the international politics of post-*Transformation* Europe begins.

However apparently dramatic, the Revolutions of 1848 did not in Schroeder's view substantially affect the Vienna settlement. Unlike the Revolution of 1789 they were soon snuffed out and provoked no interstate wars, rather coordination among the major powers once again to suppress popular unrest. But not long afterward the Pentarchy did split, as the architects of Vienna had held it never should, over which of the Great Powers of Europe was to gain predominance in the fate of the Ottoman Empire, visibly in decline and object of rivalry between them. In 1854, the war that pitted France and England, nominally in defense of Turkey, against Russia in Crimea—Austria formally neutral but effectively ensuring victory of the Western powers by pinning down Tsarist forces in Galicia—put an end to the peace of Vienna. There followed fifteen years in which its territorial settlement was then undone in three swift wars: Austria evicted from most of Italy by France and Piedmont, then from Germany by Prussia, and France from Alsace-Lorraine by Prussia with the foundation of Imperial Germany. The political upshot that followed this burial of the arrangements of Vienna had little in common with them. Russia and England, neither with any achievement to vaunt in their fight by the Black Sea and now estranged, were no longer in a position to exercise the leadership of Europe they had once enjoyed. That role now fell to Germany in the person of its chancellor, in temperament and outlook the antithesis of the statesmen of 1815.

Untouched by any of the sentiments that had moved them save one, Bismarck had no qualms about war or time for pieties about Europe. But as a ruthless practitioner of a coolly conservative

Realpolitik, he was aware of the danger to the Germany he had united of its central location in the continent, the fear it was bound to arise in its neighbors, and the risk of quarrels between them posing threats to the principles of monarchy for which they all stood. So he sought to consolidate rather than expand what he had achieved, by distraction or mediation of the powers surrounding the Second Reich—encouraging France to find compensation for its losses at home in colonial adventures abroad; binding Austria and Russia to Germany in pacts of imperial solidarity and divisions of spheres of influence; and taking care not to antagonize England where it mattered, as in Egypt. With a diplomatic skill that every other power came to respect, he created an order orchestrated by Germany offering in its own fashion a simulacrum of the Vienna system, and operating for a time as a substitute for it—even briefly recalling the Concert of Europe with the summoning of a Congress in Berlin in 1878 to resolve disputes between Russia and Austria (backed by Britain) over their respective ambitions in the Balkans, which ended with payoffs for all at the expensive of Turkey. A few years later another, less high-level conclave met in Berlin to apportion various slices of Africa to assorted European predators. Nevertheless, it was becoming increasingly difficult to hold Russia and Austria together, and when Bismarck was dismissed by Wilhelm II soon after he acceded to the throne, Germany opted for Austria, leading Russia to sign a military alliance with France. The combination Bismarck had always dreaded, exposing Germany to an attack on two fronts, east and west, was now a reality. In its turn, the successor to the Vienna system was over too. Along with their counterparts in every other major power, German diplomats would still on occasion invoke the Concert of Europe, a notion and term Bismarck disdained, while its meaning shrank yet further.

Within another decade, a mutation much more radical than the precarious equilibrium Bismarck had achieved overtook what remained of the Vienna system—no longer a modification but the negation of it. This was the rise of what Germans called *Weltpolitik* but was not their invention. It was captured by Schroeder with a lucidity and trenchancy no other historian has matched. Imperialism as such was no novelty for Europe, which had practiced it on a world scale since the end of the fifteenth century, unleashing intercontinental wars between its leading states in the eighteenth century. Under Vienna rules, however, these had been put into abeyance: colonial expansion continued, but the violence it involved was insulated from Europe—inflicted on indigenous peoples overseas without provoking conflicts between the aggressors at home. So long as the order of Vienna held good, eighteenth-century-style imperialism appeared to be—as Schroeder put it—"in remission." But with the eclipse of the Vienna system, the geopolitical partition of violence it secured gradually eroded. What emerged instead were two games played by the great powers: one, still mostly peaceful and regulated by the ideal of a Concert of Europe, in which conflicts between its members respected mutual restraints in the interest of a common good; the other, outside Europe, where conflicts were liable to go for broke in something closer to a zero-sum spirit. In the literature about it, the general name under which the second would come to pass is the New Imperialism. What this amounted to, Schroeder maintained, was the belief in every significant industrial power of the time that the future belonged to those states that controlled a major expanse of the planet and its resources beyond the confines of Europe, and only to those. Britain, Russia, and America already possessed territory on the kind of scale at which others should aim. Yet even these pioneers felt in need of more, as their actions showed. Over time, the logic of the second game prevailed over the first, as the drive for absolute gains overseas infected the pursuit of relative advantage between metropoles at home, gradually inflaming and ultimately convulsing it.

The turning point in this development, Schroeder argued, came in 1898. In that year, Britain conquered the Sudan and humiliated France over Fashoda; Germany challenged Britain with its Naval Bill; France sought understandings with Russia and Italy for partition of Austria-Hungary in the event of its collapse; the US attacked Spain in the Caribbean and the Pacific, seizing Cuba and the Philippines from it. There followed in the short order the Anglo-Boer War, the Eight-Power Expedition to crush the Boxer Rebellion in China, and the Russo-Japanese War over Manchuria— all, in Schroeder's words, illustrations of "how the ascendant ethos of imperialism defeated the declining ethos of European balance and Concert."[5] The consequences were soon patent in Europe itself: two crises over Morocco, each threatening war by France and England on Germany; Italy's seizure of Ottoman possessions in Libya and the Dodecanese; Balkan war against Turkey, followed by a second among the Balkan states themselves; Serbarmed assassination of the Habsburg heir in Bosnia; Austrian ultimatum to Serbia; detonation of the First World War.

The new imperialist game of *Weltpolitik* was played by all the Great Powers, but not symmetrically. It was a system, Schroeder pointed out, run by the Entente. Britain had long enjoyed the largest colonial empire in the world, to which it was now adding plentiful further helpings in Africa; Russia commanded a contiguous expanse of territory, from Poland to the Caucasus, Central Asia to Kamchatka, vaster than any other state on the planet. France possessed an empire stretching from the Americas to Africa, Indochina, and Oceania. They called the shots in the competition for spatial scale. The Central Powers were not in the same league. In Europe itself, Germany was a formidable power by reason of its industrial dynamism, scientific-technological advance, and military prowess. But it lacked any colonial tradition, and while bent on acquiring an overseas empire of its own, knew it was a latecomer outclassed by rivals who had begun much earlier. That was why, Schroeder argued against historical legend, its overall international conduct tended on the whole to be more moderate than the record of its opponents in the Entente. It was not so much that it was "encircled" by these older powers, as German self-pity maintained; rather Britain, France, and Russia effectively "circled it out" of the real prizes of the imperialist game. Austria-Hungary lacked any pretensions beyond the Balkans. Yet it was these two powers, he readily conceded, who were responsible for opening hostilities in 1914, and so in common opinion held ever since culpable of unleashing the catastrophe of the First World War on Europe.

Who started the war and what caused the war were, however, not the same. If Germany and Austria-Hungary were the Great Powers that fired the first shots—Austrian merely symbolic, weeks before actually attacking Serbia; German lethal against Belgium

---

5   See "International Politics," pp. 71–5, and "Stealing Horses," p. 167.

and Russia—they each believed they were acting defensively, as did the foes against whom they fought. In their case, this was not a pure illusion, for there was another side to their culpability in starting the war, the vulnerability which led them to do so. There, a twofold difference separated them from their opponents. Germany was surrounded on both sides by enemies, Russia to the east and France to the west; likewise Austria, facing Serbia to the south and Russia to the north—soon Italy to the west too. Among the combatants of 1914, their geopolitical exposure was unique: none of the Entente powers faced a similar situation. To this was added ethnic vulnerability: both empires contained allogenous populations adjoining co-nationals across the border (as did Russia, if with a nominal Kingdom of Poland within its empire, descending from the Congress of Vienna). For Schroeder these were ancillary specificities of the Central Powers, each bearing on their entry into the war but not on the causes for the war itself, which lay in the nature of the system in which all the powers were participants, and for which in the end all were punished, as in a Greek or Shakespearean tragedy. "To go beyond that conclusion, to play the blame game further by apportioning blame to particular actors, is useless, distracting, and deceptive, because the game itself was to blame."[6]

Was the First World War then inevitable? Schroeder's answer needs careful parsing. No, he declared at the outset of the third major essay in this collection; he was not going to take a "determinist" stand on the origins of the war, in which contingency played a large role. Objectively, "the war remained avoidable up to its very outbreak." Still, he went on, there were "other grounds for considering it unavoidable." To understand these, counterfactual reasoning was required—not arbitrary "what if?" speculations of what might have happened resting on idle fancy or whimsical ideas with no connection to historical realities, but "embedded" alternatives to what did happen: that is, either realistically available to actors at the time, or rationally reconstructible by historians after the event, in keeping with empirical possibilities at the time. Counterfactuals of that kind were not just a common practice of daily life but as a scholarly exercise on the past could help to

---

6   "Stealing Horses," p. 162.

explain what did happen by showing what might have happened but did not.[7] In the case of the First World War, a pregnant example was ready to hand, on which Schroeder dwelt in two successive texts.

In 1908 an agreement was reached by the foreign ministers of Russia and Austria-Hungary, Izvolsky and Aehrenthal, for a deal whereby Russia would approve the annexation of Bosnia, administered for forty years by Vienna, in exchange for Austrian approval of Russian rights of passage, long sought by St. Petersburg, through the Straits linking the Black Sea to the Mediterranean controlled by the Ottoman empire. Izvolsky, who concealed the agreement from his government, intended to add further conditions to it in due course. But before he had squared his colleagues or the press at home, Aehrenthal announced the deal, whereupon to save face Izvolsky repudiated it. Diplomatic uproar followed: France and Britain rejected any change to the status quo in the Straits, Russia refused to endorse the annexation of Bosnia, Germany eventually compelled Russia with a tacit threat of force to accept Habsburg incorporation of the province, leaving Russia humiliated and its regime and public opinion furious for revenge. The Bosnian crisis would later come to be regarded as a critical way station of Europe to the Great War.

Schroeder did not contest that judgment of its upshot, but the view he took of the agreement that led to it differed diametrically from standard accounts of its origins as a patent demonstration of Austrian aggression violating the legacy of the Congress of Berlin, enforced at German gunpoint. On the contrary, he maintained, though mooted by Russia, it was driven by Aehrenthal's desire for a durable Austro-Russian understanding in the Balkans as the stepping stone to a reconciliation of the three great Eastern monarchies in a renewed pact for peace between them—a return to the *Dreikaiserbund* of the 1870s. As such, it was in his view the last serious attempt to revive the spirit of the Vienna system and the Concert of Europe to which it had given birth, whose wreckage, for which Aehrenthal did not bear the responsibility, produced the opposite of its intention. Schroeder himself held no particular

---

7   For Schroeder's extended theoretical argument around these issues, see "Embedded Counterfactuals," pp. 91–7.

candle for Austria; at most he could be accounted an example of the "negative Austrophilia" that viewed the Habsburg polity as, whatever its obvious defects, the power with traditionally the least dangerous propensity to upset a precarious peace in Central Europe. The adage that gave its title to the essay in which he first dealt with the Bosnian crisis, now lent this book, spelt out what befell it. "A Spanish proverb says: 'Some men steal horses to great applause, while others are hanged for looking over the fence'"— which could be taken as an accurate summary of the differential effects, "not incidental, accidental, or unintended, but regular, structural, and intentional," of the imperialist game as it was practiced by 1914. Example? "In 1904–10 Japan stole horses to great applause. Austria-Hungary was hanged despite attempting the help the owner save his horses and repair his fence. It is hard to conceive a better illustration of a perverse international incentives structure."[8]

Yet what Schroeder thought Austria had attempted in the Balkans in 1908–9 contained another lesson too. It showed *en creux* what an embedded counterfactual taught about the First World War. Objectively, there existed a well-tried repertoire of measures and devices for dealing with conflicts between the Great Powers that risked becoming explosive, to ensure they did not explode. That was just the kind of conservative diplomacy—sensible compromise, practical coordination, flexible grouping—that Aehrenthal sought to pursue. Its availability spoke against the notion that war was inevitable in 1914. Subjectively, however, it was precluded by the political culture of *Weltpolitik* that all the

---

8   "Stealing Horses," pp. 159–60, 174. There is some mystery as to where and how Schroeder acquired his Spanish proverb. It is not to be found in the *Biblioteca virtual Miguel de Cervantes*. According to the *Oxford Dictionary of Proverbs*, "People may take different degrees of liberty depending on our opinion of them"; English versions of it date back to the sixteenth century, the latest employed by Rebecca West. These are all, however, milder than the saying he attributes to Spaniards, taking the form: "One man may better steal a horse than another look over the hedge" ("fence", "gate"). Might some Spaniard whom Schroeder knew have referred to the proverb conversationally, escalating it to acclamation and gallows for dramatic effect and claiming it was Castilian folk wisdom? Or would that be stereotypical Anglo projection about Spanish sensibility? He was a scrupulous scholar, so more probably there was some peninsular authority behind his attribution.

leading actors shared by then, the mentality of—when it came to a crunch—absolute gains and losses. Nothing, Schroeder argued, was so revealing of that outlook as the widespread attitude—of satisfied anticipation or resigned indifference—in the chanceller-ies of Europe to the prospect of Austria-Hungary being deleted, by breakup or collapse or takeover, from the ranks of the Great Powers. In an earlier time, that would have been unthinkable: among the cardinal precepts of the Concert of Europe, as origi-nally conceived, was the preservation of all its members. Yet in an "astonishing departure from tradition," by the time of the Belle Epoque what serious thought was ever given among its statesmen to the consequences of the disappearance of one of the constitu-ent Powers of the continent?[9] For Schroeder, when that became possible a hyperbolic war was predictable.

The present book is divided into four sections. Part I comprises the essays published by Schroeder dealing directly with the gen-eral question of how and why the First World War broke out, in chronological order of their publication. After his *incipit* of 1972, itself a response to an American colleague and more widely to conventional opinion about the conflict then and later, there fol-low three further essays that appeared in the first decade of this century, respectively in 2000, 2004, and 2007. Part II proceeds to a case study, the move—typically overlooked—of Romania away from the Central Powers toward the Entente, critical for Austria's isolation in the Balkans on the eve of the war; and then the one text that Schroeder ever wrote setting out his assessment of the respective responsibilities of the principal belligerents of 1914–15 for the immediate outbreak (as opposed to ultimate origin) of the First World War. Part III presents the two key reviews Schroeder wrote of books by other historians, each of them British—Niall Ferguson and A. J. P. Taylor—on the war and what led up to it. Part IV presents Schroeder's final unpublished writing on the conflict, on internal evidence completed in 2015, the longest text in this volume. In form it lies somewhere between a book proposal and an extended synopsis of the work he hoped to write on the war—a hybrid with which, as it happens, he had experimented

---

9   "Embedded Counterfactuals," p. 141.

before in a dry run for *The Transformation of European Politics*. Approaching ninety when he finished this, he did not live to realize the book he intended. A year before he died in 2020, he sent me the text as bearing on the interviews I planned with him: to my knowledge, the only copy that survives. Elsewhere I have explained the anomaly that I was a recipient of it.[10]

The scope of the book Schroeder envisaged was large. It would be a reinterpretation of two centuries of the European past, from 1689 to 1919, constructing a bridge between his understanding of the origins and legacy of the Congress of Vienna and his ideas about the coming and consequences of the First World War. Entitled "World War I and the Vienna System," a leading theme supplies the ironic reversal of its subtitle, "The Last Eighteenth-Century War and the First Modern Peace"—in other words, from 1815 to 1914: not progress but regression.

By the time the text was written, the historiography of the Great War had undergone a significant change since the years (1972–2007) of his four published texts on it. The intellectual consensus against which those were directed had dissolved under the impact of a series of critical studies looking at the way Russia, France, and England, as well as Germany and Austria-Hungary, had entered the war. Of these, the most comprehensive and renowned is Christopher Clark's *The Sleepwalkers* (2012), which in Schroeder's view had finally provided the "convincing alternative narrative" needed to overthrow what had hitherto been the established wisdom about the war. Not that he thought—nor would have Clark—that *The Sleepwalkers* was the last word on the war; more remained to be said. His own text, with its quite distinct framing and bearing, is sufficient indication of that.

"World War I and the Vienna System: The Last Eighteenth-Century War and the First Modern Peace" is also distinct in another way from any other historical enterprise in Schroeder's oeuvre. For as he explains at the outset, it was designed as a work backed with enough evidence to meet the standards of scholars in the field, but at the same time capable of appealing to a wider audience of lay readers. "My main reason and motive for trying

---

10   *Disputing Disaster: A Sextet on the Great War* (London and New York, 2024), 346–50.

to write the book at this late stage in my life is not the usual academic one. It derives instead from a conviction that certain things on this subject need saying, above all to a wider public and especially in America."[11] These things were of contemporary relevance. Concluding his account of the changes in the international system across two centuries, he reiterated its purpose still more explicitly and emphatically. "Even if my whole argument more or less holds up, why should anyone today care?" His answer was that he sought to show that history can be a teacher of life. "If it does not say something worth thinking about in the current world situation, it is not worth doing."[12]

In a drastically oversimplified and overstated form, the argument of his book could be rendered this way. "If you want to understand the politics that ultimately helps make wars occur and international systems break down, study World War I. If you want to understand better how a durable system of general relative peace and order can emerge, survive, and solve major problems for a considerable time, examine the Vienna System."[13] The lessons to be learnt from contrast between the two had pointed topical bearing. For in view of "the exceptionalism so deeply rooted in America's history, institutions, and popular culture, especially in its current debased and dangerous form, and the extraordinary provincialism, self-preoccupation, and superficiality this entails in world affairs," Americans in particular needed to learn them.[14]

No one reading the companion volume to this, Schroeder's writing on the country's foreign policy after the Cold War, could fail to see the direction and force of the forewarning he believed historical experience should have given the US about its conduct toward Russia and in the Middle East, in each case tragically ignored. On that note Schroeder ended what can be taken as his historiographic and political testament.

---

11   "World War and the Vienna System," p. 266.
12   Ibid., p. 350.
13   Ibid., p. 264.
14   Ibid., p. 355.

PART I

World War I as Galloping Gertie:
A Reply to Joachim Remak

In a recent article, Joachim Remak argues that modern research on the origins of the First World War, led by Fritz Fischer and his students, has distorted our view while expanding our knowledge. The search for more profound causes of the war has tended, in Remak's phrase, to make us miss the forest for the roots. World War I was really the Third Balkan War. It arose from the last of a long series of local Austro-Serbian quarrels, none of which had led to war before; it involved a series of political maneuvers and gambles typical of the great-power politics of that time, maneuvers which previously had not issued in general conflict. Only the particular events of 1914 caused this particular quarrel and this diplomatic gamble to end in world war.[1]

There is much truth in this familiar view, and considerable point to Remak's criticism of an overly determinist interpretation of 1914. Yet his version appears to me as unsatisfactory as those he criticizes. This essay, without claiming to exhaust the literature or to say anything brand new,[2] will suggest another way to look at the origins of the war, and propose a view different from Remak's, Fischer's,[3] Arno Mayer's,[4] and others now current.

---

1   Joachim Remak, "1914—The Third Balkan War: Origins Reconsidered," *Journal of Modern History* 43 (September 1971): 353–66.
2   Nor will I attempt to "prove" my case with elaborate footnotes. The references will mainly serve to illustrate the kind of sources and literature I have used.
3   Fritz Fischer, *Griff nach der Weltmacht* (Düsseldorf, 1961), translated as *Germany's Aims in the First World War* (New York, 1967); "Weltpolitik, Weltmachstreben und deutsche Kriegsziele," *Historische Zeitschrift* 199 (1964): 265–346; and *Krieg der Illusionen* (Düsseldorf, 1969). The main rival work is Gerhard Ritter, *Staatskunst und Kriegshandwerk*, 4 vols. (Munich, 1954–68), now being translated as *The Sword and the Scepter* (Coral Gables, FL, 1969–). A good survey of the controversy is in Wolfgang J. Mommsen, "The Debate on German War Aims," *Journal of Contemporary History* 1 (July 1966): 47–74; for citations of the literature, see James J. Sheehan, "Germany, 1890–1918: A Survey of Recent Research," *Central European History* 1 (December 1968): 345–72.
4   Arno J. Mayer, "Domestic Causes of the First World War," in Leonard Krieger and Fritz Stern, eds., *The Responsibility of Power* (Garden City, NY,

To start with Fischer: most of what he says about Germany and her bid for world power is true. Many of his formulations and emphases are open to challenge. He is too hard on Bethmann Hollweg and misinterprets the motives of his crucial decision in 1914.[5] He often underestimates the importance and persistence of concerns other than *Weltpolitik* in German policy, and he tends to blur the difference between Germany's prewar and wartime goals in emphasizing their continuity. But these points do not destroy his main argument. From 1890 on, Germany did pursue world power. This bid arose from deep roots within Germany's economic, political, and social structures. Once the war broke out, world power became Germany's essential goal. Fischer and his students have made the old apologias for German policy impossible.

The difficulty arises in accepting the notion, implicit in all of Fischer's work and explicitly drawn by many historians as the chief lesson of it, that Germany's bid for world power was the *causa causans*, the central driving force behind the war. Fischer never demonstrates this convincingly. His case is far more informative, compelling, and reliable on Germany's policy and national character than on the origins of the war. He may be able to tell us what Germany was like without worrying much about the policies of other powers (although even here the comparative dimension is lacking). But he cannot assume, as he constantly does, that German policy was decisive for other powers without a great deal more investigation than he has done. Moreover, Fischer's own principle of *der Primat der Innenpolitik* should have led him to assume that other powers would, like Germany, act mainly from their own indigenous drives, rather than mainly react to what Germany did, as he depicts them doing.

More important, the whole attempt to find a *causa causans* behind the multiplicity of contributing factors is misconceived. It

---

1967), 286–300; Arno J. Mayer, "Internal Causes and Purposes of War in Europe, 1870–1956: A Research Assignment," *Journal of Modern History* 41 (September 1969): 291–303.

5   Konrad Jarausch, "The Illusion of Limited War: Chancellor Bethmann Hollweg's Calculated Risk, July 1914," *Central European History* 2 (March 1969): 48–76; Fritz Stern, "Bethmann Hollweg and the War: The Limits of Responsibility," in Krieger and Stern, *The Responsibility of Power*, 252–85.

is like looking for *the* driving force behind the French or Russian Revolutions, or the Reformation, or the American Civil War. Immediately, one encounters a plethora of "causes" far more than sufficient to account for the phenomenon one wishes to explain, clearly connected with it, and yet not "sufficient" in the sense that any set of them logically implies what occurred. The fact that so many plausible explanations for the outbreak of the war have been advanced over the years indicates on the one hand that it was massively overdetermined, and on the other that no effort to analyze the causal factors involved can ever fully succeed. When on top of earlier valid arguments Fischer and his disciples insist that Germany's bid for world power was really behind it all, when Marxist historians insist that the war was the inevitable outcome of monopolistic capitalist imperialism, when Arno Mayer proposes domestic political and social unrest and the dynamics of counterrevolution as decisive, and when Peter Loewenberg argues in reply that this role belongs to the fundamental drives revealed by psychodynamic theory, one begins to suspect that all these approaches, however much valuable information and insight they may provide, cannot deliver what they promise.[6] Not only is an attempt to reduce or subordinate the various contributing factors to some fundamental cause methodologically very dubious, but also, even if it worked—even if one managed to fit all the contributing factors into a scheme of causal priority through factor analysis—this would still not give the *causa causans*.[7] For in the breakdown of a system of relations such as occurred in 1914 as a result of various intertwined and interacting forces, the system itself enters into the work of destruction. In the process wittily described by Hexter as "Galloping Gertie," the very devices built into a system to keep it stable and operative under stress, subjected to intolerable pressures, generate forces of their own which cause the system to destroy itself.[8]

---

6 "Arno Mayer's 'Internal Causes and Purposes of War in Europe, 1870–1956'—an Inadequate Model of Human Behavior, National Conflict, and Historical Change," *Journal of Modern History* 42 (December 1970): 628–36.

7 See J. H. Hexter, *The History Primer* (New York, 1970), chap. 5; Gordon Leff, *History and Social Theory* (Garden City, NY, 1971), 48–90.

8 Hexter, *The History Primer*, 118–35. "Galloping Gertie" was the popular name for the Tacoma Narrows Bridge in Washington, which collapsed in 1940

World War I seems to me clearly a case of "Galloping Gertie." Witness how statesmen and military leaders everywhere in 1914, especially in the Central Powers, felt themselves to be in the grip of uncontrollable forces. They sensed that their calculations were all futile and that what their actions would finally produce lay beyond all calculation. Remak, appreciating this fact and rejecting the search for a *causa causans*, rightly insists that the answer must lie in the narrative and in analysis within it. But his particular answer to the question, Why World War I? is similarly misleading. True, it required certain contingent events to start a war in 1914; but this does not mean the whole development was purely contingent, with nothing inevitable about it. Europe's frequent escapes from crises before 1914 do not indicate the possibility that she could have continued to avoid war indefinitely; they rather indicate a general systemic crisis, an approaching breakdown. Remak's view of July 1914 as the one gamble that did not succeed overlooks the fact that those who gambled in Germany and Austria did not expect to succeed in avoiding general war.

Thus the search for the fundamental cause of World War I is futile, while the argument that the war simply happened is unhelpful. Is there no exit from the cul-de-sac? A different question may help: not Why World War I? but Why not? War was still the *ultima ratio regum*. World War I was a normal development in international relations; events had been building toward it for a long time. There is no need to explain it as a deviation from the norm. In this sense, the question Why not? answers the question Why?

More important, it points to what is unexpected about the war and needs explanation: its long postponement. Why not until 1914? This question clearly needs answering in regard to Austria. Historians continue to exercise themselves over why the Austrian Monarchy risked its own destruction by insisting on punishing Serbia. The favorite (and very unsatisfactory) answer is that this was the kind of futile, absurd action to be expected from so decrepit an empire with so inept a ruling class. In fact, the

---

when winds induced pressures on supporting members sufficient in turn to cause the supports to generate destructive forces within the bridge.

problem is nonexistent. Preventive wars, even risky preventive wars, are not extreme anomalies in politics, the sign of the bankruptcy of policy. They are a normal, even common, tool of statecraft, right down to our own day. British history, for example, is full of them; the British Empire was founded and sustained in great part by a series of preventive and preemptive wars and conquests. As for the particular decision of June 1914, the evidence is plain that Berchtold, although often wavering, resisted the idea of a punitive war on Serbia until the assassination. With the death of Francis Ferdinand, leader of the peace party, Berchtold simultaneously ran out of alternatives, arguments, and support for any other policy, and gave in.[9] The real problem is to explain why Austria waited so long and tried so many other futile devices to stop the steady deterioration of her Balkan and great-power position before resorting to force. The idea of eliminating Serbia as a political factor by conquest, occupation, or preventive war was at least sixty years old, and constantly advanced. For over two centuries Austria had lived under the brooding threat of Russian encirclement in the south.[10] Why did she act only in the desperate situation of 1914, with all alternatives exhausted?

A similar question arises with Germany. Why, with her powerful impulse toward *Weltpolitik*, did she fail to resort to war under favorable circumstances in 1905, or 1908–9, or even 1911, and try it only in 1914, when military and political leaders alike recognized the gambling nature of the enterprise?[11] The same question, What held her back? applies to Europe in general. Fischer, Mayer, and the Marxists insist that the war did not just happen, but was caused. This is true, but so is the converse. Until 1914 peace did not just happen, but was caused. The wars that did not occur

---

9   Hugo Hantsch, *Leopold Graf Berchtold, Grandseigneur und Staatsmann*, 2 vols. (Graz, 1963); Robert A. Kann, "Erzherzog Franz Ferdinand und Graf Berchtold als Aussenminister, 1912–1914," *Mitteilungen des Österreichischen Staatsarchivs* 22 (1969): 246–78.

10   A. V. Florovsky, "Russo-Austrian Conflicts in the Early 18th Century," *Slavonic and East European Review* 47 (January 1969): 94–115.

11   As Norman Rich points out, the only way Germany could have avoided political defeat in 1905–6 was either by a more forceful diplomacy backed by the threat of war, or by war itself. Norman Rich, *Friedrich von Holstein*, 2 vols. (Cambridge, 1965), 742–45.

seem to me harder to explain than the one that did. Arno Mayer contends that we know all we need to about the European system; we lack an adequate analysis of the domestic sources of the violence that destroyed it. I disagree. We know more than we need to (although more knowledge of course is always possible and valuable) to understand in general what was impelling Europe to destruction. We neither fully understand nor appreciate the restraints holding her back, and why these gave way only in 1914.

This essay therefore deals with the question, Why not until 1914? It proposes to account for the critical difference between the system's surviving the challenges facing it and its failing to do so, by pointing to a vital element of stability within the system which in 1914 finally became destructive and generated the collapse of the system. That element, it will surprise no one to hear, was Austria-Hungary. The essay will also, briefly and sketchily, make a case for a point less trite and obvious: that a chief source of the pressures turning Austria from a stabilizing into a destructive member of the system, besides her own internal debility and Germany's policy for becoming a world power, was Britain's policy for remaining one.

The most important change in European politics after 1890, as everyone knows, was that Germany lost control of the system. Who gained the initiative she lost? For a short time, Britain seemed to; but the long-range gainers were France and Russia. Their alliance, giving them greater security in Europe, freed them to pursue world policy. Manchuria, China, Indochina and Siam, Persia, Central Asia, the Mediterranean, the Senegal, the Niger, the Congo, and the Upper Nile were the areas where Russian and French pressures were brought to bear. In every case, Britain was made to feel it.

The challenge to Britain's world leadership, coinciding with Germany's loss of control of the European system, helped conceal the latter phenomenon from the Germans themselves and contributed to their persistent belief that they could play the game of two irons in the fire and that eventually Britain would have to seek German help. Part of the challenge to Britain came from German and American industrial and commercial competition, but there was not much to be done about this. Countermeasures like imperial tariffs and economic union were likely to hurt Britain and anger the dominions rather than hamper her rivals. Besides, the main threat was to the security of the Empire, not to trade, and this danger stemmed from France and Russia. Far from threatening the British Empire in the 1890s, Germany hovered about Britain like an opportunistic money-lender, ready to offer her services at exorbitant rates and hoping for a favorable chance to buy into the firm. France and Russia competed directly with Britain and tried to drive her out of key positions. Isolated and foolish challenges like Fashoda could be faced down, but the fundamental vulnerability of Britain's position in Egypt, South Africa, the Straits, Persia, the Persian Gulf, the Far East, India, and India's Northwest Frontier oppressed the British daily. Added to this was the rise of the United States to world power and the danger of native unrest and risings in Egypt, South Africa, Ireland, and above all India. The challenges could doubtless be met, but not by the old policy, and also not by great new expenditures or tests of strength. The empire had always been acquired and maintained on the cheap, and Parliament required that it be kept so, especially now that new demands for welfare measures were being added to the old Liberal and Radical calls for cuts in military spending. As for tests of strength, the Boer War convinced most Englishmen of the dangers of isolation and the severe limits to British resources for overseas ventures.

It was therefore inevitable that Britain would meet her new problems mainly by trying to devolve some of her imperial burdens on others (the dominions or other friendly powers), and by trying to come to terms with her opponents. Bowing out gracefully in favor of the United States in the Western Hemisphere was easy and relatively painless; equally natural was the limited alliance with Japan.[12] But the main answer to Britain's difficulties would have to be a deal with her chief opponents, France and Russia. Far from representing a great break in British tradition, such a rapprochement was the obvious step for Britain, a move for which there was ample precedent and tradition

---

12   Kenneth Bourne, *Britain and the Balance of Power in North America, 1815–1908* (Berkeley, CA, 1967); Ian Nish, *The Anglo-Japanese Alliance* (London, 1966).

throughout the nineteenth century. What held it up was not British reluctance to break with splendid isolation—Salisbury, the great defender of this tradition, had been looking for chances to come to terms with France and Russia all through the 1890s.[13] It was the refusal of France and Russia to make a deal on terms acceptable to Britain, counting as they did on British vulnerability to make her ultimately come to them. It took more than a year after Fashoda fully to convince Delcassé that there was no way to get Britain out of Egypt, and five years to be ready to admit it openly. Even then the British made concessions to France over Morocco which her business community there did not like at all.[14] As for Russia, only military defeat and revolution in 1904–5, plus an expanded Anglo-Japanese alliance, finally convinced her that she must forget about putting pressure on Britain in Afghanistan. Even then, the Russians proved difficult to deal with in Persia before and after 1907.[15]

This suggests that there is no need to bring in the German menace to explain Britain's rapprochement with France and Russia. The Triple Entente was a natural development explicable purely in terms of the needs and aims of the three powers—especially Britain. Her friendships with France and Russia were ends in themselves, vital for her imperial interests, and not means of checking Germany, and remained so. Rather than seeking friendly agreements with France and Russia because of the German threat, Britain tended to see Germany as a threat because of the agreements she sought and obtained from France and Russia. Repeatedly, before the war British spokesmen's main complaint against Germany was that she resented British agreements with other powers and tried to break them up. The great

---

13 See, e.g., J. A. S. Grenville, *Lord Salisbury and Foreign Policy* (London, 1964); and Thomas M. Iiams Jr., *Dreyfus, Diplomatists and the Dual Alliance* (Geneva and Paris, 1962).

14 Christopher Andrew, *Théophile Delcassé and the Making of the Entente Cordiale* (New York, 1968); Pierre Guillen, *L'Allemagne et le Maroc de 1870 à 1905* (Paris, 1967).

15 Firuz Kazemzadeh, *Russia and Britain in Persia, 1864–1914* (New Haven, CT, 1968); Horst Jaeckel, *Die Nordwestgrenze in der Verteidigung Indiens 1900–1908 und der Weg Englands zum russischen-britischen Abkommen von 1907* (Cologne, 1968).

British fear was that Germany might lure France and Russia into her camp, leaving Britain isolated.[16]

"But you forget three things," one might reply. "Britain did not approach France and Russia until she had first attempted an alliance with Germany and failed. The agreements with France and Russia were strictly extra-European and colonial in nature, and not directed against Germany; only Germany's dangerous conduct made them into a coalition against Germany. Above all, it was Germany's direct, overt, and formidable naval challenge which forced Britain to draw close to France and cooperate with Russia in Europe."

The first point errs on the facts. The story of a missed opportunity for an Anglo-German alliance in 1898–1901 is a myth, as Gerhard Ritter argued long ago.[17] Britain never really tried for it or wanted it. Naturally she would have liked to get Germany to defend British interests for nothing, but a mutual tie was never seriously in question. There was no basis for an alliance. Lord Curzon pointed out in 1901 that the German navy was too weak to be of much help to Britain and the army was not available where Britain needed it.[18] Frances Bertie put the general political case against an alliance: it would be useful only in the extreme case of a losing British war against France and Russia, but such a war would compel Germany in her own interests to help Britain, alliance or no. Tied to Germany, Britain would lose her freedom to conduct world policy and to hold and exploit the balance

---

16   A typical expression of this fear is Sir Edward Grey's remark in October 1905 that Britain "was running a real risk of losing France and not gaining Germany; who would want us, if she could detach France from us." S. R. Williamson Jr., *The Politics of the Grand Strategy* (Cambridge, MA, 1969), 60.

17   *Die Legende der verschmähten englischen Freundschaft 1898/1901* (Freiburg, 1929); H. W. Koch, "The Anglo-German Alliance Negotiations: Missed Opportunity or Myth?," *History* 54 (1969): 378–92.

18   Curzon's argument is both typical and significant: "It [a German alliance] will mean the habitual and incessant surrendering to Germany on points where our commercial interests are concerned all over the world. What should we get from her in return? We do not want her army. Her navy is not sufficiently strong to be of much value. Austria can give us absolutely nothing and might entangle us in a fight over the Balkan Peninsula. Italy is too weak to be of any assistance." Jaeckel, *Die Nordwestgrenze*, 152.

between rival continental powers.[19] Even Lansdowne quickly saw that a German alliance would draw French and Russian antagonism onto Britain, costing her the desired rapprochement with the Dual Alliance.[20]

As for British cooperation with Germany, the only possible basis for this was the one laboriously erected by Bismarck and grudgingly accepted by Salisbury in the Near Eastern Triplice of 1887: British cooperation with Austria and Italy to uphold the Near Eastern status quo.[21] This was undermined in 1893 by the Admiralty's conclusion that the fleet could no longer defend Constantinople against Russia while a French fleet operated from Toulon in Britain's rear. Once the British government accepted this conclusion, it eliminated any possibility of serious support for Austria in the Balkans, and thus of cooperation between Germany and Britain on the continent. The only way now open for Britain in the long run to defend her Near Eastern interests, and the only one seriously pursued, was a deal with Russia.[22] It

---

19   Minute of November 9, 1901, in G. P. Gooch and H. W. V. Temperley, eds., *British Documents on the Origins of the War, 1898–1914* (hereafter cited as *BD*), vol. 2 (London, 1927), doc. 76.

20   Jaeckel, *Die Nordwestgrenze*, 152.

21   G. N. Sanderson portrays well Salisbury's resentment at being forced by Bismarck to play a role in Europe: "He resented being forced to carry Bismarck's Austrian burden at the Straits; he resented still more the consequent deflection of Russian hostility from Berlin to London. But he made a shrewd bargain by committing the Allies to the defence of Asia Minor as well as the Balkans; and as an interim defensive arrangement at the Straits the Agreement was at least as valuable to England as to Germany" (G. N. Sanderson, *Europe, England, and the Upper Nile, 1882–1899* [Edinburgh, 1965], 40–1). The agreement was really much more favorable to Britain than to Germany; as Paul Kluke points out, it marked the beginning of Salisbury's victory over Bismarck and the breakdown of Bismarck's system (Paul Kluke, "Bismarck und Salisbury. Ein diplomatisches Duell," *Historische Zeitschrift*, 175 [1953]: 295–306). But Salisbury would already in 1887 have preferred a direct deal with France to having to rely on the Triple Alliance for support; the trouble was that France's price at this time, evacuation of Egypt, was too high.

22   On the general subject, C. J. Lowe, *Salisbury and the Mediterranean 1886–1896* (London, 1965). On the breakdown of the Second Mediterranean Agreement, I disagree with J. A. S. Grenville ("Goluchowski, Salisbury and the Mediterranean Agreements, 1895–1897," *Slavonic and East European Review* 36 [1957–58]: 340–69) and Margaret Jefferson ("Lord Salisbury and the Eastern Question, 1890–1898," *Slavonic and East European Review* 39 [1960–61]: 44–60,

took somewhat longer for Britain to conclude that Italy was no real help in the contest with France over East Africa, but after 1898 she also became largely superfluous.

What happened in China, where Britain and Germany supposedly came closest to real partnership only to have Germany back out, again illustrates the impossibility of an alliance. Salisbury never designed or intended the Anglo-German Agreement of October 1900 to stop Russia in China. He wanted it to hold Germany back, keeping her out of the British sphere in the Yangtze which she hoped to penetrate, while Salisbury negotiated what he really desired, an agreement over spheres of influence with Russia. When Prince Bülow told the Reichstag in March 1901 that Germany was not obliged to oppose Russia in Manchuria and would not do so, he merely expressed bluntly the letter and spirit of the 1900 agreement. Naturally and typically, when Lansdowne's and Chamberlain's illusions were pricked, Lansdowne promptly turned to Japan, while Chamberlain became not long after the most strident Germanophobe in the Cabinet.[23]

The second point, that Britain's colonial agreements were not directed against Germany, but only became so because of Germany's conduct, is true in the sense that Britain did not want to encircle Germany but to protect her empire; this is precisely my contention. It also touches on an important truth, that Germany was not in fact the prime target of Entente diplomacy— of which more later. But what about France's and Russia's purposes in these colonial agreements? Whether Delcassé's policy of trying to encircle and isolate Germany was mainly a

---

216–21). The point is not, as both seem to feel, that Salisbury did not want to throw Austria over brusquely or act dishonestly toward her. It is that Salisbury saw absolutely no possibility of actively working with her or supporting her. He wanted an agreement with Russia and worked for it, knowing that Czar Nicholas II was already very hostile toward Austria and looking forward to her demise; Salisbury merely hoped that such an Anglo-Russian agreement could be reached without the British acting basely toward Austria or undermining her essential position. Such scruples of conscience are seldom an effective barrier against reason of state; later British statesmen would easily get over them. See also C. J. Lowe, *The Reluctant Imperialists* (London, 1967), 1: 196–204.

23   L. K. Young, *British Policy in China 1895–1902* (Oxford, 1970).

reaction to German moves[24] or the product of his own ambitions for France (undoubtedly it was both), his whole program, especially as it reached a climax in Morocco, was so overtly and rashly anti-German that most of his colleagues, including some ardent colonialists, warned him against it.[25] The British knew quite well about this aspect of French policy. They chose to accept the agreement with France for their own reasons and to let Germany worry about the European consequences. As for the Anglo-Russian Convention of 1907, its fundamental presumption was that Britain would pay Russia for cooperation in Central Asia by helping the Russians improve their position in Europe, especially in the Balkans and the Straits—directly at Turkey's and Austria's expense, indirectly at Germany's. The British knew that Russia had been exerting pressure on India in great part in order to make Britain subservient to Russian policy in Europe, and they had long been contemplating using the Balkans and the Straits as lures for Russia.[26]

It becomes even more disingenuous to claim that Britain's ententes were not intended to apply to Europe or to hurt Germany when one sees how they were used. From 1904 on, the British understood perfectly that the price of their friendships with France and Russia was diplomatic and moral support for these powers in their disputes with Germany and Austria. They gave that support even when, as often happened, they strongly disapproved of French or Russian policy. Germany and Austria, and

---

24   Christopher Andrew, "German World Policy and the Reshaping of the Dual Alliance," *Journal of Contemporary History* 1 (1966): 137–51.

25   Guillen, *L'Allemagne et le Maroc*; Andrew, *Théophile Delcassé*; Howard Sieberg, *Eugène Etienne und die französische Kolonialpolitik (1887–1904)* (Cologne, 1968).

26   Max Beloff, *Imperial Sunset*, vol. 1 (New York, 1970), 102. British thinking is illustrated by Sir George Clarke's remark in 1905: "I believe that the defense of our Indian frontier against Russia is more a matter for the F. O. than for the Indian Army. When the war is over it may be possible to give way on the Dardanelles question in return for a binding agreement with Russia as regards Afghanistan" (Jaeckel, *Die Nordwestgrenze*, 84). Indeed, the main British worry was that concessions in the Near East would not be enough to appease Russia. "Whatever we do in the way of friendliness in South East Europe or elsewhere," argued Cecil Spring-Rice in 1903, "we shall never be forgiven the crime of possessing what Russia wants to have" (ibid, 162).

France and Russia, respectively, being tied by firm alliances, could afford sometimes to restrain their partners and deny them diplomatic support. Britain, refusing all military commitments, had to give her friends moral support more unstintingly or risk seeing them go into the other camp.

Furthermore, even if Germany's encirclement was not a British aim, the "circling out" of Germany, her exclusion from world politics and empire, *was* Britain's goal in good measure. Grey and others made it clear time and again that the purpose of Britain's ententes, next to keeping France and Russia friendly, was to deter Germany from "interfering" and "bullying" in Asia or Africa, to keep her out of areas like Persia where she had no real business, to stop the Baghdad Railway, to neutralize the *baton égyptien*, and to teach Germany that she had to settle all imperial questions *à quatre*, before a united front of Entente powers. The *Auskreisung*, which Fischer portrays as the result of German aggressiveness and blunders, was precisely the outcome British diplomacy was bent on achieving.

As to Germany's naval challenge, all the facts, old and new, can be freely acknowledged.[27] There was a great German naval program aimed directly at Britain and designed to promote *Weltpolitik*. It undoubtedly became ultimately Britain's greatest naval danger (after the Franco-Russian danger faded away) and the foremost element in Anglo-German rivalry. No improvement could come in Anglo-German relations without some naval settlement. But it is one thing to see the naval challenge as a real, serious issue, sufficient to itself to compel Britain to be on guard against Germany. It is quite another to argue that it primarily shaped British policy toward Germany, or that an end to the naval race would have significantly changed British policy. The latter assumptions remain unproved. The German naval challenge did not cause the revolution in Britain's political alignments, and an end to the naval race would not overturn them. The

---

27 In addition to the valuable older works of E. L. Woodward, A. J. Marder, Oron Hale, Eckart Kehr, and others, see esp. Jonathan Steinberg, *Yesterday's Deterrent* (New York, 1965), and Volker R. Berghahn, "Zu den Zielen des deutschen Flottenbaus unter Wilhelm II," *Historische Zeitschrift* 210 (1970): 34–100.

German Navy was not really taken seriously by either the government or the Admiralty until 1906–7, by which time the Entente Cordiale was a fixture in British policy and the search for an agreement with Russia had long been under way. Nor will the naval challenge do to explain the rise of Germanophobia in Britain. The anti-Germans were clearly gaining control of the Foreign Office by 1901; popular hatred of Germany was ripe with the Kruger Telegram and the Boer War. Anti-German spokesmen in the government and the press did not need the German Navy for their propaganda, though they exploited it fully. They centered their fire on the general danger of German power, the evil of Prussian militarism, and the German bullying and blackmail of Britain since the 1880s.[28]

Nor should one ignore the fact that Germany's naval challenge was the only one among the many threats facing Britain which the British always knew they could beat. The realignment of British foreign policy came at a time when she enjoyed almost unprecedented naval superiority. The recognition in 1906–7 that Germany was now the only possible naval foe greatly improved, not worsened, Britain's strategic position; it facilitated the concentration of the fleet in home waters more than it forced it. Even the Tories, always alert for any sign of naval unpreparedness, agreed in 1905–6 that naval spending could be reduced.[29] British publicists and a hysterical public might dream of a German invasion; Sir John Fischer dreamed of Copenhagening the German fleet and, like his successor, wanted to land 100,000 men on Germany's Baltic coast in case of war.[30] Contrast the British confidence that they would be able to drive Germany from the high seas, destroy her commerce, and conquer her colonies with relative ease, with British pessimism on other scores—the knowledge that they could not hope to match American naval strength in the

---

28   Zara S. Steiner, *The Foreign Office and Foreign Policy 1898–1914* (New York, 1970).

29   Beloff, *Imperial Sunset*, vol. 1, 86–7, 103; David W. Sweet, "The Baltic in British Diplomacy before the First World War," *Historical Journal* 13 (1970): 455–7; A. J. Morris, "The English Radicals' Campaign for Disarmament and the Hague Conference of 1907," *Journal of Modern History* 43 (1971): 378–82.

30   Sweet, "The Baltic in British Diplomacy," 455–7, 482–4; Williamson, *Politics of the Grand Strategy*.

western Atlantic or Japanese in the Far East, and that the only long-range answers to the problems of Egypt and India were deals with France and Russia. Of course the British were angered by Germany's naval challenge; it was expensive, gratuitous, and worrisome. But they never doubted they could meet it; it had its domestic and foreign policy uses; it was much easier to get money voted for ships than for men and supplies to defend the North-west Frontier. All in all, it was a price Britain was willing to pay for the friendship of Russia and France, although she would have preferred not to pay at all.

Above all, no naval agreement would have ended Anglo-German rivalry or caused Britain to abandon the anti-German coalition. To be sure, Germany demanded an unacceptable price for a naval agreement, Britain's promise of neutrality in continental war. But then Britain was never willing to pay for a naval agreement, except possibly with the poisoned fruit of a colonial agreement at Portugal's or Belgium's expense.[31] If a naval agreement were concluded, the British would say, the improved atmosphere and friendly feelings it would produce would facilitate future amicable agreements on subjects of mutual interest—which is diplomatic language for "No concessions." In fact, Nicolson, Hardinge, Crowe, and other influential foreign-policy leaders were deathly afraid of a naval agreement. As Hardinge argued, the Russians "must not think for a moment that we want to improve our relations with Germany at their expense. We have no pending questions with Germany, except that of naval construction, while our whole future in Asia is bound up with the necessity of main-taining the best and most friendly relations with Russia. We cannot afford to sacrifice in any way our entente with Russia—even for the sake of a reduced naval programme."[32] Grey constantly reassured France and Russia that no agreement with Germany, naval or other, would disturb Britain's existing friendships, and he meant it.

---

31 Jacques Willequet, *Le Congo belge et la Weltpolitik (1894–1914)* (Brussels, 1962); *BD*, vol. 10, pt. 2 (London, 1938), docs. 266–9.

32 Hardinge to Nicolson, January 4, 1909, *BD*, vol. 5 (London, 1926), 550. (Also quoted in Steiner, *The Foreign Office*, 95, where it is dated March 26.)

If one needs further evidence that an end to the naval threat would not change Britain's basic policy toward Germany, the secret Anglo-Russian naval talks of June 1914 over cooperation in the Baltic and the Mediterranean supply it. Perhaps Egmont Zechlin makes too much of the impact of these talks on German policy in 1914, but the point here is what they show of British policy.[33] Britain agreed to these talks, it must be remembered, after the naval race had ended on terms favorable to her, after Germany had cooperated with her during the Balkan Wars, and while agreements with Germany over the Portuguese colonies and the Baghdad Railway were in their final stages. British writers argue that the talks meant nothing to Britain. Since her naval authorities had recently concluded that the Royal Navy would not be able to penetrate into the Baltic in case of war anyway, the conversations would lead to nothing, and were merely a political sop to Russia.[34] But that is precisely the point. At a moment when better relations with Germany seemed uniquely possible, and when Grey believed such relations would be vital to prevent war over the Balkans, Britain was willing to destroy this hope (for these talks, like the similar ones with France, had little chance to remain secret and did not), to risk creating a grave new strain with Germany, to promote Russo-French hopes and German fears of a full Anglo-French-Russian alliance, and to deliver the best possible propaganda to navalists in Germany for resuming the naval race—all in order to avoid disappointing the Russians. This marks a high point in the British appeasement of Russia that had been going on for fifteen years, and proves further that the *raison d'être* of British policy was her ententes with France and Russia, regardless of what Germany did, just as Germany was determined to try for world power regardless of what Britain did, and that rivalry with Germany was a price Britain was willing to pay for the sake of these ententes.

---

33   "Deutschland zwischen Kabinettskrieg und Wirtschaftskrieg. Politik und Kriegführung in den ersten Monaten des Weltkrieges 1914," *Historische Zeitschrift* 199 (1964): 347–55; "Die türkischen Meerengen-Brennpunkt der Weltgeschichte," *Geschichte in Wissenschaft und Unterricht* 17 (1966): 9–15.

34   Sweet, "The Baltic in British Diplomacy," 284.

"Very well," someone will say, "what of it? Britain was simply playing the game by the normal rules. Was she supposed to have appeased Germany instead? What possible concession would have done any good? In any case the anti-German coalition Britain joined was a loose, defensive one which never would have caused war unless Germany tried to break it by force, which she did. Far from refuting the Fischer thesis, you have made it more plausible. Faced with the impossibility of achieving world power and standing by peaceful means, Germany chose war. Rather than condemning British policy, you vindicate it. For whatever her motives (and what power ever acts for motives other than self-interest?), Britain was preserving the European balance of power against the unmistakable threat of German domination. That this defense was desperately needed, two world wars would seem to give adequate proof."

The argument is tenable, provided its basic premises are accepted. If Germany's main activity was her pursuit of world power; if, further, the great problem for Europe was how to cope with Germany's growing power; if the main aim of British policy, whatever its ulterior motives, was to preserve a balance of power in Europe, and the chief effect of British policy was to restrain German ambitions, then British policy was justified regardless of its motives and even of its outcome. In pursuing her own interests, Britain was also upholding the best interests of Europe as a whole, and of peace.

But in fact the premises are unsound. Of course Germany played world policy; so did every other power that could, and some that could not. The point is how Germany played it. Somehow Fischer never quite succeeds in explaining the contrast between the remarkable growth of Germany's power and wealth and her uniform failure to translate that power into corresponding diplomatic, political, and territorial gains. Even a small power like Belgium, or a would-be great power like Italy, could emerge from the imperialist scramble with impressive gains; Portugal and Holland could consolidate their possessions while hungry great powers looked on. But Germany ended up with little more than Bismarck had already gained in 1884–85, and this at the cost of weakened alliances and a ruined European position. It will not do to explain this failure simply by German aggressiveness and blunders. Who could be more aggressive and commit more blunders than Imperial Russia? Yet she survived a disastrous war, revolution, and bankruptcy and emerged by 1914 with her alliances stronger than ever and her expansion once again under way. Nor will it do to cite Germany's inconsistency, her repeated failure to know what she really wanted.[35] For the point is that no matter what Germany tried, she lost. She lost ground in Morocco when she remained passive and waited for France to come to her; she lost ground when she tried standing up for the principle of the open door; and she lost further ground when she tried to pound her fist on the table and demand compensations. Whether she tried to challenge Britain or France or Russia, or (as she did repeatedly) tried to win their friendship, she always finally succeeded in tightening the Entente against her.

The main reason for Germany's failure is not ineptness and aggressiveness, or her late start in *Weltpolitik*, or even unfavorable geography, although these are involved. It is that Germany could not pursue *Weltpolitik* all out. Each of the Entente powers could carry on a world policy without directly overthrowing the European system (although their imperialism indirectly undermined it). They could even, as the British did, indulge in the flattering belief that *their* world policy sustained the European system and made it work. But an unrestrained *Weltpolitik* by Germany, as the Germans were forced to recognize, was bound to isolate her and destroy the system upon which she had to rely for security as much as upon her army. Thus the exigencies of continental policy repeatedly imposed themselves upon Germany and restrained her.

This explains what most needs explaining about prewar German policy. The problem is not, as is often imagined, one of accounting for her reckless conduct in terms of her aggressive, imperialist character and aims. It is one of accounting for the surprising moderation of German policy until 1914, in view of her aggressive character and aims. It is clear that the Entente powers were counting upon Germany's desire for peace and

---

35   E.g., Jonathan Steinberg, "Germany and the Russo-Japanese War," *American Historical Review* 75 (1970): 1965–86.

exploiting it; even Germanophobes like Eyre Crowe insisted that she would back down before a firm front. The restraints lay, of course, not in Germany's policy or character or the supposed peace party at Berlin, but in the position and role the system forced upon her—which made it all the more important for the Entente not to overstrain the system holding her back.

The contradiction between what Germany wanted to do and what she dared do and was obliged to do accounts in turn for the erratic, uncoordinated character of German world policy, its inability to settle on clear goals and carry them through, the constant initiatives leading nowhere, the frequent changes in mid-course. It is commonly said that after 1890 Germany played the game of international politics like a plunger on the stock market, always looking for quick short-term gains. The truth is worse than this. Germany played it like a plunger looking for quick gains without making any investments, a gambler trying to win without betting. The Germans were always hoping to be paid for doing nothing, merely for being where they were; expecting to be feared and to have their interests respected because of the power they possessed but dared not exert. They wanted Britain to pay them in Africa for the trouble Germany refrained from causing Britain with the Boers. They wanted Russia to pay for benevolent German neutrality during the Russo-Japanese war, and Britain and Japan to pay for plain German neutrality during the same war. Russia and Britain were supposed to do something for Germany on account of her not penetrating Persia, and France likewise if Germany did not cause more difficulty over Morocco. The British ought to concede Germany something if she stopped building more ships. Disappointed, the Germans wondered with querulous self-pity why everyone was against them—the same mood they had often expressed before unification,[36] and which would become the national disease after 1918.

Of course German restraint was not worthless to other powers; often it was invaluable. Russia was extremely lucky to

---

36   "Germany has no friends in Europe," complained the Prussian diplomat Baron Bunsen in 1848. "No one grants aspiring Germany any favors." Holger Hjelholt, *British Mediation in the Danish-German Conflict 1848–1850* (Copenhagen, 1966), pt. 2, 20. (Translation mine.)

have Germany and Austria-Hungary covering her rear in 1904–5, and the Russians knew it. But no one pays for such services when they can be had for nothing, especially since it was not too hard to see that the real reason why Germany refrained from causing more trouble was that she dared not do so. Like it or not, she was bound to her alliances and to her Central European position. Even Italy had more freedom for *Weltpolitik* than she, and used it. For the Entente powers and Italy, alliances were primarily associations for profit; for Germany and Austria, they were of necessity associations for security.[37]

Nor can one agree without serious reservations even to the universal assumption that British policy was directed toward maintaining a European balance of power. Of course it was in one sense: Britain wanted to keep Germany from dominating the continent by either overpowering France and Russia or luring them into her camp. This was entirely legitimate and necessary, but it alone is not enough to make Britain's a real balance-of-power policy. For, quite apart from some general reservations one may have about the whole character of British equilibrist thought, the important point is that the British neither recognized nor did anything about the most critical threat to the European balance after 1900, but helped make it much worse.[38] The immediate threat to the balance in 1914 was not German power. That danger existed, but it was under control, so far as it could be by peaceful means. The impression everywhere in Europe was that the Entente powers, especially Russia, were gaining the upper hand.[39] The greater danger stemmed not from German or Russian power but from Austrian weakness. One of the few incontestable points in balance-of-power theory is that preserving the system means preserving all the essential actors in it. Equally obvious, nothing is more likely to occasion a major war than a threat to the existence or great-power status of an essential actor. Whatever the underlying causes of the

37   See esp. Fritz Fellner, *Der Dreibund* (Vienna, 1960).

38   What M. S. Anderson says of the balance of power in eighteenth-century British usage, that "very often it was no more than a phrase used to inhibit thought," seems to apply to the nineteenth and twentieth centuries as well. Ragnhild Hatton and M. S. Anderson, eds., *Studies in Diplomatic History* (Hamden, CT, 1970), 184.

39   Risto Ropponen, *Die Kraft Russlands* (Helsinki, 1968).

nineteenth-century European wars may have been, they were all touched off by a violent reaction from some declining or threatened essential actor to a menace to its existence, essential interests, or prestige. This was true of Turkey in 1853, Austria in 1859 and 1866, France in 1870, and Austria in 1914. Long before 1914 it was obvious that Austria's existence was threatened. Everyone saw her as the next sick man of Europe after Turkey. The British virtually wrote off Austria as a great power by the mid-1890s. In 1899 Delcassé tried to reach agreements with Russia and Italy in the expectation of her impending demise. From 1908 on almost everyone anticipated that the long-awaited general war would probably arise over a Russo-Austrian quarrel involving Serbia. From 1912 on the Russians and Serbs repeatedly told their Western friends that Austria's collapse was imminent, and that they intended to have the lion's share of the remains.[40]

Yet Britain's "balance-of-power" policy entirely ignored this immediate danger, and served actually to increase the threat from Germany as well. Germany ultimately might well have gone to war for world power (although she passed up chances earlier); but she was virtually bound to accept war, even provoke it, rather than let Austria go under and thus lose her last reliable ally. This was not a matter of Germany's ambitions, but of her vital interests, as the British well knew.

Once again, even if this trite contention is true, what of it? Was Britain to blame if Austria in 1914 decided to commit suicide out of fear of death, and Germany decided to join her, or rather pushed her into it? Were the Entente powers supposed to sacrifice their interests to save a rival power from succumbing to its own internal weaknesses?

As it happens, the theoretical answer to both these rhetorical questions is yes. A real balance-of-power policy would have required from the Entente precisely such a policy of restraint for themselves and controlled support for Austria, just as

---

40   E.g., in May 1914 the Russian Minister of War, General Suchomlinov, told the French Ambassador Paléologue that Russia meant to annex Galicia on Francis Joseph's death and the Czar hoped that Germany would swallow this. F. N. Bradley, "Quelques aspects de la politique étrangère de Russie avant 1914 à travers les archives françaises," *Études slaves et est-européennes* 7 (1967): 100–1.

maintaining the Near Eastern balance had always required the powers to support Turkey, not exploiting her weaknesses or seeking individual gains. It indicates the inherent contradictions of balance-of-power politics that the actions it promotes, which its proponents consider normal and natural, actually serve to undermine the balance rather than maintain it. But there is a practical answer more important than the theoretical one. The threat to Austria's existence, which I would argue was primarily international rather than internal in character, was a product in great part of Entente policy. As a result of the preoccupation of diplomatic historians with motives and aims instead of effects, both German and Entente policies have always been discussed almost exclusively in terms of the German problem, when in fact their effects were far greater on the Austrian problem. The best answer to the German encirclement myth is not that Entente policy was really moderate and unprovocative; there has been too much whitewashing of British, French, and especially Russian policy in this whole debate.[41] The answer is rather that the Entente really encircled Austria rather than Germany. Of course Germany was hemmed in and constrained. But she still had allies she controlled or strongly influenced, neutral states still leaned her way (Denmark, Sweden, Holland, Switzerland, Turkey), and she was still inherently so strong that no one wished to challenge her directly. If her bid for world power was frustrated, the more modest aim of eventually loosening the rival coalition and insinuating herself into Britain's favor was not foreclosed. Grey resisted all pressures from France, Russia, and the Foreign Office to turn the ententes into alliances, and may even have entertained the hope ultimately of bringing a chastened and more moderate Germany into the Triple Entente, as the Radicals urged.[42]

Austria, in contrast, was hopelessly encircled by 1914 and knew it.[43] Russia, supported by France, was forming a new Balkan

---

41   Fischer's *Krieg der Illusionen* is riddled with this. See also the remarks of Fritz Fellner on the Ritter-Fischer debate, in Gerald D. Feldman, ed., *German Imperialism, 1914–1918* (New York, 1972), 193–5.

42   Howard S. Weinroth, "The British Radicals and the Balance of Power, 1902–1914," *Historical Journal* 13 (1970): 653–82.

43   As Count Czernin wrote Berchtold on June 22, 1914: "Before our eyes, in broad daylight, openly and obviously, as clear as the sun, with

League around Russia's protege and Austria's worst enemy, Serbia. Romania was defecting, Bulgaria was exhausted and wavering under strong Russo-French pressure, Turkey was leaning toward Russia, Italy was cooperating with Russia in the Balkans; even Germany was a wholly unreliable support politically, and Austria's chief competitor economically in the Balkans. This isolation and encirclement resulted, moreover, principally from Entente moves and policies, always discussed as if they had nothing to do with Austria. Delcassé's policy, for example, was obviously aimed against Germany (and for a good while against Britain). But is there no significance to the fact that virtually his first move in strengthening and transforming the Dual Alliance was to seek an agreement with Russia over the spoils of the Austrian Empire, and that even after his fears of a German seizure of Austrian Adriatic ports proved groundless, he still hoped Austria's demise might give France the chance to recover Alsace-Lorraine?[44] Who was menaced by French efforts to lure Italy out of the Triple Alliance and to get her to concentrate her attention on the Balkans and *Italia irredenta*? Not Germany; Austria. Whose vital interests and security were ultimately threatened by France's move to take over Morocco? Not Germany's; only the Pan-Germans and some ardent colonialists claimed Morocco as a question of vital interest. The Kaiser, the Foreign Office, and the bulk of Germany's military, naval, and business leaders saw it as a question primarily of prestige and honor. What the French protectorate in Morocco actually did was to pave the way for Italy to attack Turkey over Tripoli and to spread the war into the eastern Mediterranean, to encourage Russia to advance her plans for the Straits, and to promote the assault of the Balkan states upon Turkey, thus raising life-and-death questions for Austria. This was not merely what happened in the event; it was what

---

shameless impudence, the encirclement of the Monarchy is being completed; under Russian-French patronage a new Balkan League is being welded together. whose purpose, today still apparently complicated, will soon appear in astonishing simplicity—against the Monarchy." Egmont Zechlin, "Die türkischen Meerengen: ein Brennpunkt der Weltgeschichte," in *Über-seegeschichte. Aufsätze aus den Jahren 1935–1964* (Hamburg, 1986), 14. (Translation mine.)

44   Andrew, *Théophile Delcassé*, 126–35.

sensible leaders foresaw and planned for, what was in good part provided for in written agreements.

It is true that Austria did not oppose either France's move on Morocco or Italy's ambitions for Tripoli. This was because, knowing that she could not stop them, she pursued the forlorn hope that, distracted by these gains, they might lessen the pressure on her, or that by supporting them she might persuade France and Italy to keep these Mediterranean moves from having dangerous repercussions for Austria in the Balkans, and to recognize her vital interests there. This policy, which had never worked for Austria throughout the nineteenth century, suffered absolute shipwreck in 1912–14, when it became apparent that all the powers, grateful though they were for Austria's restraint, intended to make her pay for everyone else's gains, and pay precisely in the only area where she had vital interests, the Balkans.

Whom (besides Persia) did the Anglo-Russian Convention of 1907 endanger? Not Germany, whose role and interests in Persia were secondary. The agreement, as intended and promoted by Britain, served to turn Russia's attention toward the Straits, the Macedonian question, and her Balkan rivalry with Austria. France's and Britain's loans to Russia, French economic penetration of the Balkans, France's arms deliveries to Serbia and Greece, and her closing her money markets to Vienna while opening them to Austria's enemies were all intended to hit Germany, insofar as they had a political purpose; but Austria was much more directly hurt. The same is true of Russia's policy, fully backed by France, of uniting the Balkan states into a league under her direction, pulling Romania and Turkey also into her camp. Intended supposedly to protect the Straits and Turkey from German influence, it served above all to destroy Austria's position. Even the Anglo-French and Anglo-Russian naval talks were directed as much against Austria in the Mediterranean as against Germany in the North and Baltic Seas. From 1912 on France was determined not to allow an Austro-Serb or Austro-Russian rapprochement, so as not to lose a valuable third front in the Balkans against the Central Powers in case of war.[45]

---

45   Ljiljana Aleksić-Pejković, "La Serbie et les rapports entré les puissances de l'Entente 1908–1913," *Balkan Studies* 6 (1965): 325–44.

Austria was therefore the actual target of Entente diplomacy. Results count more than motives. To a surprising degree, moreover, Entente statesmen knew what the effects of their policies would be and accepted them. But how was Britain responsible for this? It is easy to see why Russia, France, and Italy might want Austria weakened, but why should Britain, her old friend and natural ally, help undermine her position?

In fact, one can argue that Britain's policy (like Russia's and even, in certain respects, France's) was more anti-Austrian than anti- German. Although opposing German ambitions, the British took Germany seriously and were careful not to push her too far or trample her interests underfoot. They never took Austria seriously and were regularly ready to let her pay, or make her pay. Britain never encouraged France or Russia to provoke Germany; firmness and moderation were the watchwords. But from the mid-1890s on, she urged Russia to concentrate her power and attention on Europe, telling her that with time and patience she could become the arbiter of Europe—the worst possible threat to Austria. The British never liked Delcassé's anti-German stance over Morocco. But they worked to break up the long-standing Austro-Russian cooperation in Macedonia, valuable though they knew it to be for European peace, exploiting the Austro-Russian rift to promote a separate Anglo-Russian program for the Balkans and Turkey. Macedonia became the birthplace of the Triple Entente; it was supposed to cement the Anglo-Russian entente at Austria's expense as the first Moroccan Crisis had consolidated the Anglo-French accord at Germany's.[46]

---

46 At the first signs of an Austro-Russian rift, Hardinge commented, "The struggle between Austria and Russia in the Balkans is evidently now beginning and we shall not be bothered by Russia in Asia" (Douglas Dakin, "British Sources Concerning the Greek Struggle in Macedonia, 1901–1909," *Balkan Studies* 2 [1961]: 76). His comments on British aims in regard to Macedonia are equally clear and revealing: "We are quite hopeful about Macedonian reforms, if we can only come to terms with Russia, we shall be able to secure the cooperation of France and Italy and although Austria and Germany will at first be obstructive we have reason to believe that Germany will so dislike to see a combination of four Powers in opposition to her and Austria that she will reluctantly follow us and thus force Austria to come in also" (Hardinge to Nicolson, April 13, 1908, *BD*, vol. 5, 236–37). See also Steiner, *The Foreign Office*, 95 –7; and M. B. Cooper, "British Policy in the Balkans, 1908–9," *Historical Journal* 7 (1964–65): 258–79.

The British did not encourage France to try to recover Alsace-Lorraine; they did drop repeated hints to Russia about how cooperation in Asia would eventually help her in Turkey and the Straits. Britain welcomed the Franco-German agreement over Morocco in 1909 and showed little concern as the French first strained and then broke the Act of Algeciras so recently concluded. When Austria annexed Bosnia, legalizing a situation long existing de facto and giving up her hold on the Sanjak of Novi-Pazar in the process, Britain helped promote an international crisis over the violation of a treaty thirty years old, whose relevant provision had never been intended by Britain herself to remain long in force. The British sometimes tried to calm French suspicions of Germany. During the Bosnian Crisis and after, they impressed upon Russia that she had suffered a humiliating defeat at the hands of Austria backed by Germany—this regardless of the consequences for the balance of power and future Austro-Russian relations,[47] and despite the fact that the British knew of the prior Austro-Russian bargain over Bosnia and considered Izvolski himself largely to blame for Russia's discomfiture.[48]

While Britain in 1911 urged France to compensate Germany generously for her protectorate in Morocco, she simultaneously encouraged Russia to form a Balkan League, including Turkey, to stop Austria in Southeastern Europe. Grey rejected the idea of pulling Italy entirely out of the Triple Alliance, for fear of provoking Germany; but he welcomed Italy's cooperation with Russia and her concentration on the Adriatic,[49] and he tried to quell anti-Italian press sentiment in Britain over Italy's aggression in the Tripolitan War. While Grey cooperated with Germany during the Balkan Wars, it was often at Austria's expense, and always with great care not to offend Russia.[50] Although the outcome of these wars fatally tipped the Balkan balance against Austria, the frantic cries from Vienna for some consideration of Austria's position went unheeded as before. To Austria, the

47   Steiner, *The Foreign Office*, 87–8.
48   Hardinge to Cartwright, October 4, 1909, *BD*, vol. 9, pt. 1 (London: 1933), 74.
49   Hardinge to Bax-Ironside, October 28, 1909, *BD*, vol. 9, pt. 1, 80–1.
50   Steiner, *The Foreign Office*, 135, 146–7.

Foreign Office preached abnegation and restraint; among themselves, British leaders agreed that it would be better not to become
entangled at all in Balkan questions and Austria's selfish intrigues,
were it not that friendship for France and Russia required it.[51]
Meanwhile the British envoys at Sofia and Petersburg encouraged
a Serbo-Bulgarian rapprochement under Russian sponsorship that
would seal Austria's isolation and compel her to remain quiet. If
a partition of Turkey became unavoidable, the British recognized
that German interests would have to be taken into account.
Austria, on the other hand, had good reason to fear that Britain
would join with France, Germany, and Russia to cut her out.[52]

On the eve of the war, the Foreign Office was aware of the fear
prevalent in both Berlin and Vienna that Austria might collapse.
Far from viewing this eventuality as a danger per se, Nicolson
feared only that Russia and Germany might come together over
the spoils, and urged preventing this by a close Anglo-Russian
alliance. Grey feared rather what actually happened: a preventive
war launched by Germany out of fear of Russia's growing
strength and Austria's decline. His only answer to this was to
work with the supposed German peace party under Bethmann,
so as to conciliate Germany and get her to put still more restraining pressure on Austria. No thought of any action to help
maintain Austria's independence and integrity was entertained.
If Austria and Russia actually got into war, Grey hoped to
keep Germany and France out of it—thus holding the ring for
Russia, giving her the opportunity she had wanted ever since the
Crimean War.[53]

Finally, if one agrees with Fischer (as I do) that something can
be learned of the general character and direction of a nation's
policy before 1914 by seeing what it does and plans immediately
upon the outbreak of war, then it is significant that Britain's
contribution to the breakup of the Austrian Monarchy, the promises and concessions to Italy, Romania, Serbia, and Russia which
soon rendered it inevitable, began already on August 5, 1914, a

---

51   Ibid.
52   F. Roy Bridge, "Tarde venientibus ossa: Austro-Hungarian Colonial
Aspirations in Asia Minor 1913–14", *Middle Eastern Studies* 6 (1970): 319–30.
53   Steiner, *The Foreign Office*, 134–7; see also note 58 below.

week before Britain's declaration of war on Austria.[54] Equally
significant, while Britain always expected and even wanted a
united Germany to survive World War I, to serve both as a balance against Russia and France and as a market for British
goods, they considered Austria dispensable, reckoning freely
from 1916 on breaking her up (even if Germany absorbed the
German-speaking territories!) or on using a drastically reduced,
federated, and Slav-dominated Austria in some kind of anti-
German combination.[55]

Of course there was no great anti-Austrian plot. The British
did not think of Austria as their enemy; they tried not to think
of her at all. They did not plan to isolate and destroy her; they
simply did not concern themselves (as they never had earlier in
the nineteenth century) with the question of whether the concessions and defeats forced upon Austria before the war, and the
territorial sacrifices to be imposed on her during and after it,
would leave her viable. Britain undermined Austria's position
before the war—indeed, throughout the nineteenth century—
and assisted in her destruction during it, in a fit of absence of
mind, a state from which many British historians on this subject
have not yet emerged.[56] Austria was not Britain's concern, as
Grey repeatedly told his ambassador at Vienna, Sir Fairfax Cartwright; Britain wished to be cordial to her without entangling

---

54   F. Roy Bridge, "The British Declaration of War on Austria-Hungary in
1914," *Slavonic and East European Review* 47 (1969): 401–22; Harry Hanak,
"The Government, the Foreign Office and Austria-Hungary, 1914–1918,"
Slavonic and East European Review 47 (1969): 162–7.

55   Hanak, "The Government, the Foreign Office," 168–71; Beloff, *Imperial Sunset*, vol. 1, 206–9. On the general subject of British aims toward the
continent, see Harold I. Nelson, *Land and Power* (London, 1963); Paul Guinn,
British Strategy and Politics, 1914 to 1918 (Oxford, 1965); and V. H. Rothwell,
British War Aims and Peace Diplomacy, 1914–1918 (Oxford, 1971).

56   For example, so brilliant a book as Zara Steiner's on the Foreign Office
concentrates entirely on British attitudes toward Germany, virtually ignoring
the impact of British policies on Austria. Beloff (*Imperial Sunset*) devotes
283 pages to an admirable discussion of British prewar and wartime policy,
but mentions Austria only in passing. Only F. Roy Bridge's unpublished dissertation, "The Diplomatic Relations between Great Britain and Austria-Hungary,
1906–1912" (London, 1966), indicates the significance of British policy for
Austria.

herself. She was like China or Persia. The British had nothing against her, but she could do nothing for them, they in turn could not save her, and certainly no British interests would be sacrificed for her sake, including the only important British interest in the Balkans, keeping on good terms with Russia.

What makes Britain's responsibility for Austria's plight a heavy one, although less direct than Russia's or France's, is that Britain alone was in a position to manage the European Concert so as to control the Balkan situation. Russia was bound to be Austria's rival, Serbia and Romania bound to have territorial aspirations at Austria's expense, Italy bound at least to watch Austria jealously. These problems were there and could not be solved or spirited away. But they could have been controlled. Russia was not bound to be Austria's enemy; throughout the nineteenth century she had always found it profitable to seek a modus vivendi with Austria whenever it was plain that an aggressive course would get her into trouble. The danger regularly arose when Russia got tacit or open Western support for a forward policy, as she did before 1914. Serbia would try all she could get away with, but would not commit suicide by fighting Austria alone; Romania was entirely opportunistic, Italy not really vitally engaged in the Balkans. As for Austria, all through the century she had lived with international and internal problems that were insoluble but not fatal. There were so many dangers that her only hope was to outlive the threats and outlast her enemies; she always tried this course, and only abandoned it when it seemed too hopeless or humiliating, and violence appeared to be the only recourse. Right up to June 1914 all Austrian leaders, including those aggressively inclined toward Serbia and Italy, wanted an entente with Russia. Hence the situation was not inherently out of control, but only Britain could have exercised that control. France could not have checked Russia's diplomatic offensive, even had she wanted to; she was too dependent on Russian aid. Britain did not try, not so much because she feared losing Russia to Germany, or feared renewed trouble for India, as because she saw no reason to make the effort.

Instead, she expected Germany to do the whole job both of sustaining Austria and restraining her. It is strange that the Germans have not made more of this. Most German charges against England were baseless or highly exaggerated, most German expectations and demands from Britain absurd or dangerous. But the old, long-standing German and Austrian efforts to get Britain to bear her European responsibilities by upholding Austria have a good deal to be said for them. Never mind that Germany had selfish reasons for wanting to involve Britain, that Germany herself helped greatly to create the Austrian problem, and that German support for Austria was anything but loyal and disinterested. The fact remains that German support for Austria and restraint of her and Russia helped prevent several likely general wars, and that Austria by her very existence and her policy was restraining Germany, preventing her from playing world policy with a free hand. Moreover, only the presence of the Habsburg Monarchy holding down the Danube basin kept Germany or Russia from achieving mastery over Europe. With Austria there and determined to remain an independent great power, it was very difficult for either of them to fight each other, or dominate the other, or combine for aggressive purposes. Let Austria go under, and a great war for the mastery of Europe became almost mathematically predictable. The Germans, William II in particular, had many irrational beliefs, including the apocalyptic vision of an inevitable fight to the death between Teutons and Slavs.[57] But their fear of this contest, and the belief that Austria's impending dissolution must bring it on, were entirely rational.[58]

The main trouble with leaving the task of supporting Austria to Germany alone was not that it was unfair or exceeded Germany's resources, but that it was counterproductive for peace. The more the Germans alone supported Austria, the more she became and was considered a German satellite, against her will; the more she and Germany, instead of restraining each other, became involved in each other's largely individual quarrels, the

57   E.g., see Rich, *Friedrich von Holstein*, 215–20, 243–84.

58   In contrast, Grey's insistence in both the 1913 and 1914 crises that an Austro-Russian war over the Balkans, representing merely the struggle between Teuton and Slav for supremacy, as he put it, need not concern Britain or Europe unless Germany or France entered in, strikes one as remarkably insular and unrealistic. Grey to Buchanan, February 17, 1913, *BD*, vol. 9, pt. 2 (London, 1934), doc. 626; Grey to Bertie, July 29, 1914, *BD*, vol. 11 (London, 1938), doc. 283.

more Austria, despairing of finding help from Britain, France, or the Concert, would be prone to seek her salvation in violence, and the more Germany, fearful of Austria's demise or defection, would be tempted to push her into it—the scenario of 1914.

Only a commitment by Britain to use her influence with France to help keep Austria in existence by maintaining a balance of power in the Balkans and restraining Austria, Russia, and the Balkan states alike could have prevented this.[59] Such a policy had worked with Turkey for a long time, and she was far more vulnerable, weak, backward, despised, and dispensable than Austria. But the whole British tradition went against this. Despite many fine phrases, the British never understood what Austria's function really was in Europe, and how valuable she was to Britain. At best, Austria was for Britain a useful means to check France or Russia or to help Turkey; more often she was considered a menace to Turkey and a reactionary satellite of Russia or Germany, endangering the balance by her subservience and the peace by her reckless repressive policies. When France and Russia loomed as the chief dangers, Britain saw a united Italy and a united Germany under Prussia as the best answers. When Germany then became the chief danger, friendship with Russia and France was the solution. In both cases, Austria was forgotten or considered useless. As for the critical problem of East-Central and Southeastern Europe, the British knew little and cared less, but supposed that Austria was an anachronism and that a liberal nationalist solution would be best all round if achieved by peaceful means. Even had they better understood what was at stake, they would not have changed their policy. For to support Austria, however cautiously, would be to abandon Britain's coveted freedom from commitments, to give up that policy of a free hand toward the continent which accounted for Britain's greatness and which, only slightly modified, had worked brilliantly since

---

59   Although a number of Englishmen (Fairfax Cartwright at Vienna, Ralph Paget at Belgrade, Nicolson, and others) had long warned of the dangers involved in Austria's decline, only Francis Bertie at the last moment pleaded with Grey to put pressure on France to divert Russia from her absurd and dangerous policy of protecting her Balkan clients at all cost (Bertie to Grey, July 27, 1914, *BD*, vol. 11, doc. 192). By then it was too late, of course, and there is no chance Grey would have risked Britain's ententes by any such pressure.

1900. By 1914, all the challenges to Britain were under control. The empire and the home islands had not been so secure in two generations, all without war, great expense, or binding alliances. To this day, the thought that Britain's prewar successes in foreign policy might be connected with the final catastrophe, that in the struggle for peace, unlike her usual record in war, Britain this time won all the battles and lost the war, has not penetrated British historiography.

Yet it would be wrong to end on this note, as if Britain were especially to blame—as misleading as the current excessive concentration on Germany, and far more unfair. The basic point is that everyone saw the central threat to the European system in the decline of Austria, and no one would do anything about it. Russians, Serbs, Romanians, Greeks, and Italians all exploited it: the French thought only of their security. Even Germany made the problem worse, by promoting Austria's survival not as a European independent great power, but as a German state and Germany's satellite, and by insisting against Austrian protests that war, if it came, must be fought as a great duel to the death between Germans and Slavs. The British, meanwhile, did not want Austria to die, but hoped that if she must, she would at least do it quietly. In 1914 Austria decided not to die quietly, and once this long-postponed decision to recover her position by violence was taken, there was no stopping short of a general holocaust.[60]

The only reason for laying greater stress on Britain's role here is that objectively (although not psychologically) she had greater freedom to act otherwise and greater ability to change the outcome. The attitudes behind it all, in any case, were universal—the same short-sighted selfishness and lack of imagination, the same exclusive concentration on one's own interests at the expense of the community. Everyone wanted a payoff; no

---

60   Interestingly enough, as Egmont Zechlin repeatedly argues in criticism of Fischer, Germany (or at least Bethmann) tried to some extent early in the war to keep it a limited cabinet-style conflict. See Egmont Zechlin, "Das 'schlesische' Angebot und die italienische Kriegsgefahr," *Geschichte in Wissenschaft und Unterricht* 14 (1963): 533–56; and "Probleme des Kriegskalkiuls und Kriegsbeendigung im Ersten Weltkrieg," *Geschichte in Wissenschaft und Unterricht* 16 (1965): 69–82. But Zechlin's evidence never indicates a real chance that the war could have been limited.

one wanted to pay. Everyone expected the system to work for him; no one would work for it. All were playing the same game—imperialism, world policy, Realpolitik, call it what you will—all save Austria, and she also would have played it had she been able.[61] All believed, as many historians still do, that *sacro egoismo* is the only rational rule for high politics, that it even represents a higher realism and a higher morality, when it really is only a higher stupidity. And so the system was bent and twisted until it broke; its burdens were distributed not according to ability to bear them, but inability to resist. Inevitably the collapse came where all the weight was concentrated—at the weakest point. Two titles from Nietzsche and Nestroy sum the whole process up: "Menschlich, allzu menschlich," and "Gegen Torheit gibt es kein Mittel."

---

61   Wolfdieter Bihl, "Zur den österreichisch-ungarischen Kriegszielen 1914," *Jahrblicher für Geschichte Osteuropas* 16 (1968): 505–30; Fritz Klein, "Die Rivalität zwischen Deutschland und Oesterreich-Ungarn in der Türkei am Vorabend des ersten Weltkrieges," in Fritz Klein, ed., *Politik im Krieg 1914–1918* (Berlin, 1964), 1–21.

2

International Politics, Peace and War: 1815–1914

This chapter has a conventional approach and theme: to analyse the changing character and structure of nineteenth-century European international politics.* The procedure is less conventional: to concentrate on explaining peace rather than, as commonly happens, on explaining war. Peace is more artificial and demands more explanation. Wars sometimes just happen; peace is always caused. Moreover, understanding why the nineteenth century was more peaceful than any predecessor in European history helps illuminate why it ended in a war greater than any before.

The most obvious sign of a pacific century in Europe is its relatively few and limited wars—no general or systemic war (one involving all or most of the great powers) at all from 1815 to 1914; in two extended periods, 1815–54 and 1871–1914, no wars between European great powers. Though five wars between great powers were fought in mid-century, all important in their results, even these were comparatively limited in duration, scope, and casualties. The stability of the actors is equally striking. All the great powers of 1815 survived as such until 1914, despite some changes in rank. Except for the German and Italian states absorbed by unification in mid-century, so did most smaller states, and some new ones emerged.

Nineteenth-century international institutions and practices likewise changed in the direction of stability. Alliances, in the eighteenth century predominantly instruments for power, security,

---

*   I wish to thank Professor F. R. Bridge for many valuable suggestions and criticisms.

and concrete advantages, were used primarily for much of the nineteenth century for managing and restraining both opponents and allies and preventing aggrandizement. The nineteenth-century system not only produced durable peace where conflict had been endemic (the Low Countries, Switzerland, Scandinavia, and the Baltic, and for some time the Near East) but also succeeded at times in promoting peaceful change (for example, in the creation of Belgium). It absorbed and survived forcible change by war, and proved capable of integrating new actors, even those produced or transformed by treaty violations and war, into the system. Expansion and imperialism outside Europe, in previous centuries a direct factor in Europe's conflicts and wars, remained for much of the nineteenth century largely separated from them. Most impressive of all, this international system endured and survived the strains of a century of rapid, fundamental changes in European society—industrialization, modernization, revolutions in communications, technology, and science, the rise of the strong state, mass politicization, and the growth of liberalism, nationalism, socialism, and democracy.

The Vienna system

The explanation of this remarkable record, and of its disastrous end, begins with the Vienna system, the network of treaties, institutions, and practices developed in 1813–15 during the last Napoleonic Wars and at the Congress of Vienna. There is wide agreement on some reasons for its unusual stability. It embodied a moderate, sensible territorial settlement that satisfied the main needs and requirements of the victors (Britain, Russia, Austria, Prussia, and their lesser allies) without despoiling or humiliating France. Tied into this were comprehensive negotiated settlements of many particular disputes arising out of the wars from 1787 to 1815. These settlements, combined in a network of mutually supporting treaties, gave all governments a stake in a new system of mutual interlocking rights and obligations. Backing this was a security alliance among the great powers to defend the settlement against violation or revolutionary aggression, especially by France. Finally, an old but little-used diplomatic principle was implemented, that of a European Concert, by which the five great powers became a governing council or directory for settling serious international questions, using Concert practices such as diplomatic conferences rather than bilateral or multilateral negotiations to achieve agreed solutions.

Another feature of the settlement was equally vital though less obvious: the creation of an independent, confederated, defensively oriented European center. Throughout the eighteenth century the Revolutionary-Napoleonic era, the instability, weakness, and rivalries plaguing Central Europe (the German states, Switzerland, Austria, Poland) had spawned repeated crises and wars as internecine conflicts drew in the competing flank powers. The Vienna Congress took a series of measures to turn this critical area temporarily into a zone of peace (at the cost, to be sure, of some injustice, disappointed expectations, and future trouble). It established a German Confederation uniting the German states in a permanent defensive league under joint Austro-Prussian leadership; gave Austria leadership but not direct control of the various independent states of Italy; established and guaranteed a neutral Swiss Confederation; and maintained the eighteenth-century partition of Poland by Russia, Austria, and Prussia in a modified form. Even the Kingdoms of the Netherlands and Denmark were tied indirectly into this independent, defensive center.

If there is little disagreement among scholars about these sources of the system's stability, there is some concerning its spirit and operating principles. For many, it worked because a balance of power inhibited new bids for hegemony and monarchs cooperated against war, liberalism, nationalism, and revolution. Once these factors declined, with the balance of power shifting and new ambitions emerging, the system no longer worked. This verdict, though it contains some truth, is inadequate and misleading. The reason governments supported the equilibrium of power, territory, rights, status, obligations, and security reached in 1815 was not that they were sated by expansion or simply exhausted by war and wanted peace. It was that they had learned that war and expansion could not provide peace and security. They accepted, often grudgingly, the painful, delicate compromises of the settlement in order to achieve security in a system of rights guaranteed by law. Even in France most ministries, if not opposition groups, came to accept and support the settlement on these grounds. And when governments did need to be restrained in this era, the normal method was not balancing, confronting their power with countervailing power, but "grouping"—using Concert means and group pressure to enforce norms and treaties. In the most important crises, balancing could not have worked, for two great powers, Britain and Russia, were more powerful and far less vulnerable than the other three, and when they worked together, as they did at major junctures in 1815–48, they settled matters. In terms of power, the system was characterized by dual hegemony, British in Western Europe, Russian in the east, a hegemony that was tolerable because it was usually latent, inactive, and allowed others lesser spheres of influence.

Just as political equilibrium did not derive from balancing power by countervailing power, so conservative solidarity did not rest simply on restoring and preserving the old regime. In international politics at least, the Vienna system was not a restoration. It preserved most of the territorial, social, and constitutional-political changes brought about in the Revolutionary and Napoleonic periods, and encouraged or permitted some new ones. Only later, from 1820 on, did policies of repression of dissent and simple maintenance of the status quo dominate in Russia, Austria, and Prussia and their spheres, leading to an ideological split between a liberal-constitutional West and an absolutist East. The solidarity among governments for peace created at Vienna, which transcended and outlived this split, arose from its overall success in satisfying existing demands and harmonizing conflicting claims, based on a general consensus on the practical requirements of peace and a recognition that certain limits had to govern international competition. Rivalries and conflicting aims persisted under the Vienna system as before—Anglo-French competition in Spain and the Mediterranean, Austro-French in Italy, Austro-Prussian in Germany, Austro-Russian in the Balkans, Anglo-Russian in the Middle East. But the stakes, rules, and goals were different. Now the competition was over spheres of interest and leading influence, not territorial aggrandizement, the elimination of the rival, or total control, and preserving general peace remained uppermost. The late eighteenth-century game of high-stakes poker, which the Revolution and Napoleon had turned into Russian roulette, gave way to contract bridge.

This made Concert rules and practices effective for decades after 1815 in dealing peacefully with international problems and crises, often by repressive means and never without friction and rivalry, but without great-power war or aggrandizement. The examples can only be summarized here.

Revolts in Spain, Naples, and Piedmont in 1820–1. Three great-power conferences in 1820–2 led to their suppression by Austria in Italy and by France in Spain.

The Greek revolt in 1821–5. This profound ethnic-religious revolt and war against Turkish rule repeatedly threatened to cause a Russo-Turkish war but self-restraint by Russia and Concert diplomacy led by Britain and Austria averted it.

Revolutions in Spain's and Portugal's American colonies. All the rebellious colonies gained their independence without foreign intervention, partly because Britain with its navy deterred it, but mainly because the continental monarchies, despite their sympathy for Spain and fear of republican revolution, made no serious effort to intervene.

The Eastern Crisis in 1826–9. The intervention of Britain, Russia, and France to save the Greeks from being crushed by the Ottoman Sultan's vassal Egypt, though intended initially to end the fighting by diplomacy and prevent any great power from aggrandizing itself or acting unilaterally, instead escalated into an allied naval battle that destroyed the Turco-Egyptian forces. This led to a Russo-Turkish war, a Russian victory, and the danger that the Ottoman Empire would collapse with Russia picking up the pieces—a likely eighteenth-century-style outcome. Instead, Russia signed a peace treaty that increased its influence at Constantinople but preserved the Sultan's throne; the three allies negotiated the creation of an independent Greek kingdom; and this soon came under Anglo-French influence rather than Russian.

The 1830 revolutions. These revolutions, beginning in July in France and spreading to the Netherlands, Switzerland, Germany, Italy, and Poland, produced some violence, considerable political and constitutional change, and some international crises, deepening the East-West ideological divide. In international politics, however, the powers demonstrated restraint. They quickly recognized the new Orleanist monarchy to replace the ousted Bourbons in France, and managed Austro-French tension over Austrian interventions in the Papal State through conference diplomacy. They responded to a Belgian revolt overthrowing the United Netherlands, created in 1815 as a defence against France, by convening a London conference that, despite great obstacles raised mainly by the Dutch and Belgians, finally established and jointly guaranteed an independent Belgian kingdom, bringing peace until 1914 to an area for centuries the cockpit of Europe. Even Russia's crushing of a Polish revolt for independence passed without foreign intervention, serious international crisis, or territorial change.

New Eastern Crises in 1832–41. This time the threat to the Ottoman Empire came from the Sultan's ambitious vassal, the Pasha of Egypt, and his regime, twice defeated and facing overthrow, was rescued by European great powers, Russia in 1832–3 and four powers in 1839–40. The four powers' decision in 1840 finally to act without France led to a crisis and threat of war in Europe, apparently reviving the traditional power-political competition in the Near East and Europe. But the crisis really had more to do with rules and leadership in the Concert than power politics. France always favored a Concert to defend the Sultan but wished to lead it in partnership with Britain against Russia, the permanent threat to Turkey. Instead Britain, suspicious of French aims, preferred working with Russia, and France reacted mainly out of wounded honor and lost prestige. French preparations for war, directed against Austria and Prussia, were largely a bluff, and, when the four-power concert held fast, France backed down, with the two German powers helping it do so with honour. The crisis illustrates both the Anglo-Russian dual-hegemonic structure of the system and the effectiveness of Concert grouping strategy.

Other troubles of the 1830s and 1840s. These were a mixed bag, including civil wars in Spain and Portugal between absolutists and pseudo-constitutionalists, rising discontent and tensions in Italy, especially at Rome and between Sardinia-Piedmont and Austria, another incipient Polish revolt crushed by the Eastern Powers in 1846 and followed by the annexation of the Free City of Cracow by Austria, and a small Protestant-Catholic civil war in Switzerland. All raised contentious issues between various powers; none came close to threatening international war.

Yet to claim that the system remained effective in preserving peace is not to argue that it was unaffected or unweakened by crisis and change. The 1830s and 1840s clearly show growing tensions and friction between the powers. The cause usually given for this, as for the 1848 revolutions and the ultimate downfall of the Vienna system, is the growing ideological, political, and economic gap between absolutist and moderate liberal-constitutionalist governments and groups, and the way in which absolutist regimes, increasingly weak and threatened, tried to meet demands for political, social, and economic change and the rise of nationalism by repression rather than reform.

Basically this is true, but it over-simplifies the connection between the absolutist-constitutionalist split in domestic affairs and international relations. Historians often equate the Vienna system (the treaties, rules, and practices for conducting international politics) with the Metternich system (the absolutist prescriptions for the internal governance of states). Since Austria's chancellor Prince Metternich and his allies identified the two, using the Vienna treaties to legitimate their repressive internal and international practices, and since their liberal and radical opponents likewise tarred the two systems with the same brush, this is understandable. Nonetheless, the two were not identical or inseparable, and the actual effects of the ideological contest from 1815 to 1848 show it. Overall, the Vienna system won (peace and the treaties were preserved), while the Metternich system ultimately lost (conservative attempts to hold back constitutionalism, liberal ideas, and economic and social change lost ground throughout the 1830s and 1840s in France, the Low Countries, Germany, northern Italy, and even parts of Austria). Moreover, the ideological rifts produced heated argument but not serious international rivalries or crises between governments. All the important rivalries in Europe both antedated the ideological divide and crossed its boundaries. The ideological dispute between absolutists proclaiming a right of intervention to suppress revolutions and liberals proclaiming a doctrine of non-intervention made little difference in practice.

Regardless of doctrine, states intervened in foreign revolutions within their respective spheres of influence, or did not, according to their particular interests. The ideological contest, in other words, did not directly affect the Vienna system's capacity to manage immediate international problems, nor for the most part did it lead governments into dangerous or aggressive policies. The most reactionary great-power regime in 1815–48—Charles X's in France (1824–30)—also had the most dangerously ambitious foreign policy aims.

Yet absolutist policies did undermine the Vienna system and general peace both indirectly, adding to the pressures promoting revolution and discrediting and delegitimizing it by association with Metternichian repression, and directly, by deliberately stunting the Vienna system's capacity to grow and adapt itself to new conditions. From 1819 on Metternich and his allies took the 1815 arrangements for the German Confederation, Italy, and Poland, originally capable of change and development, and reduced them to mere instruments for preserving the status quo, leaving the system still useful for crisis management but not problem-solving. On the other side, the Utopian schemes and reckless actions of nationalist and revolutionary ideologues threatened peace even more directly, while moderate reformers, especially in Britain, gave good advice without ever intending to back it with action or to take responsibility for the consequences. Britain's Lord Palmerston, for example, was often right on the kinds of measures needed to avoid revolution in Germany and Italy; Metternich right about the dangers of urging others to apply them without considering how to manage the results. Thus its very success in preventing war and managing crises helped prepare the ground for the assault against the Vienna system.

The system undermined and overthrown, 1848–61

Unlike some revolutions, those that swept Western and Central Europe from France to the Romanian Principalities in 1848 arose primarily from internal political, social, and economic discontents and movements, not international conflicts. International politics, however, played a certain role in their origins and a bigger one in their course and outcome.

One important factor was nationalism, manifesting itself in two forms, both seeking liberation but from different bonds or restraints and for different ends. The first, voiced by peoples or leaders asserting a particular identity and chafing under foreign rule, called for national "rights" ranging from local autonomy and privileges through home rule to total independence. This kind of nationalist protest was widespread—Danes and Germans in Schleswig-Holstein, Italians in Austrian-ruled Lombardy-Venetia, Hungarians within Austria, Czechs in Bohemia-Moravia, Croats in Hungary, Poles under all three partitioning powers, Romanians under Turkish and Hungarian authority, Irish in the United Kingdom. Another kind of nationalism, voiced mainly by a rising commercial and professional middle class led or joined by free intellectuals and liberal nobles, demanded liberation from the obstacles placed in the path of the nation's political freedom, social, economic, and cultural development, and power by small, weak, or unprogressive governments. This was present in France, but strongest in Germany and Italy.

In meaning different things by national liberation and unification, the two varieties targeted and threatened different foes. The former threatened multinational empires, Austria in particular; the latter particularly targeted small princely states. The former pointed toward decentralization and federation, the latter toward amalgamation. Thus, while they might cooperate at times, the likelihood, borne out by events, was that they would ultimately clash head on. Both kinds, moreover, aroused various divergent counter-revolutionary passions and programs—anti-Polish patriotism in Prussia and Russia, particularist loyalty in Bavaria and other German states, municipal loyalties in Italy, military, bureaucratic, and religious *Habsburgtreue* in Austria, German resistance to Czechs in Bohemia-Moravia or Danes in Schleswig, Croat and Slovak resistance to Hungarian domination, and the like. Hence the inevitable result of nationalist unity movements was increased disunity and conflict.

Nationalist movements affected international politics most directly, however, not by creating or deepening conflicts within countries or between peoples, but by providing the opportunity and means for ambitious leaders and governments to pursue expansionist aims, often old statist and dynastic ones, under new revolutionary slogans. Such "nationalist" programs and the responses of governments attacked or threatened by them mainly account for the international crises and conflicts of 1848–9. The Italian revolutions directly challenged both Austrian hegemony and the 1815 system, but only when Sardinia-Piedmont took the lead and attacked Austria was there an interstate war that threatened to pull in France and become general, and, when Austria crushed Sardinia-Piedmont in 1848 and 1849, the international crisis ended. The German and Danish national causes clashed in Schleswig-Holstein, but an international crisis arose only when Prussia temporarily supported the German cause with its army, and, when Britain and Russia forced Prussia to back down, the acute crisis was over. The German National Parliament at Frankfurt developed a dangerous Great German foreign policy in seeking to unite Germany, but the great international danger lay in the Austro-Prussian rivalry over who would run it. The Hungarian independence movement was a more formidable challenge to Austria than any other because early on the Hungarian movement gained legal recognition of its rights from Vienna, albeit later rescinded. It could then declare independence and fight to retain all the historic lands and peoples of the crown of St. Stephen as a government in command of the Hungarian half of the regular Austrian army. Finally, it was Tsar Nicholas I's determination to keep revolution from his own lands and maintain Russian hegemony in Eastern Europe that ultimately doomed the Romanian risings and the Hungarian revolution, and helped prevent war in 1849–50 between Austria and Prussia over mastery in Germany.

In other words, power politics prevailed over national movements in the international arena. More surprisingly, international peace and order temporarily won out over revolution, ambition, and war. In 1850, after numerous crises, conflicts, and threats of major war, all the pre-1848 treaties, international institutions, and borders remained intact. The events of 1848–9, unlike those of 1814–15, brought about a true restoration of the old order. What made it possible and largely accounts for both the defeat of revolutions and the preservation of peace is that all the great powers resisted the temptation to expand abroad, using their armies instead to restore their internal authority. The survival and effective use of key structural elements of the Vienna order for crisis management, notably the dual-hegemonic cooperation of Britain and Russia and the application of Concert methods and principles, helps to explain this outcome.

Yet the surface restoration concealed profound changes in the international system. Crucial questions (German, Italian, and Hungarian, all part of a still larger Austrian one) had been opened up and deepened, old rivalries revived in acute form (Austro-Sardinian and Austro-French in Italy, Austro-Prussian in Germany, and Austro-Russian in the Balkans, despite their cooperation in Hungary). Liberal or democratic revolution from below was discredited, but conservative revolution from above by governments and armed force was encouraged. An insecure and adventurous republic emerged in France, with a Bonapartist conspirator, Napoleon's nephew Louis Napoleon, its President. Worst of all, the revolutions had radicalized many conservatives, formerly cautious, internationalist, and legalistic, who now saw how conservative regimes could neutralize liberalism and win over the masses by coopting nationalist goals.

This long-term perspective makes the breakdown of the Concert in the next Eastern Crisis, resulting in the first major war since 1815, appear inevitable. Yet the actual origins of the Crimean War suggest blunder and accident instead. The original confrontation between France and Russia took a long time to develop (1851–3), the issue in dispute seems superficial (nominally control of certain Holy Places in Jerusalem, really prestige and influence at Constantinople), and that issue was settled in Russia's favor before the crisis grew serious. The descent from initial crisis into actual war took almost a year (May 1853–March 1854) and went through many stages—a Turkish rejection of a Russian ultimatum, a Russian break in relations and occupation of the Romanian principalities, British and French fleet movements in support of the Turks, a Turkish declaration of war, Russian destruction of the Turkish navy, an Anglo-French offensive occupation of the Black Sea, and finally war between Russia and the Western powers. At every stage European Concert solutions, usually orchestrated by Austria, were proposed and seemed capable of solving the crisis, only to be spoiled by some new development. Yet the war did not really result from bad luck or accident; beneath a contingent process lay profound causes. Three were important without being central. France, where Louis Napoleon now ruled as Emperor Napoleon III, deliberately exploited the crisis and risked war to gain prestige, destroy the Austro-Russian alliance, acquire an alliance with Britain, and thereby enjoy security and leadership in Europe. The Turks, once confident of Western support, decided on war to relieve the constant Russian pressure on them. In Britain, domestic politics within a weak divided government under pressure from a Russophobe press, Parliament, and public opinion led to confusion and unclear decisions and actions at crucial moments. But the two central factors derived from basic policy decisions in Russia and Britain, and each rested on miscalculation. The crisis arose because Russia attempted to bully the Turkish government into formally acknowledging Russian pre-eminence at Constantinople, assuming that there would be no strong European reaction. The Ottoman-Russian conflict evolved into a major war because the British government decided at various junctures after July 1853 not to allow Russia an honorable retreat under cover of the Concert, which it knew Russia was seeking, but instead to inflict a humiliating political defeat on Russia and to weaken its position in Europe and the Middle East. This policy, which risked war from the outset and finally steered towards it, rested on two assumptions: that restraining Russia by grouping it in the Concert might preserve peace now, but would not eliminate the long-range Russian threat to the Ottoman and British empires (which was true), and that British naval and financial strength added to continental land forces (Turkish, French, and perhaps also Austrian and German) could do so fairly easily and quickly, possibly even throwing Russia back in Europe and Asia.

This proved incorrect. The war, fought principally on the Crimean Peninsula because Britain and France could not get at Russia effectively elsewhere, revealed the military weaknesses and inefficiency of all the contestants, especially Russia and Britain. The losses, though fairly heavy especially for Russia, stemmed from weather, disease, and logistical problems more than battle. When the Allies after a year-long siege finally captured the fortress of Sevastopol, France and Austria combined to force Russia to accept peace terms and to drag Britain to the peace table. The settlement reached at the Congress of Paris in the spring of 1856 reflected the limited allied victory. Russia surrendered its special treaty rights vis-à-vis the Ottoman Empire (a foregone conclusion) and had to cede a small piece of southern Bessarabia to Turkey and accept the neutralization of the Black Sea, twin blows to its prestige, sovereignty, and security.

Yet, except for France, which gained military laurels and international prestige, no principal profited from the war. Russia, suffering the effects of its backwardness, partly withdrew from European affairs to concentrate on internal reform. Britain, disappointed by its war effort and distracted by troubles in Persia and India, also partially retreated from Europe. The war, far from reducing the Russian threat to the British Empire, served to convince Russians hitherto divided on the subject that Britain was a worldwide enemy and turned them towards more expansion in the Caucasus, Central Asia, and the Far East. The Ottoman Empire, though it gained a brief respite from Russian pressure and a chance for modernization, acquired no durable Western support. The Allies disdained it during the war and abandoned it soon after, with Russia joining France in encouraging Balkan independence movements.

The main impact of the war, however, making it a turning point in international politics, was systemic and especially affected Central Europe. Austria and the European Concert lost; Prussia and Sardinia-Piedmont won. The war itself, which Austria had tried desperately to prevent, undermined the Concert and threatened Austria, an empire peculiarly dependent on international sanctions and support. The results of Austrian policy during the war proved even worse. Pressed by the Western powers to join the war and by Russia, Prussia, and the German Confederation to stay out, Austria had followed a nonbelligerent but pro-Western course that succeeded in limiting the war and preventing Russia from winning it (two-thirds of Russia's army had to be kept on its western front) but not in ending it on Austrian terms. After a peace conference at Vienna in March–May 1855 failed, Austria helped France force Russia to accept defeat and humiliating terms. In the end it made Russia an enemy by its betrayal, angered Prussia and the German states by dragging them along in its risky pro-Western policy, antagonized the western powers by refusing to fight, and convinced everyone that it was selfish, irresolute, and greedy. Yet its aim was to revive the Concert through a permanent conservative alliance with the Western powers, serving to restrain Russia, defend the Ottoman Empire, and gain British and French support for the status quo (that is, Austrian leadership) against revolution and challenges from Prussia and Sardinia in Germany and Italy. Russia, Prussia, and other states were supposed to accept this for the general peace and stability it would bring.

It was a pipe dream, of course. The Habsburg Monarchy, neoabsolutist, financially shaky, full of unrest in Hungary and Lombardy-Venetia and unsolved problems elsewhere, had neither the power nor the credibility for such a position of leadership. The program itself simply ignored liberal and national pressures and the need for change, subordinated everything to Austria's need for external tranquillity, and over-looked how unsuitable Britain and France were to be reliable partners for Austria. But the failure of this attempt to recon-struct the European Concert in mid-century on a conservative, Austrian-centered basis points to something even more signifi-cant: the absence of any liberal, Western attempt to do so. The great missed opportunity for establishing a liberal international order in Europe did not come in 1848–9—the actual liberal-revolutionary foreign policy program of those years (French, German, Prussian, Italian, Austrian, and Hungarian) were all dangerously power-political and expansionist—but in 1853–6. The Western powers' defeat of autocratic Russia afforded them a chance, if they chose, to lead Europe on a liberal path in regard to trade, nationalities problems, constitutional reform, and other policies that many had advocated for decades. But neither government had clear ideas for this task or interest in it. The British concentrated on trade, empire, domestic politics, and maintaining the continental balance of power, now mainly against France. Napoleon III's ideas about reconstructing Europe were vague, impractical, and bound up with his dynas-tic ambitions and he proved inept in executing them. The liberal moment thus passed, leaving the field to the practitioners of Realpolitik.

A further blow to Austria came with the unification and de facto independence of the Romanian principalities that Romanian nationalists achieved in 1858–9 against Austrian and Turkish opposition through shrewd maneuvers encouraged by France and Russia and grudgingly accepted by Britain. This cost the Ottoman Sultan little, for his rights had long been nominal and an independent Romania would ultimately prove a better buffer against Russia. For Austria, however, it worsened the Hungarian problem (Transylvania had a Romanian majority) and the general threat of nationalism.

Italy, however, posed a greater strategic and power-political threat. Austria's defeat of Sardinia-Piedmont in 1849 had only hardened their rivalry. Its new king Victor Emmanuel II and leading statesman Count Cavour continued the cold war against Austria and prepared for a hot one, using the Italian national cause mainly for their particular ends—military and dynastic glory and territorial expansion, the expulsion of Austria from Italy and if possible its destruction, and victory for conservative-liberal constitutional forces led by Piedmont over democratic-republican revolutionary forces in the Italian Risorgimento. Cavour's effort in 1856 to start a war against Austria with British and French support had failed, but by 1859 he had gone far to make Sardinia a leader in fiscal, commercial, and constitutional progress in Italy, to organize and co-opt the bourgeois nationalist movement, to win sympathy abroad especially in Britain, and to blacken Austria's reputation, exploiting the revolutionary discontent in Lombardy-Venetia, Austria's repressive measures against it, and its military treaties with other Italian states to paint it as the aggressor. Having goaded Austria into breaking relations, Cavour reached a secret agreement with Napoleon III in mid-1858 to provoke a joint war with Austria to expel it from Italy, expand Sardinia, and reconstruct Italy on federal lines under French influence. This was backed by a defensive alliance in early 1859. Cavour knew that he risked replacing Austrian hegemony with French, but was confident he could manage Napoleon III.

Yet, despite growing unrest in Lombardy and mobilization of Austrian and Sardinian forces on their frontier, war proved elusive so long as Austria stood on the defence of its legal rights, and the whole conspiracy was threatened when Britain and Prussia, opposed to war and worried about France, offered jointly to mediate the Italian crisis. France countered by getting Russia to propose a general congress, intended to isolate Austria and provoke a *casus belli*. The Austrians, sensing this, initially did not flatly reject a congress but insisted that Sardinia demobilize first as a precondition. Fearing isolation, Napoleon III decided in mid-April to agree and pressed Sardinia to accept this humiliation. Cavour, near despair, contemplated resigning and exposing the plot when suddenly he was rescued by an Austrian ultimatum demanding immediate Sardinian demobilization. He evaded it, Austria declared war, France honored its alliance commitment, Britain and Prussia condemned Austria as the aggressor and withdrew into neutrality, and Cavour had his war.

Austria's blunder is explained, though not justified, by its belief that it had to end Sardinia's provocations and the military, fiscal, and political pressures of cold war and mobilization once and for all, and that this was the last best opportunity. Along with this went a fatal miscalculation born of a kind of moral hubris—the conviction that Austria's cause, the defence of its legal rights against revolutionary attacks, was so obviously right and necessary for European order that Europe would in the end support it against its enemies.

Nemesis followed hubris. After the French army had defeated the Austrian in two bloody battles in Lombardy (the Piedmontese did little fighting), Emperor Franz Joseph accepted Napoleon III's offer of a truce in mid-July. Napoleon III's decision to end the war before Austria was expelled from Italy as promised was prudent. The war had proved costly and unpopular at home, the Austrian army was still in the field, Britain was growing suspicious, Sardinia was unreliable, and, worst of all, Prussia and the German Confederation threatened to intervene. His methods, however, which included deceiving Franz Joseph, worsened his existing reputation for unreliability; diplomats' tricks are one thing, sovereigns' another. Though Cavour resigned in protest over the truce, he remained in control behind the scenes and succeeded in subverting its terms so that in the final peace Sardinia-Piedmont acquired Tuscany, Parma, Modena, and the Papal Marches along with conquered Lombardy. These gains, sanctioned by plebiscites, almost tripled it in size and population. The cost was the cession to France (again dignified by plebiscites) of two smaller Piedmontese territories as compensation, Savoy and Nice. The sacrifice was painful to Italian and Savoyard patriots, but a bargain for Cavour and no boon for Napoleon. The Italian venture, as his domestic enemies pointed out, had at great cost created a new potential rival for France, while the acquisition of Nice and Savoy alienated Britain and deepened European suspicions of his ambitions.

The events of 1859–60 obviously did not create a final settlement for Italy. Austria still held Venetia, the Pope and the Bourbons still ruled at Rome and Naples, and both Napoleon III and the Austrians secretly hoped to alter the outcome in different ways. Yet it could have lasted a good while. Austria was friendless, exhausted, and racked with internal problems, Napoleon III was unready for another adventure, and Sardinia had plenty of new territory to absorb and organize. Cavour, moreover, had little interest in the south or Italian nationalism per se. It required a different kind of Italian adventurer-patriot, Giuseppe Garibaldi, the greatest of all nineteenth-century freedom fighters, to launch the next act in Italian unification, one that Cavour would take over, exploit, and finish.

In May 1860 Garibaldi led an expedition of 1,000 ill-armed volunteers from the north to Sicily to support a Sicilian insurrection against Neapolitan rule. He succeeded in driving the demoralized Neapolitan army out of Sicily and much of the Neapolitan mainland, and was checked only in late summer north of Naples. His real aim, however, was to go to Rome, overthrow the papacy, and found a democratic united Italy over which Victor Emmanuel could reign. The opportunity this presented to Cavour, who had tried secretly to stop Garibaldi while pretending to support him, was outweighed by its challenge and dangers. He, his monarch, and his allies abhorred the notion of a democratic Italy formed by popular action, but overthrowing the Pope would alienate France, outrage Catholic Europe, bring Austria back into the field with conservative support, and destroy everything that had been achieved.

Cavour's response was bold and Machiavellian. Gaining Napoleon's tacit permission, he tried first to foment an insurrection in the Papal State to justify an intervention there. When this failed, he sent the army in anyway, dispersing the papal forces and seizing most of the Pope's territory. It then invaded Naples (another neutral friendly state), and defeated the Neapolitan army, though the final mop-up took months. Garibaldi and his forces were dismissed with thanks but no reward, the Pope was confined to Rome and its environs (the Patrimony of St. Peter), and Naples, Sicily, and most papal territory were absorbed through plebiscite into a new Kingdom of Italy proclaimed in January 1861.

With all its flaws, this outcome was better than any practical alternative, and achieved with surprisingly little violence and bloodshed in the interstate wars (the internal pacification of the south was another matter). Yet, from an international stand-point, these events did less to reorganize Europe on a new national basis than to advance the destruction of the old Euro-pean order without establishing a new one. Three reasons prompt this conclusion. First, Italy was incomplete (Venice and Rome), would still have irredentist ambitions even after acquiring these, and, as a weak, ambitious would-be great power, would remain an incalculable, destabilizing factor in European politics. Secondly, France was now isolated and Napoleon III discredited as a leader and manager of the system, while old rivalries had been aggravated rather than healed (Austro-Italian, Austro-French, Anglo-French, Austro-Prussian). Finally, Cavour's actions in uniting Italy, however justified by danger and necessity, were so unscrupulous as to undermine any stable code of international conduct and system of mutual restraint unless convincingly renounced for the future—something neither Cavour, who died in mid-1861, nor his successors would or could do.

The creation of Prussia-Germany, 1862–71

As everyone knows, the Second German Reich was not unified from below but created from above by Prussia through wars that ousted Austria from Germany, destroyed the German Confeder-ation, and incorporated its non-Austrian territories into a Prussian-dominated empire. This outcome was not foreordained; other settlements of the German question were possible. Yet paradoxically, without this contingent outcome resulting in this particular Prussian-dominated Germany, it is hard to envision any stable European system emerging to replace the one finally buried in these last of the mid-century wars.

The fact that the architect of German unification, Count Bismarck, was named Prussia's Minister-President in 1862 in the course of a constitutional crisis pitting the king, the army, and the ministry against the liberal majority in Prussia's lower house demonstrates the intimate connection between foreign and domestic politics in the process. Other internal political, social, economic, and cultural factors in Prussia and Germany were involved in unification. Bismarck's motives in seeking and using power, however, were primarily international, not domestic or personal. For years he had advocated expanding Prussia's territory and power to fit its great-power needs and role, absorbing or subordinating smaller states and ousting Austria from at least north Germany and possibly the south as well.

This revolutionary program was almost certain to require war, as Bismarck recognized. Yet one cannot simply say, "Bismarck started three wars to unify Germany." He always tried other means first and as long as possible; technically Prussia was not the aggressor in any of them. Moreover, his main aim was always to strengthen Prussia and never to unify Germany entirely. Above all, he conducted policy, not as a puppeteer or visionary following his star, but as one player among many in Europe who pursued his overall goal step by step with limited means, seizing opportunities and avoiding traps as he went. The reason for organizing the story around him is not that he controlled events, but that he showed extraordinary skill and success in exploiting them.

His first big opportunity arose from another clash in 1863 between Denmark and the German Confederation over Schleswig-Holstein, which was set off by the Danish government's violation of the five-power London Protocol of 1852 and led to an armed confrontation. Though complicated, it was the sort of dispute that the European Concert had settled before, and another London conference was convened to do so. But Britain and Russia, Denmark's main protectors, were now rivals and distracted with other problems—Britain chiefly with North America, Russia with another Polish revolt. Napoleon III's opportunism and the Danish refusal to restore the legal *status quo ante* also obstructed a diplomatic solution. Bismarck cared nothing about the legal quarrel or the German national cause (in fact, viewed it in this context as a threat to Prussian interests), but saw a chance to gain something for Prussia, frustrate the German liberal nationalists trying to make Schleswig-Holstein a new north German middle state, compromise and snare Austria, and shore up his own threatened position in office. He persuaded Austria to join Prussia in intervening to settle the question as European great powers. The two powers demanded that Denmark restore the legal status quo and on its refusal sent a combined army to brush aside the German federal troops, first occupying both duchies and then invading Denmark. After a truce and a renewed London conference, which again broke down over Denmark's refusal to restore the *status quo ante*, Prussia and Austria pursued the war to victory, the peace treaty giving them both duchies in common. Austria had fought a war for conquests useful only to Prussia, thereby alienating its natural allies in Germany, further discrediting the Confederation, and damaging its reputation for conservative legality in Europe. Why, especially since Austria's foreign minister Rechberg knew how anti-Austrian Bismarck was? Partly because some Austrians hoped to lure Prussia into helping them overthrow the Italian settlement, but mainly because Rechberg, an old Metternichian conservative, saw German nationalism as the great revolutionary danger to both states and hoped that conservative Prussians such as the king would restrain Bismarck and revive the conservative Austro-Prussian partnership.

The question of the disposition of Schleswig-Holstein now became Bismarck's means for settling the larger German question by luring, dragging, or forcing Austria into abandoning all or most of Germany, or, if necessary, into fighting over who was its master. The events over the next two years by which the last alternative became reality are too complicated to relate here; besides Austria and Prussia, the other German states, France, Italy, Russia, and Britain were also involved and other issues (the Venetian and Roman questions, the Near East, and even the American Civil War and the Mexican revolution) played a role. A further complication was that Bismarck's aim was not, like Cavour's, relatively simple—to gain allies, start a war, make it as general as possible, and gamble on a favorable outcome—but to go to war only if necessary, keep it limited, prevent outside intervention, and control the outcome. His ultimate success, while demonstrating his skill, patience, and talent at playing the role of the injured party, depended on favorable circumstances. The German Confederation could not act effectively. The smaller states, though aware of the threat to their existence, were disunited, eager to hide or in some cases to follow Prussia for protection and guarantees. Napoleon III, still anti-Austrian and preoccupied with Italy, was confident that France would profit from an Austro-Prussian war. Russia, also still anti-Austrian and worried by Bismarck's warning that if he fell a liberal anti-Russian, pro-Polish ministry would take over, remained benevolently neutral. Italy would join any war against Austria for territorial gains, though it feared being caught fighting alone. The British preferred peace, but had other concerns overseas and mainly worried about French expansion. Austria, once it failed to secure Prussian help to recover Lombardy in exchange for Schleswig-Holstein, fell back on a stubborn, passive policy of defence, trying without success to rally German and European support against Bismarck's white revolution.

Thus the most serious obstacles Bismarck faced on the road to confrontation were domestic—overcoming the king's and others' scruples about a "civil war" in Germany and the fiscal problems caused by the ongoing budget fight in parliament. These concerns probably account for the diplomatic truce concluded with Austria in August 1865. By February 1866, however, the king was converted to war, and in April Prussia concluded a short-term offensive treaty with Italy threatening Austria with a two-front war and assuring that at least at the outset France would not intervene. By June, these and other pressures on Austria helped Bismarck maneuver it into taking the initiative in the final clashes over mobilization and Schleswig-Holstein that dissolved the Confederation and brought on war.

The war quickly proved disastrous for Austria and its German allies. Prussian superiority in mobilization, training, tactics and strategy, and some weapons (notably the new breech-loading rifle) far outweighed Austrian advantages in artillery and cavalry. After easily dispersing the lesser German forces and winning nearly all the early engagements, the Prussian army crushed the main Austrian one at Königgrätz (Sadowa) in early July. Bismarck, bent on harnessing the fruits of victory before outsiders, especially France, could intervene, quickly concluded a truce over the opposition of the king and some military men, making peace with Austria on terms often considered astonishingly moderate. Austria suffered no territorial losses but had to accept the dissolution of the Confederation, extensive Prussian annexations in north Germany, and a Prussian-led North German Confederation. The south German states were to be allowed their own confederation if they wished. In simultaneous separate negotiations with these south German states, Bismarck largely negated this option by tying them to Prussia in tight military alliances. In north Germany neither Prussia's allies nor its victims were given any choice. Hanover, Schleswig-Holstein, Nassau, and Frankfurt (four million inhabitants) were simply annexed to Prussia and the other small states (with another four million) incorporated into the North German Confederation. Preventing France from interfering in this revolution in the German and European balance of power was trickier, but Napoleon's indecision, French blunders, and Bismarck's wiles enabled him to evade France's search for compensations.

The settlement is often pictured as settling the struggle for supremacy in Germany; as a piece of luck for Austria, offering it a new lease on life when its last hour seemed to be striking; as a temporary stage on the road to final unification of Germany; and as the prelude to the next likely or inevitable war with France. Only the first of these verdicts is acceptable without major reservations. The war of 1866 did make Prussia master of Germany and a leading great power in Europe, a result all but a few diehards in Germany and Europe soon came to terms with and accepted. As for the second, Bismarck's treatment of Austria was realistic, but hardly generous. He took everything he wanted, aware that taking more would have imperilled his real ends. True, he wanted Austria to survive—not as a future ally, however (this is a myth), but as a defeated, vulnerable foreign state useful for holding down Southeastern Europe and for keeping nine million

Catholic Austro-Germans out of a predominantly Protestant, Prussian-controlled Germany. Bismarck, moreover, always recognized the obvious fact that the dissolution of Austria would have revolutionary consequences for Germany and Europe, making Prussia's position between France and Russia even more dangerous, and that the idea of a Greater Germany was a bad, un-Prussian dream.

Austria's fate admittedly could have been much worse, and the settlement helped it survive—but at considerable cost. With its historic reason for existence, its German and Italian mission gone, and its strategic position vis-à-vis Prussia hopeless, its only reasons to exist were the power-political ones of security and expansion, now directed to the southeast against Russia. The internal effects of defeat were mixed. It accelerated the historic compromise with Hungary reached in 1867, which changed Austria into a dual Austro-Hungarian monarchy, bringing some immediate relief on the Hungarian question but creating other long-range problems. The albatross of Venetia was ceded to Italy despite Austria's land and sea victories over the Italians in 1866, in fulfilment of a prewar treaty obligation to France made to secure French neutrality. Yet, if 1866 temporarily eased Austria's worst nationality problems, it created a dangerous new one: divided loyalties among Austro-Germans looking towards Berlin.

The most doubtful views are seldom debated: that 1866 was bound to be temporary, a halfway house on the road to final unification with the south German states, and that this would probably require war with France. True, both these ideas were widely believed in 1866 and after. The North German Confederation was deliberately kept provisional so that the south German states could easily enter. In France, meanwhile, Prussia's shocking victory, France's humiliating failure in the aftermath, and the obvious new military threat to the east destroyed the pro-Prussian party at court and turned once indifferent Frenchmen into strong opponents of Prussian expansion. Yet further German unification and a Franco-Prussian confrontation over it would become inevitable only if the 1866 status quo proved untenable against the tide of German nationalism, if France decided to stop it by force, or if Prussia used violent means to promote it. None of this happened after 1866. Neither great power sought a confrontation. Prussia passed up a favorable opportunity for a national war with France in 1867 over Luxembourg. France, after meeting more rebuffs in its quest for compensation and a Prussian alliance, tried repeatedly for a defensive alliance with Austria and Italy or a united European diplomatic front against Prussia, but failed. Britain, Russia, and Austria all wished to preserve the status quo of 1866 in Germany and avoid further war. Most important, the German national movement went temporarily into reverse after 1866 in south Germany. Liberal nationalists lost ground in elections; particularist anti-Prussian parties came to power in Bavaria and Württemberg. Meanwhile particularist opposition to Prussia in north Germany declined and the North German Confederation proved such a success that many, especially liberals, called for making it permanent.

Thus, if one cannot confidently say that the 1866 settlement could have lasted and further unification been delayed for years or decades, neither can one assert the contrary. Some signs clearly pointed to this possibility, and Bismarck himself spoke of it. Moreover, the crisis that led to Franco-German war in July 1870, especially Bismarck's campaign to put a Hohenzollern prince on the vacant throne of Spain, seems highly contrived in comparison to his usual policy. He had gambled before, but only when he had to, after carefully preparing for every possible contingency and rigging the odds in his favor. His scheme here involved numerous uncontrollable risks and was virtually bound to blow up in his face, as it finally did. While his exact motives cannot be established with certainty, a sensible guess is that he, like Cavour in 1860, was gambling less to gain a prize, unification with south Germany, than to avert a loss, the possible defection of Bavaria to the Austro-French camp, which would have indefinitely postponed unification, dealt Bismarck a grave political defeat, and made the liberals in north Germany harder to handle. In any case, the collapse of his maneuver in Spain followed by French exposure of it spawned a European crisis and threatened Bismarck with public humiliation and possible dismissal. He escaped by using France's foolishly aggressive response to enflame French national pride and German national honor against each other. When France compounded its folly by declaring war first, the reluctant south German governments were swept along into war by the nationalist tide.

This war, though bloodier, was initially as one-sided as that of 1866. Unpreparedness and strategic confusion in the French army, combined with efficient German mobilization and movements and the German ability to throw large numbers of trained reservists into combat, led by early September to the defeat, capture, or immobilization of all three main French armies. This failed to end the war, because Napoleon III, captured with one army at Sedan, was overthrown by revolution at Paris, a Provisional Republic was established, and new armies were raised and guerrilla tactics used to liberate French soil. But revolutionary élan proved insufficient to defeat the German army. Paris was besieged and starved into submission and the French pleas for foreign intervention fell on deaf ears. Italy instead seized Rome after the French troops protecting the Pope had been evacuated. The Pope responded by retiring to the Vatican, breaking relations, and remaining technically at war with Italy till 1929. Russia also took advantage of the war to repudiate the Black Sea clause of the Paris Peace of 1856. With Britain and Austria denouncing this, a London conference was convened with Prussia and France participating. Here the war in France was ignored despite French protests, Russia was rebuked for unilaterally violating a treaty, and the clause in question was abrogated. Meanwhile Bismarck negotiated with the south German states, especially Bavaria, on the constitution of a new federal German Reich enabling William I to be proclaimed Emperor of Germany at Versailles in mid-January 1871. A Franco-German truce in late January enabled the French provisional government to crush a rising of the Paris Commune; the final peace treaty followed in May. By nineteenth-century standards it was a harsh peace, imposing on France a heavy indemnity and the loss of Alsace and part of Lorraine, old German Reich territories acquired in the seventeenth and eighteenth centuries.

The war of 1870–1 is often considered to have substituted Germany for France as the hegemon of Europe, and to have created a lasting Franco-German enmity because of the annexation of Alsace-Lorraine. Obviously both interpretations are partly true, but they need qualification. Except possibly briefly in 1856–9, France had not been a hegemon in Europe since 1812, and Germany was at best an insecure half-hegemon after 1870. As for Alsace-Lorraine, while it remained an open wound (though by 1914 it was slowly closing) and obstructed any real Franco-German rapprochement, it never constituted the main problem estranging France and Germany. That problem, created in 1870 and lasting until the 1950s, was French insecurity vis-à-vis Germany. Even the return of Alsace-Lorraine, as 1919–39 would show, would not solve this problem; only French armaments and alliances could, and these would in turn make Germany insecure. Bismarck's main argument for annexation reflected this: since France would never accept its defeat, Germany needed a better defensive frontier. In other words, 1870–1 created a classic security dilemma; Alsace-Lorraine merely symbolized it and made it worse. Theoretically, this security dilemma could have been solved in one of three ways. First, France like Austria after 1871 could have given up trying to achieve security against Germany as an impossible task, and leaned on Germany for protection instead. For that, France was still too strong, independent, proud, and capable of alliances. Secondly, France and Germany could have become so closely integrated economically and politically that war between them would become impossible. The political and economic conditions for this would not arise till the 1950s. Thirdly, the mutual military threat could have been kept manageable by maintaining a rough parity in military capability between the powers, limiting them to a narrow common frontier, and preserving a sizeable territorial buffer between them. This was the situation created by the 1866 settlement, destroyed in 1870.

Thus the disappearance of the independent south German states becomes one of the most important changes of 1870–1 for the European system. As intermediary bodies, they had been useful not only for Franco-Prussian relations, but for Austro-Prussian, Russo-Prussian, and even Italo-Prussian ones as well. Absorbing them into Imperial Germany even worked against Bismarck's fundamental purposes for expanding Prussia. His goal was not power and territory mainly for their own sake, but in order to disentangle Prussia, freeing it from pressures and threats inseparable from its exposed geographic position by making it a true great power and master in its own house,

Germany. The war of 1866 had achieved that, giving Prussia all the power and position it could safely use for this purpose. It enjoyed complete control of north Germany, close military, political, and commercial ties with the south, and a Europe in which all the great powers, including even Austria and France, were ready (if grudgingly) to live with this outcome provided Prussia went no further. The war of 1866 also gave Prussia something Imperial Germany never had: the chance for a vivifying idea, a European mission for which to use its new power. That mission, inherited from Austria, which had never effectively fulfilled it, was to organize, lead, and defend Germany as a whole, including its independent states, and keep Central Europe at peace. Victory in 1871, in contrast, gave Germany more power than its neighbors were comfortable with, and no clear European mission for which to use it, leading others both to fear that power and to try to enlist it for their purposes, creating the very entanglements Bismarck had sought to avoid.

As for Bismarck, he derided the very notion of a European mission, but did come later to regret the annexation of Alsace-Lorraine and entertain doubts about the internal solidity of the Reich he had created. Convinced, not least by his difficulties in making peace in 1871, that Germany had now gone as far as it dared, he now turned Germany's interests purely into making the new system work. No one else was available for this managerial task; it is doubtful that anyone else would have tried.

The Bismarckian system in operation, 1871–90

Bismarck's first expedient for keeping France isolated and Germany and Europe at peace was to revive the spirit of conservative monarchical solidarity, encouraging an Austro-Hungarian-Russian entente and then joining it to make the Three Emperors' League (1872–3). This proved a weak reed. A brief and artificial "War in Sight" crisis in 1875, in which Bismarck, worried by France's rapid fiscal and military recovery, tried a small intimidation campaign against France only to have Britain and Russia warn Germany instead, revealed that reviving the Holy Alliance would not ensure Russian friendship. The more serious Eastern Crisis of 1875–8 would destroy the Three Emperors' League, forcing

Bismarck into a new strategy: diverting European rivalries away from Germany to the periphery, with Germany helping to manage and settle them.

This Eastern Crisis like earlier ones grew out of the Sultan's lack of control in the Balkans, making it easy for risings against local authorities to turn into mass revolts and nationalist movements along ethnic and religious lines, drawing in great powers and new Balkan states alike. This time revolt began in Bosnia-Herzegovina in 1875, where it persisted, and spread to Bulgaria in 1876, where it was suppressed by Ottoman irregular forces by methods exaggeratedly depicted in Europe as the "Bulgarian Horrors," producing a strong public reaction against the Turks, especially in Britain and Russia. To this point Russia and Austria, encouraged and supported by Germany, had been working in distrustful partnership to get European and Turkish agreement on a program of European-supervised reforms to pacify the region. Their proposals, inadequate in any case, were foiled by British coolness, Ottoman resistance, and the rebels' persistence in revolt. The Bulgarian Horrors, however, temporarily made it impossible for the British government openly to support the Turks, while Tsar Alexander II felt that he had to act to restore Russia's prestige and satisfy its public opinion. He appealed to Bismarck to repay Russia's support in 1866 and 1870 by keeping Austria neutral in a Russo-Turkish war. Bismarck refused, insisting that Germany needed both its great neighbors equally and could not allow either to be weakened. This forced Russia to agree with Austria on the conditions under which it could punish the Turks indirectly by encouraging and supporting a Serbian attack. But, despite Russian leadership and volunteers, the Turks defeated Serbia and had to be stopped by Austrian and Russian pressure—another frustration for St. Petersburg. After more failures to reach a European Concert settlement, Russia in early 1877 worked out a broader agreement in which Austria consented to a Russian war on Turkey to liberate the eastern Balkans, provided that Russia annexed no major territories itself, established no large satellite state, and gave Austria Bosnia as compensation. The conditions and concessions almost made the game not worth the candle, but cumulative frustration brought Russia to declare war in April 1877.

An initial threat of British intervention against Russia passed when it became obvious that Germany and Austria would remain neutral. Stiff Turkish resistance, however, stalled the Russian offensive for months; not until January 1878 did the Russian army finally crush the Turks and appear about to take Constantinople. Another flurry of Anglo-Russian crises passed without war in January–February 1878. A much worse one arose, however, when Russia concluded a peace treaty with the Sultan at San Stefano in March that flagrantly violated its agreements with Austria-Hungary. For the first time it joined Britain in confronting Russia; already militarily and financially exhausted, Russia faced a war it could not possibly win.

Why the Russian government allowed its negotiator, an ardent Pan-Slav, to conclude such a treaty is unclear—perhaps as a sop to nationalist opinion, or perhaps conservatives at the Foreign Ministry decided to let their opponents try their program and learn the consequences. In any case, Russia, needing to retreat, seized on Bismarck's offer to help revise the treaty at a European Congress. At Bismarck's insistence, Russia and Britain worked out a preliminary agreement to ensure success. On this basis the Congress of Berlin—the most splendid since Vienna—met in June–July. Hard negotiations led to agreements on the crucial issues. The huge Bulgaria of San Stefano dominating the Balkan map was greatly reduced and divided into two portions, one semi-independent of Turkey, the other merely self-governing, and Austria was invited to occupy and administer Bosnia-Herzegovina under Turkish sovereignty *sine die*. Many other territorial and other Balkan, Near Eastern, and Black Sea questions were also settled.

Two common criticisms of the Berlin Congress are that by adopting half-measures on Bulgaria, discarding the ethnic principle on which the Treaty of San Stefano was based, it prolonged unrest and condemned the Balkans, especially Macedonia, to decades of future conflict, and that Bismarck in siding secretly with Austria and Britain forced a humiliating settlement on Russia. Neither complaint is persuasive. In following ethnic lines, San Stefano ignored or violated many other strategic, political, religious, and contractual considerations, making the treaty intolerable to Britain, Austria, Serbia, Greece, and Romania, a sure prescription for new and wider war. Allowed to stand, it would have destroyed the balance of power in the whole region through Russian domination of Bulgaria, the Balkans, the Straits, and Turkey. The Berlin Treaty proved useful precisely because it was a series of half-steps and compromises that satisfied few entirely but left the door open for further change. As for Bismarck, the real Russian grievance was not that he failed to be an honest broker but that Russia wanted an ally. Helping it escape an impossible position was not enough. Nor was it Bismarck's fault that Russia's gains from fighting were apparently less valuable than Britain's and Austria's from neutrality. At the crucial juncture they held the stronger hands. Two real lessons emerge from the crisis and settlement: the European system required a manager— how war would have been avoided without one, one cannot tell; and Bismarck, by playing the honest broker and diverting rivalries to the periphery, had not succeeded in disentangling Germany or winning security and gratitude.

The collapse of the Three Emperors' League in this crisis and the strained relations with Russia that ensued pushed Bismarck a stage further in his quest for managerial expedients, from monarchical solidarity in 1871–5 and honest brokerage in 1875–8 to controlling alliances. After deliberately exacerbating the quarrel with Russia to convince Emperor William that an alliance with Austria-Hungary was necessary, in 1879 Bismarck concluded the defensive alliance the Austrian government had long sought. He promptly used it, however, to force Austria back into unwilling partnership with Russia and Germany in the Three Emperors' Alliance of 1881. This worked for a time to manage Russo-Austrian rivalry in the Balkans. Bismarck's proposal that they simply divide the Balkans along east-west lines was impractical because their various overlapping interests, strengths, and weaknesses in the region made a division into separate spheres of influence impossible and undesirable for either, but the competition could be controlled, especially if both were tied to Germany. Other Bismarckian alliances of restraint and management developed in 1881–3. Italy, at odds with France over territory, trade, and colonies, allied with Austria-Hungary and Germany in a Triple Alliance in 1882, forcing Austrians and Italians to manage their rivalry. Romania concluded a secret alliance with Austria-Hungary acceded to by Germany, and in 1881 Vienna took its small neighbor Serbia, or rather Serbia's prince, under its wing. Meanwhile Bismarck took advantage of Anglo-French rivalry in Africa to improve relations with France, and maintained reasonable relations with Britain, despite an acrid dispute arising over entering the colonial race in Africa in 1884.

This system of limited alliances of restraint seemed to give Germany great control over European politics with little danger or commitment. Yet it was a complicated, entangling, and fragile system, as the next crisis over Bulgaria in 1884–7 would prove. The Bulgarian Crisis was complicated and sometimes tragicomic in details, but fairly simple in origins and essence. Russia, ruled by the narrowly autocratic Alexander III (1881–94), managed by heavy-handed interference to alienate its loyal and grateful satellite principality, lost control of it to Bulgarian nationalists, suffered painful prestige defeats, and chose to blame its troubles on Austria and indirectly on Germany. Out of this arose a kind of "I dare you" Austro-Russian confrontation, which destroyed the Three Emperors' Alliance. Bismarck had to find another way to keep France and Russia apart at a time when revived French and German nationalism, Franco-Italian hostility, Anglo-French rivalry in Africa, and Anglo-Russian rivalry in the Near East and Central Asia further threatened the peace. The combination he came up with in 1887 was his most elaborate and artificial. He encouraged an Anglo-Italian agreement for maintaining the status quo in the eastern Mediterranean, which Austria later joined. This served to draw in Britain, reassure Austria and Italy, and check France. A renewal of the Triple Alliance served the same ends. An agreement between the same three powers to work for the status quo in the Near East drew Britain as close to Austria as it would ever go in a commitment to resist a Russian advance in the Balkans. But earlier in February Bismarck had concluded a secret Reinsurance Treaty with Russia promising German neutrality if Austria attacked Russia and German support for Russian interests and aims in Bulgaria and the Straits.

This was obviously a system of balanced antagonisms, but that does not say much. Bismarck always considered balanced antagonisms the essence of international politics. Now, however, he was no longer balancing existing antagonisms, but promoting antagonistic policies so as to balance them and keep Germany the arbiter. Moreover, while the Reinsurance Pact did not technically violate Germany's commitments under the Dual Alliance, it did leave both sides uncertain which side Germany would support if it came to war. Granted, the juggling act preserved peace and was far better than the preventive war against France or Russia some German leaders urged and Bismarck rejected. But it did not arrest a further sickening of the peace in 1888–9 and a gradual rapprochement between Russia and France. Intense economic competition in the latter stages of the so-called Great Depression (1873–96) and a Russo-German customs war contributed to this. One cannot tell whether Bismarck, had he remained in office, could have devised new expedients to keep France and Russia apart and to avoid a choice between Austria-Hungary and Russia or Britain and Russia; toward the end he tried some unsuccessfully and was considering others. By Bismarck's fall in March 1890 in a power struggle with Germany's new erratic Emperor William II, however, most of his room for foreign policy maneuver and all his domestic support was gone; most Germans greeted his fall with a sigh of relief. Probably, therefore, even Bismarck could not have managed the European system much longer. But the new Wilhelmian style would certainly be worse, and, since the only plausible alternative to German leadership was the detached, balance-of-power, muddle-through style of Britain, the question was not who would next manage the system, but whether anyone would at all.

Imperialism and world politics, 1890–1907

The initial results of Bismarck's fall and William II's "New Course," though dramatic, did not seem dangerous. Germany's abrupt decision not to renew the Reinsurance Treaty with Russia led in 1891–4 to a Franco-Russian defensive alliance against Germany and Austria—a major turning point in the system, but also an apparent return to normalcy, restoring a balance of power in Europe. The alliance, moreover, put more pressure at first on Britain, Russia's and France's main imperial rival, than on the German powers; for the most important development of the 1890s was that center stage in international politics shifted away from the continent to the wider world and a scramble already under way over it, the "new imperialism."

The hotly debated questions of what caused "new imperialism" and what effects it had on the various European and non-European actors cannot be discussed here. In so far as they relate to our theme, the course of European international politics, the answers are fairly easy. "New imperialism" for one thing, was not new, but an acceleration, after a slowdown from 1815 to about 1870, of a pattern of Western penetration and partial domination or conquest of different sections of the non-European world beginning in the fifteenth century. "New imperialism" speeded up the process, took in new areas (most of Africa, parts of East and Southeast Asia, and the Southwest Pacific), brought in new imperialist actors (Germany, Italy, the United States, Japan, King Leopold II of Belgium), and re-energized older ones (Britain, France, Russia, Spain, Portugal, and the Netherlands). As to its causes and motives, they were so many, powerful, and closely intertwined that better questions than "Why?" are "Why not?" and "Why just then and not earlier?" The answer to the latter is that at this time certain barriers (political, economic, commercial, and above all scientific, technical, medical, and military) restraining European penetration and expansion declined or disappeared. As for its causes, all the positive explanations (military and political strategy, European great-power competition, the pull of the periphery, the breakdown of traditional regimes and societies, the push of local imperialisms, men on the spot, turbulent frontiers, the white man's burden and manifest destiny, racism, the struggle for markets, the patterns of European economic development and competition, imperialism as a lightning rod for European energies, and so on) are true and apply at various points; none is the sole or main answer.

Hence the focus here must be on what imperialism did within the international system and to it. First and foremost, at least for two or three decades, it acted as a safety valve. Just as mass emigration from Europe, mainly to the New World, helped to prevent social and political revolution in the nineteenth century, so "new imperialism" helped keep the Bismarckian and post-Bismarckian system going without general war. The second, ultimately more important, impact was to help make the system unworkable and a general war likely if not inevitable. This apparent paradox cannot be explained by narrating the events of imperialism (impossible here anyway), but only by analyzing its two stages and why they affected international politics as they did, illustrating this with brief looks at particular crises and the shifts in European alignments they engendered.

Imperialism initially served as a safety valve because from the early 1870s until the mid-1890s or later it involved less a struggle between different states for critical territories and positions of power than a hunt for prizes, like an Easter egg hunt, carried on in fierce competition on the ground between individuals in and out of governments (entrepeneurs, firms, explorers and adventurers, settlers, careerists in politics and the military, and so on), but pursued more cautiously by most governments, usually aware of the dubious value and high costs of acquisitions. Even where imperialist ambitions and programs clashed, deals and compromises were the normal outcome; there seemed enough for everyone, and losers could be compensated, elsewhere.

The reasons for imperialism's ultimate destructive impact are more numerous and complex. First, interstate competition inevitably heightened as the available prizes dwindled. Pre-emptive actions to seize prizes and shut competitors out, always prominent, grew in frequency and intensity and became the dominant rule of the game. Secondly, even originally amicable deals and shared arrangements tended to break down and to produce crises and confrontations as governments sought sole possession and exclusive control rather than shared influence and exploitation (for example, Anglo-French Dual Control in Egypt; Franco-German cooperation in Morocco; the Berlin-to-Baghdad Railway; the Anglo-Russian Convention in Persia). Thirdly, as imperialist activity expanded, even ordinary commercial or political activity by one state in an unclaimed area became for another power a threat to its rights, interests, and security. Examples include British feelings, colonial and metropolitan, about Germans in South Africa; Russian and British concerns to keep Germans out of Persia, Mesopotamia, and eastern Anatolia; Britain in Egypt and the Sudan, France in Morocco; most dangerous of all, Russia and Austria mutually in the Balkans. Fourthly, and most importantly, "new imperialism" combined with other late nineteenth-century trends in economics, science and technology, communications, and the art of war to make world policy the dominant ideology and strategy in international politics. The survival, security, and prosperity of states in the twentieth century was believed to depend upon securing a world position, which for great powers meant the ability to compete with the established world powers, Britain, the United States, and Russia, around the globe; for lesser powers, having at least a seat at the imperialist table and share in the game.

World policy (*Weltpolitik*), often discussed as if it only or especially concerned Germany, was in fact almost universal. The enormous territorial growth of the British Empire before, during, and after the First World War represented its world policy— expansion of formal empire in order to sustain the old informal paramountcy now challenged by Russia, the United States, France, Germany, and even Japan. Russia's imperialism in Central Asia and the Far East was its world policy for meeting British and German challenges and compensating for its economic and technological lag. French imperialism was a world policy for reversing its relative decline, recovering the status and prestige lost in 1870, and keeping up with Germany and Britain. The American world policy was the most overt and unselfconscious of all—a claim to exclusive hegemony over a whole hemisphere, soon extended to the Pacific. Japan, Italy, and even Austria-Hungary succumbed to the world-policy virus; Spain, Portugal, the Netherlands, and the king of Belgium, though without illusions that they could compete with the great powers, were determined to stay in the game or enter it.

Thus "new imperialism," beginning as a relatively safe (for Europe) scramble for prizes outside Europe, turned into a deadly struggle for world power and position central to European politics. Germany's world policy became the most important, not because it acted in a particularly reckless or aggressive way (at least until 1914 it was more cautious than most) but because its attempt to compete with Britain, America, and Russia for world position was bound to fail. It would have been surprising had Germany not tried for world position; miraculous had it succeeded at a game rigged by geography and history against it in comparison to Britain, Russia, France, the United States, and even in some respects Japan. Germany, like France, was handicapped in naval and colonial rivalry with Britain, by a late, inferior starting position, the lack of a historic tradition and outlook, and above all a geographical position both less suitable for projecting its power outward and requiring constant division of effort between activity abroad and defense at home. These same handicaps account for Germany's lack of success in imperialist combinations and alliances. German tactics and methods, true, were often counterproductive (though their failings are frequently exaggerated), but no improvement in tactics and methods could have produced success.

The shift to world policy had profound implications. The traditional nineteenth-century European power game had been played for relative advantages, often relatively modest or symbolic ones, and was usually deliberately stopped or held short of decision—an irreversible victory for one power or side or the decisive defeat or elimination of one side or any essential actor. The struggle for world power was different, with higher stakes and goals (victory for the next century), with a structure favoring certain powers on one side in the European game and disadvantaging those on the other, and with a strong tendency toward a final outcome and the elimination of competitors.

Understanding its results requires looking briefly at three international crises of imperialism and how they affected European alignments. The first and least important was the Fashoda Incident, an Anglo-French confrontation in 1898 over the Sudan. The British came to Fashoda in southern Sudan following a military conquest of the Sudan from Egypt, occupied in 1882; the French occupied it first from the western Sudan and West Africa. For Britain the vital stake was not the Sudan itself, but strategic pre-emption—barring any possible threat to the Suez–Red Sea route to India and ending France's attempts to challenge its position in Egypt. France's policy, like its government, was incoherent. A small, secretive group of ardent colonialists and military men aimed to extend the French Empire from west to east across Africa, denying Britain control from the Cape to Cairo. The government, which failed to control this group's activities, wanted to pressure the British into negotiations on Egypt as a way to improve France's colonial and European positions generally. The British government, moreover, was willing and prepared to fight; the French was not, having assumed that a colonial question could not become a *casus belli*. The outcome, a humiliating French retreat, had two main effects on European politics. It did not, as often said, pave the way for an Anglo-French colonial and political entente (in fact, it delayed it), but it forced the French eventually to recognize that, if they wished an entente with Britain, it would have to be on British terms. At the same time, the direct threat of European war between great powers over a colonial issue raised the temperature and stakes of colonial and world competition.

The roots of the second crisis, the Second Anglo-Boer War of 1899–1902, go back much further, to British conquest of the Dutch Cape Colony during the Napoleonic Wars and the Anglo-Boer political and cultural dash that subsequently developed. Though as always the immediate origins of the war from 1896 to 1899 are debated, the main cause is dear enough: the determination of the virtually independent Boer Republics to maintain their independence versus Britain's determination to maintain its exclusive supremacy in South Africa, threatened by the economic growth of the Republics, by forcing them into union with the British Cape Colony after previous British attempts at federation through annexation, persuasion, and attempted coup had failed. (Both white communities, of course, ruled and exploited the blacks and coloreds.) Britain's political and military pressure finally prompted the Boers to open the fighting, but they only anticipated the British in doing so. The war, though costly to Britain militarily and politically (world opinion and most governments with the exception of the American and German ones favored the Boers), ended in British victory and the preservation of its supremacy—for a time. Ironically, when a Union of South Africa was formed in 1910, it brought to pass the very Boer domination of all of South Africa that the war had been supposed to prevent, with consequences reaching down to present times.

The war's direct consequences in international politics were relatively few. That constant bogeyman of the British press, public opinion, and many politicians, the German threat, was here non-existent. Germany's policy, as opposed to its press and public opinion, was consistently pro-British, the government hoping to become Britain's colonial partner. Hence Russia and France, which considered forming a continental league against Britain, could do nothing, while the British government, having fobbed Germany off with a fool's deal over the Portuguese colonies in Africa, cashed in on German inaction while evading German advances. Thus the war again demonstrated the strength of Britain's imperial position, but also, in convincing the British that such ventures were costly and limited friendships better than isolation, helped pave the way for its later ententes.

The last crisis, the Russo-Japanese War of 1904–5, had major effects impossible to discuss here on Russian, Japanese, Chinese, and Korean history, the rise of anti-Western movements in Asia and elsewhere, the development of modern land and sea warfare, and much more. Here again we must concentrate on its impact on the international system, which was also profound. Under the impact of European penetration and foreign and civil war, the Chinese Empire decayed from the mid-nineteenth century while Japan rapidly adapted to Western penetration and modernized. In the Sino-Japanese War of 1894–5 the Japanese completely defeated China and imposed heavy losses on it. Russia, which had earlier reached the Pacific and established a base at Vladivostok and was rapidly building a Trans-Siberian Railway to connect it with Europe, organized an intervention with Germany and France, forcing Japan to surrender gains that would have given it dominant influence at Beijing. Russia's victory and Japan's humiliation threw China into the arms of Russia, which gained a series of political, financial, and military advantages in China in 1896–7 worrisome to other European powers, especially Britain. The contest for influence escalated in 1898 into a scramble for concrete concessions at China's expense (naval bases, commercial spheres and settlements, railway and other concessions, and so on). The competition, touched off by Germany and joined by almost everyone, was won by Russia, which gained from China the very military and commercial positions in South Manchuria it had forced Japan to disgorge in 1895. Meanwhile, from 1898 to 1900 the so-called Boxer Rebellion, a vast, diverse revolt against foreigners, missionaries, and partly the Chinese government itself, spread sporadically across China. Crushed by foreign troops especially from Japan, the movement served only to accelerate both the imperialist scramble and the Chinese government's decay, with Russia again making the greatest gains. Defeating the insurrection in Manchuria, it militarily occupied the zones of its earlier railway concessions and seemed bent on remaining indefinitely. At this same time it was also penetrating Korea.

Diplomatic efforts to check Russia, including Anglo-American efforts to promote an "Open Door" in China and an Anglo-German agreement of 1900 in support of it, proved ineffective. The British government sought an agreement with Russia recognizing each other's informal spheres of influence in northern and central China respectively, but Russia was not interested. Only Japan, most directly threatened by Russian imperialism, organized for resistance. After provisional agreements and alliance negotiations with Russia had broken down, Japan concluded a limited defensive alliance with Britain in January 1902, ensuring that, if war came, Japan would at least face only one European foe. Before opting for war, however, the Japanese again sought a deal with Russia, essentially on terms of conceding Russia Manchuria for a Japanese free hand in Korea. Arrogance, divided counsels, confusion, and sheer incompetence kept the Russian government from taking Japan seriously until too late. In February 1904 Japan declared war and attacked the Russian naval base at Port Arthur in Manchuria.

The war surprised the world and shocked Russia by a series of Japanese victories, hard-fought and bloody on land in Manchuria but overwhelming at sea. The Russian naval base at Port Arthur was conquered and two Russian fleets destroyed or captured. By mid-1905, however, with Russia facing bankruptcy and revolution at home and Japan nearing the end of its slender resources, both sides needed peace. The peace treaty mediated by the United States satisfied neither but benefited both. Japan gained the Russian concessions in southern Manchuria and a free hand in Korea, which it proceeded to annex and colonize in 1910, while Russia escaped from the war without an indemnity just in time to deal with impending bankruptcy and the worst outbreaks of revolution in European Russia. The real losers were Korea, soon to be a Japanese colony, and China, now facing the Japanese threat alone, and the great winner in international politics, through pure luck, was Britain. A war that Britain had not wanted and that at one point had threatened to drag Britain in brought it huge gains: an end to the Russian threat in China, an extended Anglo-Japanese Alliance in 1905 protecting India, and the chance to deal with a chastened and weakened Russia over Central and Western Asia. The result of this was an Anglo-Russian Convention in 1907 that divided this whole area, especially Persia, into British and Russian spheres of influence, tacitly but effectively excluding Germany.

This last development marked the culmination of "new imperialism's" impact on Europe's international politics: the transformation of alliances and alignments between 1890 and 1907 begun by the Franco-Russian alliance, advanced by Italy's partial defection from the Triple Alliance in the direction of France in 1899–1902, further developed in the Anglo-French colonial agreement over Egypt and Morocco in 1904 known as the Entente Cordiale, and finished with the Anglo-Russian Convention. Germany, in 1890 still the center of European alliances with only an isolated France as a clear opponent, by 1907 found itself isolated with only a weakening, vulnerable Austria-Hungary as a safe ally, France and Russia as its clear opponents, and Britain leaning towards their side. Frustrated in world politics, it faced the threat of encirclement in Europe.

The standard view is that Germany brought this on itself by its dangerous growth in power, its restless, incalculable policies, and especially its attempts to make gains through pressure and threats. Two supposed major instances of the latter are its bullying of France during the First Moroccan Crisis of 1904–6 in an attempt to break up the nascent Anglo-French Entente Cordiale, and its construction from 1898 of a High Seas Fleet that challenged the British navy in Britain's home waters. Both German policies unquestionably proved counterproductive. The Moroccan Crisis drove the British and French closer together, leading to Germany's isolation and diplomatic defeat at the international Conference of Algeciras, and the naval race had much the same effect internationally and met a British naval build-up that Germany could not match.

This much in the standard view is indisputable: German policy and tactics often irritated and antagonized others, and its leaders operated from two wrong assumptions—that Anglo-French and Anglo-Russian rivalries in colonial and world affairs were irreconcilable, so that Germany could exploit them to its advantage, and that a great battle fleet would not only help Germany protect and expand its commerce and empire, but also make it more attractive as an ally, especially for Britain, and make it too risky for anyone (again especially Britain) to attack Germany. (There were also less defensible motives for fleet-building. Admiral Tirpitz, the fleet's architect, hoped to defeat Britain in war, and the Kaiser and much of the nationalist public saw a great fleet as a symbol and requirement of Germany's greatness. However, the risk and alliance theories were the ones followed by the government as a whole.) But it is one thing to show that Germany blundered and had dangerous aims; quite another to prove that these really caused the outcome, or that, had Germany not made them, the overall outcome would have been drastically changed. The difference between these two propositions is illustrated by the most important instance of Germany's aggressive provocations, the naval race. Certainly German policy was a challenge that greatly heightened Anglo-German antagonism. But, if we ask whether Germany could have been expected not to build a fleet, or if without this naval race Britain would not have made its ententes with Germany's rivals, the answers are anything but clear. Naval expansion from the 1880s on was a worldwide phenomenon—American, French, Russian, Japanese, even Italian, Austrian, and Turkish. Britain's own naval program was guided more by technological and fiscal imperatives than the need to respond to Germany's. The patterns of Anglo-German world antagonism, moreover, were set before Germany began building its fleet, and did not change when in 1912–13 Germany effectively dropped out of the race. Most important, the main reason for Britain's ententes with Germany's rivals, as scholars have increasingly shown, was not to check Germany but to save the British Empire.

In short, the main explanation for the transformation of alliances and alignments is structural. Once the Great Game changed from European balance to imperialist world politics, Germany was bound to lose relative to others no matter how it played the game. Besides the handicaps mentioned earlier, Germany had few individual cards to play compared to others. The fact that Russia and France were serious colonial rivals of Britain worked, contrary to German belief, to Germany's disadvantage. It compelled Britain to deal seriously with France and Russia, especially after they allied in 1894, and to pay something for their cooperation or a limit to their hostility, while Germany had nothing to sell. The Germans were constantly trying to extort payment for services that the British neither needed nor wanted, when Britain wanted Germany to stay out of world politics, confining itself to Europe, where it belonged. As illustration of this, 1901–2, the point in the Boer War at which, according to the leading study of Anglo-German antagonism, the British began clearly to identify Germany as an enemy, was also the point, according to the best studies of German policy during the Boer War, when Germany was trying hardest to convince Britain that Germany was the friend Britain needed. Added to Germany's uselessness to Britain as a partner in world politics was its economic challenge, the rapid growth in industry, commerce, and technology that made it a successful competitor in numerous British-dominated markets. In Britain and elsewhere the perception was that Germany was likely to dominate any sphere that it could penetrate or share, giving Britain, France, and Russia, even incipiently the United States and Japan, a common interest in keeping Germany out.

In short, the competitive-cooperative pattern of imperialist world politics naturally favored a collaboration among Germany's rivals to its disadvantage. Witness the formal and informal agreements and cooperative actions in various regions of the world in 1890–1907 serving to exclude or restrain Germany: Anglo-Portuguese in South Africa, Anglo-American in Latin America and the South Seas, the actual working of the Anglo-Japanese alliance in China, Anglo-French-Russian dealings over the Ottoman Empire and the Berlin-to-Baghdad Railway. The clearest instances are also the most important. The Entente Cordiale of 1904, as a colonial agreement, was clearly anti-German—designed to end Germany's ability to interfere with British control in Egypt and to exclude Germany from an action in Morocco (an international question in an area in which Germany had strong interests) for which France had consulted every other party but Germany. The Anglo-Russian Convention of 1907 was likewise designed to exclude Germany from Persia and to ensure Anglo-Russian cooperation to check Germany in the Near and Middle East generally.

This does not suggest any anti-German conspiracy, exonerate Germany or justify its actions, imply sympathy for it, revive the old war-guilt question of the First World War, or support the German war-innocence lie in response to it. It merely applies to international politics a principle we take for granted in commerce: firms that perceive an advantage in combining to eliminate or neutralize a formidable competitor are likely to do so. Germany lost the game of world politics primarily because other major players shared an interest in making Germany lose, a result that reflects the normal nature of unregulated competition in the imperialist marketplace. Recognizing this, we can ask the next more crucial question: could this outcome have been insulated from continental European politics and kept from causing a European war? That is, could Germany have been brought to accept and live with its defeat in world politics, without resorting to violence to reverse it?

Many historians say "No." That is, without adopting a determinist view, they point to the actual events and developments of 1908–14 as evidence that Germany refused to accept this outcome and ultimately chose war to reverse it, and cite deep-seated flaws in German politics and society as responsible for this: the dangerous ambitions and erratic impulses of the Kaiser and his court, military independence of civilian control, deep social and political rifts and chronic political crises, the unreformed Prussian and Imperial constitutions, radical middle-class nationalism, militarist and authoritarian elites and traditions, the political immaturity of Germans generally, and so on. Undeniably these traits (far from unique to Germany) made it dangerous before the First World War, and help explain what it did during the war and after it down through the Second World War. However, they do not suffice to answer the question, a counterfactual but central and unavoidable one, of whether Imperial Germany could have been restrained in Europe despite its having lost the world game.

There are reasons for answering "Yes, conceivably it could." First, Germany's defeat in world policy was relative and incomplete.

Excluded from certain spheres and activities and barred from some gains and colonies, it nonetheless continued to compete fairly successfully economically in most markets, enterprises, and consortia and had reasonable prospects of continuing to do so. Secondly, it was still unclear before 1914 what the prizes of the imperialist contest it had lost were actually worth and how long they would last, and already apparent that some acquisitions, including Germany's own colonies, represented assets of little or no value.

A third reason, however, is decisive historically: the actual international competition before and after 1907 demonstrated that Germany could be effectively restrained. Nothing that Germany actually *did* after 1890, as opposed to its attitudes, tactics, and latent aims and ambitions, was as reckless, aggressive, and legally unjustifiable as many of the actions taken by others, especially its opponents—the British in East, Central, and South Africa or Western and Central Asia; the French in North, West, and Central Africa; Italians in Ethiopia and Libya; Americans in the Caribbean, Latin America, and the Central and Southwest Pacific; the Japanese in Manchuria, Korea, and China; or Russians in the Far East and Central Asia. The only great power that was less aggressive in the imperialist scramble than Germany was Austria-Hungary, and its restraint, unlike Germany's, can be explained mainly by internal weaknesses. Clearly Germany was being successfully restrained by the international system. The contrast between Germany's uncomfortable situation, its dangerous potential, and its actual moderation in conduct shows up strikingly in Germany's military establishment. Constitutionally the military was dangerously uncontrolled; the strategy the High Command had adopted for fighting a probable two-front war (the Schlieffen Plan) was terrifyingly reckless. Yet repeatedly in times of crisis Germany's military leaders showed caution, advising the government against exploiting relatively favorable chances for war in 1904–5, 1908–9, and 1911 and actually neglecting a badly needed expansion of the army until 1912–13.

Thus the European balance system, though strained by the pressures and outcome of the world-policy game, was still working to prevent a great war in Europe. Restraining Germany was the key to this, not because Germany was the only important actor, or the only one that needed restraining, but because by 1907 only Germany was likely to decide to launch a war out of frustration or desperation, or was in a position to do so. This European balance game, however, would not long survive or succeed if the same kind of unregulated competition that had led to a decisive outcome in the world-imperialist contest came to prevail in it. Preventing this implied four basic conditions or rules. First, victory in the world game must not be used to gain a decisive advantage in the European game. Secondly, international competition, hitherto diffused outside Europe or along its periphery and conducted mainly by political and economic weapons, with military force being used mainly against non-Europeans, must not become concentrated directly on Europe and conducted by military confrontations there. Thirdly, European alliances and alignments must remain fairly flexible and permeable to be useful for managing crises, and not become rigid blocs preserved at all cost for security, rendering each alliance's policy hostage to its weaker and more threatened members. Fourthly, a rule implicitly recognized and followed throughout the nineteenth century, effective in preventing or limiting wars, must remain in force: all essential actors must be preserved regardless of shifts in relative advantage, and the European Concert must keep this goal foremost in settling disputes.

The international history of 1908–14 demonstrates how all these vital rules for preserving general European peace were broken.

The descent into the maelstrom, 1908–14

The Bosnian Crisis of 1908–9, which started the fatal slide, arose from an action, Austria-Hungary's annexation of Bosnia-Herzegovina, that should never have caused serious international trouble at all. It aimed to remove an anomaly that had existed since 1878—Austrian occupation and de facto rule of these territories under nominal but empty Ottoman sovereignty—and thereby to consolidate the status quo and eliminate one flashpoint in the Balkans. It was accompanied by a retreat from a more advanced Austrian military position (the Sanjak of Novi-Pazar); had the annexation been accepted and endorsed by the other powers (as it had been in principle more than once since 1878 by Russia and Germany) it might have helped check the cold war that had been developing since 1903 between Austria and its neighbor Serbia. Most important, it was the product of a deal negotiated between the Russian and Austro-Hungarian foreign ministers Izvolski and Aehrenthal on the former's initiative, to help Russia regain the security and prestige lost in 1904–6 by defeat and revolution. Essentially it traded Russian consent to the annexation for Austro-Hungarian support for changes at the Turkish Straits favorable to Russia. Successfully carried through, it could have revived the restraining partnership between Russia and Austria that had kept them at peace and the Macedonian conflict and other Balkan issues on ice during the period from 1895 to 1907.

Instead, this potentially valuable bargain broke down, creating a crisis that foreshadowed that of 1914 and precipitated the arms race and alliance competition that brought 1914 on. The deal failed partly because of the actions of one of the principals, but also because of actions of those not party to the bargain. When Austria announced the annexation in October 1908, Prince Ferdinand of Bulgaria seized the occasion to declare Bulgaria's final independence, which was taken wrongly as proof of Austro-Bulgarian collusion. The Turks and Serbians protested violently against the annexation, but their protests could have been ignored or managed. Far worse was the fact that Izvolski did not make the deal in good faith, intending once Austria announced the annexation to call for an international conference to consider it, thus forcing Austria to pay for the annexation with further concessions. In Izvolski's absence, however, other members of the Russian government convinced the Tsar, who had given his consent, that the deal would outrage public opinion in Russia. Meanwhile Izvolski discovered that the British and French governments were unwilling to support Russia on the Straits issue. Disavowed by his regime and foiled of his hoped-for prize, Izvolski claimed that he had been tricked by Aehrenthal and called for a conference to discuss the annexation as a unilateral violation of the 1878 Treaty of Berlin (already by Austrian count violated thirty-two times). The French reluctantly endorsed the call for the sake of the alliance; the British did so more heartily in support of the Ottoman Empire.

To see Russia at the height of this imperialist age ask Britain and France to help it defend the sanctity of the Treaty of Berlin is rather like watching Bluebeard summon Don Juan and Casanova to a joint defense of the honor of Sadie Thompson. But, combined with Turkey's protests and economic boycott and Serbia's mobilization to back its demand for compensation, this international pressure put Austria-Hungary under considerable strain, forcing it to call for support from Germany, whom Aehrenthal had kept largely in the dark to show Austria-Hungary's independence. Germany responded, seeing the chance to teach Russia how useless Western support was. Thus a potentially useful bargain spawned a serious crisis and test of strength and will between opposed alliance systems.

Russia, still too weak to fight Austria, much less Germany, was bound to lose. France declined to recognize the *casus foederis,* and the British, though pleased to see Russia alienated from the German powers and focused on the Balkans rather than Central Asia, never intended more than limited diplomatic support. Hence once Austria had faced down the international opposition, bought off the Turks, threatened force unless Serbia demobilized, recognized the annexation, and pledged to cease its hostile and subversive activities, Russia either had to make its Serb clients comply, or stand by while Austria invaded Serbia, or fight a hopeless war. The Russian government asked Germany to intervene, hoping that it would build Russia a golden bridge for retreat. Germany did, but it was an iron one—a warning that Russia's only way out was to make Serbia back down. It did, ending the crisis but leaving Russians determined never to suffer such humiliation from the German powers again, sentiments the British and French encouraged.

The Bosnian Crisis had profound effects. It irreparably poisoned Austro-Russian relations, further exacerbated Austro-Serbian ones, tended to make Austria-Hungary even more dependent on Germany, and established a pattern by which crises became tests of the opposed alliance systems. Worst of all, it launched a race in land arms, an arena relatively quiescent in previous decades with greater attention given to naval armaments. Russia gave the initial impetus to this arms race, initially to recover from 1905, later with a great program adopted in 1912–13 aiming at clear superiority over both German powers combined by 1917. Germany, which for a variety of reasons had not expanded its army proportionate to its population, launched a major expansion in 1913, as did the French with the introduction of three-year service. Even Britain and Belgium were caught up in a competition involving weapons, training, and offensive strategies and war plans as well as numbers. Austria-Hungary, which tried to compete but could not because of its fiscal, political, and constitutional-dualist problems, felt itself falling from the ranks of great powers. Italy, which also tried with even less success, never really attained that status. With the arms race went a militarization of diplomacy; all subsequent crises were prolonged and marked by mounting levels of tension and antagonism, difficult, unsatisfactory resolutions, and a quest for victory for one's own bloc.

The Second Moroccan Crisis (or "Agadir Incident") of 1911 exemplified this. The initial French provocation, a direct takeover of Morocco in violation of recent treaties, was answered by German gunboat diplomacy to back its demand for compensation. An ostentatious British warning to both parties, but most directly to Germany, not to shut Britain out of any agreement raised the tension and stakes still further. In the final settlement, France gained Morocco with only minimal compensations to Germany, but the main result was to heighten both German frustration and French fears and to tighten the links between Britain and France to include naval cooperation and military consultation. The takeover of Morocco had a further snowball effect, actually foreseen and to some degree prepared for in advance. Italy now cashed in on its position between the two camps and its pledges from both sides to seize Libya, nominally Ottoman territory, not because Libya was concretely worth anything, but to raise its own prestige and ease a current domestic crisis by expansion abroad. Though the great powers reacted calmly—the Austrians took Italy seriously as a foe, and they were glad to see it distracted in North Africa—this aggression also escalated. Unable to pacify the nomadic tribes in the Libyan desert, Italy declared war on the Ottoman Sultan, formally annexed Libya, and carried its military operations into the Straits and the eastern Mediterranean, the most dangerous flashpoint in Europe.

This Italian move, perhaps the single most irresponsible action by a major power before 1914, paved the way for the worst prewar crisis, caused by the two Balkan Wars of 1912–13. Russia contributed to it in 1912 by promoting a Russian-led Balkan League, which ultimately included Serbia, Bulgaria, and Greece, to give Russia exclusive leadership in Balkan politics. The French, tardily informed of Russia's initiative, immediately recognized it as a recipe for war against the Ottoman Empire and a direct challenge to Austria-Hungary, but went along for the sake of their alliance. Russia did not want a Balkan war (in fact, it hoped to bring the Turks in), but its Balkan clients, assured of Russian protection and seeing Turkey weakened, halted their bitter struggle among themselves over Macedonia for a joint attack on Turkey in October 1912.

This set off a year-long crisis far too complicated to relate here. From a systemic standpoint, European diplomacy, which failed at the last minute to prevent the war, barely managed in the end to prevent a general war, but the European Concert, acting through a London conference chaired by the British Foreign Secretary Sir Edward Grey, can hardly be said to have controlled the course or outcome of events. By December Turkey's forces had surprisingly collapsed, forcing Russia to intervene to stop the Bulgarians or Greeks from taking Constantinople and Austria and Italy to check the Serbian-Montenegrin-Greek advance into the proposed independent principality of Albania. Then Russian and Concert pressure failed to prevent a new war among the victors over the spoils. In mid-1913 the Serbs and Greeks, joined by the Turks and aided by Romanian mobilization and intervention, completely defeated the main victor of 1912, Bulgaria, and seized most of the spoils. The Treaty of Bucharest in August, reached largely without Concert control, ended this second war but not the crisis. A prolonged Austro-Serbian confrontation over the Serbian seizure of territories designated for Albania brought them closer than ever to actual war before an Austrian ultimatum forced a Serbian withdrawal.

Peace had been saved, but barely, and the whole European balance had been changed. In the Balkans Austria-Hungary had suffered a huge defeat. Serbia, its worst enemy, emerged from the wars almost doubled in size and confidence, while Bulgaria,

Serbia's rival, was exhausted and impotent. The Ottoman Empire, the only state representing no potential threat to Austrian interests, was now virtually gone from the scene; Romania, hitherto a secret ally, was alienated, openly independent, and ardently courted by Russia and France. Italy, nominally an ally but actually a rival in the western Balkans and Adriatic, competed directly with it for control of Albania. As for Russia, though delighted by the reversal of 1909, it saw its own gains as unstable until the Balkan League was strengthened and extended and incomplete until Russia controlled the fate of the Turkish Straits. It therefore bent its efforts, now with open French support, on reconciling Serbia and Bulgaria, adding Romania and Turkey to the league, keeping Austria-Hungary isolated, and combating German influence.

In the Western, especially British, view Concert diplomacy in 1912–13 was a success, and a recipe for managing future crises. Britain had restrained Russia, Germany had held back Austria, a general war had been averted, and the overall balance of power preserved. The Balkans were not Britain's problem, and Austria's plight was its own concern and Germany's. The worst danger to Britain, the defection of Russia to Germany and a resultant continental league, seemed more remote than ever. France's President Poincaré was equally satisfied for somewhat different reasons. The two alliance blocs had survived intact, with the Russo-French one this time proving more solid, effective, and successful than the Austro-German. Maintaining these blocs rigid and unchanged was the key to peace and security. Germany, which had cooperated with Britain in the hopes of promoting British neutrality vis-à-vis the continent, by late 1913 had become sufficiently pessimistic on this score and about Austria-Hungary's plight to back the latter's demand for strong support to arrest its decline.

Thus by 1914 the vital prerequisites for peace were being systematically negated and those for war fulfilled. The combination that had brought the Triple Entente success in imperialism was now effective in Europe, with Russia and France expecting to attain military superiority by 1917 and Britain, though declining a direct alliance, aligned firmly with them, partly to maintain a European "balance," but mainly to retain friendships vital to its world position. Power-political competition, once diffused on the periphery, was now deliberately concentrated on the two most dangerous fault-lines in Europe, the Rhine and the Balkans. Flexibility and permeability in alliances were replaced by a conscious separation and opposition of military blocs, intended to eliminate uncertainty and miscalculation but actually working to tie Russia's policy and fate more tightly to Serbia, France's to Russia, Germany's to Austria-Hungary, and ultimately Britain's to France. Most important, one essential actor, Austria-Hungary, had concluded from bitter experience that Concert diplomacy was no longer a means to preserve its great-power status and vital interests, but a fatal snare: the other great powers, including Germany, used it to make Austria pay the collective costs of international settlements and to paralyze its capacity for action still further. Hence its government resolved to break with the Concert and to arrest its decline through strong independent action, and the German government, equally pessimistic about its one remaining ally, resolved to support it.

The scenario this suggests, in which by 1914 the question had become less whether or not general war would break out, but when and how, seems too determinist, and its implication that Austria and Germany acted out of desperation and exhaustion of alternatives sounds like an old, discredited whitewash. No such charge can apply in regard to the immediate origins of the war in the so-called July Crisis sparked by the assassination of Archduke Francis Ferdinand by Bosnian Serb terrorists. Each stage of it was contingent; each involved conscious governmental decisions that conceivably could have gone otherwise. This applies to the decision of the Austrian government to change its original plan of action from one of forcing Romania back publicly into alliance to one of eliminating Serbia as a political factor in the Balkans; to Austria's demand for German support and Germany's blank cheque; to Austria's ultimatum to Serbia and Serbia's decision partly to reject it; to Russia's advice and consent to this decision; to Austria's declaration of war on Serbia; to Russia's partial mobilization against Austria followed by full mobilization against Germany; to Germany's declaration of war on Russia; to its implementation of the Schlieffen Plan by the invasion of France and Belgium, and to Britain's declaration of war on Germany. Throughout this process the Central Powers held the initiative and other powers reacted to it; they started the war.

Yet the answer to "Who started the war?" does not constitute an answer to "What caused the war?" For this one needs to get beyond the usual answers, all in different ways true but also inadequate, to one that underlies them all and yields more insight. There are three such broad answers, which, oversimplified, go as follows. First, Austria and Germany caused the war by gambling on a local war to recoup their losses and gain or regain hegemony in Europe (behind which reckless gamble, it is often said, lay a desire to save their unreformed domestic structures by foreign policy victories). Secondly, Europe stumbled into war through an accumulation of unresolved conflicts, rivalries, unreconciled purposes and ambitions, hatreds, pressures, and entangling commitments that had repeatedly threatened war earlier and finally escaped control this time. The third is closer to a satisfactory answer but still inadequate: war came because the rules, norms, and practices of European politics had become so ruthlessly competitive that the very devices used to prevent war actually helped cause it. The alternative answer suggested here, which includes parts of all the above while rejecting others, is of European governments to do certain specific things necessary to keep peace viable, while at the same time repeatedly doing things that made war likely, so that the resources for peace were finally exhausted.[2]

The explanation in terms of Austro-German aggression, correct for the July Crisis, will not do as an overall answer for various reasons; only the more important will be mentioned here. First, that it begs the question of where aggression begins, and who is attacking or defending the status quo. The initial aggressive act in the crisis itself came from Serbia, part of a

---

2 An analogy: this is like explaining a man's fatal heart attack by going from saying (a) it was caused by overexertion, to (b) it was a coronary thrombosis caused by a blocked artery, to (c) it resulted from a long history of high blood pressure, to (d) it was caused by his consistent failure to take his medicine or his doctor's advice on smoking, diet, and exercise. One could concede that the first three explanations are all true, but still insist that only the last is satisfactory in human, historical terms.

program of state-sponsored terrorism in the service of a Great Serb nationalist program and ideology directed against the very existence of Austria-Hungary. The answer also ignores the questions of whether Austria-Hungary and Germany could have afforded not to make some kind of drastic response to their situation in 1914, or been expected not to, and what alternatives not involving the risk of crisis and general war still existed. Most important, this answer with its aggressor/defender distinction assumes that the two sides at this juncture were playing two different games, one bellicose, the other peaceful, when all were really playing essentially the same game by much the same rules. No power desired general war, but all preferred it to other outcomes. Serbia preferred war to abandoning its anti-Austrian national program, Austria-Hungary preferred it to a further decline in its status and security, Russia to another "humiliation" like 1908–9, Germany to the collapse or defection of its last major ally and a prospective military inferiority to France and Russia, France to the loss of its Russian alliance and instant inferiority to Germany, Britain to the defeat or defection of France and German domination of the continent. All saw existing trends (and the status quo in international politics is always a trend on which calculations are based, not a static condition) in similar fashion, and concluded that the game was approaching a turning point in the near future. Three powers, seeing victory ahead, favored a "peaceful" continuation of the "status quo." Two others sensed impending defeat and determined to change it.

All, moreover, had the same requirement for "peace": that their rivals accept their victory. Without question Austria-Hungary and Germany, in trying for a local war in 1914, consciously risked a general war and in a sense opted for one. But their opponents were gambling similarly in the longer term. Serbia and Russia wagered directly and France and Britain tacitly (the latter trying not to think about it) that somehow Austria-Hungary's demise, which all anticipated, would occur quietly and that Germany would accept both this demise and its resultant inferiority to its foes—a gamble less obviously aggressive, but just as risky and foolish as the Austro-German one. In a sense, the European powers went to war in 1914 because they thought alike and agreed with one another.

As for saying that the war resulted from mounting pressures, strains, enmities, and crises until one finally got out of hand, the trouble is simply that there is too much evidence right to the end that governments acted on the basis of calculation. They knew what they were doing, however much they might feel that they had no other choice.

This seems to confirm the third explanation: war came because imperialism, mass politics, fervent nationalism, cut-throat economic competition, all-out arms races, and Social Darwinism had made international relations too ruthless for peaceful compromise and coexistence. Certainly this answer comes closer; this essay seems to point to it. Yet here again the evidence shows that these conditions had arisen well before 1914, and that governments even in 1914 were not the helpless pawns of them.

A deeper answer lies not in what finally triumphed in 1914, a *va banque* spirit in international competition, but in what finally disappeared, means and institutions for limiting the stakes and assuring that competition would remain within tolerable limits. In other words, the better question is not "What caused the war in 1914?" but "What had stopped war until 1914, and no longer could?"[3] The First World War is often explained as resulting from Germany's growth in power and bid for hegemony, so that stronger deterrence of Germany (for example, a clear advance warning by Britain that it would stand by France) might have preserved peace. But Germany and Austria-Hungary thought they were losing, not winning, the power competition in 1914; Germany especially saw this as its last good chance to avert defeat in the near future. Moreover, the Germans anticipated and reckoned with a British entry into the war sooner or later. Most important, deterrence, which doubtless had helped stop Europe at the brink on previous occasions, was tried in 1914 and failed. The fatal problem was the absence not of deterrence but of assurance. Europe had remained generally peaceful throughout the nineteenth century not by the natural workings of the balance of power, but by restraints on it—a system of rules, norms, and practices enabling actors, especially the great powers, to act on

---

3   To resort to another medical analogy: this is like asking not what particular disease killed a patient, but why his body's defenses against it succumbed.

the assumption that rivalry and competition, though inescapable, would not destroy them. The original Vienna system of guarantees had broken down and been discarded, but new versions of deterrence/assurance had emerged or survived providing enough such confidence to keep the system going. By 1914 that belief was gone, replaced by the conviction that the next, inevitable war would be one fought not within limits by governments, but to the death by whole peoples—a belief that helped postpone war till 1914 and bring it on then. The fund of assurances and mutual restraints had run out; everyone's hopes for peace rested on making others accept the unacceptable. July 1914 marks not just the onset of war, but the exhaustion of peace.

3

Embedded Counterfactuals and World War I as an Unavoidable War

This essay, though it may seem to do so, does not take a determinist stand either on counterfactual reasoning and contingency in history in general or on the origins of World War I. On the war, though its conclusions differ from R. N. Lebow's argument that it could readily have been avoided, it agrees with Lebow's views on many points and concedes a large causal role in all great events in history, including World War I, to contingency, chance, and particular choices.[1] It even argues that in a certain objective sense the war remained avoidable up to its very outbreak, and presents other grounds for considering it unavoidable.

It also broadly agrees with Philip Tetlock's and Aaron Belkin's views on the necessity, unavoidability, and potential utility of counterfactual reasoning in historical study.[2] The difference between my views and theirs lies in the practical rather than the theoretical realm. While in general accepting the Tetlock-Belkin analysis of the various types of counterfactual reasoning and the basic tests to use for them, I will suggest a different notion about how and where to apply counterfactual reasoning concretely to historical explanation, as a better way of showing historians the value of counterfactual reasoning for accomplishing their task. That task (here I agree with the historians who are skeptical about it) is not to speculate on what might have happened in

---

1   R. N. Lebow, "Franz Ferdinand Found Alive. World War I Unnecessary," unpublished paper presented at the Mershon Center, Ohio State University, February 4–5, 2000.

2   Philip E. Tetlock and Aaron Belkin, eds., *Counterfactual Thought Experiments in World Politics* (Princeton, 1996), chap. 1.

history, but to shed light on what actually did happen, why it did, and what it means.

As for whether World War I ever became unavoidable, and if so, when and why, once again the point I wish to make is a practical more than theoretical one. Clearly there were contingent events and developments occurring and important choices being made in 1914 right up to end of the July Crisis. One can undoubtedly make a case, as Lebow has done, that some vital events in the causal chain, such as the assassination of Franz Ferdinand, could easily not have happened. It is more difficult, but not impossible, to argue that vital decisions could have been made differently. But this fact in itself does not make the war avoidable, because it does not cancel the practical limits to the avoidability of outcomes in human affairs. To term an outcome inevitable often means no more than to say that the time when it could have been avoided is past—that the kinds of decisions, actions, or chance developments required to avert it, though possible earlier, have become so unlikely or unthinkable as to rule out any plausible scenario for avoiding it.[3] This is an obvious point, yet it is not easy or commonplace to apply it to particular developments in history, especially major ones like the outbreak of great wars or revolutions. My hope is to use a particular application of counterfactual reasoning to history to show one specific way in which World War I by 1914 had become unavoidable.

---

3   An illustrative analogy: an attempt to drive an old automobile with faulty brakes and steering down a steep mountain road with no guard rails will not necessarily end in an accident. If the dangers of such an attempt are ignored and all the many decisions and moves necessary to avoid an accident are not taken, however, at some point a crash becomes inevitable. This kind of practical, commonsense reasoning is frequently used by historians. Orlando Figes, e.g., in his *A People's Tragedy: The Russian Revolution 1891–1924* (New York, 1997), repeatedly points to junctures where the revolution could have been avoided, but also shows why the necessary steps were not taken or contrary ones were, and ascribes this failure above all to the thought and actions of the conservative forces ruling Russia and to the personality, character, and beliefs of Tsar Nicholas II. These are contingent factors; so was the occasion of the revolution in March 1917—riots over bread shortages in St. Petersburg at a time when flour supplies were still available. Yet by this time a revolution had become inevitable.

The case for "embedded" counterfactual reasoning

The Tetlock-Belkin theses seem to assume that the way for historians or other scholars to apply counterfactual reasoning to historical exposition and explanation is to pose the question, "What if?"—that is, to imagine or conceive of a way in which a particular event or development could have unfolded differently, and to ask, "What if this had happened? What further changes would have resulted?"[4]

A working historian, however—even if, like me, he agrees that counterfactual elements are logically implied in all explanation, including historical explanation—may have serious qualms about this procedure. The reason is that though it is logically defensible to think up counterfactual questions with which to confront the historical record, the exercise seems pointless or at best of limited value from a practical standpoint because even so-called easily imagined variations introduced into the complex matrix of historical developments can change so many variables in so many unpredictable or incalculable ways, leading to so many varied and indeterminate consequences, that the procedure quickly becomes useless for helping us deduce or predict an alternative outcome. Tetlock and Belkin of course see the problem and deal with it in terms of abstract logic. Yet my feeling is that the procedure's practical limits and problems sensed by the working historian are not sufficiently grasped.

The difficulty, as noted, is that if the variation is really important, involving a central component or variable in the historical equation, introducing it will alter so much of the complex web of history that the results of omitting or altering that crucial variable become incalculable. If the variation introduced, however, is minor, sufficiently precise and limited enough that its immediate consequences can be calculated with confidence, its implications for general historical explanation or for suggesting

---

4   Tetlock and Belkin, *Counterfactual Thought Experiments*, 4, 8; "Counterfactual Outline," Mershon Center, Ohio State University, February 24, 1997. The same assumptions seem to reign in Niall Ferguson, ed., *Virtual History: Alternatives and Counterfactuals* (New York, 1999).

any important alternative outcome are unlikely to be important. A major counterfactual, in other words, will change too much, and a minor one too little, to help us explain what really did happen and why, and why alternative scenarios failed to emerge, the only sound reasons for using counterfactual reasoning. Thus using this kind of "What if?" counterfactual procedure might well have the perverse and ironic effect of confirming ordinary historians in their resistance to counterfactual reasoning and strengthening their tendency to see history as the result of pure contingency and chance.

One might of course reply that if historians cannot or will not recognize the presuppositions and assumptions involved in the explanations they offer, other scholars will have to identify and analyze them, and subject them to various tests, including those of counterfactual reasoning. Again I agree, up to a point. The alternative kind of counterfactual reasoning I will suggest might help historians get over the tendency toward a naive pragmatic empiricism. Yet it would be rash of scholars in other fields to suppose that because a particular historian fails to give compelling theoretical grounds for being dissatisfied with a particular counterfactual procedure, his or her concerns can be safely ignored. Practitioners may well sense from experience and schooled intuition that a plausible idea or theory will not work in their field, even if they have difficulty articulating theoretical reasons why. Moreover, the principal contention here, that some major easily imagined counterfactual variations in particular sections of history change so much that the entire subsequent development becomes incalculable, while other variations, just as easily imagined, make no significant difference at all, can readily be illustrated in any period of history.[5]

---

5   One such illustration comes from the War of the Second Coalition (1798–1801) in Napoleon's era. Suppose that Napoleon had been killed or captured during this war, either in battle or at sea on returning from Egypt or by conspirators after he seized power—all easily imagined variants in history. No amount of historical research and reasoning could enable us to tell what the consequences of his death would have been. But suppose that he had lost the final major battle of that war at Marengo in June 1800—again something easily imagined, for it nearly happened and was only averted by the disobedience of his orders by a subordinate general. Here one can show by concrete

One can get around the difficulty, I suggest, by a different concept and method of counterfactual reasoning. It starts by conceiving of counterfactuals not as non-history (that is, imagined or virtual as opposed to real history, what might have happened rather than what did), but rather as *real* history, an integral part of history, embedded in history both in the actual experience of historical actors and in those constructions or reconstructions of history constantly made not only by scholars but also by everyone who reflects on the past. History, like life itself, is lived, acted, made, and relived and reconstructed in the face and presence of counterfactuals. Historical actors in all arenas of life constantly think, calculate, decide, and act in the face of uncertainty; they repeatedly ask the question, "What if?" try to answer it, and make decisions and act on that basis. Historians take this for granted. They know instinctively (or are quickly taught) that historical actors regularly face an uncertain, open future. Recognizing this, they must portray and analyze that situation and show why and how actors responded to the questions, choices, and alternatives they faced as they did. If they are at all sophisticated, they also realize that carrying out this task requires not merely trying to discover and analyze the actors' thought worlds and the role played by their counterfactual questions and calculations, but also framing and posing their own counterfactual questions as to what might have happened had the actors answered their counterfactual questions differently. Thus in seeking to discover the real nature and results of the actual choices made by actors in the face of their uncertainty and their counterfactual questions, historians must use their advantages of hindsight and historical evidence to ask counterfactual questions of their own, such as: What other decisions and actions could the historical actors have made under the existing circumstances? To what extent did they recognize and consider these? What circumstances made these choices or alternative courses genuinely possible or merely specious and actually unreal? What might the alternative results of these choices have been? The real

---

evidence that reversing the outcome of this battle would not have changed the main outcome of the war, overthrown Napoleon's rule, or altered the course of history much at all.

justification for the use of counterfactual reasoning in history and the best answer to those who reject it is the fact that historians cannot faithfully convey the real nature and results of historical decisions and actions simply by constructing a factual narrative of "what happened" without confronting the various counterfactuals, both those faced by the actors and those necessarily posed by the historian, integrally embedded in that story.[6]

This understanding of counterfactual reasoning not only justifies its use but also suggests how it ought to proceed. The first task is to discover and analyze the counterfactual questions actually seen and faced by the historical actors themselves. This part is so obvious, normal, and ubiquitous an element of historical research that it needs no discussion here. The second step, less obvious but no less necessary, involves looking carefully at the reconstructions and explanations of historical events and outcomes offered by historians (especially oneself) with the specific aim of discovering and analyzing the implicit and explicit counterfactual questions and assumptions they contain. The next assignment is to test rigorously these counterfactual assumptions and scenarios that historians wittingly or unwittingly pose, by means of the kinds of tests and criteria Tetlock and Belkin suggest and the same types of historical evidence as are employed to construct the "factual" story. By ferreting out and analyzing the overt or concealed counterfactuals embedded in historians' reconstructions and explanations of history, I contend, we can both better explain the actual course of historical events and better judge whether the counterfactual possibilities envisioned by the actors and those constructed and used by historians were sound or illusory. In short, it can help us better understand both

---

6   This argument agrees in part with Niall Ferguson's call (in his introduction to Ferguson, *Virtual History*, 86–7) for historians to consider only plausible unrealized alternatives and to examine these rigorously on the basis of valid evidence. He goes too far, however, in insisting that "We should consider as plausible or probable *only those alternatives which we can show on the basis of contemporary evidence that contemporaries actually considered*" (italics in original). This is too restrictive. As the discussion of World War I later will illustrate, the historian's purview includes both those possibilities and alternatives contemporaries saw and considered, and those they failed to see at all or to consider seriously.

what did happen in history and why this particular thing rather than some other possible thing occurred.[7]

This kind of counterfactual reasoning has other advantages as well. It represents something historians regularly do, whether or not they are fully aware of it, and thus is a method that, once understood, they can hardly reject. Most important, it seems to me to fit the nature of history, recognizing its openness and uncertainty for the actors themselves while insisting at the same time that history's outcomes, though not predetermined, can and must be explained by causes. It thereby takes seriously both the contingent and the determinate character of the past; respects both the extent and the limits of its range of possibilities. It depicts history as unfolding in an indeterminate way, the product of unpredictable human conduct and material circumstances, but not as kaleidoscopic chaos. It offers a way of distinguishing between genuine and specious counterfactual scenarios, showing that while much could have happened differently, not everything, including many of the things historical actors and later historians have thought were possible, could have happened. It fits our sense, learned from life as well as history, that at some point some things once indeterminate do become inevitable.

I now need to illustrate how a certain degree and kind of inevitability in history applies to the origins of World War I (not demonstrate it, which might be impossible and would certainly

---

7 Once again this general principle can be illustrated by an example from the Napoleonic era, the object of much counterfactual speculation, the Battle of Waterloo and the possible results of a Napoleonic victory rather than defeat there. I think it can easily be shown that a French victory in this battle could not possibly have changed the fundamental balance of military forces, overwhelmingly favorable to the allies, or their willingness to prosecute the war to victory, and therefore it could not have significantly altered the ultimate outcome of the war, as many have supposed. However, a Napoleonic victory, by prolonging the war and making victory more costly for the Allies, would almost certainly have destroyed the Vienna peace settlement concluded just before Waterloo and have resulted in a far harsher, less stable peace settlement resembling that of 1919, with many of the latter's unfortunate consequences. In other words, Wellington's victory was not critical for the ultimate outcome of the war but it was vital for saving the peace. The evidence is too extensive to discuss here, but is summarized in Paul W. Schroeder, *The Transformation of European Politics, 1763–1848* (Oxford, 1994), 548–58.

take too long).[8] The topic suits the purpose for several reasons. First, the story is very well known and does not need to be expounded in detail. Second, though the scholarly debate over the origins of the war which raged for decades after 1914 has not completely died out, a clear consensus view has emerged which denies that the war was inevitable and ascribes its origins to specific avoidable choices and actions taken by particular actors. Hence it represents a good challenge. Third, it illustrates particularly well the potential value of detecting and analyzing embedded counterfactuals, the surprising results it can lead to, and the dangers of failing to do so. Finally, in asking whether this world war, a major source and cause of Europe's subsequent relative decline, was avoidable, it suggests further major counterfactual questions it will not attempt to answer, namely, whether absent World War I European world supremacy would have lasted a considerable while longer and World War II have been avoided.

My treatment of this huge subject must be brief and sketchy, little more than an outline, and is bound to seem dogmatic in some places and trite in others. It will start by discussing the current prevailing view of the origins of the war, analyze and criticize the counterfactuals embedded in it, and from this develop a divergent view.

The standard explanation and its counterfactuals

By common agreement, the direct proximate cause of World War I was the German and Austro-Hungarian decision that Austria-Hungary issue an ultimatum to Serbia in July 1914 following the assassination of Archduke Franz Ferdinand by Bosnian nationalists with connections to Serbia. The German powers intended by this ultimatum to provoke a local war against Serbia and eliminate it as a political factor in the Balkans, thus shifting the balance there and in Europe generally in favor of themselves. Without necessarily intending to start a general war, the German powers

---

8   This is my reason or excuse for the paucity of footnotes and the fact that many will be expository notes rather than references to the enormous scholarly literature on this subject. Though I think I know the literature reasonably well (not exhaustively—no one does), this is not the place to prove it.

consciously risked provoking one by this initiative, as actually happened.

Disagreement persists over the motives and attitudes prompting this go-for-broke gamble, with some historians emphasizing the fear and desperation felt by leaders in Germany and Austria-Hungary, others stressing their aggressive aims and their hopes that they could either get away with a successful local war or win a wider one. This disagreement makes little difference in deciding whether this war was avoidable, however, because everyone agrees that Germany and Austria-Hungary, whatever their reasons, *chose* to take this gamble; they were not forced into it. This belief implies a counterfactual: they had viable alternatives, could have chosen other ways to protect their interests without risking a great war. A similar consensus prevails that the other great powers, Russia, France, and Britain, reacted essentially defensively to the German-Austrian move and had little choice other than to do so in self-defense, given their vital interests and the unmistakable challenge presented them. The counterfactual scenario embedded in the consensus explanation thus ascribes to Germany and Austria-Hungary a choice of alternate strategy or strategies by which they could reasonably have hoped to protect their vital interests by peaceful means, while denying that the other major actors had practical alternatives for saving peace once the Central Powers launched their initiative.

To be sure, few attribute the German-Austro-Hungarian gamble purely to aggressive expansionism, militarism, and paranoia, or deny that the international situation was becoming increasingly unfavorable and dangerous for the Dual Alliance in 1914. The consensus view, in fact, uses this to help explain the Austro-German action, while denying that this justifies it or renders it necessary, claiming among other things that Germany and Austria-Hungary had themselves largely created the dangers threatening them by failing to reform internally while pursuing unrealistic, aggressive policies abroad. Again this involves an implied or stated counterfactual: even as late as 1914 the Central Powers could have changed their policies and thereby made themselves more secure within the existing international system without overthrowing it.

Consensus historians recognize further that Germany, already in 1914 largely isolated diplomatically and threatened with encirclement by the Triple Entente, faced an imminent future threat, that once Russia had completed its announced plans for military expansion, scheduled for completion by 1917, the German army would be numerically as decisively inferior to those of its opponents as the German navy already was on the sea. But the consensus view claims that Germany had largely created this perilous situation for itself by the aggressive world policy it had followed ever since Bismarck's fall in 1890. Its naval race with Britain, its restless quest for colonies, bases, and spheres of influence around the globe, and its frequent resort to bullying and threats, all designed to give Germany hegemony over Europe and a world position competitive with those of Britain, Russia, and the United States, provoked the alliances, ententes, and armaments races, first at sea and then on land, by which Germany now felt encircled and threatened. Since these dangers arose primarily from Germany's policies and actions (here comes another important counterfactual), different German policies could over time have reduced or eliminated them. Even as late as 1914, had Germany realized that none of its neighbors intended to attack it or violate its rights and had it decided to give up its drive for world power, pursuing instead a sensible, moderate policy focused on economic expansion, it had good chances to enjoy a reasonably secure, prosperous, and honorable place in the European and world international system. In fact, prominent historians have argued that Germany's economic dynamism was so great that it needed only a prolonged period of peace to achieve mastery in Europe.[9]

Almost everyone also recognizes that Austria-Hungary faced even graver dangers than Germany, and that these were less obviously the result of its own actions, at least in the international arena. The Habsburg Monarchy before 1914 was growing steadily more isolated politically and diplomatically and losing its great-power status and reputation. Two allies, Italy and Romania, were unreliable and hostile, the latter to the point of open defection.

---

9   Some leading historians who maintain this are Martin Kitchen, A. J. P. Taylor, Volker Berghahn, and J. C. G. Röhl.

Its most important ally, Germany, was the Monarchy's most serious economic rival, especially in the Balkans where Austro-Hungarian interests were concentrated, and the Germans tended both to dominate Austria-Hungary politically and strategically and to ignore its vital interests. Austria-Hungary's military security against a host of possible or probable enemies (Serbia, Russia, Italy, Russia's ally France, and even Romania) depended totally on receiving major, timely help from Germany in case of war. Yet given Germany's own threatened military position facing a likely two-front war, Germany's gambling offensive strategy for fighting it (the Schlieffen Plan), and the fact that the Dual Alliance lacked a military convention or an agreed and coordinated military strategy, how much actual military help Germany would provide its ally was anyone's guess. Meanwhile Austria-Hungary's long-standing security problem had been further worsened by the disastrous outcome of the two Balkan Wars in 1912–13. The Peace of Bucharest in August 1913 left Austria-Hungary with no reliable partner in the last region, the Balkans, where it still counted as a great power and had its most vital interests. The Ottoman Empire was virtually expelled from Europe, while Bulgaria, which the Austrians counted on to check Serbia, was defeated and exhausted, Rumania alienated, the new Kingdom of Albania a basket case and albatross around Austria-Hungary's neck, and Italy an active rival in Albania and the Adriatic with irredentist claims on Austrian territory. Even Germany had not given its ally steady support during the prolonged crisis, but had held Austria-Hungary back in order to preserve general peace and pursue its own particular aims. Meanwhile Austria-Hungary's worst rivals and enemies, Russia, Serbia, and Montenegro, had emerged from the Balkan Wars stronger, more confident, and more hostile, and Russia, aided by its ally France, seemed poised to consolidate its dominance over the entire region by expanding the Balkan League it had earlier sponsored and thereby promoted the Balkan Wars in the first place. The decline in Austria-Hungary's strength and status, obvious to everyone, enabled other powers to ignore its interests, to exploit its internal problems, especially the nationalities conflicts, to raise irredentist claims on the Monarchy's territory, and in Serbia's case, to wage a cold war of propaganda and a guerilla

war of terrorist subversion against it. They further spurred dissatisfied nationalities and groups within Austria-Hungary to
demand concessions from the Austrian and Hungarian governments, sometimes soliciting foreign support for them, thus
exacerbating the already grave problems of governance in both
halves of the Monarchy and inducing anger and hopelessness in
those who remained *Habsburgtreu*. Most important, Austria-
Hungary, far more than Germany, had fallen hopelessly behind
in the land arms race then reaching a crucial stage among the
great powers in Europe (only Italy was worse off, and Italy was
only a would-be great power). Given Austria-Hungary's limited
economic and fiscal resources and the restrictions imposed on its
military exertions by the parliamentary system in both halves of
the Monarchy and the autonomous position enjoyed by Hungary,
there was simply no hope for it to catch up. It thus faced the
prospect of fighting a great war against several foes with only
doubtful German support and under conditions of hopeless
inferiority.[10]

No historian to my knowledge denies the gravity of Austria-
Hungary's situation; various factors in it are regularly invoked
to explain its go-for-broke gamble in 1914. Yet many also
contend, as they do with Germany, that Austria-Hungary had
largely brought this on itself. For decades or generations it
had failed or refused to solve its own internal problems, especially the nationalities conflicts, and thus exposed itself to
irredentist subversion and external threats. It had made this
worse by a stubborn, aggressive defense of outworn positions
and untenable claims in foreign policy (its so-called Pig War
against Serbia before 1908, its annexation of Bosnia in 1908, the
subsequent humiliation of Russia in 1909, its refusal to reach
reasonable compromises with Serbia, Montenegro, and Italy

---

10   On the military situation, see David Stevenson, *Armaments and the
Coming of War: Europe, 1904–1914* (Oxford, 1996); David G. Herrmann, *The
Arming of Europe and the Making of the First World War* (Princeton, 1996);
and Norman Stone, *The Eastern Front, 1914–1917* (New York, 1975). For more
general depictions of Austria-Hungary's critical position, see F. R. Bridge, *The
Habsburg Monarchy among the Great Powers, 1815–1918* (New York, 1990);
and Samuel R. Williamson Jr., *Austria-Hungary and the Origins of the First
World War* (New York, 1991).

during the Balkan Wars of 1912–13, the hopeless attempt in 1913–14 to create a viable new Balkan satellite in Albania). Once more the consensus verdict, by implication more than explicitly, posits a major counterfactual: though by 1914 the hour was late, the Monarchy's one remaining chance to survive its crisis was not the use of force, either internal or external, but reform in the direction of federalism, turning itself into a more free and democratic union of peoples and recognizing the interests of the other nationalities besides those of the master races, the Germans, Hungarians, and Italians.[11]

Thus in both cases the supposedly counterproductive and dangerous foreign policies of Germany and Austria-Hungary culminating in their gamble in 1914 are linked to a wider problem and at least partly explained by it: the failure or refusal of their regimes to reform and modernize in order to meet their internal political and social problems. Instead these regimes chose to stay in power, preserve their existing social order and the interests of their respective elites, and manage their internal social and political divisions and problems through an assertive, expansionist foreign policy (a resort to so-called secondary integration and social imperialism).

These explanations, in assigning Germany and Austria-Hungary the primary responsibility for causing the threats against which they decided to act in 1914 and explaining their policies as directed as much against internal problems as external dangers, add (as noted) further counterfactuals to the original counterfactual thesis, that these two powers had means and choices for protecting their legitimate interests in 1914 other than aiming for a local war and risking a general one. To lay these out for Germany: (a) Had Germany not conducted a reckless, aggressive pursuit of world power for decades before 1914, its general interests and position in world politics would not have been threatened as they were or were perceived to be in 1914. (b) Had Germany pursued political reform and social integration rather than manipulated social imperialism and secondary integration at home, its government would not have needed to pursue a reckless,

---

11   Examples of historians who argue along these lines are Solomon Wank, Vladimir Dedijer, Steven Beller, Alan Sked, and Leo Valiani.

aggressive foreign policy for domestic-political reasons. (c) A more democratic, liberal, and well-integrated Germany using peaceful, normal ways of protecting its legitimate interests would not have encountered enmity and opposition from the other great powers, especially from Britain and France as fellow democracies, but would have been welcomed as a partner for peace and prosperity in Europe and the world.[12] Somewhat similar counterfactuals apply to Austria-Hungary. A reformed, more progressive and democratic Monarchy pursuing wiser policies toward its nationalities and a more conciliatory foreign policy could have solved or managed its internal and external problems to such an extent that it would have both been less vulnerable to pressures and threats from its opponents and have encountered fewer such threats, thus eliminating the need for the suicidal gamble of 1914.[13]

The counterargument and its counterfactuals

First, a logical and methodological point: If, as I claim, these counterfactuals are embedded in the consensus scenario and logically implied by it, then those who advance this view have an obligation to back them up, showing by research, analysis, and evidence that these counterfactual propositions are at least reasonable, more probable than not. The burden of proof lies on them to do this, not on others to disprove them. By and large this has not been done. Historians have usually devoted close attention first to determining the facts on the origins of the war, both immediate and long term, and then to linking the outbreak of the war to the German-Austro-Hungarian initiative in July 1914,

12   This view is expressed most clearly by the authors mentioned in note 10 and in general by Fritz Fischer and his school; it is more nuanced but still present in Wolfgang J. Mommsen, *Grossmachtstellung und Weltpolitik: die Aussenpolitik des Deutschen Reiches, 1871–1914* (Frankfurt am Main, 1993); and Klaus Hildebrand, *Das vergangene Reich: Deutsche Aussenpolitik von Bismarck zu Hitler, 1871–1945* (Stuttgart, 1995).

13   Besides the historians mentioned in note 12, this view still dominates the nationalistic historiography of the successor states, Serbia, Czechoslovakia, Romania, and to some extent Poland, as represented in Adam Wandruszka and Peter Urbanitsch, eds., *Die Habsburger-Monarchie 1848–1918*, vol. 6, *Die Habsburgermonarchie im System der Internationalen Beziehungen*, pt. 2 (Vienna, 1993).

both by connecting that initiative to their particular situation and aims in 1914 and by trying to show how their general situation and aims derived from their previous foreign and domestic policies and actions. In other words, starting from a correct initial premise that the German powers' initiative was the immediate proximate cause of the war, they have then constructed a plausible case that this initiative derived from and was caused by a general situation which also primarily resulted from German and Austro-Hungarian actions and policies over a much longer term. The null hypothesis stated or implied in this argument, however, has not been systematically laid out and examined, nor have the counterfactuals embedded in it been analyzed and researched in detail. No serious attempt has been made to back up the (hidden, implied, unarticulated, but real and logically necessary) claim that absent those supposedly decisive German and Austro-Hungarian policies and actions, the general situation in 1914 would have been different in the ways the consensus view contends.

Whatever the reasons for this disparity, so long as the counterfactuals clearly, logically, and necessarily implied in the consensus argument have not been researched and analyzed with the same care as the other so-called facts in the case, both the argument making the German-Austro-Hungarian initiative the main cause rather than merely the occasion for war and thus making these powers primarily responsible for it, and the argument that the war was inherently avoidable, the result of particular decisions that could have been made differently, remain unproved. Absent this analysis of the embedded counterfactuals, we do not know whether in fact the leaders of Germany and Austria-Hungary had any real freedom to act otherwise than they did, or what difference it would have made (*ex hypothesi*) had they done so.

The argument could stop here, with a claim that the consensus case for World War I as an avoidable conflict remains unproved and with a call for more research. While this might be prudent, it would be inconclusive and not very interesting or helpful. Instead I will attempt three things. The first is to show that the counterfactual assumptions and implications of the consensus view are not only largely unexamined and unproved, but also improbable and in some instances untenable. The second is to lay

out an alternate set of counterfactual conditions and performances necessary if war were to be averted both in 1914 and for
some indefinite but significant period thereafter. The last is to
argue that this (counterfactual) set of conditions and actions
required *ex hypothesi* for avoidance of a general war in that era
not only was not recognized, accepted, or carried out by the
various actors at this time, but also that the existing international
system, that is, the circumstances, political culture, and rules and
practices that then prevailed in international power politics,
worked to make it highly unlikely that these necessary steps
would or could have been taken. This makes it in turn almost
impossible to construct any plausible counterfactual historical
scenario by which the war could have been avoided, and thus
justifies terming the war inevitable.[14]

Obviously this is a tall order. The counterargument against
the consensus view will have to be as bare-boned as the previous
exposition of that view, or more so. It starts with conceding (in

---

14   An illustrative analogy, inevitably inexact, might help indicate where the
argument is going. Suppose that one intends to challenge the verdict of an
inquiry into a fatal accident in which an automobile carrying a number of
passengers plunged off a cliff on a steep mountain road—that verdict being that
the accident was caused by two passengers who had sent the car over the cliff in
their efforts to seize the wheel by force. One might challenge that verdict in
several ways: by arguing that the defects in the car's brakes and steering made it
unlikely that it would make the trip safely in any case; by contending that the
car was already out of control and heading toward the cliff when the two intervened; or by claiming that their attempt to seize the wheel was only part of an
ongoing struggle over control of the car which made a crash likely at some point
anyway. None of these claims, however, even if true, would prove that an accident was inevitable or disprove that their effort to seize the wheel was the
proximate cause of the accident, and that they therefore bore the prime responsibility for it. If, however, one could do the following: first, show what kind of
driving conduct would have been required for this car to make this trip without
accident; second, show that none of the passengers who were struggling to
control and steer the car displayed this kind of driving conduct; third, show that
this was because for all of them the most important goal was not finishing the
journey safely, but getting control of the car and determining its final destination
against the wishes of some passengers; and finally, that the actual attempt to
seize the wheel came when the two were convinced this was their last chance not
to be kidnapped and possibly killed by the others; then, I think, one could argue
that the verdict, even if technically correct, was substantively misleading, and
moreover, that under these conditions an accident was unavoidable.

fact, insisting) on several points basically correct in the standard view concerning the immediate origins of the war—that the German-Austro-Hungarian initiative of July 1914 aimed at a local war and risked a general war with the aim of reversing the prevailing trends in international politics by violence, that this launched the great-power crisis resulting in general war, that during the July Crisis the other great powers were primarily reacting to the Central Powers' initiative, and that without this particular Austro-German initiative no local or general war would have developed *at this particular time*. But these points have long been obvious. The key question regarding both responsibility for the war and its avoidability is the counterfactual one implicit in the consensus case: the question of whether other choices were available to the Central Powers at that time which, under the existing rules and conditions of the game, offered them an opportunity to satisfy their security needs reasonably without risking a major war. If so, they chose war when it was avoidable—if not, then not.

The related question, whether they were also responsible for creating the insecurity that prompted them to gamble, is not strictly speaking relevant to the question of inevitability of the war, though it is to that of ultimate responsibility for it. If they themselves largely created the general situation that made a desperate gamble their only hope for survival, one might argue that this made war in 1914 in a sense unavoidable—they were bound soon to do something desperate that would touch it off—but also that they were responsible for it even if they had no better choice at that time. Yet though this question of responsibility is less central for our purposes than the first, the two are so closely related that even a *prima facie* case against the consensus argument, to be coherent, must deal with both. Therefore I will deny both sets of counterfactuals. That is, in addition to denying that Germany and Austria-Hungary had viable alternatives in 1914, I will also briefly state some reasons why they were not chiefly responsible for creating the critical security challenges they faced in 1914, why different policies on their part would not have substantially changed their situation, and why the existing international system precluded other reasonable peaceful alternatives for meeting the threats they faced.

I start with an assertion that will sound deliberately provocative, even outrageous, but that in my view represents a reasonable,
almost self-evident interpretation of historical evidence. In the
whole period from about 1890 to 1914, the international *policies*
and *actions* of Germany and Austria-Hungary, as distinct from
their aims, attitudes, gestures, language, and ambitions (especially those of Germany) were actually more restrained and
moderate than those of any other great power. One cannot point
to specific German or Austro-Hungarian *actions* between 1890
and July 1914 that were as aggressive, expansionist, imperialist,
law-and-precedent-breaking, and belligerent as many of those
taken during this same period by every other major power—
Russia in East Asia and Central Asia, Britain in East and South
Africa, Southeast Asia, and Central Asia, France in West, Central,
and North Africa and Southeast Asia, Italy in North and East
Africa and the eastern Mediterranean, the United States in
Central America, the Caribbean and the Western Pacific, and
Japan in East Asia. The same point holds, *mutatis mutandis*, for
a number of small powers, notably Serbia, Greece, Bulgaria, and
Montenegro.

This of course does not make Germany and Austria-Hungary,
especially the former, peace-loving defensive status quo powers.
Germany was as active a participant in the colonialist-imperialist
scramble of the era as it could be, while Austria-Hungary would
have liked to participate, tried to do so on an informal basis, and
did join half-heartedly in the open imperialist scramble toward
the end, but never had the means to pursue it seriously. Both
powers had active foreign policies and pursued aims by no means
limited to preserving the status quo. Germany in particular constantly sought gains and repeatedly made attempts at achieving
them—seldom, however, pursuing its initiatives consistently or
very far or succeeding in doing more than arouse fear, resentment, and opposition from other states. Behind its various
restless impulses lay the overall goals of *Weltpolitik*. This meant
for Germany essentially a policy of maintaining its security in
continental Europe (which, given Germany's central location,
required at least half-hegemony there) while simultaneously
making gains in world power and position (colonies, bases,
markets, a formidable navy, and alliances) that would make it

competitive in the twentieth century with Britain, Russia, and the United States. Both goals were to be achieved with the aid of Germany's military and economic power, but mainly by means of shrewd diplomacy and power politics—using Germany's key position in Europe and the free hand it supposedly gave her to exploit what Germans supposed were irreconcilable rivalries between Britain, Russia, and France, so that Germany could reach favorable deals and arrangements especially with Britain. Austria-Hungary's main aims were necessarily more defensive— to preserve its territorial integrity, independence, and great-power status against many serious challenges and threats, particularly in the one area where it still had vital great-power interests and some imperialist ambitions, the Balkans and Near East. Its policies, toward the other great powers if not lesser ones, were correspondingly more conciliatory.

Yet to dwell, as most historians do in explaining the origins of World War I, on what the Central Powers wanted and tried to do is largely beside the point. The salient fact is that throughout 1890–1914 their various initiatives, regardless of their nature and intent, regularly failed—failed either relatively in the sense of yielding them only limited gains at high long-term costs (for example, Austria-Hungary's annexation of Bosnia in 1908 or Germany's Berlin-to-Baghdad Railway project), or absolutely in the sense of ending in defeat and greater insecurity for one or both (for example, the two Moroccan Crises and the two Balkan Wars).

Equally striking is the contrast in this regard between their experience here and that of the other great powers. The latter were able to gamble, commit serious blunders, provoke wars, experience serious setbacks and defeats, and not only survive their gambles and failures but often reap long-term profit from them. The French, though they were humiliated by Britain at Fashoda, escaped unscathed from this foolish gamble and eventually gained the colonial deal and entente with Britain they wanted. Two overt, dangerous French challenges to Germany in Morocco launched serious crises, but ended by improving France's colonial and European positions. Britain used the threat of war successfully to compel France to back down over the Sudan and Egypt, got away with an aggressive, badly run war in

South Africa, and forced the Germans to accept their terms in Persia and Mesopotamia. The Russian government pursued an especially reckless imperialist policy almost everywhere, especially in the Far East, and yet not only survived the disastrous war and the crippling revolution in 1904–6 its policies had brought upon it, but by 1914 was not only pursuing its old imperialist goals in the Balkans and the Turkish Straits more boldly than ever, but also exploiting its new accord with Britain to encroach on Persia, and even laying the foundations for a revival of Far Eastern expansion. Italy's reckless adventure in Ethiopia in 1896 led it to a humiliating defeat—and subsequently to a rapprochement with France that enabled Italy thereafter to play off both sides in the European alliance system for the benefit of Italian interests in Africa, the Mediterranean, and the Balkans. Eventually this policy emboldened Italy to commit what was arguably the most cynical and dangerous act of imperialist aggression in the whole prewar period, condemned by everyone—its attack on the Ottoman Empire in Libya and the Dodecanese in 1911–12, an act directly linked with the two Balkan wars and World War I itself. Yet Italy emerged from this adventure with no concrete losses and handsome territorial gains. Japan's risky, all-out gamble in 1904–5 in launching a preventive war against Russia paid off handsomely. The US war against Spain in 1898, a war against a state that posed no threat to the United States and was thus surely avoidable even if in some respects justified, paid off even more handsomely at almost no risk.

This will doubtless be seen as an argument drawn from a familiar exculpatory tradition: the contention that Germany and Austria-Hungary were not as imperialist, reckless, or aggressive in the prewar era as other powers—to which the obvious answer is that they were imperialist, reckless, and aggressive where and when it really counted, in Europe in 1914. Let me say emphatically (I have the impression that this is an instance where one must shout in order to be heard) that this is not my point. The argument has nothing whatsoever to do with the character of German and Austro-Hungarian policy as compared to those of other powers. It has to do with who was really controlling the system, making the rules, and running the show, and thereby directly challenges the consensus case making the German powers primarily responsible for the security threats they faced in 1914 and contending that they could have warded off these threats by peaceful means. For it establishes that Germany and Austria-Hungary were not in control of the international system, but being restrained and controlled by it. The initiative and leadership in European politics from 1890 to 1914 always lay with their opponents, increasingly so as time went on. The standard reply, that the Central Powers lost control because of their own blunders and provocative acts, breaks down in numerous ways. It is a circular argument; it begs the question; it smacks of the ethic of success; it ignores the patent evidence that Germany's and Austria-Hungary's policies and initiatives regularly failed regardless of their character, whether aggressive and provocative or moderate and conciliatory;[15] it fails to specify concretely what different policies could have led to success, or explain how and why they could have. In more theoretical terms, it ignores a fundamental argument advanced by realists in international relations theory, an argument not always valid but here supported by strong evidence: that systemic factors, the distribution of power, vulnerability, and opportunities within the system, account for the major power-political patterns and outcomes of international politics more than do the character and aims of the individual actors. Logically and methodologically it errs in applying its principle of the primacy of domestic influences and interests not only to explain decisions in foreign policy (which is always in principle legitimate), but also to account for outcomes in international relations, where systemic factors must be taken into account. Finally, it errs by applying this dubious principle of the primacy

---

15   Good evidence for this is found in Harald Rosenbach, *Das Deutsche Reich, Grossbritannien und der Transvaal (1896–1902)* (Göttingen, 1993), who shows that Germany's policy toward Britain on the important issue of South Africa regularly produced British hostility and counterproductive results no matter what the Germans were trying to do or how; and Konrad Canis, *Von Bismarck zur Weltpolitik: Deutsche Aussenpolitik 1890 bis 1902* (Berlin, 1997), who demonstrates the same point on a wide range of other issues. Other instances illustrate the point. German efforts to put pressure on France over Morocco or to work in partnership with France there both failed equally; so did German efforts to work with Britain in the Berlin-to-Baghdad Railway scheme; so did Austro-Hungarian attempts either to conciliate and cooperate with Russia in the Balkans, or to put pressure on her.

of domestic politics one-sidedly, to the Central Powers far more than to the Entente.

The moral of all this is simple: to understand international outcomes from 1890 to 1914, one must stop looking first and foremost at what Germany and Austria-Hungary were doing, and concentrate on the powers who held the initiative in world affairs, basically running the system and making it work for them. One must further assume, barring evidence to the contrary, that their policies were primarily internally motivated, driven essentially by their own needs, purposes, and interests, and that Germany and Austria-Hungary, who could not and did not control events, were reacting to what the other powers were doing more than the other way around. Research on the policy of the various Entente powers done from this standpoint serves to confirm this judgment and produces a picture very different from the standard one.[16]

The distortions produced by focusing on Germany and Austria-Hungary as the prime movers in the international system are not remedied but made worse by stressing the domestic pressures and unsolved internal problems supposedly driving their foreign policies. Regardless of the extent to which this explanation may be justified (obviously their foreign and domestic policies were inextricably interwoven; in the case of Austria-Hungary, the distinction between foreign and domestic policy virtually breaks down), such a concentration on their internal problems in explaining their policies and motives simply reinforces the fundamental error of making these powers the prime movers within the system. The key to explaining the German powers' policies lies not in what their governments and their constituent interest groups and elites would have liked to do, but what they found

16 For example, on British policy, David French, *British Strategy and War Aims, 1914–1916* (London, 1986); Keith M. Wilson, *The Policy of the Entente* (Cambridge, UK, 1985); and Keith Neilson, *Britain and the Last Tsar: British Policy and Russia, 1894–1917* (Oxford, 1995). For France, see, e.g., J. C. Allain, *Agadir 1911: Une crise impérialiste en Europe pour la conquête du Maroc* (Paris, 1976); Raymond Poidevin, *Les relations économiques et financières entre la France et l'Allemagne de 1898 à 1914* (Paris, 1969); Jean-Louis Miège, *Le Maroc et l'Europe (1830–1894)* (Paris, 1961); and J. F. V. Keiger, *France and the Origins of the First World War* (London, 1983).

themselves compelled to do. It makes better sense to analyze British, French, Russian, American, Italian, and Japanese policy in terms of domestic pressures and influences, for each of these governments had more effective choices and room to translate its desires into some kind of action.[17] It also bears remembering that the foreign policy/domestic politics nexus works both ways. Domestic pressures influence and shape foreign policy, but success or failure in international politics and foreign policy also strongly influence domestic politics. This was obviously the case in prewar Germany, where the government's perceived failures in foreign policy promoted dissatisfaction throughout the political spectrum, with right-radical groups and special interests especially calling for strong action to defend the country's interests.[18] If the danger to the regime and governing elites arising from foreign policy failure was serious for Germany, it was life threatening for Austria-Hungary. The steady erosion of the state's independence and international prestige not only encouraged dissident elements to press their claims and weakened the attachment of the loyal and dominant ones, but at the same time encouraged foreign governments to advance irredentist territorial claims and to promote internal discontent and subversion within Austria-Hungary and, in the Serbian case, to support terrorist resistance within it, and encouraged almost every government to ignore or oppose its interests in international crises.[19] To contend

---

17   It might well be that had Germany and Austria-Hungary been less constrained by prevailing circumstances, their prewar policies would have been more aggressive and dangerous than those of their opponents, at least Britain and France. I myself am inclined to believe this, given the German and Austro-Hungarian record during World War I, when some of the prewar restraints ceased to operate, and the joint German-Austrian record in 1933–45. But this does not apply to the period before 1914, when they were so constrained.

18   David Blackbourn and Geoff Eley, *The Peculiarities of German History: Bourgeois Politics and Society in Nineteenth-Century Germany* (Oxford, 1984); Geoff Eley, *Reshaping the German Right: Radical Nationalism and Political Change after Bismarck* (New Haven, CT, 1980); Marilyn S. Coetzee, *The German Army League: Popular Nationalism in Wilhelmine Germany* (New York, 1990).

19   In Russia's case this was particularly true of its support of pro-Russian Ruthenian nationalism in East Galicia and the Bukovina and of some Russian official support and much public and press support of Czech and South

that the internal problems allegedly motivating the Central Powers' aggressive, dangerous foreign policies should have been handled instead by internal reforms is to ignore the extent to which, especially for Austria-Hungary, developments in the international arena contributed to those internal problems and made them unmanageable without foreign policy success.

This is (to repeat) not an attempt to blame their opponents for the failure of German and Austro-Hungarian statecraft that terminated in their July 1914 gamble.[20] It is instead an attempt to get beyond the old, tired blame game by showing that the root cause lies deeper than the policies of either the Central Powers or their rivals. It derives from the overall character of the international game being waged and the fundamentally unfavorable geopolitical position Germany and Austria-Hungary occupied within it.

That game requires at least a thumbnail description here. It comprised two simultaneous contests, inextricably intertwined and interdependent but with differing characteristics, stakes, and rules. The first was that of the old European balance of power. By 1914 this had evolved into an extremely competitive, zero-sum contest played for very high stakes (national survival) and at great risk (general war among populous industrialized states possessing mass armies); yet until just before 1914 certain minimal restraints or norms of international conduct left over from the Vienna era still prevailed. These norms, combined with prudence derived above all from fear of a general war, served to restrict the competition in Europe between individual powers and rival alliance systems to one waged for relative advantage

---

Slav nationalism. On the Serbian anti-Habsburg program, see especially Wolf-Dieter Behschnitt, *Nationalismus unter Serben und Kroaten, 1830–1914* (Munich, 1980); and Katrin C. Boeckh, *Von den Balkankriegen zum Ersten Weltkrieg* (Munich, 1996).

20   Once again, in anticipation of a plausible objection, let me make clear that just as I am not arguing that Germany and Austria-Hungary, had they not been under severe pressures in international politics before 1914, would have pursued moderate, peaceful policies abroad (see note 17), so also I do not claim that had there been no outside pressures on them or interference in their domestic problems, they would have solved or managed them more successfully. The opposite is more likely. But this also irrelevant to what happened before and in 1914.

rather than decisive victory; the powers aimed to ensure them-selves victory in case of war and an upper hand in imperialist competition, but not to conquer or eliminate one's rivals. The notion of preserving a balance of power, still widely held as an ideal though each power defined the desired balance differently and pursued it in opposed, incompatible ways, rested on a general recognition that even a victorious great war would be terribly risky and costly and might prove counterproductive, creating new international dangers by destroying the existing balance or eliminating essential actors. Thus the game resembled high-stakes poker played by heavily armed men bent on winning but reluctant to raise the stakes too high, both to avoid losing them-selves and to avoid provoking others facing impending bankruptcy into kicking over the table and starting a gunfight. As a result, there was a certain unspoken, consensual limit on the size of the bets and a general assumption that over major issues some com-promise involving a minimal level of satisfaction for everyone, or at least all the great powers, should emerge. This last remnant of the old European Concert principle remained alive, though barely so, in the two Moroccan Crises, the Bosnian Crisis, and the diplomacy of the Balkan Wars.[21]

Another game was being played alongside European balance-of-power politics, however, called imperialism or world politics (different names for the same thing). Its stakes were shares in the economic, military, political, and territorial control and exploita-tion of the non-European world; its goals and rules resembled the board game Monopoly; and it evolved differently from its companion game. The nineteenth-century European balance game began in 1814–15 with conservative monarchical coopera-tion against war, revolution, and territorial change and gradually evolved by 1914 into almost unrestrained zero-sum competition. Imperialism, always present throughout the nineteenth century but only taking center stage after about 1870, started out then as an individualistic scramble, carried on initially more by individ-uals and firms than governments, for goods supposedly free for the taking. This made imperialism at first a win-win contest for

---

21　Richard J. Crampton, *The Hollow Detente: Anglo-German Relations in the Balkans, 1911–1914* (Atlantic Highlands, NJ, 1979).

governments, less dangerous and more cooperative than the European balance game, in some ways a safe outlet for drives and energies too dangerous to be employed in Europe. Hence late nineteenth- and early twentieth-century imperialism sometimes led to confrontations but seldom to wars between European states (even the wars that occurred between European powers and the colonized peoples and states were usually small-scale affairs)[22] and often to deals dividing the spoils between certain claimants.[23]

Yet in the end European imperialism was more rapacious than ordinary balance-of-power politics, quite apart from the rapacity it showed to colonized peoples and territories. Unlike the European game, its primary aim was not security and relative advantage, but clear gains and acquisitions, which as time went on increasingly drove states to seek unchallenged control of particular areas, shutting others out. To be sure, sharing-out agreements continued to be made up to and through the Great War—consortia to build railways, carry on commercial activities, or exploit mineral resources in China or the Ottoman Empire, agreements to permit other powers commercial access to one's own colonies, international or bilateral deals over Egyptian, Ottoman, or Chinese customs, and others. Yet not only were these agreements often a *pis aller* necessary to avoid dangerous conflicts or to share prizes too expensive or troublesome to exploit exclusively. They were also usually monopolistic or

---

22 Bruce Vandevort, *Wars of Imperial Conquest in Africa, 1830–1914* (Bloomington, IN, 1998); Thomas Pakenham, *The Scramble for Africa, 1876–1912* (London, 1991).

23 The examples are almost too numerous to mention. The numerous Anglo-French contests over West and East Africa always ended in deals; even their dangerous confrontation at Fashoda led eventually to their colonial bargain of 1904. Franco-German confrontations over Morocco eventually led to a colonial bargain, though it left behind hostility on both sides. The Anglo-German contest of 1884–5 over Southwest Africa ended similarly; so did later ones over South Africa, though the Germans ended up with worthless paper concessions. The Anglo-Russian conflict over Persia and Central Asia led to their Convention of 1907, though that did not end the rivalry; the Baghdad Railway dispute eventually led to an Anglo-German agreement. Even Russia and Japan ten years after going to war over East Asia came to an agreement for coordinating their imperialist aims in China.

semi-monopolistic in character, dividing up regions so as to exclude others and enable each partner to monopolize its own sphere. Moreover, even this element of cooperation tended increasingly to break down into confrontation or open conflict. New Imperialism, in short, tended inexorably toward exclusive paramountcy and control. Witness the aggressive extension of the American Monroe Doctrine in the Western Hemisphere (Cuba and the Caribbean, the Panama Canal, Venezuela, Brazil) and the Pacific, extending even to the Philippines; the British version of their own Monroe Doctrine, informal but effective, in much of Africa, India, and elsewhere; France's preemptive extension of its exclusive control from Algeria to Tunisia and Morocco; Russia's version of exclusive empire in Central Asia, tried less successfully in Manchuria, North China, and Korea, where Japan countered this with its own program. The Anglo-Russian Convention of 1907, which tried to avoid conflict and ensure cooperation by dividing Persia and Central and South Asia into clear-cut spheres, led to far more friction than cooperation between the two imperialist partners.

This points to further crucial differences. European balance-of-power politics before 1914, even at its most competitive as in its rival security alliances, was supposed to keep all the necessary players in the game and to last indefinitely with no decisive end-point. The players had established, relatively fixed, legally recognized positions and well-known, comparable assets and opportunities, making the idea of regulating competition among them by an equilibrium of forces thinkable, though not necessarily feasible. European imperialist politics, in contrast, was designed to keep some players in the game while driving others out. Its conclusion, with final winners and losers, would come when all the available world spoils were divided up, promoting a dominant spirit of *Torschlusspanik*—panic at the closing of the gates—from early on. Finally, the players started from very different starting points with vastly different, almost incommensurable and noncomparable assets, liabilities, and opportunities. When the serious game began after 1870, Great Britain began with a vast empire and many opportunities for further expansion, but at the same time with a new formidable challenge facing it. Its vast, far-flung possessions and the informal character of its paramount position in much of Africa and Asia, both stemming from a period in which it had no serious rival in naval, industrial, and commercial terms, made the British Empire now vulnerable and hard to defend against new competitors at a time when Britain was gradually losing its industrial supremacy, and the efforts necessary to defend it might undermine the very commercial strength and prosperity on which the Empire ultimately depended and which it was supposed to promote. Two other powers, Russia and the United States, had extensive empires that were mainly continental and hence less vulnerable, giving them both considerable security and potential for further expansion. France had a substantial colonial empire and numerous opportunities for expansion, but relatively little power and capital to expend on them. Other actors (Spain, Portugal, and the Netherlands) had residual empires they were determined to retain and exploit but could not defend against serious challenge. Finally, new players having no prior stake and widely varying capacities nonetheless entered determined to play (Germany, Japan, Italy, the King of Belgium, and toward the end Austria-Hungary). Even this does not exhaust the roster of players. Those who became targets of imperialism—China, the Ottoman Empire, various African states and empires—did not simply react passively, but developed their own programs, sometimes expansionist-imperialist ones (Great Serbia, Great Bulgaria, the Greek *Megali Idea,* Pan-Turanianism, and the like).

All this ensured that the imperialist game, unlike the European one, could not be played according to more or less rational rules and calculations leading to some sort of balanced power and satisfactions, but would end in clear winners and losers. Moreover, while the high stakes of the European balance game, the fact that the survival of the nation was at risk in any general war, made for caution, the high stakes in imperialist politics, based on the general conviction that a nation's future survival and prosperity in the coming century depended on acquiring world power and position, had an opposite effect. Since the immediate danger of a great war breaking out over imperialist quarrels seemed small, imperialist competition encouraged strategic and tactical boldness, going for broke.

This relates to our main question, because in order to judge whether Germany and Austria-Hungary had alternative policies available by which they might have averted the threats they faced in 1914 and eliminated any need to gamble, one must appraise how much intrinsic chance they had to succeed in these two interlocking games from an earlier point—say, 1890—at which both games became more seriously competitive. In the European balance game, in my judgment, their basic starting positions, strengths, and liabilities gave neither much chance for significant gains and assured Austria-Hungary in particular of difficulty in holding its own regardless of what it did. The most fundamental miscalculation German leaders made was their expectation that Germany's central position in Europe would help it exploit rivalries between other powers and make itself indispensable to both sides, at a profit. That geographical position (as Bismarck had recognized—it gave him his nightmare of coalitions) was instead mainly a handicap, forcing both powers always to reckon with the likelihood of a two-front war (in Austria-Hungary's case a multi-front one), increasing their vulnerability and limiting their freedom of maneuver and alliance capability. Centrally located as they were, they could make firm commitments only to each other or to weaker states needing their support, such as Italy and Romania. They also had an additional liability often ignored in the literature: unlike all the other important powers save the Ottoman Empire, they had territories other states and/or peoples coveted and in certain instances claimed by right. In Germany's case, this meant France (Alsace-Lorraine), Denmark (North Schleswig), and the Poles (Polish Prussia). Austria's case was far worse: Italian nationalists claimed the Veneto and Trentino, Istria, and parts of Dalmatia; Russian nationalists and leaders, including the Tsar, wanted to solve the Ukrainian problem by annexing East Galicia and the Bukovina; Serbia claimed all the Austro-Hungarian territories populated by Serbs or Croats; and Romania had its eyes on Transylvania.

To be sure, these claims and velleities did not immediately threaten Germany's and Austria-Hungary's territorial integrity. Like other notions some Russians had about the Turkish Straits or East Prussia and Prussian Poland or some British and French had about Germany's colonies, these aims were likely to come into play, and did, once war broke out, but no one save radical Serbian nationalists and their backers in the Serbian military and in extreme Pan-Slav circles in Russia wanted a war to achieve them. Throughout the prewar period the Central Powers, especially Germany, remained too strong for other powers to challenge them too directly in Europe. In other words, their basic situation was unfavorable but not disastrous; it was likely that they would lose in terms of relative security and advantage, but unlikely that they would forfeit their positions as European great powers. This pretty much sums up the outcome of European great-power politics from 1890 to 1910. Given their basic situation at the outset, its unfavorable course for them was natural and normal if not strictly predictable, readily understandable without invoking particular blunders or provocations on their part as explanations. Nor is there ground to suppose that other policies on their part would necessarily have changed this result very much.

If the question is what basic chances for success they had in the imperialist world politics game from about 1890 on, the answer could well be the familiar bon mot about their wartime situations in 1917: in Berlin it was serious but not hopeless; in Vienna it was hopeless but not serious. Almost everything in their geopolitical situation worked against them for success in imperialist expansion: no initial foundation in terms of colonies, overseas trade, bases, and readily projected naval or military power; an unfavorable geographic location with only limited access to one ocean, easily blocked by rivals in case of war; an exposed position in Europe which forced them to limit their commitments and be risk-averse in the world game, making them unattractive as imperialist partners and tempting as targets; and internal divisions and weaknesses hampering both, especially Austria-Hungary. Germany had only one of the requirements for success in the imperialist world game, a vibrant growing economy, and Austria-Hungary, though growing economically, did not enjoy even that.

Just as important as these liabilities in insuring their defeat were the rules of the imperialist game and the way the other powers played it. The dominant fact—obvious yet somehow frequently overlooked or, if noticed, not taken seriously—is that the other imperialist great powers, Britain above all, but also Russia, France, Italy, and to some extent the United States and later Japan, played the imperialist game to make Germany and Austria-Hungary lose, as part of their strategy to win. The common German charge that the Triple Entente deliberately encircled Germany in Europe was false, at least so far as Britain was concerned, but another charge, that Germany and Austria-Hungary were deliberately circled out of world politics as much as possible, is obviously true. The Anglo-French Entente Cordiale in 1904 was intended to keep Germany from interfering with exclusive British and French control in Egypt and Morocco. British efforts from 1890 on to reach an agreement with Russia over the Middle East, culminating in their 1907 convention on Persia and Central Asia, were designed to prevent German penetration of this region—an aim Russia shared. Much of British foreign policy on South Africa was directed at keeping Germany from interfering there at all, whether as a partner or as an opponent. France deliberately set out to do the same vis-à-vis Germany in both Moroccan Crises, violating international agreements of 1880, 1906, and 1909 in the process. The United States worked with Britain in Latin America, the South Seas, and the Far East to limit German influence. The British and Russians collaborated against Germany on the Baghdad Railway and fought especially hard against German influence at Constantinople and in Mesopotamia. Russia, encouraged by Britain and aided by France, worked from 1907 on to check Austro-Hungarian influence in the Balkans and especially after 1911 to eliminate that influence entirely. Russia, Britain, Japan, and the United States all tried to check German economic and political expansion in China and the Far East. In the prewar scramble for concessions in Asiatic Turkey, all the other powers, including Italy and Germany, worked against Austria-Hungary.

Of course this is not evidence of a sinister anti-German or anti-Austro-Hungarian conspiracy. These tactics broke no rules because these *were* the rules, the way to play the imperialist game for fun and profit. One no more needs to invoke an anti-German or anti-Austro-Hungarian conspiracy to account for this pattern than one needs to talk of conspiracies to account for monopolistic and oligopolistic combinations and strategies in the business world, or to explain how these often target particular firms and sometimes drive them out of business. Everyone recognizes these tactics as part of the game.[24] The pattern, however, does further undermine the view that German and Austro-Hungarian policies were primarily responsible for the threats to their interests and security, and that Germany could have achieved its needed place in the sun had it followed less aggressive and provocative policies. This is like arguing that firms being deliberately driven out of business by others could have saved themselves by following less aggressive and provocative policies toward their competitors. It ignores both the concrete evidence to the contrary and the basic rules and nature of the game.

A similar unrealism afflicts the related argument that Germany, even if it lost the contest in power politics, would nonetheless have survived and prospered simply by continuing its current rate of economic growth, becoming in a few more years of peace an economic hegemon in Europe too powerful for the others to challenge. This argument, on the surface plausible, seems to ignore certain facts, such as the precarious nature of Germany's economic achievements and prosperity in an age of intense competition and frequent booms and busts (German economic growth was being surpassed by the United States at the same time and at much the same rate as Germany was surpassing Great Britain, and Russia had the fastest rate of industrial growth before 1914); or the fact that the more German trade and exports grew, the more dependent the German economy became on external markets and imports for further growth and survival, and the more vulnerable it became to military threats to these. Since British leaders calculated that they could destroy German overseas commerce and ruin Germany's economy by a naval blockade and made this their primary strategy in case of war, it was reasonable for Germans to feel vulnerable to this threat

---

24 It is somewhat surprising that historians and other international relations scholars, especially of the realist persuasion, do not automatically see this and apply it to the pre-1914 scenario, considering how commonly micro-economic competition between firms is used by realist theory as an analogy for the structure and operation of international politics.

regardless of how much economic power and wealth they amassed. Indeed, the wealthier they became, the more that sense of threat would grow. Fear of loss, as psychologists have long established, is a more powerful motivator than hope of gain. But even apart from these considerations, obvious yet inexplicably widely ignored, the most important thing here is to understand the counterfactual question. It is not, "How would the European and world economies have developed had peace lasted for some years after 1914?" That question is both too loaded with indeterminate contingent variables to be answered, and not relevant here. The question is rather, "In the real world of 1914, could Germany's leaders and public reasonably have been expected to rely for their security against foes already superior to Germany on the sea and expected shortly to achieve superiority also on land on the prospect or possibility that if peace lasted long enough, Germany's economic dynamism would protect it against these strategic and military threats?"

The answer to this question seems self-evident to me, but it is apparently not so to others, and so one needs to look at its underlying assumptions and implications. To rely on this expectation, German leaders would have had to be confident not merely that Germany would win the current economic competition, but also that a generally free, liberal world economic order with open access for everyone to international trade, especially overseas, would endure indefinitely, regardless of developments on the European and world strategic and military stage and regardless of whether Germany could if necessary support its economic interests with political and military weapons. This assumption simply flies in the face of the facts. It assumes that Smithian free-market liberalism by 1914 had decisively triumphed over neo-mercantilism, protectionism, and economic imperialism, when in fact all the major powers save Britain believed in protectionism and mercantilism rather than free trade. Even Britain practiced a form of imperialist protectionism, and most states were more protectionist than Germany. It assumes that Germany's rivals would have peacefully come to terms with Germany's economic domination, when in fact they were already worried by Germany's economic progress and took active measures before the war, especially in Russia and France, to avoid becoming

economically dependent on Germany.[25] It assumes that the prewar
international economic system operated largely independently
of European high politics and military strategy and would continue to do so, when in fact everyone believed that a strong state
and a strong economy required each other and that it was the
government's duty to bring the nation's political, military, and
economic resources together to promote its national interests.
Tariff wars, discrimination against foreign goods and enterprises, and attempts by governments to promote their nationals'
economic interests or to use these interests to promote their
political and strategic ends were central to the age of imperialism. Even the British, who still adhered to free-trade principles,
relied on their naval supremacy and empire as a hedge against
dangerous competition or decline.

In other words, this counterfactual holds that the Germans,
of all people, should have believed and trusted in the message of
Norman Angell's prewar book *The Great Illusion:* that growing
interdependence in the modern capitalist economy had rendered
war obsolete, counterproductive, and unthinkable. True, Angell
was right in criticizing the reigning neo-mercantilist, protectionist, and militarist doctrines of his day, but he also ignored power
political realities and their connection to economics then and
since.[26] The counterfactual argument that Germany could have

---

25   Fritz Fischer's well-known thesis (*Griff nach der Weltmacht: Die
Kriegszielpolitik des kaiserlichen Deutschland*, 3rd ed. [Düsseldorf, 1964]; and
Krieg der Illusionen: die deutsche Politik von 1911 bis 1914 [Düsseldorf, 1969])
of a continuity between Germany's prewar drive for world power and the imperialist war aims program it developed and pursued in 1914–18 may go too far
in making Germany's wartime aims the actual motives for its prewar policy. Yet
it is hard to deny that the aims Germany developed in wartime reflect what its
elites were already thinking about before 1914 as to how Germany might solve
its problems in case war arose. If we apply this same argument to the Allies, it
tells us something important about their prewar attitudes toward Germany's
economy. Prominent in the British, French, and Russian war aims programs
were measures to break Germany's economic power while at the same time
somehow preserving Germany as a market for their own economies. Along
with the works of David French and Keith Neilson cited above (note 16), see
especially G. H. Soutou, *L'Or et le Sang: Les buts de guerre économiques de la
Première Guerre mondiale* (Paris, 1989).

26   See the Forum in the *American Historical Review* 94, 3 (October
1993): 1106–42, an exchange between Carl Strikwerda and Paul W. Schroeder

broken up or loosened the alliances or quasi-alliances against it by more moderate, patient policies and conduct has similar problems. Granted, Germany's opponents genuinely perceived Germany as unpredictable and dangerous, and were acting partly to counter that threat. But this does not mean that Germany could have removed that perception and changed its opponents' policies simply by becoming somehow more moderate and conciliatory in its behavior. Germany posed a threat particularly to Russia and France mainly because of where it was located and the power it possessed rather than by its policies, and their alliances and ententes were intended to meet this objective, structural threat by giving the Entente powers a margin of military preponderance over Germany. Any signs of German restraint would and did serve as proof that these alignments were working and should be continued. Besides, as already noted, these combinations had important uses in world politics. Their central value for Britain was to help preserve the British Empire by maintaining Britain's good relations with France and Russia so as to curb both their colonial rivalries with Britain and German competition. Preserving the so-called balance of power in Europe was part and parcel of this policy. In other words, the anti-German alliances and ententes were so intrinsically valuable for the Entente powers for both their security in Europe and their world-imperialist purposes that German good behavior would not have made them give them up, and that German attempts to undermine or loosen them, or even join them, served as more proof that Germany was treacherous and dangerous. The history of prewar politics shows this. The cognitive biases apparent in the consensus view—the ascription of more freedom of choice to one side (in this case Germany) than to the other, and the belief that it could easily have changed its policy and thereby have induced the other side to change too—are familiar to political psychologists.

All this concerns only the German side of the problem, on which most historians concentrate, ignoring thereby the more

---

on the former's article, "The Troubled Origins of European Economic Integration: International Iron and Steel and Labor Migration in the Era of World War I."

immediate and pressing half, the Austro-Hungarian problem.[27]
The counterfactuals embedded in the consensus view involving
Austria-Hungary are even stranger than those for Germany, and
receive less scrutiny. But in a way this is not surprising, for in
regard to Austria-Hungary the consensus case with its embedded
counterfactuals rests on assumptions so unwarranted as hardly
to deserve discussion. A good example is the notion that internal
reforms could have solved the nationalities disputes within
Austria-Hungary and thus given it the needed power and cohesion to survive the ruthless competition of European and world
politics. This assumes two things: that nationalities conflicts of
the kind that have troubled the Habsburg Monarchy and other
multinational states in modern times are soluble by any means,
and that internal reforms, if they succeed in promoting greater
domestic harmony, also make a state stronger for foreign policy
purposes.[28] No support is offered in theory, argument, or evidence for either assumption, and none is available. In fact, the
Austrian government launched many reforms between 1867 and
1914 that helped make the Monarchy a progressive, modernizing
state in important respects—a thriving culture, a growing
economy, an advanced educational system, and a political system
that, though riddled with conflict and tensions, respected civil
rights and included democratic features. But these reforms also,

---

27   The problems this causes are illustrated by Niall Ferguson's recent revisionist and controversial book on World War I, *The Pity of War* (New York,
1999). Ferguson actually makes some sound and important, if not really new,
points about the origins of the war, mostly directed against the prevailing
German-war-guilt thesis. The trouble is, however, that because like most other
historians he virtually ignores Austria-Hungary and Eastern Europe, he not
only misunderstands the origins of the war but advances an unsound counterfactual argument that a German victory would not have been so bad for Europe
or the British—indeed, that it might have averted later disasters—and that
Britain would have done better to stay out of it. Critics have generally ignored
the sound points in his case and pounced on the unsound ones in reaffirming
the conventional verdict about Germany as the main architect of the war.

28   As Geoffrey Hosking notes in his *Russia: People and Empire 1552–1917*
(Cambridge, MA, 1997), 397, Tsarist Russia tried to solve its nationalities problems before World War I by repression and Russification; Austria-Hungary
tried to solve its by concessions. Neither policy worked, and the problem may
simply be insoluble.

inevitably, hampered rather than aided the Monarchy's efforts to conduct a strong foreign policy. The more freedom its many peoples, factions, and parties enjoyed to contend for their particular rights, status, and share of power within the Monarchy, and the more parliamentary (and thereby more chaotic) its politics became, the less chance there was to unite everyone on a single foreign policy agenda, or to raise the taxes needed to keep Austria-Hungary competitive in the European arms race, or to prevent foreign governments and groups from intervening in the Monarchy's nationalities conflicts, and the nationalities themselves from exploiting this.

Even more implausible is the suggestion that successful internal reforms, whatever these might have been, would have lessened the hostility or changed the aims of its opponents abroad. Russian nationalists and the Russian government were not interested in protecting the rights of Ukrainians (so-called Ruthenes) in East Galicia; their concern was to prevent Ukrainian nationalism from spreading from East Galicia and the Bukovina to Imperial Russia, and the ideal solution was to annex these territories to Russia. Much the same holds for Italian nationalists and their irredentist claims, as well as Romanian nationalists, to say nothing of the Serbs. This has nothing to do with the question of whether Austria-Hungary should have done something more or different to meet its internal problems; it means only that meeting its internal problems would not have significantly changed the attitudes or actions of its opponents.

The central weakness in the counterfactual case on Austria-Hungary, however, parallels the one in regard to Germany: it ignores the basic rules and nature of the game. Austria-Hungary's competitors and opponents were acting with regard to the Monarchy essentially on behalf of their own interests and aims, not in reaction to what it did. Austria-Hungary could have prevented this only by changing the nature and stakes of the game to make this unprofitable—which was what it finally tried to do by its July 1914 gamble. One more feature of the standard counterfactual scenario deserves mention: that it leaves the two sides of its case, the German and Austro-Hungarian aspects, unconnected when they are in fact tightly interwoven. It suggests a counterfactual solution for Germany's security problem, namely, that it show greater restraint, moderation, and patience toward its opponents and accept some temporary military and strategic insecurity while seeking its future security through the relaxation of tensions in Europe and German economic growth. For Austria-Hungary it suggests domestic reforms to strengthen it politically and militarily so that it could better defend its interests against external challenges. Leave aside for the moment the inherent flaws in these proposals, already discussed, and ask simply how they fit and work together. The answer is: They do not—they contradict each other. Suppose *per impossible* that Austria-Hungary could before 1914 have achieved the internal cohesion and economic strength to keep up with the others in the arms race; how would that have fit in with a simultaneous effort by Germany to try to cool the arms race? It would have been obviously and directly contrary to it—the main reason being that the fixed policy of all three Entente powers was to consider Austria-Hungary as simply Germany's subordinate ally, no matter how desperately the Austrians pleaded that they were pursuing an independent policy, so that a stronger, more confident and assertive Austria-Hungary automatically meant in St. Petersburg, Paris, and London a stronger, more dangerous Germany.[29] Or consider the impact of German efforts to conciliate its opponents on Austria-Hungary's security problem. The historical evidence is clear: such efforts by Germany made Austria-Hungary's problems worse. What Russia wanted as proof of German moderation and cooperation, also demanded by Britain, was that Germany restrain Austria-Hungary in the Balkans. Germany's refusal in Russia's eyes to restrain Austria-Hungary in 1909 was the source of massive, permanent Russian resentment. When Germany did restrain its ally from 1910 to 1913, thereby helping prevent a general war and temporarily improving Russo-German and Anglo-German relations, that also contributed hugely to

---

29   A good example of this is the Entente powers' reactions to the expansion of the Austro-Hungarian navy in the Adriatic before 1914. Entente leaders knew perfectly well that the Austrians were building solely against the Italians, their nominal ally, and had no thought of challenging Russia, France, or Britain on the sea. Never mind; Austria-Hungary was Germany's ally, and therefore its navy, like its army, must be regarded as simply part of the joint enemy forces in the coming war.

undermining Austria-Hungary's position and fueling frustration and despair among its decision-makers. Or consider the suggestion that Germany should have relied on peaceful economic expansion for its future security. One of Germany's most important economic targets before 1914 was the Balkans and the Ottoman Empire. German economic expansion there directly threatened Austria-Hungary's trade, prosperity, and independence more than those of any other state, serving to encourage Austria-Hungary's opponents, Serbia in particular, and push Austria-Hungary toward violent countermeasures.

These points are important not just as further instances of the internal contradictions in the consensus scenario and the ways it neglects the Austro-Hungarian problem, but as evidence of a profound misunderstanding of the German problem as well. Those who insist that Germany was mainly responsible for the Central Powers' gambling strategy in 1914, even though Austria-Hungary conceived that strategy, demanded German support for it, and finally launched it, argue that Austria-Hungary could not possibly have acted without German help, and that since Germany gave its ally a blank check, subsequently pressed Austria-Hungary forward, and never really tried to restrain it, Germany was chiefly responsible. Once again the embedded counterfactual assumptions demand examination. There are at least two, closely related: first, that the German government, if it genuinely wanted peace, could have rejected Vienna's demand for support, regardless of Austro-Hungarian warnings that a denial of support would critically affect the alliance, future Austrian policy, and the survival of the Monarchy as a great power; second, that Germany, in the interest of general peace, could and should have detached its security and great-power status from Austria-Hungary's survival as a great power—a survival that Germans, like everyone in Europe, including especially the Austrians, considered genuinely threatened.

It is hard to conceive how these assumptions could be defended. They seem to contradict everything known about the history of German and Austrian relations in Central Europe, the connection between this problem and the wider problems of relations with Russia over Eastern Europe and the Balkans, and the nature of European international politics, both political and military.

Above all they strike one as an impossible way to promote durable European peace. In a more peaceful and stable earlier era, Bismarck recognized and acted upon an insight fully confirmed by history since 1914: that breaking up the Habsburg Monarchy or eliminating it as a great power, regardless of how this happened and whether or not Austria deserved it, would have revolutionary consequences for Germany and Europe as a whole. That insight is here ignored. The surprise is not that Germany recognized this community of fate in July 1914 and backed Austria-Hungary's desperate gamble; the decision to do so had essentially been taken earlier in 1914. The surprise is rather that the German government earlier tried for a long time to ignore its ally's problems or to sweep them under the rug, even in various ways helping make them worse, and that only now it seriously reckoned with the consequences for Germany of Austria-Hungary's continued decline and potential collapse or defection as an ally.

The crowning anomaly in the consensus view and its counterfactuals lies thus in its ignoring precisely what the July Crisis most clearly proves: that Germany could not ignore the Austro-Hungarian problem even though it wished to, because the German and Austro-Hungarian problems were Siamese twins, and part of still wider and more complex Central and East European and Near Eastern problems, so that an attempt to solve or manage the German question and the question of European peace without seriously dealing with the Austro-Hungarian problem was an attempt to play Hamlet without the Prince of Denmark.

An account of the origins of the war with different embedded counterfactuals

The argument thus far seems to suggest that the war was inevitable for the following reasons:

(a) The nature of the European power game and of Germany's and Austria-Hungary's respective positions within it made its actual outcome by 1914, namely, relative loss, frustration, and looming danger for Germany and even worse decline and immediate peril for Austria-Hungary, likely from the outset.

(b) Similarly, the nature of the imperialist game and of Germany's and Austria's positions in it made its actual outcome, that Germany would lose relative to its rivals, but not absolutely or fatally, while Austria-Hungary risked losing completely, even more likely.

(c) Yet these unfavorable outcomes and trends were probably not enough individually and by themselves to make the two powers risk a general war in order to reverse them. This is suggested by the fact that on several occasions previously (1904–5, 1908–9, and 1912–13) they passed up opportunities for war when their chances for success were better than they were in 1914. Nevertheless, given the facts that these two games were tied together both objectively and in their perception, and that the Central Powers, like others, believed that both contests were critical to their ultimate survival, security, and prosperity as great powers, their belief that they were losing and declining in both made it likely that at some point they would take some risky action to reverse the trend. Any immediate, overt challenge and threat to the independence, integrity, and great-power status of one or both of them, such as arose on June 28, 1914, would increase that likelihood dramatically.

(d) Since their rivals shared their assumptions regarding the nature, rules, and stakes of the combined European-world politics game and were therefore equally determined to maintain their favorable positions or improve them, any German-Austro-Hungarian initiative to reverse the existing trends of the game was almost certain to meet strong resistance and produce a direct collision between the two sides. The tense, crisisladen atmosphere of prewar politics, with many vital issues unresolved and major developments in flux, made it virtually certain that occasions for confrontations and clashes of interest would arise. These facts, plus the high stakes on both sides and the absence of any mutually acceptable compromise of their irreconcilable purposes, entitle one to consider a general war as inevitable sooner or later.

This view comes close, but it is too determinist or determinist in the wrong way. It makes the decisive element the nature, rules, and stakes of the prevailing game of international politics and the objective conditions under which the various actors entered it and played it out. The version I propose locates the determining element elsewhere—not in the international game itself, which still could conceivably have continued for some time without general war and without radical changes in its rules, but in the political culture of the era and in certain dominant beliefs about the prevailing game.

Let me try to show the subtle difference by an analogy, inevitably inexact but perhaps useful for illustration. Compare World War I to a train collision involving five trains, all in a race to reach the station first or at least to avoid coming in last. The strict determinist view just outlined holds that they collided because all five were on intersecting tracks, the only way to avoid an accident was for at least one or two of them to give way to the others and thereby lose the race, and all considered this action with its predictable outcome unacceptable. An indeterminist view would hold that the trains, though running on unsafe tracks at dangerously high speeds with obsolete equipment operated in certain instances by reckless engineers, were not running on intersecting tracks but parallel ones set dangerously close together. Hence a collision was not inevitable but could only arise by accident (say, if one of the trains left the tracks or swayed into another one) or by deliberate recklessness. My version holds that while all five trains involved in the race were running together closely enough that all would be involved in any accident, only three of the five were on a potential collision course. These three, however, had been in similar races over this same terrain a number of times before, and knew how an accident could be avoided—when to slow down, what signals to give, what switches or side-tracks to take, and so on—actions that involved some active coordination between themselves and at least passive cooperation from the other two trains in the race. What caused the collision in this instance was a refusal by the engineers on all five trains at critical moments to take the steps their experience told them were needed to avoid an accident. They failed to act out of a shared conviction that the game no longer allowed for such actions—that they had become futile and counterproductive, would cause them to lose the race, and were in any case not their particular responsibility. This collective mentality and fixed attitude made the collision unavoidable.

Notice that this last version shifts the focus from, "Who or what caused the train wreck?" to "Who or what caused the failure to avoid it?" Applied to World War I, the focus is changed from, "Who or what caused the outbreak of war?" to "Who or what caused the breakdown of peace?" For many reasons impossible to discuss here, I contend that explaining peace rather than war should be the prime emphasis in studying war and international politics in general. But regardless of this claim as a broad principle, the aim here is solely to show in a prima facie way that the distinction makes sense and that World War I is better explained as the breakdown of peace than the outbreak of war. The analysis intends to show how the war had become unavoidable not because the forces and impulses driving the different powers toward it had become irresistible, but because the actions needed to avoid it had become unthinkable. Consistent with the theme of this essay, the argument involves counterfactual reasoning.

The strict determinist argument sketched out earlier holds that under the circumstances prevailing by 1914 the German powers were virtually certain sooner or later to try to reverse the prevailing trends pointing toward an outcome unacceptable to them through violent means that would risk general war, and that the others were equally certain to resist this strongly, resulting in war. To see why this comes close but misses the target, one needs to ask two closely related counterfactual questions. First, what plausible circumstances might have led Germany and Austria-Hungary in 1914 to decide once again, as they had done several times before, to try other less provocative and dangerous ways of defending their security and vital interests? Second, what actions, plausible under the circumstances, might the other powers have decided to take before or during the July Crisis suitable to deter and/or dissuade the German powers from a course risking war?

These counterfactual questions seem to give the game away to the indeterminists, opening the door wide to many suggestions and alternative scenarios commonly encountered in the literature. Things would have been different had the assassination attempt failed, or had the Austro-Hungarians agreed to stop their attack on Serbia at Belgrade, or had Russia given the Serbian government different advice, or had Britain given Germany a clear warning that it would enter the war on France's side, and so on. However, the argument made earlier, that all the major actors were fundamentally driven by long-term concerns based on shared assumptions about the nature, rules, and stakes of the game and a shared understanding of where that game was headed, closes the door against that kind of general speculation about contingencies. If one side by 1914 was determined to reverse the prevailing trend and avert the predicted ultimate outcome even at the grave risk of war, and the other side was equally ready to accept war rather than let that happen, then different individual events and actions at the time of the July Crisis would only have altered the occasion, timing, and form of the final collision, not averted it, *unless the different events and actions also changed these shared assumptions, beliefs, and expectations.* The real questions therefore are, first, whether such a change in these reigning collective European mindsets and understandings about international politics was possible at all before or during the July Crisis, and second, what alternative policies, decisions, and actions conceivable in terms of the minimal-rewrite rule and compatible with historical evidence might have effected this change, that is, might have altered the reigning perceptions of current and future trends sufficiently on both sides, especially on the Central Powers, to change their views of what could and must be done. The strong determinist position denies that any such shift was possible; the indeterminist one denies that any was necessary. The view advanced here is between and beyond both. It is that, objectively and historically speaking, strategies and tactics were still available to the great powers that might have averted a collision by changing crucial prevailing mindsets, but that subjectively, in terms of what the actors considered conceivable and feasible, they were not—and therefore war was inevitable.

The first step in testing this is establishing just what needed to change in the mindsets of what particular actors. The consensus view holds that only German and Austro-Hungarian attitudes needed to change; that view, as we have seen, will not do. But did virtually everything in the whole situation have to change? The determinist view fits the common impression that Europe by 1914 was a tinderbox filled with explosive material waiting for a spark, so that war could have broken out over any one or any combination of many issues or causes. That picture is also misleading. Actually, Europe in June 1914 was near general war, as it had been repeatedly since 1908, but it was not yet at the brink or certain to go over it, and most of the conflicts that divided the great powers were not such as to set off a war. In fact (here again comes counterfactual reasoning) no convincing scenario can be constructed by which most of the issues in dispute could have caused a general war, either alone or even in combination. One could compile a long list of issues—Anglo-German naval rivalry, Alsace-Lorraine and other irredentist territorial claims, military threats, colonial and commercial rivalries, historic national hatreds, ethnic and racial animosities—that were serious, sufficient to create hostility and tension, but not matters over which any great power wanted or intended to fight, or for which it could plausibly start a war. Instead, only three great powers contemplated starting a general war under any circumstances—Russia, Germany, and Austria-Hungary—and their respective grounds for doing so were limited and specific. Russia was willing, though not eager, to fight for two reasons: to prevent any other power from gaining control of the Turkish Straits (witness its willingness to use force to prevent its own allies and associates, Bulgaria and Greece, from seizing Constantinople in the first Balkan War, and its strong stand over the Liman von Sanders affair in early 1914); and to prevent what the Russian government, driven by a nationalist press and so-called public opinion, viewed as another humiliation like that of 1908–9 in the Balkans at the hands of the German powers. Germany was willing to go to war rather than allow its army to become decisively inferior to those of its foes, either through Russia's successful completion of its armaments program or by Austria-Hungary's collapse or defection, or both. Austria-Hungary's will for war was the most desperate and dangerous of all. Although with good reason it feared general war more than any other great power, its leaders had already concluded by early 1914 that it could not tolerate any further deterioration of its great-power status and its Balkan position, particularly through more challenges and provocations from Serbia. These were the only issues that could have caused general war in 1914, and they did cause it. The question of the avoidability of war therefore rests neither on whether some impossible set of sweeping changes in the whole international situation occurred, nor on whether certain particular contingent events involved in the outbreak of war in July 1914 could have gone differently, but on the specific question of whether these particular great powers could have been deterred and/or dissuaded from risking general war for these particular reasons.

The answer is "Yes." It arises not from theory or speculation, but solid historical evidence. The first thing to recognize is that these problems were not new to these powers, but old and familiar, almost standard; they had repeatedly caused wars or threatened to cause them before.[30] Twice in the previous century (1809 and 1859) Austria had gone to war rather than accept a further decline in its great-power status and position and more threats to its prestige and rights. In 1756 Prussia had deliberately launched a preventive war against Austria and Russia rather than wait for an overwhelming coalition to jell against it.[31] Russia had been ready in the Bulgarian Crisis of 1884–7 to fight Austria rather than accept another supposed humiliation at its hands. Not only were the essential dangers in 1914 familiar, almost commonplace; so were the theater, the terrain, and the three players. Ever since 1763 at the end of the Seven Years War, when Russia and Prussia had fully emerged as recognized great powers, these three states had dominated Central and Eastern Europe, competing over territory, interests, influence, leadership, and security. This area, even during the Napoleonic Wars, had been constantly the main focus and center of European politics. The issues that dominated the Austro-German-Russian relationship and threatened the peace in 1914 had *mutatis mutandis* been vital for them the whole time.

But if the issues and dangers were familiar, so were the remedies. The astonishing fact (astonishing both in itself and in its

---

30   This is the point, in the analogy of the train wreck, of noting that the engineers of the three trains had been over this terrain previously and knew what caused wrecks and how to avoid them.

31   Lest one suppose that these historical examples counted for little in 1914, Johannes Burkhardt argues convincingly that analogies with Prussia's situation in 1756, 1813, and 1870 were very prominent in German thinking in 1914. "Kriegsgrund Geschichte? 1870, 1813, 1756—historische Argumente und Orientierungen bei Ausbruch des Ersten Weltkriegs," in Johannes Burkhardt et al., eds., *Lange und kurze Wege in den Ersten Weltkrieg* (Munich, 1996), 9–86.

being so widely ignored) is that the 150 years of Austro-German-Russian relations after 1763 represent a story not of constant rivalry, conflicts of interests, struggles for power and influence, and frequent tensions and crises leading to war, but of constant rivalry, conflicts of interests, struggles for power and influence, and frequent tensions and crises resulting in *peace*. Between 1740 and 1914, Austria and Russia, always rivals in the Balkans, often rivals elsewhere as well, frequently at swords' points, *never* fought each other, except for two occasions in 1809 and 1812 when they were dragged by Napoleon into half-hearted campaigns that they would never have entered on their own. The same is true between 1762 and 1914 for Prussia-Germany and Russia. Austria and Prussia fought two short wars over Germany, to be sure— one indecisive in 1778–9, the other decisive in 1866. Yet within thirteen years of the latter they were again allies, as they had been most of the fifty years before 1866—without ever ceasing to be rivals. In the same way Austria and Russia and Germany and Russia were frequently allies though always rivals.

Thus the central story in European international history from 1763 to 1914 is this remarkable Austro-German-Russian *peace*. Nineteen fourteen must be seen first and foremost not simply and generically as the outbreak of general European war, but as the breakdown of that specific long peace. To explain the war, scholars must first explain it, understand what maintained and revived it so long, often against improbable odds, and then, having done this, ask themselves whether the measures and devices that had previously served to maintain this Austro-German-Russian peace no longer would work in 1914, or whether (as I believe) they simply were not tried.

To attempt any such serious analysis here would stretch the already elastic bounds of this essay beyond the breaking point. I will therefore merely make some general points, more by assertion than by argument. First, the procedures and principles of European diplomacy used for dealing with such problems as these, especially those of the European Concert, were well known. Where seriously tried, they still worked even in 1914. One vital issue capable of causing war in 1914, that of the Turkish Straits, was actually handled successfully in this way. Russia's warnings to Bulgaria and Greece to stay away from the Straits and its success (with British and French support and restraint) in inducing Germany and the Ottoman Empire to back down on the Liman affair under cover of a face-saving formula without using force against the Turks were examples, if risky ones, of traditional Concert diplomacy on the Eastern question. The underlying principles behind both were traditional: that Russia had special interests in the Straits and could not allow others besides Turkey to control them, but could rely on diplomacy and the Concert to defend its interests and was not allowed to act unilaterally or by force. True, the other fighting issue for Russia, that it would not tolerate another humiliation in the Balkans at the hands of Austria-Hungary and Germany, and the corresponding fighting issue for Austria-Hungary, that it could not endure any further undermining of its great-power position in the Balkans or challenges from Russia and its client Serbia, were far more difficult to handle, not merely because of the mutually incompatible perceptions and enflamed public opinion on all sides, but also because (in my view) Russian perceptions were one-sided and unjustified. The widespread belief that Russia's rights had repeatedly been violated, its prestige and honor challenged, and its security and historic mission in the Balkans threatened ever since 1908 by the German powers simply does not square with undeniable facts. In 1908–9, as even more in 1904–6, Russia had been lucky to escape dangers of its own making, that the Central Powers could have exploited but did not. Since then Russia had been mainly winning in the Balkans and getting away with a very bold offensive policy. Yet this was far from the first time that Russia had blamed difficulties largely of its own making on Germany and Austria (witness the Eastern Crisis of 1875–8 and the Bulgarian Crisis of 1884–7) or that Austria had seen Russian pressure as an alp that it had to shake off at almost any cost (the Crimean War). Historically, there were tested ways of handling such problems short of war.[32]

As for Germany's fear of Russia, here again one must distinguish between the irrational fear of being overrun by barbarian

---

32   For example, France was held back from war over the Near East in 1840 and Russia from war with the Ottoman Empire over Greece in 1821–3 and with Austria over Bulgaria in 1885–7 by just such collective pressure.

hordes from the East and the concomitant belief in a great, inevitable Teuton-Slav struggle for mastery in Europe, and the concrete and rational fear of being hopelessly outmanned by 1917 by the combined Russo-French armies and those of their allies. Diplomacy could not directly combat the former fear, but it could have done something to manage the latter, even within the existing alliance structure. For instance, there could have been some informal equivalent for Germany of Bismarck's Reinsurance Treaty with Russia in 1887, assuring Germany that France and Britain would not support a Russian attack on Germany, as Bismarck had reassured Russia that Germany would not support a British-Austrian offensive against it.

The other requirement for simultaneously deterring and reassuring Germany concerns Austria-Hungary, and brings us to the heart of the problem. One can hardly overemphasize the destabilizing effect of the conviction among German leaders by 1914, one promoted by the Austrians themselves, that Germany must now use its ally or lose it—stand by it now at any risk and cost, or expect shortly to have to fight without it because of Austria-Hungary's defection, paralysis, or breakup. It is difficult enough to imagine a counterfactual scenario in which Germany with its powerful, irresponsible military, its erratic, impulsive monarch, and its semi-authoritarian, deeply divided government and society would have calmly stood by while Russia and France completed their efforts to achieve military superiority over it. It is quite impossible to imagine Germany doing so while it simultaneously was losing its last remaining useful ally. The implication is clear: one indispensable key to restraining Germany and in general to preventing a major war was stabilizing Austria-Hungary's international status by doing something serious about the Austro-Hungarian problem.

The common reply to this assertion, or rather, dismissal of it, is that Austria-Hungary's decline and eventual collapse were irreversible, the result of its internal decay and impossible to solve or arrest by international politics and diplomacy. As already indicated, I deny the premise, as do other scholars more expert on Austro-Hungarian internal affairs than I. Austria-Hungary's problems and weaknesses were real and would not go away or be cured, but they were not of themselves destroying it or even keeping it from being a working political entity, functioning far more soundly in most respects, for example, than Russia or its Balkan neighbors or Italy. It was the combination within the cauldron of European international competition of internal and external pressures on Austria-Hungary and the purposeful exploitation of these by other states that was ruining its international position. It is simply not true—in fact, nonsense—to say that European international politics could do nothing about this or about preventing a war that might arise out of it. Were this principle true, the Habsburg Monarchy would not have survived a number of crises in its long, crisis-riddled existence. It had repeatedly been saved in the past by support, usually passive but sometimes active, from various members of the European family of states including Russia who recognized that its disappearance would bring with it incalculable consequences and insoluble problems.

Yet making this simple historical observation, or citing the traditional balance-of-power principle of the need to preserve in order to maintain a viable international system, risks confusing the central issue to the advantage of those whose interest it is to confuse it. The question is not whether the Habsburg Monarchy could have been saved in 1914, or should have been, or whether other powers including its rivals should have done something concrete to save it. My own view, indicated earlier, is that the Monarchy did not need active intervention by anyone in its internal problems in order to survive and continue to muddle through, as it had done for most of its existence with fair success. Quite the contrary—it needed less intervention and pressure from outside. But regardless of this, the real question is whether, in the face of mounting evidence of the possibility or likelihood of the collapse or paralysis of so essential an actor as Austria-Hungary, the members of the European international system had reasons, incentives, precedents, and devices for taking some kind of action to manage and control the process and international consequences of so mammoth a change, or whether they were bound simply to let it happen and see what emerged from the wreckage.

Thus correctly posed, the question answers itself, and not on the basis of any moral considerations, but on those of history and elementary state self-interest. The Austro-Hungarian problem in its *international* dimensions and repercussions was precisely the sort of question with which the international system was supposed to deal, and could have dealt. Historical precedents abounded in 1914 for the systemic European management of the problems and dangers presented by declining and threatened vital units. They varied widely, of course, from brutal measures like planned partitions of the declining units with more or less balanced compensations to the more powerful ones (Poland and the German Empire in the late eighteenth and early nineteenth centuries) through less brutal, more controlled management (the Ottoman Empire in the Balkans and North Africa) through measures of joint guarantee and protection (Belgium, Switzerland, Denmark, and for a considerable period the Papal State). What was unprecedented was what actually happened before and during 1914—the ignoring of this issue, the absence of any collective European response to the prospective downfall or disappearance of a central actor like Austria-Hungary, a contingency long and widely foreseen and predicted. That was a great, astonishing departure from tradition. What could and should have been done to manage the international aspects and consequences of the Austro-Hungarian problem over the longer term is of course controversial, as is whether any feasible international action would have been effective. But it is not hard to propose measures, plausible on their face, for short-term action in 1914, that is, for a European intervention following the assassination of Franz Ferdinand to stop the incident from escalating into a dangerous confrontation and war. Something certainly could have been attempted to satisfy Austria-Hungary's prestige and honor and to compel Serbia to conform at least outwardly to its international commitments to act as a good neighbor.[33] Since

---

33 To be sure, there are historians, not merely Serb nationalists but others as well, who deny any Serbian responsibility for the assassination, arguing *inter alia* that Austria-Hungary had brought it on by the provocative character of the state visit to Sarajevo. Niall Ferguson (*Pity of War*, 146n3) quotes A. J. P. Taylor's remark that if British royalty had chosen to visit Dublin on St. Patrick's Day during the Troubles, they could also have expected to be shot at. Let me amend Taylor's analogy to make it conform better to Austria-Hungary's position: Suppose that the United Kingdom in 1914 was not separated from the continent by the English Channel, but had as its direct neighbor in the

the particular steps Austria-Hungary demanded—a serious investigation of the ties between the assassination plot and Serbia's
government, its nationalist organizations, and its military intelligence, followed by concrete measures to prevent future
provocations, would not and probably could not be carried out
by Serbia no matter what its government promised, and since
Russia's attitude meant that they also could not be undertaken
by Austria-Hungary without provoking an international crisis,
the obvious conclusion, based on historical precedents, would be
that Europe acting in concert would ask Austria-Hungary to
turn its cause and demands over to them, and then carry through
seriously an investigation of the terrorist attack and any required
sanctions on Serbia. The nineteenth century provided ample
precedent for international action to compel smaller states,

---

southeast, where the Low Countries are, an independent Kingdom of Ireland.
This Kingdom of Ireland, though small and backward, was fiercely combative,
violent, and conspiratorial in its politics, and committed to an ethnic integral-
nationalist hegemonic state ideology calling for it to unite all Irishmen under
its rule. Its definition of "Irish" included other Celts in the UK (Scots, Welsh-
men) on the grounds that they were really Irish corrupted by an alien regime
and religion, and it taught its children in school that large parts of the UK really
belonged to the Kingdom of Ireland and should be liberated. To this end its
nationalist press waged a propaganda war against the UK calling for its overthrow and dissolution, and its military intelligence arm, operating secretly and
without control of the government, supported dissidents and revolutionary
organizations in the UK, and trained and armed terrorists to operate there. This
Kingdom of Ireland was allied with and supported by Germany. When the
decision to send the Prince of Wales on a state visit to UK Ireland was made in
London, the Irish royal government, knowing that some form of Irish terrorist
action was being planned and being unready for a war but not daring for internal reasons to act decisively to prevent one, gave a vague warning to London
that the visit might have bad results. But London also knew that a cancellation
of the planned state visit, designed as a measure to support and encourage UK
loyalists in British-ruled Ireland, would be exploited by the royal Irish press and
nationalist organizations as more proof of British cowardice and weakness and
a further spur to Irish rebellion. Would the UK government under these circumstances have cancelled the visit? Or, when the Prince was assassinated by a UK
Irishman who had contacts with the royal Irish military intelligence and when
the entire royal Irish press and public hailed this act as a glorious patriotic deed,
would British leaders have shrugged their shoulders and said, "Well, we asked
for it?" One need not know the actual British response to Irish acts of rebellion
like the Phoenix Park murders or the Easter Rising to guess the answer.

however innocent they might claim to be and however righteous their cause, to stop challenging great powers and causing international crises, just as there were precedents for requiring great powers to act through the international community and not take the law into their own hands. Greece and other Balkan states, for example, had repeatedly been compelled by joint great-power intervention to stop irredentist campaigns against the Ottoman Empire, and the Ottomans prevented from taking revenge on their rebels and enemies. Russia was more than once required in the nineteenth century to turn its cause and national honor in the Balkans over to the European Concert to defend. The fact that this procedure did not always work or was not always tried makes no difference. It was there, it could and did sometimes work, and in some instances like this one it was the only thing that could have worked (the only means, for example, that could have prevented the Crimean War, and almost did).

Yet in a way this discussion too, however necessary it is to clear the ground, is irrelevant and distracting, for the obvious, overriding fact is that before and during 1914 no action of this sort was tried, seriously considered, or even entertained. The danger of war steadily increased, the European powers were quite aware of the crucial specific source of that danger in the Austro-Hungarian problem, they knew about the kinds of measures used in the past and still available to meet such dangers, and collectively they did nothing. This inaction is the most important development in prewar diplomacy and in the July Crisis. It also strikingly illustrates both how counterfactual reasoning can serve the vital historical purpose not of telling us what might have happened, but of illuminating what really did happen, and why one needs to see 1914 not as the outbreak, of war but as the breakdown of peace. Every account of the July Crisis discusses the crucial delay between July 5, when Austria-Hungary received Germany's support for its ultimatum to Serbia, and July 23 when the ultimatum was actually delivered. Some have speculated that the delay was fateful in allowing the initial shock of the assassination to wear off (which is doubtful—the Serbian and Russian reactions, the decisive ones, would have been the same earlier). But another delay, far more fateful and inexplicable, is hardly mentioned or discussed in the vast literature. For a full month after the assassination, the powers did absolutely nothing in concert to prepare for or deal with the possible or likely consequences of this sensational event. Everyone knew that Austria-Hungary and Serbia were mortal enemies, that they had gone to the brink of war at least four times in the past five years, three of them in the past year, and that Russia was Serbia's ally and protector and Austria-Hungary's main enemy. Yet when something occurred that anyone could see might set off this long-envisioned war, the Entente powers averted their eyes, went about their other business, waited for whatever Austria-Hungary and Germany might do, and insofar as they thought about the incident at all, shrugged their shoulders and hoped for the best. Meanwhile Austria-Hungary and Germany took actions that set off the war.

This argument seems paradoxically to prove the precise opposite of what was promised and intended—to show that the war was not inevitable. For if the means for a serious attempt at avoiding it were known and available, as I have just argued, then the root cause of the war must have been contingent, have lain in a collective failure to apply them.

But of course that collective inaction in 1914 is neither inexplicable nor really contingent. Behind the failure to act lay precisely those shared assumptions and convictions about the nature, stakes, and reigning course of the international contest earlier cited as the reasons why determinists consider the war objectively unavoidable, by virtue of the *force des choses*. I contend only that the pressure of events did not make war objectively unavoidable by making peaceful choices impossible in the face of hard realities like security threats, alliance commitments, and arms races, but made it subjectively unavoidable by fatally constricting what all the actors would entertain as a conceivable, rational course of action in the face of this crisis or any other like it. The particular reasons why the various powers did not even consider taking any of the steps mentioned above to anticipate a crisis and manage it collectively are familiar and obvious. Austria-Hungary and Germany were determined to reverse the existing trend in international politics they considered fatal to them, and saw in this crisis a final chance to do so. The Entente powers equally saw in this crisis a danger to the existing trend favorable to them and were equally determined not to allow it to be reversed. Russian policy, seen by Russians as a defense against German and Austro-Hungarian aggression, was resolutely bent on maintaining and extending Russia's control over the Balkans. French policy was rigidly fixed on maintaining the existing alliances and therefore doing nothing to weaken the Franco-Russian one.[34] Britain's was fixed on maintaining its ententes, both in order to check Germany in Europe and avoid threats to the British Empire—the latter aim, the primary one, requiring maintaining the entente with Russia at all cost.[35] But behind these familiar positive reasons for failure to act collectively, there was a still more fundamental negative one. No one believed that a sane, rational policy allowed any longer for this kind of collective response. Anyone who tried to suspend the rules of power politics, of "every man and every alliance for himself, and the devil take the hindmost," was a fool and would earn the fool's reward. Hence to ask any British, French, Russian, Italian, or even German leader to sacrifice or subordinate particular interests and opportunities of theirs for the sake of some sort of collective action to stabilize the international position of Austria-Hungary so as to lessen the chances of a general war was to ask the impossible and absurd—to ask them to commit political suicide at home and to be laughed at and swindled abroad. Stabilizing Austria-Hungary's position was really not anyone's business except that of Austrians and Hungarians, or perhaps Germans if they wished to do so for their own power-political reasons. This profound practical indifference to the survival of a vital actor such as the Habsburg Monarchy was, to repeat, a break with tradition. It did not represent normal Realpolitik, but constituted a different concrete definition of it, a different collective attitude toward international politics.[36] The

---

34   See Keiger, *France and the Origins of the First World War*; and J. F. V. Keiger, *Raymond Poincaré* (New York, 1997).

35   See the works cited above, note 16, and also David French, *The Strategy of the Lloyd George Coalition, 1916–1918* (Oxford, 1995).

36   The history of the politics of World War I illustrates this dramatically. Imperial Germany was the great threat and object of hatred for the Allies, especially in the West; Austria-Hungary was taken much less seriously. Yet these same Allies never intended to eliminate Germany as a state, or even take away enough territory to cripple it as a major power. All, in fact, hoped to have Germany as a junior political and economic partner in the postwar era. In

power whose final break with the Concert principle proved decisive, Austria-Hungary, was also the last and most reluctant to
abandon it, because it was the one most dependent on it and on
collective international support and restraint to survive. This
outlook was evident before 1914. One of Foreign Minister
Aehrenthal's chief aims in 1908 had been to revive the old Three
Emperors' League and the moribund Austro-Russian entente in
the Balkans by a deal with Russia over Bosnia and the Straits.
Even in 1914 this idea was far from dead. The original Austrian
proposal for reversing the current disastrous trends in the Balkans
called for political rather than military action and was changed
only in the wake of the assassination (though how much difference this would have made is debatable).[37] During the July
Crisis itself Austro-Hungarian leaders hoped against hope that
Russia might let it get away with a local war against Serbia, and
if Russia did, they intended to use the opportunity to seek a

---

contrast, the territorial aims of the Allies were directed overwhelmingly against
Austria-Hungary in the interest of gaining and keeping lesser allies—Serbia,
Italy, Romania, and ultimately the Czechs and the Poles. This went on until,
in a marvelous instance of the irony of history, the Western Allies decided in
1916–17, when faced with Russia's defeat and the possibility of a German
victory, that it would be nice to get Austria-Hungary, by this time on its last legs
and totally dependent on Germany, to defect, help defeat Germany now, and
balance against Germany in the future. The only thing more astonishing than
the notion that this absurd eighteenth-century-style volte-face was possible is
the fact that some able historians take it seriously as evidence that Britain and
France never meant real harm to Austria-Hungary and always wanted to
preserve it. John Grigg, *Lloyd George, from Peace to War, 1912–1916* (London,
1983); French, *Strategy of the Lloyd George Coalition*; Harry Hanak, *Great
Britain and Austria-Hungary during the First World War* (New York, 1962).

37   The Matscheko memorandum of June 1914, changed after the assassination to be used against Serbia, called for joint Austro-German pressure on
Romania to commit itself publicly to the Austro-German alliance from which
it had just defected. It has been interpreted by some, including F. R. Bridge, as
showing that Austria-Hungary contemplated a political rather than military
solution to its problems until after June 28 (see his *Habsburg Monarchy*, 334–5).
My view is that the original plan, a proposal to force Romania, now independent, to do what it was never willing to do even when it was a secret ally, would
certainly not have solved Austria-Hungary's problem and was almost as
likely to escalate into a general crisis as the actual Austro-German initiative did.
Paul W. Schroeder, "Romania and the Great Powers before 1914," chapter 5 of
this volume.

fundamental rapprochement with Russia through negotiations for a joint solution to both the Balkan and the Ukrainian problems.[38] There is a tragic appropriateness about Austria-Hungary's breaking at last with the Concert principle and thereby destroying itself and Europe with it, like the blinded Samson pulling down the pillars of the temple, just as there is about Tsarist Russia's acting upon the shibboleths of its honor and its alleged historic mission of protecting the Balkan Slavs rather than its true state interests, thereby signing its own death warrant.[39]

To argue for the inevitability of World War I on this ground is, to repeat, *not* to blame Britain, Russia, and France for it while exonerating Germany and Austria-Hungary, or to characterize the former as more blind and reckless than the latter. It is an attempt to root the disaster deep in a political culture that all shared, which all had helped to develop, and upon which all acted in 1914, Germany and Austria-Hungary precipitating the final descent into the maelstrom. It is to see the origins of the war as finally a tragedy more than a crime, though crimes were surely involved; as inevitable by reason of wrong beliefs, hubris, and folly too broadly and deeply anchored in the reigning political culture to be recognized, much less examined and changed. The tragedy of its origins thus connects with the tragedy of the war itself in its hyperbolic protraction and destruction, evoking, like Shakespeare's *Romeo and Juliet,* the verdict, "All are punished."

---

38   John Lloyd, "Österreich-Ungarn vor dem Kriegsausbruch," in Rupert Melville et al., eds., *Deutschland und Europa,* vol. 2 (Munich, 1993), 661–83; Günther Kronenbitter, "'Nur los lassen'. Österreich-Ungarn und der Wille zum Krieg," in Burkhardt et al., *Lange und kurze Wege,* 159–87.

39   For a convincing argument that Russia had never had the kind of vital interest in the Balkans that its Orthodox and Pan-Slav publicists claimed, and that throughout the nineteenth century it had repeatedly become involved in costly complications there against its best interests, see Barbara Jelavich, *Russia's Balkan Entanglements 1806–1914* (New York, 1991).

4

Stealing Horses to Great Applause: Austria-Hungary's Decision in 1914 in Systemic Perspective

This essay does not present new research or attempt to revise the many recent and earlier accounts of the immediate origins of the war in 1914 and Austria-Hungary's role in it. On these scores, as will be seen, it basically agrees with the reigning view. It instead proposes a reinterpretation of the general causes of the war and the nature of Austria's decision, mainly by using well-known faces from familiar chapters of history, but viewing them and the international system from a different perspective. It therefore emphasizes not what Austria-Hungary did in 1914 and how its actions affected the international system, but rather what happened in the international system in the quarter-century before 1914 and how this affected all the actors, Austria-Hungary in particular.[1] The cryptic reference in the title to stealing horses,

---

1 For this reason and given the wide-ranging character of the essay, in which almost every sentence includes a fact or judgment on which a large literature exists, I will keep the footnotes to a minimum, using them only for points that I believe need grounding. On Austria-Hungary's role in the longer-range and immediate origins of the war, essential works include F. R. Bridge, *The Habsburg Monarchy among the Great Powers, 1815–1918* (New York, 1990); Bridge, *Great Britain and Austria-Hungary, 1906–1914: A Diplomatic History* (London, 1972); Samuel R. Williamson Jr., *Austria-Hungary and the Origins of the First World War* (New York, 1991); and Günther Kronenbitter, *Krieg im Frieden: Die Führung der k.u.k. Armee und die Großmachtpolitik Österreich-Ungarns 1906–1914* (Munich, 2003). Three excellent studies dealing with prewar Austro-Hungarian policy especially toward its Triple Alliance partners are Michael Behnen, *Rüstung, Bündnis, Sicherheit: Dreibund und informeller Imperialismus, 1900–1908* (Tübingen, 1985); Jürgen Angelow, *Kalkül und Prestige. Der Zweibund am Vorabend des Ersten Weltkrieges* (Cologne, 2000);

as will be seen, applies to the international system rather than to Austria-Hungary.

The reinterpretation must begin with two methodological views or working principles almost universally accepted by international historians. The first is that foreign and domestic policy are inextricably interwoven and interdependent. One cannot analyze the foreign policy of a state or government without factoring in the economic, domestic-political, social, ideological, cultural, and other internal factors that influence it. From these emerge the interests and aims that the government and its leaders seek to protect and advance in its foreign policy. Endorsing this principle does not mean asserting the primacy of domestic politics or subordinating other strategy, military, and diplomatic factors in foreign policy to it, but simply accepting that these elements are interwoven and inseparable. The second working principle is that the central task in international history involves analyzing the foreign policy decision-making process, explaining above all how and why statesmen, governments, and ruling elites made the decisions they did.

These two principles, self-evidently true, seem to apply with particular force to Austria-Hungary before 1914. Nowhere else do domestic conditions, above all the multi-national composition of the state and the resultant nationalities conflicts within it, seem more obviously the decisive determinants of foreign policy. In Austria's case, the very distinction between foreign policy and domestic issues and interests proves artificial and unworkable. Every question of domestic politics, constitutional authority, economic interest, and above all national identity

---

Holger Afflerbach, *Der Dreibund: europäische Grossmacht- und Allianzpolitik vor dem Ersten Weltkrieg* (Vienna, 2002). Important essays are in Helmut Rumpler and Jan Paul Niederkorn, eds., *Der "Zweibund" 1879: das deutsch-österreichisch-ungarische Bündnis und die europäische Diplomatie* (Vienna, 1996). On the race in land armaments that contributed heavily to the spiral into war, David Herrmann, *The Arming of Europe and the Making of the First World War* (Princeton, 1996), is good, and David Stevenson, *Armaments and the Coming of War: Europe, 1904–1914* (Oxford, 1996), even better. There are many older and recent accounts of the origins of the war, bur the most satisfactory general treatment still seems to me James Joll's *The Origins of the First World War* (London, 1984).

turned in some important respect into a foreign policy question directly affecting its security, strategy, alliances, and international prestige. Equally plainly, the question of who actually made and influenced foreign policy decisions in Austria-Hungary and how they did so becomes especially crucial and complicated, given the peculiar constitution of the Dual Monarchy and the way its two autonomous halves worked together, or failed to do so.

Therefore most historians addressing the question, "What led Austria-Hungary to decide and act as it did in 1914?" point to these two areas: the juncture between its foreign policy and its domestic situation, and the workings of its particular foreign policy decision-making process. Most would say that the Austro-Hungarian government decided to act as it did in 1914 because the Monarchy's ruling elite came to believe that the Monarchy's interwoven external and internal problems and challenges, especially those in its South Slav regions and those emanating from Serbia, Romania, Russia, and Italy, had become unmanageable and intolerable, calling for drastic action to change Austria-Hungary's situation, and that the special nature, composition, and interests of this elite strongly influenced both this conclusion and the choice of a violent rather than peaceful solution.

I agree in general with both this approach and this verdict, so far as they go. Yet these two methods of studying international politics (in this case, Austria-Hungary's decision), i.e., interweaving the interdependent factors of foreign and domestic policy and analysing the foreign policy decision-making process, important though they are, are not exhaustive or sufficient. The results and conclusions they yield represent at best penultimate truths, and penultimate truths, taken as final, have a way of hiding and obstructing deeper ones, especially in history. A deeper answer to the questions of what caused Austria to choose the policy it did in 1914 and how that choice should be interpreted, I contend, comes not simply from studying Austria's foreign and domestic situation and its decision-making process, vital though this is, but from also looking carefully at the prevailing rules of the European system. When that is done, one sees that in choosing to act as it did, Austria was not breaking those rules or overturning the prevailing system, but finally following it.

So broad an argument obviously has to be presented here in bare-bones fashion, without very much scholarly evidence or detail. It starts therefore with propositions that are widely accepted.

First, Austria-Hungary started the war, deciding in 1914 deliberately to provoke a local war with Serbia, in the knowledge that this risked a general war. Moreover, Vienna, not Berlin, was the main locus of this decision. This latter point is more controversial; many have argued that since Austria could not have acted without Germany and Germany could have stopped Austria but instead after July 5 urged it forward, Germany was therefore the real center of the decision. Furthermore, Germany had its own reasons for wanting at least a major shift in the balance of power and deliberately risking a general war to achieve it. This reasoning is not in the end persuasive, however. Austria made the original decision on its own and demanded rather than requested German support, and did so in the knowledge that Germany by denying it would do unacceptable damage to the alliance and thereby further imperil its own position. The question of German responsibility is really a separate one; the initiative for provoking a local war at the risk of general war came from Vienna and remained there.

Given Austria-Hungary's notorious weakness and vulnerability, this decision in itself seems hard to explain. Other well-known facts make it still stranger. Before 1914, Vienna had repeatedly rejected this course. In the previous decade, it had had numerous opportunities for a local or a general war that in objective military-strategic terms offered much better chances of success. Yet when it took the plunge under unfavorable conditions in 1914, it did so at the urging of some who had actively opposed it earlier.

Austria-Hungary furthermore launched the war with no positive program of war aims. True, no great power government in 1914 had a set of aims for which it was ready or eager to fight, much less deliberately to start a war. Yet they all had given thought to what concrete gains they ought to seek once the Great War that had long been anticipated broke out. Hence, all the other original belligerents, including Serbia, quickly developed concrete war aims programs. So did later entrants—the Ottoman Empire, Italy, Bulgaria, Greece, Romania, Japan, and China. Even neutral Belgium, brought into the war solely by the German invasion, soon developed extensive plans both for territorial changes in Europe (including claims on the neutral Netherlands going back to 1839) and for colonial gains. Austria-Hungary, however, started the war without such a program, and the program it did develop during the war in regard to Poland and the Balkans was mainly a reaction to military events and Germany's actions rather than a set of concrete aims of its own, intended primarily to preserve Austria-Hungary's status as an independent great power and to avoid becoming a dependent satellite of Germany. The lack of positive war aims is illustrated by the very aim for which it decided on war, eliminating Serbia as a political factor in the Balkans. Even among themselves Austrians could not define precisely what this phrase meant—annexing Serbia, dividing it, reducing it to satellite status, partitioning it with Bulgaria, or something else. The other major objective that other great powers and some lesser ones pursued before and during the war, that of gaining overseas colonies and improving their world position, though present in Austria-Hungary before the war to a lesser degree than in other great powers, almost disappeared once it started.

The obvious reply to these points is that Austria-Hungary's war aim was not to make positive gains, but to eliminate threats. Yet this fact, too, has remarkable aspects. While opting for war against Serbia, Austria-Hungary neither intended nor expected thereby to eliminate the main military threat it faced, that from Russia, even if the war proved sucessful. The Monarchy's decision makers, though they did not really expect Russia to accept a local Austro-Serbian war, hoped that Russia would do so and wished, if general war were avoided, to use the crisis to work out a new compromise with Russia over the Balkans and the Ukrainian question.[2] In other words, they expected to continue to have to coexist with Russia as a great power. This differs from the other great powers' expectations. Britain, France, and Russia expected a victorious war to eliminate the main threat to their security by reducing Germany's power, and developed their war

---

2   John Leslie, "Österreich-Ungarn vor dem Kriegsausbruch," in Ralph Melville et al., eds., *Deutschland und Europa in der Neuzeit*, vol. 2 (Stuttgart, 1988), 670–84.

plans accordingly. German leaders, at least in their optimistic moments, expected military victory to make Germany dominant on the continent, ending the threat of encirclement and insecurity. The Russians expected war to end Austria-Hungary's very existence as a major power. Austria, however, did not expect to eliminate Russia as a great power and potential rival. Even the Austrian Chief of Staff Conrad von Hötzendorf, a constant advocate of preventive war, much preferred to target lesser threats, Italy and Serbia, rather than Russia. In opting for a violent solution to their problems, Austrians seem to have accepted the permanence of the Russian threat and hoped to contain it by breaking up the Balkan League, ending the Serbian challenge, restoring Austria's alliance with Romania, and demonstrating that their alliance with Germany was unbreakable and invincible, so that Russia would go back to their previous mutually restraining relationship, and perhaps even to the old Three Emperor's League.

This unusual Austrian attitude toward its main enemy was more than matched by its strange stance toward its ally Germany, both before and during the war. No other great power was more one-sidedly dependent on its main ally than Austria-Hungary, and none feared that ally as much. While differences, tensions, and suspicions certainly existed among the Entente powers, they did not privately refer to one another, as Austro-Hungarians did to Germany, as "the enemy to the North." No other great power, furthermore, feared as much as Austria-Hungary did that a victory achieved in partnership with this ally might destroy its great power independence as surely as defeat.[3]

Two further facts: first, Austria-Hungary, along with Russia and Italy, had especially powerful reasons to fear that a great war, especially if it were prolonged or unsuccessful, would bring on revolution. Second, Austria more than any other great power had previously endeavored to maintain its position and status and manage its many international threats and challenges mainly by defending the legal status quo, practicing peaceful diplomacy,

---

3   Holger Herwig, *The First World War: Germany and Austria-Hungary, 1914–1918* (London, 1997); Gary Shanafelt, *The Secret Enemy: Austria-Hungary and the German Alliance, 1914–1918* (New York, 1985).

seeking international support, and invoking the Concert of Europe to deal with international problems and defend Austrian interests. Provoking even a local war would therefore undermine these international assets and tools and starting a general war would surely destroy them.

Thus, a decision remarkable enough on its face becomes even more baffling on closer examination. The great power with the most to lose and least to gain from war, weaker than any other in terms of its resources in relation to its security needs and challenges, and most inclined by its character, position, and requirements to be conservative, pacific, and risk averse in foreign policy, deliberately started the very war it had been trying to avoid and thus willfully caused its own destruction. It appears, as it has often been described, a case of committing suicide out of fear of death.

A historical comparison may possibly be useful. This was not the first time in the nineteenth century Austria suddenly decided to precipitate a war it had been trying to avoid and thus brought disaster down on its head. One previous instance is obvious. In 1859 Austria, apparently on the point of winning a diplomatic victory in its conflict with Sardinia-Piedmont and Piedmont's ally France, provoked a war by issuing a deliberately unacceptable ultimatum to Sardinia-Piedmont. The result was to isolate Austria, save Sardinia-Piedmont's premier Count Camillo Cavour from defeat and resignation, and bring France, which had seemed about to defect from its alliance, into a war in which Austria was quickly defeated and set on the road to expulsion from Italy. The other instance, less obvious, seems even more suicidal than its decision in 1914. In 1809 Austria decided to go to war with Napoleon and his Empire—this despite the facts that Austria had already suffered disastrous defeat in three previous wars with France, Germany and Italy were wholly in Napoleon's grip, Prussia had recently been crushed and Russia defeated in a war Austria had declined to join, Russia was now Napoleon's ally, and the British, besides being remote from the continental theater, otherwise preoccupied, and unable to help, were basically indifferent to Austria's fate. As a result, Austria suffered another crushing defeat and an even more humiliating peace treaty, and managed to avert the danger that Napoleon would extinguish the dynasty and divide the Austrian Empire only at the cost of becoming Napoleon's subservient ally.

This historical comparison seems merely to make the problem of 1914 worse, requiring three apparently inexplicable decisions to be explained instead of one.[4] A historian who looks for common features, however, will quickly find them. Here are some similar attitudes shown by Austria's leaders in the three cases:

1. a perception of an intolerable, growing threat to Austria's great-power security and status stemming not from the danger of immediate or direct attack by its enemies, but from the unrelenting pressure of encirclement, isolation, subversion, and exhaustion—death by a thousand cuts;

2. a keen awareness of Austria's internal weaknesses, especially its political, national, financial, and military ones, and a recognition that a war, especially a long war, would heighten the dangers of revolution and the overthrow of the dynasty;

3. a widespread consensus reached on the eve of the decision that Austria's foreign policy in the preceding years, which had been risk averse and directed at avoiding war by conciliation, had not merely failed but had made Austria's position worse;

4. a strong show of resolve by certain political and military leaders, whose optimistic appraisals of Austria's immediate military situation and its chances for success were not accompanied either by adequate military preparations or by clear ideas on how the planned preventive strike and quick victory would produce long-range security and advantages;

5. a similar short-term optimism in regard to the international political constellation—the hope that somehow quick successful action by Austria would break up the opposing alliance or produce allies for itself;

6. finally, a consensus that peaceful remedies were exhausted, leading former opponents of war to join the war party or fall silent.

---

4   Geoffrey Wawro finds a fourth instance in the Austro-Prussian War of 1866—"The Habsburg Flucht nach vorne in 1866: Domestic Political Origins of the Austro-Prussian War," *International History Review* 17, 2 (May 1995): 221–48. The case, however, does not seem to me really comparable to those in 1809, 1859, and 1914.

Yet these parallels, even if they illuminate the background of the decisions and suggest that all three are instances of the familiar strategy of desperate flight forward, do not explain the particular choice in 1914.

Certain inadequate answers have been proffered. One, formerly common and still occasionally encountered, is that it was typical for nineteenth-century Austria to behave thus, reacting too slowly and too late to danger and then plunging ahead in headstrong, obstinate panic. Napoleon said this; Henry Kissinger suggests it.[5] This is not to explain the problem, but to dismiss it. Another answer, earlier alluded to, is that this kind of action is not rare in international politics—many wars arise from attempts by a threatened declining power to reverse its decline through violence. Yet to show that something happens fairly frequently is not to explain why it does, or why the same power should commit the same suicidal blunder three times in a century.

The serious attempts to interpret and explain Austro-Hungarian policy in 1914 divide roughly into two camps, one primarily emphasizing internal factors and motives and the other primarily external ones. To summarize and oversimplify both positions, the first holds that the assassination of Franz Ferdinand coincided with an approaching crisis and breakdown in Austria-Hungary's creaking, semi-paralyzed state machine, and thus served to bring to a climax the spiraling, converging problems that were making the Dual Monarchy progressively more and more ungovernable—the failure of the 1907 electoral reform, the breakdown of parliament in the Austrian half, the necessity of emergency rule, an unsatisfactory turn in a weak economy, the persistent unsolved problem of Austro-Hungarian relations, and above all critical nationalities problems, those with the South Slavs and Romanians in particular. The decision to provoke a war with Serbia therefore represents a policy of secondary integration and manipulated social imperialism in which a failed, bankrupt leadership and ruling elite sought to save itself, rally its loyal followers, and distract attention from its insoluble internal problems by a flight forward into war. The other view is that the 1914 decision was motivated primarily by traditional foreign policy

---

5   Henry A. Kissinger, *Diplomacy* (New York, 1994), 194–96, 211–12.

considerations of security, military strategy, and the determination to remain an independent great power and act as one.

The latter view seems to me more satisfactory. True, Austria-Hungary did face the problems emphasized by the former interpretation and some leaders hoped if it came to war that a successful war would help solve and manage them. Yet these factors, though present, were not decisive in opting for war. The issue is not critical to this essay, however, because the aim is to show that a third reason was more basic than either.

It is interesting that these two lines of explanations (whose differences I have over-sharpened here—there is no reason why they cannot be reconciled) converge tacitly on one point: Austria-Hungary's decision was wrong. Some judge it harshly as driven by class-bound prejudice, arrogance, and a determination to defend entrenched privilege and power. Others are more sympathetic, inclined to see it as a blunder understandable in view of the extreme pressures to which Austria-Hungary was subjected and the narrow choices available to it. Nonetheless, there is considerable agreement that other decisions and options were available, that this decision was a wrong, disastrous one, and that it had horrendous consequences for Austria and Europe. Which of the two labels for Austria-Hungary's decision in 1914, crime or blunder, is more fair and accurate is again not important for this essay, for it argues that the decision in one important sense was neither—that, understood within the context of international history, it was the correct, right decision.

The term "correct" or "right" as used in this context must be carefully defined. It does not mean "morally and legally justifiable." To reach any such conclusion would require delving into legal, philosophical, and ethical issues impossible to deal with here. Nor does "right" here mean "sensible, prudent, representing a rational choice of ends and reasonable correlation of means and ends." One might well argue forcefully that Austria-Hungary's policy was none of these things and point to its results as proof. Yet one could grant this and still contend that Austria-Hungary's decision was right in this respect, that it made a correct, accurate assessment of the nature and direction of the prevailing international system and of Austria-Hungary's position within it, and it recognized that some such course of action as it took in 1914 was the only serious choice left available to it.

This is not the sort of conclusion historians readily embrace. Most, including international historians, are nominalist pragmatic empiricists, suspicious of abstract entities like "the system," fond of historical contingency and averse to any hint of determinism. They work on the reasonable assumption that historical actors face an uncertain, undetermined or under-determined future in which they almost always have alternatives open and real choices to make. The claim therefore that Austria-Hungary did not have viable alternatives in 1914 faces major hurdles both in terms of the facts and evidence needed to back it and in regard to its assault on most historians' working assumptions. To back it up would require two things. The first would be to show that the courses of action proposed as alternative ways which Austria-Hungary could have met its challenges peacefully, whether these involved internal reforms or a different diplomatic strategy or a combination of both, are at best specious and offered Austria-Hungary no real chance of success, and that its leaders were correct in finally recognizing this. I have tried to defend this position elsewhere and for reasons of time cannot present that case here.[6] The second and more important task, central to this essay, is to show that those who argue for alternative possibilities and courses of action ignore or underrate the international system as a limiting factor and a determinant of outcomes in international politics, and thereby overestimate the possibilities of Austria-Hungary's acting differently and solving or managing its problems largely on its own.

This argument, it must be conceded, cannot be made simply on the basis of objective facts and evidence, but involves certain definitions and assumptions that can at best only be rendered plausible in an essay like this. These are that in international politics the term "system" refers not merely to relationships of power and influence between the actors and the institutions through which power and influence are exerted, but also and importantly to a more intangible set of widely shared assumptions

---

6   Paul W. Schroeder, "Embedded Counterfactuals and World War I as an Unavoidable War," chapter 3 of this volume.

and expectations as to what rules and norms prevail and govern the shared practice of international politics. These "rules of the game" enter significantly into the calculations and decisions leaders and elites make, and constitute an incentives structure by indicating what kind of conduct is likely to have consequences of success or failure, reward, toleration, or punitive sanction. They rest in good part on a political culture always subject to changes, both subtle and violent. Despite an inevitable vagueness and uncertainty, one can detect and define a certain ethos or underlying spirit and code behind them, a governing collective mentality, set of reigning assumptions and expectations, and resultant prevailing rules and norms of the game.

This definition of "international system" may be vague and abstract, and I will not try to illustrate it here with historical examples, because the case of Austria-Hungary's decision in 1914 is supposed to do so. But if it is accepted at least provisionally *ex hypothesi*, two further considerations follow. In international politics, domestic factors influence foreign policy decisions, and these decisions aim at certain outcomes, but in an important sense, while actors propose, the system finally disposes, that is, determines the outcomes by limiting the range of options and outcomes possible. That system, moreover, never involves a level playing field with clear rules and an impartial umpire, or a smooth billiard table where the outcome is determined by the mechanical interactions of the balls. The rules are made and changed as the games go on by the players themselves, especially the most powerful and successful ones. The table is thus always rigged. In 1914, I contend, the table was rigged to make Austria-Hungary lose. It was therefore a rational choice, though made too late and executed badly, to attempt something drastic to change the rules and alter the tilt of the table, even at the risk of knocking it over and ending the game.

First a brief statement of how the system was rigged to make Austria lose, followed by an argument to support it. A Spanish proverb says: "Some men steal horses to great applause, while others are hanged for looking over the fence." The proverb can be read as an ironic observation on how unfairly the law, systems of justice, and life in general sometimes work. Here it is offered as an accurate summary of how the European international system actually was working by 1914. Its rules had been so fashioned and bent that certain states could steal horses to great applause while other states were hanged for looking over the fence. This result was not incidental, accidental, or unintended, but regular, structural, and intentional.

The name given to the horse-stealing game was imperialism (or its synonym, "world policy"). The best way briefly to envision the basic difference in the ethos and the attendant rules, norms, and incentives structure of the latter nineteenth-century European states system and those of imperialism is to see it as the difference between high-stakes poker played by heavily armed men out to win but nonetheless aware of conventional limits on their bets and in agreement on the importance of keeping all essential players in the game, and the board game Monopoly, in which players aim to maximize gains through the elimination of rivals.[7]

The imperialist game, to be sure, had been played for centuries, but in the earlier decades of the prewar era it remained what it had been most of the previous centuries, a game largely separate from the main game of European international politics, or attached but auxiliary to it. The Anglo-Russian Great Game in Asia and the Anglo-French competition for colonies during much of the nineteenth century illustrate this. They were played chiefly outside Europe, governments were initially less centrally involved in them than individuals, firms, or particular interests, and their stakes were not generally critical in the game of European politics. So long as imperialism remained an ancillary game, it did not destroy or directly undermine the European system and could even help preserve it by offering an outlet for European expansionist energies and material for profitable deals and combinations among various powers. This held true even though the game was always so constituted that some powers could steal more horses than others and some could only stand

---

7   For a good mordant discussion of the imperialist ethos, especially in the relation between great powers and the objects of imperialism, see Gordon Martel, "Afterword: The Imperial Contract—an Ethology of Power," in A. H. Ion and E. J. Herrington, eds., *Great Powers and Little Wars: The Limits of Power* (Westport, CT, 1993), 203–25.

and look over the fence, since those whose horses were being stolen were non-Europeans and outside the states system.

After 1890, however, this game with its imperialist ethos and rules not only became more ruthlessly competitive and involved higher stakes; it also gradually took over as the main game in European politics itself and increasingly involved stealing horses claimed by other Europeans. This development, emerging clearly about the turn of the century, made the game of European politics more competitive, dangerous, and likely to end in a great war. Even this heightened level of imperialist competition, however, did not of itself necessarily lead to general war. It was in fact sustained for a time without general war, and could have been sustained even longer, simply because of the high barriers holding back a general war between great powers in an age of mass politics, industrialization, major advances in military technology, and huge armies. But the next stage that occurred in the first decade of the twentieth century, partly through natural development and partly by design, heightened the danger by transferring the imperialist game with its special ethos and rules to Europe itself. The contest over imperial prizes abroad was absorbed into, and instrumentalized for, a larger struggle for domination and control of the European system, and with it the world. Even that was not all. From 1907 on, this struggle to control the European balance came to focus, again partly through natural developments and partly by design, on the most explosive part of Europe, with its most intractable problems, the Balkan Peninsula. It thus targeted Europe's most vulnerable and exposed great power, Austria-Hungary.

This completed the cycle of change in the nature of European politics over several decades. First an imperialist ethos accompanied European politics; then it invaded it and came to pervade it and replace the older one; then the game itself was transferred back to Europe, with control of the European system for security and survival becoming its essential stake; and finally that contest was concentrated on Europe's most dangerous and vulnerable point. This long process, like a poisonous snake circling back upon itself and sinking its fangs into its own tail, made Austria-Hungary's decision in 1914 a rational choice and response to its situation.

This, in brief, is the argument. Much of its particular content is familiar and conventional, but its conclusion is not. One can anticipate certain reactions—that this argument is selective in its use of facts and evidence and unrealistic in its approach to international politics. Moreover, it fails in particular to recognize that European imperialism is as old as the European system and integral to it, that European politics has always been driven by power and interests, not ideals, and that ruthless competition and survival of the fittest rather than normative rules and restraints have always governed it. The argument in addition is moralistic, applying inappropriate moral standards selectively to some actions and certain powers, and biased in favor of Austria and against some other states (Britain, Russia, Serbia).

The less serious charges, those of bias and moralism, can be met quickly. Both strictly speaking are irrelevant—a scholar may be subjectively biased and moralistic (in this case, pro-Habsburg) and still interpret the issues and evidence correctly. In any case, the issue here is not the character of the Habsburg Monarchy, or its alleged historic European mission and whether it was fulfilling or betraying it, or whether it could and should have survived with what results, or any other such questions. The issue here is solely how best to understand the Austro-Hungarian decision in 1914, and whether, as claimed here, this requires above all understanding the prevailing nature and rules of the European system.

As for the charge of moralism, this interpretation does suggest a moral view of the origins of World War I—that it is like a Greek or Shakespearean tragedy. To go beyond that conclusion, to play the blame game further by apportioning blame to particular actors, is useless, distracting, and deceptive, because the game itself was to blame. But this moral judgment also is strictly speaking irrelevant to the question of causation.

A more serious charge is that this account of the changes in international politics and their impact on Austria-Hungary's decision is unrealistic in failing to see that the developments briefly described earlier as perverting and undermining the normal European game and its rules actually represented normal Realpolitik and constituted no reason for Austria-Hungary to overthrow the game. The answer, drawing on basic international relations theory, is that the judgment that Austria-Hungary made

a correct rational choice in 1914 under the conditions of the prevailing European system rests theoretically on a conventional
realist approach to international politics, which starts with the
rational actor model. It assumes that states are the primary
actors in international politics, that they can for analytical purposes be considered unitary rational actors, and that they decide
and act primarily on the basis of cost-benefit utility analysis.
Their calculations therefore must include an appraisal of the
incentives or payoff structure of the prevailing international
system, and routinely do so. My claim is that over decades the
incentives structure of the European international system was so
warped by imperialist competition as systematically to reward
conduct subversive of stability and peace and to penalize conduct
designed to uphold them. I contend further that this process of
distortion of the system led to the general crisis situation of
1914 focused on the Balkans and targeting Austria, and that the
crisis produced by this process made Austria's decision for preventive war a rational, appropriate one in terms of the prevailing
rules and incentives of that system. Such an argument is therefore
plainly, in terms of theory, an attempt to describe what happened
in strictly realist terms. To refuse to take this factor of the systemic incentives structure into account, instead assuming that
the decision must necessarily have been wrong or unjustified
because it started a great war with horrendous results and that
there must have been a better way for Austria-Hungary to seek
its reasonable goals, is to be unrealistic and moralistic.

But theory of course will not get us far; the central question is
historical. Did a change in the system such as I have posited
occur, or has international politics always been essentially a
struggle for power, security, and advantage played with rules
and incentives based on a survival of the fittest? The evidence, I
hold, shows clearly that until late in the nineteenth century a
European system with a different payoff structure prevailed.
True, the ethos of the Vienna era and its solidarity order had
since the mid-century given way to the Realpolitik of Napoleon
III, Cavour, Bismarck, and others. Yet the system continued on
the whole to discourage and penalize attempts to steal horses and
to encourage and reward those who stopped looking over the
fence, at least within Europe. Bismarck himself led in restoring

and maintaining this system for self-interested reasons. The evidence of this is familiar to historians and too extensive to rehearse—Russia and Britain in 1875 warning Germany off another war with France and France off a war of revenge for Alsace-Lorraine; Bismarck refusing to promise neutrality to Alexander II in a Russo-Austrian war because Germany could not allow either of them to be destroyed; Russia being forced to retreat from its violation of the Budapest Accords in 1878 and Germany trying to build a golden bridge for its retreat; various instances, especially in the Near East, in which ambitious smaller powers willing to start a great fire if they could roast their particular marshmallows in the ashes were controlled. Until about 1890, perhaps somewhat beyond this, the incentives structure of the European system continued to sustain a tolerable level of international relations in which, in general, policies of not stealing horses paid off and vice versa.

The New Imperialism beginning in the early 1870s and escalating thereafter ultimately changed this. In a sense, it was bound to, for imperialism and an international system are intrinsically alien, imperial rule being the logical contradictory of membership in a community of independent, juridically equal units. More important in practical terms was the principle on which New Imperialism came to operate, namely, that those who stole horses deserved to win while those who only looked over the fence deserved to lose out. This principle became an explicit part of international law with the Berlin Congo Conference of 1885, making legal colonial possession a matter of successful theft—finding a territory no other so-called civilized state had taken and appropriating it by effective occupation or the appearance of it.[8]

This had a much greater impact on the ethos of the late nineteenth century system than the imperialism starting in the late fifteenth century, involving major seizures of territory especially in the New World, had had earlier. For most of the fifteenth to the early seventeenth centuries the European system or society of states was only being formed. Not until the early eighteenth

8   Stig Förster et al., eds., *Europe and Africa: The Berlin Congo Conference 1884–1885 and the Onset of Partition* (Oxford, 1989).

century can one detect any serious regulative principle in it (the so-called balance of power); not until the late eighteenth century did the system embrace both Western and Eastern Europe, even then the rules and norms were almost as rapacious in Europe itself as in the colonial arena. Moreover, only in the late nineteenth century did so many powerful states compete for empire on so broad a scale and in so frantic a manner. Furthermore, an unwritten rule in the Vienna era that lasted into the latter part of the century had erected a certain separation of imperialist activity from European international politics. The imperialist ethos, though applied with drastic effects to lesser breeds without the law, had no great impact on the incentives structure of the European system.

Two developments at the end of the century ended this separation. The first was the virtually universal triumph of the belief that the survival and prosperity of European states in the twentieth century would depend on their success in world policy, i.e., imperialism. This doctrine sharply raised the stakes and tempo of an already heated competition. The second was a series of dramatic events serving to demonstrate that the ethos and tactics of imperialism, hitherto largely confined to the extra-European world, now applied equally to European or Europeanized powers as well, and thus drastically altering the unwritten understandings and incentives structure of the European system.

The best date for marking this sea change is 1898—not, of course, that everything important happened in this calendar year, but that in 1898 many developments began, combined, and jelled to prove that an imperialism already red in tooth and claw abroad would now infect relations between European peoples and states. The British conquest of the Sudan that year in the most glorious and bloody of what Bismarck once called Britain's sporting wars demonstrated the power-political lesson aptly summed up by Hilaire Belloc: "Whatever happens, we have got the Maxim gun, and they have not." A direct aftermath and consequence of this conquest was the Fashoda Crisis, teaching the French government to its astonishment and chagrin that the unwritten rule prevailing in European politics since 1815, that European powers might quarrel over colonial territory but not go to war with each other over it, no longer held. Britain was not only ready to go to war with another European great power over territory in Africa, but also would neither negotiate over that power's claim to the territory nor allow the rival any face-saving compromise. The British resort to *Machtpolitik* was successful. The German Naval Bill of 1898 demonstrated that Germany, pursuing its *Welt- und Machtpolitik,* proposed to challenge British naval supremacy more seriously than anyone had done since the Napoleonic Wars. The Second Anglo-Boer War (1899–1902) was clearly foreshadowed already in 1898 by the British government's firm decision to bring de facto independent South African republics of European stock into its Empire by military force if necessary, and its willingness to respond with force to any European interference. In 1898, Théophile Delcassé took over the French Foreign Ministry and immediately began working to transform the Russo-French alliance from a defensive instrument into a general weapon of world policy. One of his first moves was to seek agreements with Russia and Italy on partitioning Austria-Hungary should it collapse, so as to prevent Germany from getting particular portions of it.[9] In 1897–8, European imperialism in China, already underway, escalated sharply from a competition mainly over trade and dominant political influence into a scramble for territorial concessions and naval bases. This touched off a great Chinese revolt, the Boxer Rebellion, leading to further Western intervention and imperialism, and ultimately in 1904 to the Russo-Japanese War. The year 1898, finally, included the Spanish-Cuban-American War in which the United States defeated Spain and ended Spanish misrule in Cuba only to bring it quickly under its own domination, expand the American empire in the Caribbean and Pacific, and seize the Philippine Islands, provoking an insurrection and war that killed thousands of Filipinos.

In every one of these cases, horse stealing paid off. Breaches of precedent and the use or threat of force never led to any international sanctions or resistance. Concern for how these actions would affect the international system and the relations between

---

9   Christopher Andrew, *Théophile Delcassé and the Making of the Entente Cordiale: A Reappraisal of French Foreign Policy 1898–1905* (New York, 1968), 126–9.

its members never served as a deterrent; if anything, it acted in certain instances as a spur to action. The rule was no longer the traditional "*Do ut des*" ("I give so that you give"), and still less "Do to others as you would have them do to you"; but "Do to others what they might do to you, but do it first."

The Spanish-American-Cuban War illustrates particularly well how the ascendant ethos of imperialism defeated the declining ethos of European balance and Concert. The centenary observances and discussions of the war in 1998 and publications since have re-examined various effects of the war on Cuba, the Caribbean, Latin America in general, the Philippines, and above all the United States in its rise to world power. One aspect has received little attention: the impact of this disastrous, humiliating war on Spain. Historians of Spain tell us that this war was a major step in the decline and downfall of the Spanish monarchy that led in turn to military dictatorship in the 1920s, the ill-starred Republic of 1931–6, and civil war and semi-Fascist dictatorship under Franco from 1936 on.[10] International historians know that in the 1880s and 1890s fear of a revolution in Spain and concern about how to prop up the feeble Spanish monarchy and thereby avoid European complications were a persistent if minor theme in European politics. Two small incidents illustrate that concern, and the difference it made in two eras. In the 1880s a dispute arose between Spain and Germany over the Caroline Islands in the Pacific, arousing the public in both countries and leading to republican agitation in Spain. Bismarck could have forced Spain to yield. Considering, however, that to do so would damage Germany's reputation and undermine the feeble Spanish monarchy, endangering European peace, the notoriously hardheaded realist Bismarck proposed settling the issue by Papal arbitration, and, as Bismarck intended, Pope Leo XIII decided in favor of Spain.[11] In April 1898 the Austro-Hungarian foreign minister Count Agenor Goluchowski tried to organize a

10   Sebastian Balfour, *The End of the Spanish Empire, 1898–1923* (Oxford, 1997); Sebastian Balfour, "The Impact of War within Spain: Continuity or Crisis?," in Angel Smith and Emma Davila-Cox, eds., *The Crisis of 1898* (New York, 1999), 180–94.

11   Hans-Ulrich Wehler, *Bismarck und der Imperialismus* (Cologne, 1969), 400–7.

European Concert mediation of the Spanish-Cuban and Spanish-American conflict so as to prevent a Spanish-American war and help the Spanish monarchy survive. The effort went nowhere. The United States rejected mediation, Spain refused to give way entirely to American demands, Germany and Russia feared jeopardizing their commercial relations with the United States, and Great Britain, concerned over South Africa and actively engaged in appeasing the Americans, wanted nothing to do with it. The British government later claimed credit in Washington for having foiled a continental European attempt to interfere. Imperialism easily trumped European balance and Concert.[12]

The Spanish-Cuban-American War involved Austria-Hungary only in a minor way, to be sure. In general, it had little directly to do with the late-century developments marking the triumph of the imperialist ethos. Preoccupied with its domestic nationality problems and crises, it could not compete seriously in the imperialist scramble for power and territory overseas and was already seen itself as a possible target of partition. Its efforts later to join the scramble for imperialist prizes, largely for prestige reasons, were half-hearted and proved unsuccessful.[13] Nonetheless, Austria-Hungary had a vital role to play in European international politics in the critical years around 1898. In 1897, in agreement with Russia, it began a decade of wary Austro-Russian cooperation in damping down the revolutionary insurrection in Macedonia and the growing rivalry and clashes between various Balkan states and peoples over it, to keep the Balkans on ice and avert an Austro-Russian clash there.[14] Here the ethos of Concert and balance trumped imperialism.

Naturally, Austria-Hungary had particular reasons and interests of its own for promoting peace with Russia and restraining

---

12   F. R. Bridge, "Great Britain, Austria-Hungary and the European Concert on the Eve of the Spanish-American War," *Mitteilungen des Österreichischen Staatsarchivs* 44 (1996): 87–108.

13   F. R. Bridge, "'Tarde venientibus ossa': Austro-Hungarian Colonial Aspirations in Asia Minor 1913–14," *Middle, Eastern Studies* 6, no. 3 (October 1970): 319–30; Wolfdieter Bihl, "Zu den österreichisch-ungarischen Kriegszielen 1914," *Jahrbücher für Geschichte Osteuropas* 16, no. 4 (1968): 505–30.

14   Steven W. Sowards, *Austria's Policy of Macedonian Reform* (Boulder, CO, 1989).

revolt and ethnic conflict in the Balkans at this time, the main ones being a serious domestic crisis with the Czechs and growing problems with Hungary. The question, however, is what kind of incentives and rewards an international system must provide in order for it to survive durably and work effectively to control conflict and promote general stability and peace. The policy Austria-Hungary adopted in the Macedonian question, which it followed fairly faithfully until 1907, when Russia under British pressure and with Italian encouragement abandoned their agreement, involved cooperating with its most dangerous rival in the area of their sharpest historic competition in order to manage a critical problem, keep their rivalry within bounds, and preserve the general peace, even while the Austrians knew that this policy offered their opponent the opportunity to make gains elsewhere that would enhance its overall power. A policy such as this must pay off in some clear benefits for both sides if the rival parties are to continue their cooperation and if the international system and peace are to endure. Russia gained major direct benefits from this Austro-Hungarian stance. With their European and Balkan flanks secure, the Russians were able to concentrate on imperialist expansion in the Far East, and when this venture led them into a disastrous war and revolution, Austria-Hungary's guarantee of neutrality and cooperation paid off still more handsomely in helping the regime survive. Austria-Hungary's payoff for its cooperation in Macedonia then and later consisted, as leading Russians conceived it, in the opportunity to survive a while longer, provided it could do so by its own resources.

This is not to portray Austria-Hungary as a victim, which would be inappropriate and irrelevant. It merely asks, to repeat, how long an international system with the kind of ethos and attendant rules, norms, and incentives that emerged around the turn of the century could be expected to last, or states like Austria-Hungary, even if they depended on it to survive, could be expected to continue sustaining it in the face of adverse payoffs.

The year 1898, of course, marked only the point at which the ascendancy of the politics of imperialism over those of European balance and Concert became clear. It would take far too long here to show how almost every subsequent major event and development in European politics further promoted the triumph of an imperialist ethos and fit into its pattern of perverse, destructive payoffs. The list is a long one: the Second Anglo-Boer War and its outcome; the course of Western imperialism in East Asia culminating in the Russo-Japanese War; the results and aftermath of that war, bringing great gains to Japan, colonial occupation to Korea, new threats to China, revolution to Russia, and immense benefits in various theaters (East Asia, India, Central Asia, Europe, and the high seas) to Britain—an instance in which a state could profit by simply being a silent partner to another's horse stealing; the Anglo-French Entente Cordiale and the accompanying French deals with Italy and Spain on Morocco, designed to exclude Germany; the succeeding French move to gain control of Morocco and isolate Germany, leading to the First Moroccan Crisis and a partial French victory; the Anglo-Russian Convention dividing up Persia and Central Asia, again intended to exclude Germany; the French takeover in Morocco and the Second Moroccan Crisis of 1911; Italy's cynically aggressive attack on the Ottoman Empire in Libya, soon extended, in total disregard of the international consequences and dangers, to the Turkish Straits and the Dodecanese Islands; Russia's moves to isolate Austria and control the Balkans through its Balkan League; the Serbian-Bulgarian-Greek offensive alliance aimed directly against Turkey and indirectly against Austria-Hungary, which Russian diplomacy promoted, and the two Balkan Wars it prompted. All these well-known developments fit the pattern already seen. Those who set out to steal horses, unless stopped by other horse stealers by threat or superior force, were rewarded; those who held back lost out and were punished.

Two major developments do not obviously conform to the pattern—the Anglo-German naval race and the Berlin-to-Baghdad Railway. Even these, however, do not contradict it and basically fit in. The German naval challenge to Britain represented an attempt to better equip Germany for horse stealing, i.e., for competing with Britain for empire and world position. The German bid failed because Germany faced too many other challenges to concentrate fully on it and the British had the resources and will to defeat it. The Berlin-to-Baghdad Railway scheme ended in an apparently peaceful compromise because

Russia and Britain had previously secured the prizes in Persia, Central Asia, and the Ottoman Empire most important to them and decided that it would be too costly and dangerous to exclude Germany from a share of the economic spoils in Anatolia—an instance of the shared horse stealing not uncommon in the New Imperialism.

Without trying to expound and defend this interpretation of the whole period from 1900 to 1914 further here, the central point concerning the ultimate impact of the ethos, collective mentality, and incentives structure of imperialism on the international system in general and on Austria-Hungary in particular, can be illustrated through one major development, the Russo-Japanese War. Russia's policy toward Japan in East Asia from 1895 to 1903 bears a striking similarity in certain respects to Russian policy toward Austria in the Balkans from 1909 to 1914. That is, in both cases Russia did not want a war or desire the physical elimination of its rival. It simply wished to keep its opponent isolated, hold it off, fob it off if necessary with meaningless assurances and agreements, and over time consolidate its hold over the area in dispute until its control became so strong that the opponent would have to recognize and accept it. One difference between the two instances, so far as Russian policy is concerned, is that in East Asia Russia encountered some resistance from outside powers, notably Britain, while in the Balkans it was encouraged and aided by Serbia, France, Britain, Italy, and Romania.

The difference between the two cases that most affected the respective outcomes, however, lies in the way Russia's opponents, Japan and Austria-Hungary, reacted to Russia's moves. The Japanese government came to understand Russia's policy in East Asia and its ultimate consequences for Japan early on and decided, after much debate and considerable hesitation and division, that Japan must either obtain a satisfactory, reliable agreement with Russia dividing the spoils (essentially Korea for Japan, Manchuria for Russia) or fight. When the Japanese government concluded that it could not obtain the deal it wanted from Russia, well before the possibilities of peaceful negotiation with Russia were formally exhausted, it chose not, as Austria-Hungary did in 1914, merely to take actions to protect its interests at the risk of war (such as occupying Korea), allowing Russia to decide on its response. Instead, it chose all-out, immediate preventive war, attacking Russia suddenly and with all its might. In terms of my metaphor, the Japanese saw that under the current imperialist system it was foolish to look over the fence, see a chief preparing to steal horses one coveted oneself, try to reach agreement on shared theft, and failing this fall back on the hope that the horses would not be stolen after all or that one could simply steal a few oneself without fighting the other thief. The rational though risky course was to attack the other thief first, drive him off, and then steal the horses oneself. And that policy worked.

Contrast this with Austria-Hungary and Germany's reaction to the war, especially to Russia's severe defeat at Japan's hands and the paralyzing Russian Revolution that followed in 1905–6. Recall that many historians (including me) interpret the joint Austro-Hungarian and German decision in 1914 as tantamount to opting for, if not directly starting, a preventive war. Historians also agree (though many ignore its implications, slide over it, or explain it away) that Germany and Austria-Hungary in the previous decade had passed up several better opportunities for preventive war or other drastic actions to improve their position. These arose in 1912–13, 1911, 1908–9, and best of all in 1904–6. At this juncture, with Russia mired in a losing war and revolution, Germany could have used the First Moroccan Crisis to attack France and Austria-Hungary could have acted to punish Serbia for its anti-Habsburg moves in 1903 and force it back into line without having to worry about Russian intervention at all. I do not contend that they had no good reasons, domestic, foreign-political, and strategic, not to do this—they did. My point instead is two-fold: first, that their decision against preventive war at this juncture and later (against prominent advocates of it in both countries) saved the system and preserved general peace, and furthermore, that in 1904–6 they consciously followed a policy precisely the reverse of preventive war, that of helping to prevent the collapse of their main rival.

This is no exaggeration. Austria-Hungary's and Germany's conduct in 1904–6 saved the Tsarist regime. The only way the Russian government could put down the revolution was to scatter its army away from the western front all over European Russia.

The only way the premier Count Sergius Witte could persuade Russia's military authorities to do this, who on general principles strongly opposed using the army for police duty and to repress revolution, was to assure them that there was no chance of a German or Austrian attack.[15] Any Austro-German or Austro-Hungarian mobilization or threat on Russia's western front would have sufficed to paralyze this use of the Russian army and bring the regime down.

Once again, Austria-Hungary had particular reasons at this time for not exploiting Russia's desperate situation, above all its own threat of civil war in Hungary. Nonetheless, both German powers courted and supported Russia rather than threatening it and using the crisis to solve their internal problems through secondary integration, and (to repeat) the policy they followed in this crisis is the kind any system needs to preserve peace and the existence of essential actors. In international affairs, results count more than motives and intentions.[16]

The results here, however, demonstrate the adage that in that era, no good deed went unpunished, for the payoff both powers received was entirely negative. Even before the revolution was finally quelled and political order restored, Russia had turned to the Entente powers for vital financial aid and ideological support and friendship, and within months of its survival, the Russian regime had abandoned its decade-long cooperation with Austria in Macedonia and launched its own campaign for reforms in partnership with Britain.[17] Within a year, the Russian foreign

---

15   William C. Fuller, *Civil-Military Conflict in Russia, 1881–1914* (Princeton, 1985), 129–68, especially 138–9.

16   Given these facts and Austria-Hungary's goal of reviving the Three Emperors' League, Michael Behnen's view (*Rüstung, Bündnis*, 109–13) that the Austro-Russian neutrality agreement of October 1904 represented a victory for Austria-Hungary, clearing the decks for a possible dash with Italy, seems to me strained.

17   While the general story is well known, two points worth noting here are: (1) that Austria-Hungary participated substantially in the French-English loan in 1906, thus helping save the Tsarist regime from having to make further concessions to the Russian liberals and the Duma; (2) that other powers—Italy, France, and Great Britain—had long worked to break up the Austro-Russian partnership in the Macedonian question or insert themselves into it, even while recognizing that it was good for general peace. See Behnen, *Rüstung, Bündnis*,

minister A. P. Izvolski was complaining bitterly that Austria's proposed railway in the Sanjak of Novi-Bazar (a project that Izvolski admitted Austria-Hungary was entitled by treaty to carry out) represented "a bomb rolled between his legs."[18] To sum up: in 1904–10, Japan stole horses to great applause. Austria-Hungary was hanged despite attempting to help the owner save his horses and repair his fence. It is hard to conceive a better illustration of a perverse international incentives structure.

There is an obvious objection to this line of argument. It appears to disregard one of the most important events and developments of the prewar era, and one that destroys the portrayal of Austria-Hungary as the victim of the imperialist ethos, because it shows Austria-Hungary at this time doing major horse stealing of its own. In 1908, it annexed Bosnia-Herzegovina in violation of the Treaty of Berlin, provoking the Bosnian Crisis of 1908–9. Out of this, historians agree (and I concur), grew fatal developments contributing directly to war in 1914—an even more bitter and incurable Austro-Russian enmity and rivalry, heightened Austro-Serbian tensions, a spiraling land arms race, and a chain of events in the Balkans and Mediterranean that led to the ultimate explosion.

Rather than ignoring the Bosnian Crisis, I was saving it, to present it as evidence for my thesis that the ultimate ground for Austria-Hungary's decision in 1914 and therefore the deeper cause of the war was the triumph of an imperialist ethos and incentives structure over the earlier ethos of balance and Concert in European international politics. In explaining why, I ask your indulgence for recounting how my own views on this subject have changed. It shows, if nothing else, how revisionist views may in time and under examination become more radical rather than moderate.

368–71; Sowards, *Austria's Policy of Macedonian Reform*, 78–81; Douglas Dakin, "British Sources on the Greek Struggle in Macedonia," *Balkan Studies* 2, 1 (1961), 76–77.

18   Sowards, *Austria's Policy of Macedonian Reform*, 84–87; F. R. Bridge, "Izvolsky, Aehrenthal and the End of the Austro-Russian Entente," *Mitteilungen des Österreichischen Staatsarchivs* 29 (1976): 315–62. Behnen's account (*Rüstung, Bündnis*, 419–37), though very critical of Aehrenthal and Austrian policy, makes clear that if the Sanjak project was a bomb at all, it was rolled between Italy's legs, not Russia's.

A central problem for historians of the Bosnian Crisis has always been how to explain why the annexation of Bosnia-Herzegovina, which changed the existing power-political situation hardly at all, had such crucial international effects. Under the Treaty of Berlin of 1878, Austria-Hungary had already occupied and administered the provinces sine die for thirty years, exercising what amounted in practical terms to full, permanent possession and governance and largely transforming the provinces in the process. No one expected the occupation to end; annexation by Austria had long been anticipated and even foreseen in various treaties. A formal transfer of sovereignty to Austria-Hungary from the Ottoman Sultan, who had lost effective control over the provinces long before 1878, would seem in this era of high imperialism, replete with overt land grabs, major conflicts over disputed territory and rights, and not a few violations of treaties, to be an insufficient cause for such huge consequences.

Many historians, to be sure, don't see this as a problem. The annexation had the consequences it did, they argue, for two main reasons: first, because Austria-Hungary's move was ill-planned and ill-prepared, executed badly, and when it encountered trouble pushed through by Austria-Hungary and Germany with ultimative threats to Serbia and Russia that left deep, abiding resentment; and second, because it was inherently an aggressive, imperialist move intended to shift the balance of power in the Balkans and indirectly in Europe in favor of the Dual Alliance. It unquestionably violated the letter of an important international treaty and negated the residual rights of the Ottoman Empire and the nationalist hopes of the Serbs. In particular, it was designed to take advantage of Russia's weakness following its lost war and revolution in order to assert Austro-Hungarian primacy over the whole western half of the Balkans, to check Italian and Serbian pretensions, and to foster an Austro-German economic *Drang nach Osten*.

On the basis of some research on the question, though relying mainly on more thorough work by other scholars, I have earlier argued that this interpretation clashes with too many facts to be persuasive. Most of the points I and others have made are familiar, and some need not be rehearsed here. The important ones, boiled down, are: the crisis arose out of an Austro-Russian bargain initially proposed by the Russian Foreign Minister A. P. Izvolski, freely negotiated and entered into by him, and approved by the Tsar. Izvolski and his second-in-command Charykov knew well in advance of Austria-Hungary's intention to annex Bosnia-Herzegovina, believed that Russia could not stop it and even had no legal ground to do so, and made the bargain in order to obtain a concession important to Russia. Baron Alois Aehrenthal, the Austro-Hungarian foreign minister, though he bargained hard, did so in good faith—more so than his Russian counterpart, who always intended to betray the agreement by later seeking further concessions from Austria-Hungary on top of the agreed quid pro quo. Aehrenthal's main motives for the move, moreover, were domestic-political and defensive rather than power-political and aggressive, and directed against Italy and Serbia but not Russia. From a purely power-political, military, and strategic standpoint, moreover, the annexation marked a retreat from any alleged Austrian *Drang nach Osten* rather than an advance. True, Aehrenthal miscalculated the reactions in the Ottoman Empire, Serbia, and Russia, but Izvolski's miscalculations proved far worse, and he actively lied to cover himself and save his position. It was not Austria-Hungary's or Germany's fault, moreover, but that of France and Great Britain that Russia failed to get its intended payoff. The Russian government, not the Austro-Hungarian one, changed its mind and repudiated the original bargain. As to the charge of treaty violation, the Treaty of Berlin had repeatedly been violated and revised ever since its inception thirty years before, sometimes at the instigation, or with the connivance of the states that now denounced this violation.

In other words, my previous argument was essentially that the annexation of Bosnia-Herzegovina was so mild and relatively innocuous an instance of imperialism (indirect informal imperialism, to use the language of Michael Behnen and others) that it should never have caused a crisis at all, but would in a saner international system have been accepted and allowed to succeed.

I still believe this, but no longer consider this the most effective reply to critics or, more important, the best way to understand the real meaning and significance of the Bosnian Crisis for the international system—in particular, how the crisis concretely

illustrates the dash between the old European and the new imperialist ethos and incentives structure in international politics.
Impressive and invaluable though the detailed research on the
crisis by many scholars has been, there is a way in which the
intense focus on the immediate story in all its details and close
analysis of the moves and countermoves of the various players,
examining their respective motives, aims, strategy, and tactics
and how these intersected and reacted with each other as the
crisis evolved, can make one miss the forest for the trees, overlook
what it reveals about the evolution of the European international
system. The current dominant tendency is to interpret the decision to annex Bosnia-Herzegovina and to strike a deal with
Russia as a move within the ongoing imperialist competition and
thus judge it an ill-prepared attempt to make Austria-Hungary
once more a serious player in the new imperialist game, a
strategy that blew up in Aehrenthal's face because of his own
bad planning and execution and Austria-Hungary's weaknesses
and vulnerability. This is certainly one tenable way to interpret
the evidence; Aehrenthal and the Austro-Hungarian government
were unquestionably caught up in that era and spirit and compelled to try to compete within it. But it is important also to
understand the Austro-Hungarian move from a broader systemic
perspective at the same time. From that perspective, the initiative
must be seen as Aehrenthal's attempt to escape the imperialist
game and to revive the ethos, rules, and incentives of the Bismarckian era in international politics.

Almost everything about the move and the Austro-Russian
bargain fits this interpretation, beginning with Aehrenthal's
central foreign policy purpose: to restore good relations with
Russia, revive the Three Emperors' League (which Michael
Behnen calls Aehrenthal's pet idea [*Lieblingsidee*]), and renew
Austro-Russian cooperation in the Balkans. Aehrenthal, more
pro-Russian than any Austrian foreign minister at least since
Count Rechberg in 1864, perhaps in the whole nineteenth century,
had in mind a return not to the barely concealed or open Austro-
Russian rivalry of the late 1870s and 1880s, but to the wary
partnership of the early 1870s, when Austria and Russia buried
the hatchet following Germany's unification in order, among
other things, to become more independent of Germany—which

was another of Aehrenthal's leading aims. The goal of monarchical solidarity against revolution prominent in the 1870s fits equally
well. Aehrenthal was certainly more intent on supporting the
Tsar's authority than Izvolski, eager to cultivate the conservative-
liberals in the Duma and the aristocratic liberals in London and
Paris. The bargaining between Aehrenthal and Izvolski in 1908
bears strong similarities to the Austro-Russian bargaining over
the Eastern Question in 1876–7. The presuppositions of the
bargain reached in 1908, at least on Austria-Hungary's side, were
those that Bismarck had then repeatedly urged on both sides
without success: that they tacitly divide the Balkans into their
respective spheres, cooperate in holding down rebellions, and
mutually act in the spirit of "*Do ut des,*" with Austria-Hungary
recognizing Russia's special interest in the Straits and Russia
recognizing Austrian interests in the western Balkans and the
Adriatic. True, the 1908 agreement was asking for trouble in
leaving out the other great powers, ignoring Italy's desire to play
an active role in Balkan affairs, overriding Ottoman concerns
(where, incidentally, Russia's demand for a special status at the
Straits represented a far greater threat to the Turks than Austria-
Hungary's extinction of the Sultan's purely formal rights in
Bosnia-Herzegovina), and paying no attention to Serbian nationalism or the wishes of Bosnia-Herzegovina's inhabitants. But all
these traits also characterized the politics of the Bismarckian era,
especially in regard to the Balkans, and contributed to its success
in warding off general war.

As to the claim that the annexation represented a serious violation of an important international treaty, the main point is not
that this charge was overblown and unusually hypocritical in this
era of high imperialism, but that it fundamentally mistakes the
general nature and purpose of treaties in the Bismarckian era.
They were not expected to last forever, but intended to be revised
and if necessary canceled to meet changing needs and circumstances. The operating rule, one of Bismarck's favorite axioms,
was "*Pacta sunt servanda rebus sic stantibus*" (Pacts must be
observed so long as conditions remain the same). This applied
to the entire Treaty of Berlin, consciously devised as a provisional solution to an immediate crisis and subjected to repeated
revision by negotiation and unilateral action almost from the

day it was concluded. One of the many ironies in the Bosnian Crisis is that Great Britain, which had throughout the 1870s and 1880s done its best to promote and exploit Austro-Russian rivalry for its purposes heedless of the danger for European peace, and had under Gladstone in the early 1880s and Salisbury in 1885 led the charge to revise or overthrow central provisions of the Berlin Treaty, would in 1908 ardently defend that treaty's sanctity against the very change it had advocated a generation earlier.

To heighten the irony further, the provisions of the Berlin Treaty granting Austria-Hungary the right to occupy and administer Bosnia-Herzegovina sine die, violated in 1908, were specifically intended to be impermanent. Everyone knew at the time that they were a fig leaf for Austro-Hungarian annexation and expected annexation to follow quickly. The British advocated this, Russia accepted it, Germany and Russia formally recognized Austria-Hungary's right to do it in 1881 and 1884, and no power at that time would have thought of opposing it. If, as claimed, Austria-Hungary in 1908 ignored Ottoman rights, Serbian outcries, and the wishes of Bosnia's inhabitants, it did so far more openly in 1878–81, touching off a serious rebellion, and did so with the approval of the international community.

That last phrase is a key one. For ultimately the Bismarckian system rested on the formal or informal acceptance of treaty revisions by the European family of states as a way of coming to terms with change while avoiding general war, whether the changes came about through negotiation or unilateral acts such as the Russian repudiation of the Black Sea clauses in 1870 or the Bulgarian unification coup in 1885. This understanding about the international community's needing to accept change and those making changes needing to seek its approval was part of the agreement reached at Buchlau in 1908, and Aehrenthal accepted the obligation more genuinely than did Izvolski. Austria-Hungary, like Germany and unlike Britain and France, was ready to support Russia's proposal for a change in the status of the Turkish Straits and to accept a conference like the London Conference of 1871 to sanction its action in Bosnia-Herzegovina, provided the conference would grant it without unacceptable conditions.

This is not intended to portray the ethos, rules, and incentives structure of the Bismarckian age as ideal for meeting international problems and crises, even in that era. They were simply better for general peace and stability than what followed. Still less should Aehrenthal and the Austro-Hungarian government be seen as shining examples of honesty, restraint, and cooperation in a lawless era. Holger Afflerbach's characterization of Austro-Hungarian policy in this era as half-Machiavellian and half-defensive is apt, and can be understood as a natural consequence of the Monarchy's situation and special nature. It was caught in a dangerous, escalating competition in which it was losing and becoming steadily more insecure, and it was therefore strongly tempted to regain ground by the same tactics and strategies others used against it, but at the same time aware that this ruthless Darwinian competition was killing it. Aehrenthal's policy thus resembles the half-piracy, half-legality characteristic of Austrian actions in the 1790s vis-à-vis the Polish question, the French Revolution, the duel with Prussia in Germany, and the wars against France and Napoleon. Austria-Hungary wanted to restore the earlier nineteenth century rules for obvious self-interested reasons; it depended on those rules or something like them for survival. Never throughout its history as a great power since the late seventeenth century had Austria been able to meet its many dangers and threats solely or mainly by its own power. Its security had always depended not only upon powerful allies, but also on international consent—what I have called elsewhere "negative Austrophilia" meaning thereby not positive support for Austria from other powers or their active willingness to defend it, but at least their grudging, half-contemptuous recognition that whatever its virtues and shortcomings, Austria fulfilled functions in the European system difficult or impossible to replace by anything else and that it therefore needed to be accepted and at least minimally supported and kept alive.[19] That minimal level of support or toleration required systemic restraints at least as durable and powerful as those of the Bismarckian era. The Bosnian Crisis, I

---

19   Paul W. Schroeder, "Comment: The Luck of the House of Habsburg: Military Defeat and Political Survival," *Austrian History Yearbook* 32 (2001): 215–24.

contend, arose out of an Austro-Hungarian attempt to revive those restraints and that ethos within that system.

The disastrous outcome of that effort proved that this simply could not be done. The single biggest reason why not is that the Russians simply did not want any durable agreement with Austria-Hungary. lzvolski wanted only a temporary one that he could turn to Russia's advantage, in order to restore Russia's prestige and enhance his own. Other Russians, especially the military and parliamentary leaders, the Prime Minister Peter Stolypin, and Tsar Nicholas, decided that any agreement with Austria-Hungary that offended so-called "public opinion" or appeared to betray the cause of their Slav relatives was out of the question. How much this decision was affected by the Russian fear of Germany and of being drawn into dependence on Germany through rapprochement with Austria-Hungary is more difficult to say. That Italians and Serbs would resist any revival of earlier nineteenth-century norms is obvious; so would other small ambitious states. France during this period had no active rivalry with Austria-Hungary and no desire to fight for Russian interests in the Near East, but its fear of Germany, determination to retain Russia as an ally, and desire to break Italy away from the Triple Alliance outweighed everything else. Germany, though it would have liked to revive the Three Emperors' League in order to split the growing coalition against it, would not be restrained by its partners and in the end decided to use the Bosnian Crisis to teach Russia a lesson. As for Britain, throughout the nineteenth century it had almost always opposed any alignment between Germany, Austria, and Russia and tried to break it up. The current German naval threat to Britain and the German threat on land to the continental balance of power, combined with the looming Russian threat to the British Empire, made this policy even more a self-understood necessity. The oft-debated question of which factor weighed more in British policy, its Empire or the continental balance of power, is almost impossible to answer because both concerns fit seamlessly together, and here the question is irrelevant in any case. Alongside these overriding British interests, Austria-Hungary's existence and its European functions did not count—or rather, Austria-Hungary counted only as Germany's ally.

The Bosnian Crisis is significant therefore not simply because more than any other crisis it started Europe's fatal descent into the maelstrom, but even more because it involved the last serious attempt to turn European policies around by reviving its previous spirit and ethos, and the attempt not merely failed miserably, but confirmed and accelerated the trend it was meant to reverse. As a result, Austria-Hungary was bound to conclude that it must do something drastic to change a system that was slowly but surely strangling it. In 1914 as in 1809, it waited too long. Not every reckless gamble is irrational; it may be rational to choose one form of death over another—and, as has been observed, Austria-Hungary committed suicide not out of fear of death, but out of fear of the hangman.[20] The hangman was not a particular enemy power, but the international system.

---

20   Helmut Rumpler, *Eine Chance für Mitteleuropa: Bürgerliche Emanzipation und Staatsverfall in der Habsburgermonarchie* (Vienna, 1997), 604.

PART II

5

Romania and the Great Powers before 1914

There are several points about Romania's position in the European system just before World War I, well known to all scholars, which only need to be stated as the background to the main point of this essay.* In 1913 Romania's successful military and diplomatic intervention in the second Balkan War brought her not only significant territorial gains and greatly enhanced prestige, but gained her a key, almost dominating position in the Balkans, recognized as such by friends and opponents, small and great powers alike. Romania's success involved, and partly resulted from, a fundamental realignment of her position and policy. Since 1883 attached to the Dual Alliance, she now became de facto independent and even leaned toward the Triple Entente, without denouncing her secret alliance with Austria-Hungary. This shift in alignment yielded Romania great advantages at little cost. Since the German Powers were reluctant to snap the remaining thread to Bucharest, Romania continued to enjoy the residual benefits of her alliance, especially her connection to Berlin, while shaking off its obligations. Meanwhile, both sides in the European and the Balkan power struggles ardently courted her, and she gained valuable moral support and potential military aid from Russia and France in maintaining the advantageous status quo of 1913. Romania's realignment meant a decisive shift in the Balkan balance of power in favour of Serbia and Greece against Bulgaria and, to an extent, against Turkey; it also meant an important loss for

---

* A paper presented at the Romanian-American Historical Conference, Suceava, August 19–21, 1974.

the Triple Alliance and gain for the Triple Entente in the European balance. Finally, Romania's shift in 1913 to a more overtly independent, national policy was part of a line of development leading to her ultimate entry into World War I and, after many vicissitudes, her achievement of national unification.

All these points hardly need elaboration or proof. This paper will propose a thesis more open to dispute. It will suggest that Romania's change in policy and alignment was even more significant than is often recognized. In support of this contention, this essay will survey how the European great powers viewed Romania's change in policy and position before World War I, and reacted to it, beginning naturally with Austria-Hungary.

Till early 1913, the Kingdom of Romania did not represent a serious foreign problem for the Monarchy, but rather on the whole an asset. This statement needs qualification, of course. Internally, the Romanian problem in Hungary was one of the most intractable, if not the most explosive, of the Monarchy's nationalities problems, and it was growing steadily worse. Romanian national struggle in Transylvania had long worried Austria, and any signs of active support from within Romania for the movement always made her very anxious. Throughout the nineteenth century, Austria focused much attention on the Romanian Principalities, trying to keep them within her sphere of influence and to prevent them from falling under Russian domination, or becoming nationally united, liberal, or revolutionary. The mere mention of certain dates—1821, 1829–34, 1848–9, 1853–6, 1857–9, 1866–8, 1877–8, 1881–3—reminds one of the times in which the Romanian question in its various forms constituted a pressing problem for Austrian statecraft. Yet when all this is said, it still remains clear that before 1913 Austrian leaders, desperately worried about many other problems, were not nearly so concerned about Romania. There were implicit problems, of course; public opinion was not favorable to the Monarchy, as it never had been; the defensive alliance of 1883 was a highly secret and, in a sense, artificial tie.[1] Yet the Austrians looked on Romania

---

1   For surveys of Austro-Romanian relations and Austrian policy just prior to the war, see Ion Gheorghiu, "Relaţiile dintre România şi Austro-Ungaria în anii 1908–1914," *Studii şi Articole de Istorie* 11 (1968): 137–52; and Willibald

as safely in their camp, and had too many pressing troubles to worry about remoter ones. The relative lack of concern for Romania is apparent in the Bosnian annexation crisis of 1908–9. The Austrian Foreign Minister Count Aehrenthal genuinely desired to take into consideration the interests of all the powers affected by the annexation, Russia, Turkey, Italy, even Serbia— but Romania received no attention at all.[2] Only occasionally in 1908–9 did he voice any concern for the impact of Austrian policy on Romania, arguing at one point, for example, against the Chief of Staff Conrad von Hötzendorf's proposals for draconic action against Serbia with the point that too severe a policy might promote the hitherto chimerical idea of a Balkan League not only in Bulgaria and Turkey, "but even perhaps in Romania."[3] Austrians noted with appreciation but no surprise the favorable attitude of King Carol and his condemnation of British policy. The German Chancellor Prince Bülow supposed that Austria could use Romania as well as Bulgaria against Serbia if strong action proved necessary.[4] No reward for Romanian loyalty figured in Austrian plans. Both Aehrenthal and the Germans refused in late 1909 to guarantee Romania compensation at Bulgaria's expense if Bulgaria acquired Macedonia, and warned that if Romania provoked or attacked Bulgaria, she was on her own.[5]

This confident, almost insouciant, attitude toward Romania persisted into late 1912, even after Austria learned of the existence of the Balkan League and war clouds grew thick over the Near East. The Austrian minister at Bucharest, Prince Fürstenberg, warned Aehrenthal's successor Berchtold already in May 1912 that Romania's growing dissatisfaction might lead her to drift

---

Plöchl, "Die Balkanpolitik des österreichisch-ungarischen Monarchie am Vorabend des ersten Weltkrieges," *Balkan Studies* 6 (1965): 281–92. On the origins of the Austro-Romanian alliance, see Ernst Rutkowski, "Österreich-Ungarn und Rumänien 1880–1883," *Südost Forschungen* 25 (1966): 150–284.

2   See, for instance, Ludwig Bittner et al., eds., *Österreich-Ungarns Aussenpolitik von der bosnischen Krise 1908 bis zum Kriegsausbruch 1914* (Vienna, 1930), vol. 1, nos. 40, 75. (Henceforth cited as *OUA*: to keep the footnote citations within reasonable bounds of length, published documents will be cited only by name of the publication, volume, and number of the document.)

3   Ibid., nos. 752, 799; vol. 2, no. 1718.

4   Ibid., vol. 2, no. 1518.

5   Ibid., nos. 1713, 1732, 1740.

toward Russia if she were not appeased. But Berchtold was reassured by a visit to Sinaia in September, and the Austrian Chief of
Staff General Schemua saw no military danger from the direction
of Bucharest, though plenty elsewhere.[6] Foreign observers supposed that Romania's role in the crisis would be to join with
Austria and Turkey to restrain Bulgaria and prevent war.[7]

The smashing victory of the Balkan League over Turkey naturally made some differences in Austria's attitude. Not only
Fürstenberg, but also other ambassadors like Marquis Pallavicini
at Constantinople warned that Romania must be satisfactorily
compensated if the alliance were to hold. Hence Berchtold
undertook simultaneously to satisfy Romania and to win over
Bulgaria, trying also (without success) to get Berlin to support
this policy.[8] But the attempt to keep Romania happy and loyal,
though genuine enough, meant no fundamental change in Vienna's attitude and expectations. A great deal of evidence, which
need not be reviewed here, shows that Austria subordinated the
appeasement of Romania to the main aim of splitting the Balkan
Leage and winning over Bulgaria, and that she still expected
Romania to be on her side if a general crisis and conflict developed.[9] Therefore it is not surprising that Austria's support at
Sofia, Petersburg, and elsewhere for Romania's claims vis-à-vis
Bulgaria won her little gratitude at Bucharest. Still less is it surprising that with Germany urging and following a line opposite
from Austria's (i.e., anti-Bulgarian, pro-Romanian, pro-Greek,
and even to an extent pro-Serb), Austrian pressure for a Romanian-
Bulgarian agreement failed both at Bucharest and at Sofia. The
only surprise is that Austria should have persisted in courting
Bulgaria not only in the face of repeated warnings from many
quarters that it was undermining the Romanian alliance, but also
despite Berchtold's serious doubts that Bulgaria would prove a

---

6   Ibid., vol. 4, nos. 3527, 3773, 3869.

7   See, for example, G. P. Gooch and H. W. V. Temperley, eds., *British
Documents on the Origins of the War 1898–1914*, vol. 9, pt. 1 (London, 1933),
207–10, 539–40. (Henceforth cited as *BD*.)

8   *OUA*, vol. 4, nos. 4226, 4418–19, 4442, 4673; vol. 5, nos. 5809, 5961,
6081–82.

9   Some of the documents making these points clear are ibid., vol. 4,
nos. 4693–9, 4710–16, 4719; vol. 5, nos. 5806, 5903, 6022–3, 6025.

useful or reliable ally.[10] Plainly the Serbian danger mesmerized Vienna, virtually excluding all else. As Count Hoyos at the Ballplatz finally told Fürstenberg on the eve of the second Balkan War, there was no help for Romania's displeasure. Austrian interests regarding Serbia ran counter to those of Romania, and required that Bulgaria be as strong as possible.[11]

The failure of Nicholas II's attempt to mediate between Bulgaria and Serbia and their drift into war represented an illusory triumph for Austro-Hungarian diplomacy; but her failure to keep Romania from intervening in the war changed it into a disaster. Austria's pleas to Berlin, her warnings to Romania that she would destroy her alliance with Austria and Germany and that Russia would intervene on Bulgaria's behalf, and her desperate last-minute attempts to get Bulgaria to grant what Romania demanded for neutrality, proved useless.[12] Romania not only escaped Austria's control, but also insured Bulgaria's crushing defeat and Serbia's victory by her intervention. Reports even reached Vienna of Romania's setting up border defense units on her Hungarian frontier.[13]

Romanian intervention in the second Balkan War marks the phase at which Austria began really to take Romania seriously as a problem, though still without basically changing her policy. Berchtold hid his bitterness while the war and negotiations went on, even supporting Bucharest as the site for the peace conference, hoping thereby to get Romania to sponsor Austria's ideas for the peace settlement and to limit Serbia's gains and Bulgaria's losses. All was for naught. The treaty turned out even worse than Austria had feared, the idea of a Bulgarian-Romanian rapprochement now that Bulgaria had been humbled got nowhere

---

10 Not only Berchtold, but also the Austrian minister at Sofia, Tarnowski, doubted that Bulgaria could ever be fully lured away from Russia—ibid., vol. 6, nos. 6627, 6901, 6989. On the Berthtold-Conrad dispute over policy toward Romania, see Horst Brettner-Messler, "Die Balkanpolitik Conrad von Hötzendorfs von seiner Wiederernennung zum Chef des Generalstabes bis zum Oktober-Ultimatum 1913," *Mitteilungen des Österreichischen Staatsarchivs*, vol. 20 (1967), 190–1, 222–5.

11 *OUA*, vol. 6, no. 7399.

12 Ibid., nos. 6862, 7194, 7453, 7463, 7486, 7515, 7649.

13 Ibid., no. 7220.

at Bucharest, and lacking German support Austria's campaign for European revision of the treaty collapsed almost before it began.[14]

The period from the Peace of Bucharest to the outbreak of World War I was for Austro-Romanian relations a descent into the maelstrom. Nothing worked for Austria; increasingly she lost control. Germany remained intractably anti-Bulgarian, persistently advising Austria to conciliate Serbia and to attach her along with Romania and Greece to the Dual Alliance.[15] The problem for Austria became less one of keeping Romania loyal than of preventing her from joining and heading a Balkan League promoted by Russia and France; less one of forming a Romanian-Bulgarian combination against Serbia than of preventing an overt Romanian-Serbian military alliance. Even without such an alliance, Austrians realized that Romania would almost certainly enter any new Balkan war if Turkey attacked Greece or Bulgaria Serbia.[16] A Russian-Romanian marriage project raised a new danger, even though it did not materialize.[17] The military implications of Romania's defection for Austria were horrendous. Hitherto all her calculations had been based on Romania's cooperation; now she faced another sizeable potential enemy on a non-fortified frontier. Throughout the tense months of 1912–13 Austria had at least been able to concentrate her military measures on possible action against Serbia and/or Montenegro; henceforth her attention and strength would have to be divided even in the Balkans.[18] In October 1913 Berthtold recognized Romania as well as Serbia as a state with irredentist aims against the Monarchy. Though Austria's military attaché at Bucharest, Hranilovic, insisted that irredentism presented no military danger until and unless the Romanian government supported it and encouraged agitation in Transylvania, after the breakdown of

---

14   See ibid., nos. 7724, 7922, 7964, 8016, 8079, 8157, 8227, 8282, 8345.

15   Ibid., vol. 7, nos. 8708, 8990, 9009, 9025.

16   Ibid., nos. 8908 and 9261; British Minister at Bucharest Barclay to Under-Secretary Nicolson, February 11, 1914, Public Record Office, FO 800/372.

17   OUA, vol. 7, no. 8480.

18   See Wilhelm Deutschmann, "Die militärischen Massnahmen im Österreich-Ungarn während der Balkankriege 1912/13" (PhD dissertation, Vienna, 1965).

Count Tisza's talks with Romanian leaders over Hungarian policy in Transylvania in March 1914, the Romanian government seemed to Austrian observers to be doing precisely this.[19]

Vienna did not remain passive in the face of the deteriorating situation, but tried to remedy it in three main ways. First Count Ottokar Czernin, who enjoyed close ties to the Austrian heir-apparent and had a good reputation as an anti-Magyar at Bucharest, was appointed minister to Romania, with the mission of preparing the way for a clarification and reaffirmation of the Austro-Romanian alliance, to include the publication of the secret treaty. Second, as a means to this end, the Hungarian Minister-President Tisza launched talks with Romanian representatives from Transylvania to try to defuse the increasingly explosive Romanian national problem. Finally, Austria directed even more strenuous efforts to convincing Berlin that the Austro-German rift in Balkan policy was ruining Austria's entire great-power position, and that Romania could not be regained for the Dual Alliance, as Berlin advocated, by means of an Austrian reconciliation with Serbia.

As everyone knows, the first two efforts failed entirely. The last effort finally succeeded, with disastrous consequences all round. The story of Czernin's activity is nonetheless fascinating for its insights into Austrian attitudes, and the mounting despair and bewilderment of Austrian policy. Czernin threw himself energetically into the task of reviving the Austro-Romanian alliance, setting great store by the Tisza-Romanian talks and rightly insisting on the inseparable connection between foreign and domestic policy in both countries. To the common Hungarian argument that the treatment of Romanians in Hungary was only a pretext for the Kingdom's disaffection with Austria, Czernin responded that the point was really irrelevant. Whether Transylvania was pretext or genuine cause, without progress on it, no progress would be made at Bucharest on the larger issue of the alliance relationship. But while Czernin had a clear view of the problem, he also wished to let Romania feel the iron fist in the velvet glove. By late 1913 he already was urging an immediate

---

19   *OUA*, vol. 7, nos. 8779, 9338, 9463, 9471, 9489, 9491, 9496, 9525, 9543, 9567.

either-or showdown with Romania, which Berchtold and the Germans considered premature. By early 1914, with the Tisza-Romanian talks heading for breakdown, he was ready to discard even the velvet glove, and to use Romania's fear of Bulgaria and the threat of an Austro-Bulgarian alliance to frighten Romania back into line.[20] With the collapse of the Tisza-Romanian talks and the surge of anti-Austrian propaganda tolerated by the Romanian government which followed it, there ensued a triangular debate over policy between Czernin, Tisza, and Berchtold. The minister at Bucharest denounced with desperate fervor what he saw as a policy of helpless inactivity at Vienna, and proposed all sorts of measures to bring Romania around, including waging a preventive war on Serbia or forming an iron ring with Romania and Serbia against Bulgaria, guaranteeing the frontiers of both states and thus tying them to the Monarchy. His pleas culminated, in the wake of the Tsar's and Sazonov's visit to Constanta in June, in his well-known cry of despair of June 22: under Russian-French patronage a new Balkan League, headed by Bucharest, was being welded together which would imprison and strangle the Monarchy.[21] Tisza, unwilling to admit the connection between Romania's attitudes and Hungary's nationalities policy, argued that the danger, grave though it was, could be averted by a calm, consistent policy of detaching Romania from Serbia and turning her and Greece against Serbia and/or Bulgaria. Above all, Germany had to be converted to full support of Austrian policy.[22] Berchtold, though more sympathetic to Tisza's ideas than Czernin's, correctly saw difficulties in every solution and came more and more to rely on convincing Germany that something had to be done—exactly what, was not clear.[23]

---

20   The most important and characteristic documents are ibid., 9032, 9039, 9051–2, 9138, 9169, 9385.

21   See especially ibid., nos. 9463, 9600, 9615; vol. 8, nos. 9668, 9845–47, 9874, 9902. While one can see from some of Czernin's ideas why Professor Robert Kann once termed him "an aristocratic desperado," it is only fair to Czernin to say that he was often bold and honest enough to express hard truths his compatriots would not face.

22   Ibid., vol. 7, no. 9482.

23   Ibid., nos. 9413, 9482, 9521, 9565; vol. 8, no. 9639.

Only in German attitudes could Austria detect any improvement. By mid-June 1914 Germany, long a subterranean economic and political rival of Austria all over the Balkans and the Near East, had finally come to admit the seriousness of Austria's position and to accept the necessity of drastic action to stop the rot.[24] The Ballplatz, contrary to Czernin's supposition, had not been deaf to his pleas and cries of alarm; foreign observers had long noted that the defection of Romania worried the Viennese government and press more than anything else.[25] Vienna now prepared a course of action to propose to Berlin to retrieve Austria's great-power position. It was directed, significantly, not at eliminating Serbia but at herding Romania back into line. The origins and development of the proposal, embodied in a memorandum of June 24 by Baron Matscheko, are well known. The plan basically called for forcing Romania to choose either for or against the Triple Alliance. As compensation for an open Romanian allegiance to the Austro-German camp, Austria would give Romania a territorial guarantee against Bulgaria and try once more, with Romanian assistance and through political and economic concessions, to improve relations with Serbia. Only if Romania refused the offer would Austria proceed to fortify Transylvania and, with Germany, to try to erect an alliance with Bulgaria and Turkey to block the Russo-French encirclement policy. As is also well known, it was this proposal to Germany which, drastically changed and sharpened after June 28, formed the basis of Francis Joseph's appeal to William II, elicited the German blank check of July 5, and led to the disastrous results which followed.[26]

---

24   F. R. Bridge, *From Sadowa to Sarajevo* (London, 1972), 360–5; Frank Weber, *Eagles on the Crescent* (Ithaca, NY, 1970), 39–48; Fritz Fischer, *Krieg der Illusionen* (Düsseldorf, 1969), 599–600, 608–12.

25   See, for example, *Documents diplomatiques français, 1871–1914*, 3rd series, *1911–14* (henceforth cited as *DDF*), vol. 9 (Paris, 1929), no. 281; *Die internationalen Beziehungen im Zeitalter des Imperialismus: Dokumente aus den Archiven der Zarischen und der Provisorischen Regierung* (henceforth cited as *IB*), vol. 1, pt. 1 (Berlin, 1931), no. 244.

26   *OUA*, vol. 7, nos. 9627, 9918, 9984; H. B. A. Petersson, "Das österreichisch-ungarische Memorandum an Deutschland vom 5 Juli 1914," *Scandia* 30 (1964): 138–90.

Some scholars have emphasised the sharp difference between the program Austria envisioned on June 24 and the one she chose after the assassination of Franz Ferdinand. The former called for a diplomatic-political campaign directed at Romania, designed to restore Austria's position in the Balkans over the long term, involving no hint of the use of force and no overt challenge to any other great power. The latter envisioned an immediate punitive war to eliminate Serbia as a political factor, thus directly challenging Russia and entailing the high risk of a general war.[27] Without denying that there were differences, I prefer to emphasize the essential continuity and logical connection between these two phases of the planned Austro-German offensive, and to contend that the assassination did not basically change Austrian strategy, but only rendered explicit and brought more quickly into play what was implicit in the earlier plan. First of all, the decision either to force Romania to become a publicly declared ally of Austria or, failing this, to consider her an enemy and to prepare for possible hostilities against her represents for Austria an admission of defeat, a declaration of diplomatic bankruptcy, just as much as the later ultimatum to Serbia did. For it constituted a tacit admission that without Romanian support or some adequate substitution for it, Austria was isolated in the Balkans, unable to play a great-power role there or to defend her vital interests. The need therefore somehow, by whatever means necessary, to regain a lost position of strength was as clear in the first plan as in the second.

The second and more conclusive point, however, is that the June 24 diplomatic offensive had no chance of success, as Austrian appraisals of the situation made clear. Romania could no longer be brought back into the Austro-German camp either by lures or threats. All the Austrian representatives had reported that anti-Austrian sentiment in the government, almost all parties, the army, and the public had gone too deep for this. What Austria proposed to offer Romania, a guarantee of her frontiers, Romania already effectively enjoyed through the support of France, Russia, Serbia, and Greece, and the sympathy of Germany and

---

27   See, for example, Friedrich Stieve, ed., *Der diplomatische Schriftwechsel Iswolskis, 1911–1914*, vol. 3 (Berlin, 1926), nos. 706–7.

Great Britain. Even Bulgaria cared far less for the Dodrudja than for Macedonia. As for Austria's promise to Romania to try once more for better relations with Serbia, not only was nothing likely to come of this, but also everyone knew, including the Austrians, that what Austria and Romania meant by good Austro-Serbian relations were two different things, and that what Serbia meant was yet another. Austria meant that she would extend a benevolent paternalist protection to a Serbia that resolved to live inoffensively under her protection. Romania meant that Austria must accept the independent nationalist Serbia Romania needed to keep Bulgaria in check. Serbia meant a period of normal relations and profitable trading during which Serbia would consolidate her gains and wait for the weakening and collapse of the Monarchy.

Thus the German powers had no effective lures to use with Romania; they equally had no efficacious threats. Treating Romania as an enemy and fortifying the Transylvanian frontier would only have driven her into Russia's and France's arms and promoted Romanian irredentism. As for an Austro-Bulgarian-Turkish alliance, not only was it doubtful that this could be achieved, but the Austrians, especially Berchtold, saw clearly that a weak, exhausted, unreliable Bulgaria and an equally decadent and unreliable Turkey provided no adequate substitute for Romania. Obviously, moreover, the attempt at such an alliance would merely have promoted the open anti-Austrian Balkan alliance headed by Romania which Austria most feared, leaving her position worse than before.

In short, the Austrian plan of June 24, even though it did not explicitly envision a resort to violence in order to regain a lost position of strength, paved the way for it and logically required it. Had the assassination not intervened, and had the Austro-German political offensive been tried, its failure would have quickly compelled the Central Powers to seek the sort of ground for preventive war that the assassination gave them.

If all this is accepted, it supports the contention that Romania's defection from Austria and Germany was an important element in the political confrontation just before the beginning of World War I. It was not that Romania had come by 1914 to be as grave a threat to Austria as Serbia was, so that it was only a question of which enemy to strike first. The Serbian threat was clearly paramount for Austria—Serbian enmity more virulent, the South Slav question more acute, Serbian irredentism more dangerous, Serbian propaganda and subversion more persistent. The point is rather that the loss of Romania at once increased the danger from Serbia (the chief gravamen of Austria against Romania was that she had formed a de facto alliance with Serbia) and destroyed Austria's ability to continue to live with the Serb problem and somehow to manage it. Whatever one thinks of Austrian policy, she had been living with the Serbian problem for over sixty years, had repeatedly been tempted to solve it by violence, and had always drawn back from the brink. As early as the Crimean War Austrian generals were advocating the same "solutions"—either absorbing Serbia, destroying her, or reducing her to impotence—which Conrad and others urged from 1908 on. It was the loss of Romania, more than the assassination of Franz Ferdinand, which made the decisive difference for Austria between further postponement, living with the Serbian challenge and hoping somehow to outlive it, and the determination to settle the problem once and for all, at all costs.

Before asking whether anything could have been done to stop Austria from thus committing suicide out of fear of death, one needs to review another side to Romania's role in great-power diplomacy—the attitude and actions of the Entente powers. The Austrian thesis, of course, was that bribes, plotting, and pressure from Russia and France had produced Romania's defection, and would ultimately bring her into a Russian-led Balkan League. How much truth was there to this contention?

Not a great deal. Of course Russian policy was as anti-Austrian at Bucharest as elsewhere, and the Russians had long been aware of the advantages that would accrue from luring Romania away from the Dual Alliance. Yet until the second Balkan War, Russia's main aim was to preserve and control the Balkan League, in particular her Slav brothers in Bulgaria and Serbia. Her chief concern with Romania was to prevent her, as a supposed tool of Austro-German diplomacy, from breaking up the League and promoting a Bulgar-Serb war. This helps explain the negative attitude taken by Russia and her partners in the Triple Entente to most of Romania's demands for compensation at Bulgaria's expense. Only when the Tsar's arbitration failed to prevent a

Bulgarian-Serbian war in June 1913 did Russian policy come to concentrate on producing a Romanian break with Austria, so as to be able to use Romania to control Bulgaria and protect Serbia.[28] With the success of this policy manifest after the Peace of Bucharest, Russia made every effort to woo and flatter Romania, to detach her still further from Austria, to try to get from her a promise of neutrality in case of an Austro-Russian war, and to pave the way for a full Balkan alliance under Romanian leadership and Russian patronage.[29] Yet one should really not speak of a triumph of Russian diplomacy in Romania. Russia had not produced the Austro-Romanian break, only profited from a situation not of her making. Moreover, she had by no means achieved her final goal by July 1914. While Romania was willing to cooperate with Serbia and Greece to preserve the status quo and curb Bulgaria, she was not ready to break openly with the Dual Alliance (Germany still had considerable influence, if Austria did not) and still less ready to head a Russian-sponsored Balkan League. The Russian Foreign Minister Sazonov knew of the continued existence of the secret treaty with Austria, and though he became reasonably sure it was a dead letter, he could not be absolutely certain. Moreover, Romania's realignment created problems as well as opportunities for Russia. Romania as well as Serbia and Greece opposed the concessions to Bulgaria which some Russians urged in order to bring Bulgaria back into the Russian fold. Russia's efforts to reconcile Bulgaria, Serbia, and Romania proved as ineffective as Austria's in the other direction. An independent Romania, moreover, would hardly prove a docile instrument for solving the Straits Question in Russia's interests. Russia could congratulate herself on Austria's defeat and discomfiture, and claim rightly that what she had gained in Romania was more important than what she had lost in Bulgaria; but the fact remained that Austria's defeat in 1912–14 did not necessarily represent Russian's victory. Austria had lost the

---

28   British ambassador to Russia Buchanan to Undersecretary Nicolson, private, July 9, 1913, Public Record Office, FO 800/368.

29   *IB*, vol. 1, pt. 1, nos. 81, 94; pt. 2, no. 146; *DDF*, vol. 9, no. 250; I. V. Bestuzhev, "Russian Foreign Policy February–June 1914," *Journal of Contemporary History* 1 (1966): 95, 99–100.

ability to play a great-power role in the Balkans and to defend her interests there by 1914; but Russia had not gained the ability to order events her way (the Balkan Wars had repeatedly proved this) and she was not likely to achieve it.[30]

Much the same verdict applies to France. That is, the French in 1913–14 did all they could to expand and exploit Romania's break with Austria and to turn it to their purposes, but they were not responsible in any major way for producing it, nor were they able to achieve all they wanted out of it. The French minister at Bucharest, Blondel, had by his own admission been working steadily since 1908 to split Romania from Austria, but for a long time he had received little encouragement from his government, and numerous admonitions to prudence. Up to mid-1912, in fact, France generally acted more to restrain Russia in the Balkans than to push her forward. Though the Quai d'Orsay supported Russia in the Bosnian Crisis for the sake of the alliance, privately French statesmen were extremely critical of Izvolski's blunders, and the way in which they threatened to drag France into a general war for Russian interests and prestige. Though ready to welcome and encourage the drawing away of Bulgaria and Romania from Austria toward Russia,[31] France was not willing to encourage Russia in any adventures.

An important change came in mid-1912. The Premier, Poincaré, had already made clear that he no longer saw any use in preserving a special relationship with Austria as a means to restrain both Germany and Russia.[32] Now he learned about the Balkan alliance system that Russia had helped to forge. Poincaré understood perfectly the import and anti-Austrian point of the whole arrangement, and the danger to European peace it represented. He also learned from his general staff, however, that Austria was very unlikely to react to it in a belligerent way, and that in case of war the prospects for the Entente were good. Hence he decided to support Russia in her Balkan policy for the sake of the alliance, come what may. From this time forward France represented

---

30   *IB*, vol. 1, pt. 1, nos. 184, 187, 198, 295, 354, 358; pt. 3, 167, 182, 238; Fischer, *Krieg der Illusionen*, 504–11.

31   *DDF*, vol. 1, nos. 373, 376.

32   Ibid., vol. 2, nos. 218–19.

a goad rather than a curb in Russia's Balkan plans. This was part of Poincaré's desire, for both domestic and foreign policy purposes, to display the solidarity and strength of the Triple Entente on every possible occasion.[33]

Initially this change in French policy meant no major change in her attitude toward Romania. In the interval between the Balkan Wars, Poincaré, like almost everyone, regarded Romania as a potential weapon in Austria's hands, which therefore had to be neutralized.[34] Up to the eve of the second Balkan War Blondel feared that Romania, under Austrian pressure, might sell her neutrality or even cobelligerence to Bulgaria.[35] But Blondel worked tirelessly to promote a Romanian mobilization and intervention against Bulgaria, despite several cautionary instructions from the Foreign Minister Pichon.[36] Some French diplomats, like the brothers Cambon and even the anti-Austrian ambassador at Vienna, Dumaine, saw how provocative the Tsar's assumption of a patronage over the whole Slav world was to Austria, and were worried about overt French support for Russia.[37] Nonetheless, Blondel was doubtless working in Poincaré's directions, if not in Pichon's, and his policy succeeded.

After the Peace of Bucharest, virtually all the pretense of neutrality in Balkan affairs which France had hitherto maintained was dropped. Blondel's anti-Austrian activity became more indefatigable than ever, and where Pichon had endevored to rein him in and had rejected the French ambassador at Petersburg Delcassé's proposals for joint Russo-French military and financial aid to Romania, Pichon's successor Doumergue openly hailed and publicized the pro-Entente trend in Romanian politics. French economic policy in Romania, hitherto one of cooperation with Germany, now turned to open competition. The French

---

33   Ibid., vol. 3, nos. 264, 314, 359; D. R. Mathieu, "The Role of Russia in French Foreign Policy, 1908–1914" (PhD dissertation, Stanford, 1968), 143–63. Evidence of France's anti-Austrian policy in 1913 is plentiful in *Isvolski's Briefwechsel*; see, for example, vol. 3, nos. 658, 666, 1080, 1082–3, 1093, 1095, 1101, 1107, 1111, 1114–15, 1118–19.

34   *Isvolski's Briefwechsel*, vol. 3, nos. 659–60.

35   *DDF*, vol. 7, no. 54.

36   Ibid., nos. 68, 73, 135, 149, 165, 195, 220, 253, 267, 268.

37   Ibid., nos. 103, 115, 194.

followed the Hungarian-Romanian talks intently, and reacted to their collapse with relief and delight. The chargé of the French Consulate-General at Budapest even proposed that France support the Hungarian opposition independence party, in order further to weaken Austria-Hungary and the Dual Alliance. Yet in all this, France was exploiting Romania's switch in policy rather than causing it. At times even Blondel, though delighted with the whole trend of events and convinced that it was irreversible, felt that Russia was unwise to force the peace and to try to exercise a tutelage over Romania, instead of simply taking advantage of her new independence and commanding position.[38]

Thus the Austrian charges about a Russo-French policy of encirclement were justified, as were her fears of its eventual success—but her belief that her predicament was due to Entente machinations was not.

As for the third member of the Triple Entente, Great Britain, not even the Austrians could consider her responsible in any causal sense for Austria's defeat in the Balkans. Britain, in fact, was the one member of the opposing camp with whom Austria by 1914 still hoped to keep on good terms; Austrian diplomats frequently referred to the traditional friendship between the two nations and praised the loyalty and fair play of Foreign Secretary Sir Edward Grey in his mediation efforts during the Balkan Wars.[39] Britain's importance in regard to Romania lay not in any active role she played in the Balkans, for she had none. It lay rather in the special position she held within the Triple Entente, which, despite much pressure from France and Russia and considerable sentiment within the Foreign Office, she refused to turn

---

38 Ibid., nos. 280, 288, 293, 324, 333, 364; vol. 9, nos. 13, 15, 62, 109, 179, 181, 356; vol. 10, nos. 6, 238, 397, 416; Mathieu, "Role of Russia," 164–7; Fischer, *Krieg der Illusionen*, 616–22; Raymond Poidevin, *Les relations économiques et financières entre la France et l'Allemagne de 1898 à 1914* (Paris, 1969), 671–5, and "Note sur les ententes et les rivalités financières franco-allemandes en Roumaine 1900–1914," *Bulletin de la Faculté des Lettres de Strasbourg* 46 (1968): 589–93.

39 In this the Austrians perhaps gave Grey somewhat more than his due; he meant to be fair and impartial, but above all had to keep on good terms with Russia. See F. R. Bridge, *Great Britain and Austria-Hungary, 1906–1914* (London, 1972).

into an alliance, and within the European balance, where Britain still retained far more than other great powers a free hand and ability for maneuver.

On Romania and the Balkans, one must distinguish between British policy and British opinions and reactions. British policy was simple. She would not become involved in any purely Balkan questions (as opposed to questions touching the Straits, Asiatic Turkey, and the Mediterranean, where her interests were important). Where she could not help becoming involved diplomatically in Balkan crises, her aims were twofold: to preserve the present alignment of powers (which meant keeping Russia at least reasonably happy), and try to keep Balkan conflicts from escalating. In practice, this made British mediation in Balkan disputes moderately anti-Austrian; though the British by and large had no real animus against Austria, she turned out regularly to be expected to pay the price for keeping Russia happy and preventing disputes from developing into general war. On the other hand, British policy in the Balkans was not anti-German; German economic and political penetration there was not resented as it was in Persia or Asiatic Turkey. In fact, the British government had so little concern for Balkan developments for their own sake that British comments on these events have almost the value of those of a neutral observer.

In the main, the British saw what others did, and reacted to it in similar, if much more detached, fashion. Until early 1913 they viewed Romania as safely in the Austrian camp and hoped that Romania's influence would help restrain Austria from forceful intervention. They also expected that Austria and Russia would both be able to control their respective satellites and bring about a peaceful Romanian-Bulgarian settlement in the spring of 1913.[40] They quickly recognized the switch in Romania's position in mid-1913 and its disastrous results for Austria; insofar as they were interested in this development at all, they praised Romania's new role as an independent power holding the balance and helping to preserve peace. But what emerged from the struggle

---

40   See, for example, Buchanan to Nicolson, October 31, 1912, PRO, FO 800/359, and Nicolson to Sir Fairfax Cartwright, ambassador to Austria, April 2, 1913, FO 800/364.

between Romania, Bulgaria, and Serbia was intrinsically unimportant in British eyes compared to the maintenance of Turkish rule in Asia; this might affect the loyalty of the Muslim population in India.[41]

The British took the Russo-Austrian struggle over the Balkans somewhat more seriously than they did inter-Balkan rivalries. On this question a good many British agents were openly anti-Austrian in sentiment, and either pro-Russian or in favor of the Balkan peoples against the Monarchy (a lingering echo, perhaps, of the Gladstonian tradition). Buchanan at Petersburg and Bax-Ironside at Sofia certainly encouraged Russian efforts to create a Balkan League against Austria, and may have made some small contribution to its realization in 1912 and to Russian efforts to re-establish it in 1913–14. While Ralph Paget, minister at Belgrade, was anti-Serb and Sir Francie Bertie, ambassador at Paris, was critical of the excessive Russophilia of Nicolson, no one of importance in the Foreign Office or diplomatic service, once Fairfax Cartwright had been removed from Vienna, could be called pro-Austria.[42] Yet while there was undoubtedly a pro-Russian and anti-Austrian bias in the British view of the Russo-Austrian struggle over the Balkans, the British outlook was determined less by sympathies either for Russia or for the Balkan peoples (the Serbs were far from popular at London) than by the acceptance of what the British considered undeniable realities. The first of these realities was that for the sake of peace the present alignment of the great powers had to be maintained. The second was that by early 1914, if not before, Russia's victory in the Balkan power struggle was already certain and Austria's

41   For illustrations of these British attitudes, see Nicolson to Cartwright, July 8, 1913, FO 800/368; Nicolson to Marling, chargé at Constantinople, July 9, 1913, ibid.; Goschen, ambassador to Germany, to Nicolson, October 9 and 17, 1913, and January 21, 1914, FO 800/370 and 372; and Nicolson to Bax-Ironside, minister at Sofia, May 25, 1914, FO 800/374.

42   For examples of the attitudes mentioned, see BD, vol. 9, pt. 2, no. 287, and vol. 10, pt. 1, nos. 358 and 374; memorandum by Bertie, June 23, 1913, PRO, FO 800/161; Bax-Ironside to Nicolson, April 8, 1912, and July 11, 1913, PRO, FO 800/356 and 368; Cartwright to Nicolson, June 20, 1912, FO 800/357; Nicolson to Bunsen, ambassador to Austria, March 2 and 16, 1914, and Nicolson to Bax-Ironside, May 25, 1914, and Bax-Ironside to Nicolson, June 17, 1914, FO 800/373.

defeat sealed. Indeed, an early breakup of the Monarchy was very likely. It would obviously be utterly foolish for Britain to bet on a horse that had already lost, or to urge anyone else to do so.[43] The third reality was that it was very useful to Britain that Russia occupy herself with consolidating her gains in the Balkans, for this would distract her from forward moves in Asia.[44] The final, and most important, reality was that while there was a danger of a violent reaction by Austria and Germany to Austria's defeat in the Balkans and her threatened demise,[45] there was nothing at all Britain could do to stave off this violent Austro-German reaction other than to remain militarily prepared herself, to maintain her ententes, to urge prudence and moderation on all sides, and to encourage Germany to restrain her ally. Thus Britain, convinced of the impossibility and undesirability of any British intervention to control developments in the Balkans, tended even more than other powers, when she saw what was coming, deliberately to avert her eyes.

This attitude, which persisted even long after Sarajevo, can hardly be praised for imagination and initiative. Yet it would have taken remarkable vision and leadership for any British government to have followed any other course. In any case no one can lay any positive responsibility on Britain's shoulders for the destruction of Austria's great-power position and for her consequent suicidal venture.

---

43   A good example of this conviction is found in a private letter of Nicolson to Sir Charles Hardinge, former Permanent Undersecretary and then Viceroy of India, on July 2, 1913. After discussing Austria's understandable dismay at the Tsar's proclamation of a virtual protectorate over all the Slavs, Nicolson remarked: "My own idea is that whatever developments the present situation may assume there is little doubt that sooner or later all these Slav States will feel it necessary to come into the orbit of Russia and not remain in an attitude of hostility towards her. Moreover, Austria is far too weak a reed for them to rely upon. Pessimistic prophets predict that the next Empire which will go to pieces will be that of Austria-Hungary" (FO 800/367).

44   E.g., see Hardinge to Nicolson, Simla, May 16, 1913, ibid; "I devoutly hope that Russia may be preoccupied for some years to come in the Near East with the interests of the Slav races, so that those who favour a forward policy in Asia may receive no encouragement."

45   See Nicolson to Bunsen, March 30, 1914, and Bunsen to Nicolson, April 10, FO 800/373.

If the preceding argument is correct, it would seem that I, often considered an incorrigible Austrophile, have served the Monarchy very badly. Her case now appears worse than before. If the decisive blow to Austria's great-power status and position was the loss of Romania rather than the growth of the Serbian menace; if the loss of Romania was primarily due to Austria's own foreign policy and her internal problems and failures, and not to the actions of Russia and France; if Romania's desire for greater independence was normal and legitimate within the prevailing rules of the international system, and her policy defensible in terms of her own interests and the maintenance of peace; and if the only answer Austria could find to this adverse development was the basically aggressive policy of either forcing Romania back into a tight alliance, or treating her as an enemy and forming a combination against her—a policy which led naturally and logically to the final punitive-war strategy of 1914—if all this is true, what possible defense can be offered for Austrian policy? One can at least make a prima facie case for punitive action against an incorrigible enemy; but what excuse can one give for bludgeoning an ally who no longer wants to stay in the partnership?

All this, I think, is true; there is no good case to be made for Austrian policy in 1914, any more than there was finally in 1859 (which is not to say that she was always wrong and always the aggressor). But this also seems to me not a very important point, or at least far from the most important one. For Austrian policy might be seen as indefensible and at the same time as virtually inevitable; the chief issue might be not whether her decisions and Germany's could be justified, but whether they might not have been anticipated and headed off. Here the main point about the reaction of the Great Powers to Romania's realignment seems to me to resemble Sherlock Holmes's famous point about the dog that significantly failed to bark in the night. It concerns not what the powers thought and did about this development, but what they failed to think and do about it. As has been seen, all the powers readily understood the crucial nature of Romania's change of alignment. All saw how it undermined Austria's position in the Balkans and her great-power position as a whole. All saw that Romania had now become the key to the Balkan balance. All reacted to this development with reactions ranging, as we have seen, from Austria's frantic despair to Britain's detached approval. Yet no government addressed itself to the most obvious and critical question of all: how was this new, crucial development to be managed? How, that is, could it be harmonized with the overall European balance, incorporated into the prevailing international system, without raising the already fearful strains upon that system to the point of explosion? No one thought of this problem, or suggested doing anything about it. Austria and Germany thought only of reversing the defeat they had suffered, Russia and France only of exploiting and expanding the victory Romania's new policy represented, Britain only of not getting involved.

It might be supposed that this is merely typical of the prevailing atmosphere and conduct among the great powers at this time, when everyone could think only of winning and not of preserving the system. But this is not quite true. There were times when the great powers at least thought about longer-range considerations, even in 1914; when they warned of dangers threatening the whole system, and urged action to avoid or defuse them. Instances are familiar to everyone. The British refused to turn the Triple Entente into a Triple Alliance, in part because this would seem too overt a challenge to Germany. Both Britain and France declined to try to get Italy openly to abandon the Triple Alliance, on much the same ground. There were constant warnings before 1914 of the dangers of allowing Austro-Russian rivalry in the Balkans, or Astro-Serbian hostility, to develop unchecked. At least isolated voices can be found who suggested means of containing these explosive rivalries. Until the world war broke out, no one, not even Russia, was willing openly to thrown the question of the Straits or of Asiatic Turkey onto the table, because of the dangers to general peace such an action would contain. Yet I can find no instance of anyone's suggesting that if Romania was to leave the Austro-German camp and to lean toward the opposing side, some means would have to be found to make this loss tolerable to the losers, or the whole system might be undermined.

A discussion of what could conceivably have been done in this direction would go beyond the bounds of this paper. Perhaps nothing was even theoretically possible—though I myself am inclined to believe that in this particular area of devising means to save the face of losers and to keep a system going despite major changes and adjustments, the resources of diplomacy are almost unlimited. The impossibility, I would suggest, was contextual and situational in 1914, not intrinsic. But this question must be left aside as unanswered, if not unanswerable. The main point remains that everyone in 1913–14 saw what Romania's change in alignment meant—and no one among the great powers acted in a European sense to manage it.

6

Prudence vs Recklessness: Assessing Responsibility for World War I

The debate over the Great War's origins persists to this day, despite a century of controversy, a massive literature, and considerable general agreement about how the war started and who started it.[1] Though research continues to turn up new details, it has long been clear that among the great powers it was the Central Powers, Germany and Austria-Hungary, who initiated the so-called July Crisis—for a majority of scholars, Germany more than the Dual Monarchy, for others (including me), Austria-Hungary more than Germany.[2]

The debate, however, is really not over who or what initiated the crisis, but who or what was behind it, what aims, decisions, drives, and actions by which powers genuinely caused the war. One line of interpretation, the majority view, sees the main force behind events in Germany's drive for world power, i.e., for hegemony in Europe and a world position in the twentieth century competitive with the existing world empires of Britain, Russia, and the USA. This German bid for power coincided in 1914 with Austria-Hungary's decision to confront the various foreign and internal challenges and threats facing it and to reassert its position as a great power by eliminating its most challenging and dangerous small neighbor, Serbia. A minority view (also mine) sees the main

---

1   Samuel R Williamson Jr. and Ernest R. May, "An Identity of Opinion: Historians and July 1914," *Journal of Modern History* 79, no. 2 (2007): 335–87.

2   Francis R. Bridge, *The Habsburg Monarchy among the Great Powers 1815–1918* (New York, 1990); Samuel R. Williamson Jr., *Austria-Hungary and the Origins of the First World War* (New York, 1991); Günther Kronenbitter, *"Krieg im Frieden": Die Führung der k.u.k. Armee und die Großmachtpolitik Österreich-Ungarns 1906–1914* (Munich, 2003).

cause as a general breakdown of the international system and its collective restraints and rules, prompting two great powers to conclude that they had to act forcefully now to meet the mounting threats against them even at the grave risk of general war, and the others to believe that this gave them no choice but to respond in kind—thus the downward spiral into general war.

The two master narratives, despite agreements on many facts and questions, and variations and differing emphases within each, are really about what was still possible within the system and what happened to it in 1914. One narrative claims that the Central Powers smashed it. Peaceful remedies for their problems and alternative courses of action were still open to them in 1914; absent their actions, war need not have developed at this time or later, and the system could have soldiered on. The other narrative claims that while certain contingent events (e.g., the assassination attempt against Archduke Franz Ferdinand) could doubtless have gone differently, the supposed alternative choices available to the Central Powers were illusory, and barring some highly improbable change in outlook and attitudes throughout the system and a serious collective effort to change the game as it was being played, the possibilities of further peaceful development were blocked and a general conflict was in the cards.

Each master narrative, therefore, involves an analysis also of the course of international history over the previous quarter century, and these too diverge. The versions that stress Germany's and Austria-Hungary's responsibility allege a long record of aggressive and dangerous actions on their parts—Germany's naval challenge to Britain, German bullying and threats against France in both Moroccan crises, Austria's annexation of Bosnia-Herzegovina and Austro-German humiliation of Russia in the Bosnian Crisis, German attempts to penetrate and dominate the Ottoman Empire and the Middle East, Austria's persistent economic and political pressure on Serbia and military threats against it after 1903, especially in the Bosnian Crisis and both Balkan Wars, and of course the final Astro-Hungarian ultimatum backed by Germany in July 1914.

Proponents of the "systemic breakdown" argument, like me, not only interpret many of these same events and developments differently but also cast a wider net for the war's causes. The list of things alleged to have helped destroy vital rules and restraints and ruin the system as a civil association include for example, Anglo-French colonial rivalry in Africa, culminating in the Fashoda Crisis of 1898 to 1899;[3] the Spanish-American War in 1898 and its extension to the western Pacific; Russia's imperialism in the Far East and Japan's resort to preventive war to stop it, 1895 to 1905; the Second Anglo-Boer War, 1899 to 1902, and the succeeding incorporation of the Boer Republics into a Union of South Africa; France's challenges to Germany in each of the two Moroccan Crises; the breakdown of Austro-Russian cooperation in the Macedonian question in 1906 to 1907 and Britain's policy in response; the Anglo-Russian Convention of 1907 on Persia and Central Asia, especially in relation to Germany; Russia's promotion of a Balkan League under its protection in 1912, the French reaction to it, and its impact on the Ottoman Empire, the Balkan states, and the whole Near East; Italy's attack on the Ottoman Empire, in 1911 to 1912, first in Libya and then in the eastern Mediterranean and the Straits;[4] Britain's agreement with Germany in December 1912 to postpone Concert intervention in the first Balkan War until the warring states had fought it out to a conclusion; Russia's preparations for war against the Ottoman Empire if it refused to yield on the Liman von Sanders issue; the heightened rivalry and strains between Britain and Russia over Persia, with both, especially Russia, threatening the Persian government; the Anglo-Russian talks in 1914 on potential naval cooperation against Germany in the Baltic; and the Russian and French efforts in 1913 to 1914 to wean Romania away from alliance with the Central Powers and into their camp.

What purpose is served by presenting these two bareboned lists of alleged crimes against the system? Both doubtless prove that the game of international politics from 1890 on was one of intensive

---

3 Christopher Andrew, *Théophile Delcassé and the Making of the Entente Cordiale: A Reappraisal of French Foreign Policy, 1898–1905* (New York, 1968); Roger Brown, *Fashoda Reconsidered: The Impact of Domestic Politics on French Policy in Africa, 1893–1898* (Baltimore, 1970); Ronald Robinson and John Gallagher, *Africa and the Victorians: The Climax of Imperialism in the Dark Continent* (New York, 1961).

4 Richard J. B. Bosworth, *Italy: The Least of the Great Powers* (London, 1979); Richard J. B. Bosworth, *Italy and the Approach of the First World War* (New York, 1983).

imperialist competition, full of dangerous crises. But everyone already knew that; no one has ever disputed it. Everyone also agrees that the war did not arise, at least directly or primarily, over colonial-imperialist competition outside Europe. The great colonial-imperialist powers and rivals, Britain, France, Russia, Italy, Japan, and the USA, all ended up eventually on the same side. The main struggle for power in the years before 1914 was on the Continent and between land armies, and the most critical danger was the rivalry between the three great Central and Eastern European monarchies over Southeastern and Eastern Europe.

As a proponent of the "systemic breakdown" thesis, I do not merely accept these points; I insist on them. To believe that High Imperialism lay at the root of a systemic breakdown in international politics by 1914 has never required believing that struggles over colonies and empire directly caused the war or constituted its main issues. The question is what kind of practices, reigning assumptions, and rules of the game were part and parcel of High Imperialism and became thereby common, accepted, and legitimate. The purpose of seeing these two lists of gravamina side by side is not to decide which powers were more to blame for the war, which state's motivations and purposes were legitimate or illegitimate, revisionist or status-quo-oriented, aggressive or defensive, etc. ad infinitum. Questions such as these have long passed the point of diminishing returns and proved a cul-de-sac. The point of the comparison is to raise again the issue of the nature and role of the system. Can the war be understood best as a system effect of a simple, common kind, resembling many in the seventeenth and eighteenth centuries—the outcome of so complete a breakdown of any systemic rules and practices that could have held it back that general conflict sooner or later became highly likely, if not absolutely inevitable? Did state actors in 1914 and before regularly pursue substantive goals of such a nature and by such means as to make it impossible for international politics to continue for long as the practice of a civil association dedicated to keeping the practice going?

To some this will seem a deceptive maneuver, substituting a new set of terms claimed to be more objective and intersubjectively verifiable than the old, but actually just as laden with value choices, ultimately unanswerable questions, and subjective judgments as the old. Instead of asking whether certain policies and actions were aggressive or defensive, designed to provoke war or preserve peace, one now asks whether they supported or undermined the operation and survival of the international system as a civil association. What difference does this really make?

To see how it can help in a concrete way, try a thought experiment. Assume *ex hypothesi* that, as argued here, in order for tolerable peace and stability to prevail in international politics, the individual states participating in it and pursuing their individual substantive goals must simultaneously also act as members of a civil association working to maintain the practice, and that this requires members, especially the great powers, to have shared formal and informal understandings on acceptable rules, norms, and practices, a general agreement on what limits have to be observed and joint responsibilities fulfilled, and the ways to do this. In other words, they must understand at least in general terms certain necessary minimal rules of the game and be willing to follow them.

Now apply this assumption concretely to the July Crisis and the quarter century of international politics earlier. Ask the same question of each important action, decision, and policy. Can it be defended as a legitimate way to play the game, something compatible with the international system operating as a civil association?

This is not an unreasonable or inappropriate test. It is often applied, though seldom explicitly articulated. Those who contend that the Central Powers caused the war by their policies and actions in 1914 implicitly assert as a principle or general rule that a great power cannot legitimately confront a small neighbor, especially one allied to a rival great power and under its protection, with ultimate demands that it hopes and expects will be rejected, in order to have a plausible pretext for a war to eliminate that neighbor as a political factor in the region. Why not? Because it is dishonest, aggressive, bullying, bellicose? These are epithets; they may be deserved, but are not reasons. The reason is that any such action constitutes so egregious a violation of essential rules of the international system as a civil association as to destroy it. You cannot adopt such a policy and expect the other players to swallow it and let the game continue.

I agree. On what the Central Powers did, the principle involved, and the immediate consequences, the argument is sound. They acted like two players in a Wild West high-stakes poker game who, losing the game and convinced that it was deliberately rigged against them, kick over the table and draw their pistols, preferring to shoot it out rather than let it go on as before. But then this same principle and reasoning must be applied to all the actions, decisions, and policies of all the other actors as well, in the July Crisis and before, to determine whether these too can be defended or not as legitimate ways to play the game and maintain the system as a civil association. Before assuming that the Central Powers actions were decisive in wrecking the game by violating its essential prevailing rules, one needs to determine what were by 1914 the prevailing rules and consider the possibility that by then the principles on which the Central Powers acted were already the actual prevailing rules.

Look at Serbia. It is remarkable that a century after 1914 a wide scholarly consensus should agree that Germany and Austria-Hungary were responsible for starting the war, and no such consensus prevail in regard to Serbia's policy, conduct, and role. Here was a state created and enlarged not merely by its own efforts in war, revolution, and ethnic cleansing, but also by international recognition and action. It had been rescued more than once from military disaster by great powers, including Austria-Hungary. It was built on a state ideology of extreme romantic ethnic-integral nationalism. Its goal, ostensibly Serb unification, was actually in practical terms a Balkan mini-empire in which Serbs ruled over minorities of Albanians, Macedonians, Bulgarians, Croats, Hungarians, and Germans.[5] It targeted all its neighbors at one time or another for territorial acquisitions, principally first the Ottoman Empire, then later Austria-Hungary. Well before 1914, it laid claim in its propaganda and public instruction to large portions of Austro-Hungarian territory. In defiance of clear treaty obligations, it openly encouraged revolutionary movements and secretly supported terrorist activity in Austria-Hungary, and in 1914 was indirectly involved in the assassination of the heir-apparent to the

---

5   Wolf D. Behschnitt, *Nationalismus bei Serben und Kroaten 1830–1914: Analyse und Typologie der nationalen Ideologie* (Munich, 1980); Katrin Boeckh, *Von den Balkankriegen zum Ersten Weltkrieg: Kleinstaatenpolitik und ethnische Selbstbestimmung auf dem Balkan* (Munich, 1996).

throne, the worst blow short of war that could be struck against the Dual Monarchy. Can anyone suggest a rule of principle to justify this conduct as compatible with maintaining the system as a functioning civil association?

Or look at Russia. The main debate has been over the purpose and timing of its partial and general mobilizations in July and their role in the outbreak of war, but this is less important than what it generally aimed at in the crisis and what advice and support it gave Serbia. One thing that was clear in the crisis, or should have been, was that any peaceful settlement would have to include satisfaction for the Dual Monarchy in the form of serious penalties for Serbia and effective restraints on its future conduct. The one thing clear about Russia's reaction was its determination not to allow the Dual Monarchy to gain this, not out of sympathy for the Serbs or their actions (many Russians considered them dangerous troublemakers) or for reasons of Russian security and strategy, but because any such Austrian success would damage Russia's prestige and leadership in the Balkans and offend Russian public opinion and its national honor. Again one has to ask, "Can you play the game this way very long and expect it to survive?"

The same refrain applies in lesser degree even to France and Britain. True, France did not give Russia an explicit blank check in 1914, but it had already given Russia its blank check in 1912 and repeatedly confirmed it thereafter, unwilling to do anything that might possibly jeopardize the Russo-French alliance against Germany. Understandable though this is, it breaks a cardinal rule of crisis management: that one must be ready to restrain and manage not only one's opponents but if need be also one's allies. Britain also did not encourage Russia to back Serbia, but made no attempt to control or curb it either. Preoccupied with a crisis in Ireland, serious internal disagreements over what role if any Britain should play in a possible European war, the Russian challenge in Persia, and the danger of losing Russia to Germany, the British government did not consider an Austro-Serb-Russian quarrel important or its concern.

Even better proof of the widespread, virtually universal indifference to the system and its function as a civil association by 1914 is the fact that for twenty-five days after the assassination, nothing whatever was done to mobilize the European Concert for purposes of mediation, intervention, or control. In the wake of so explosive an event, following closely on a decade of mounting tensions and rivalry elsewhere, an escalating land arms race, constant crises, and three wars in the Balkans and the Near East that threatened to become general wars within less than three years, such inaction is almost incomprehensible. The usual explanations (e.g., that Britain, France, and Russia were lulled into it by vague assurances that Austria would not do anything rash) are pitifully inadequate. The reality is that in Europe, especially in the West, the reigning attitude toward Austria-Hungary and the Balkans was indifference—"Not our problem." This indifference, moreover, did not arise in 1914; it rose from broken rules, shattered precedents, and violations of norms accumulated over a quarter century of unrestrained High Imperialist competition.

Some final reflections on moral judgments, prudence, and recklessness

No matter how it is stated, this argument will sound to many like the excuse once offered by some, especially Austrians and Germans— "Everyone broke the rules and undermined the system, and so no one is especially guilty or responsible for the outcome." By this sleight-of-hand, one might complain, the mountain of evidence bearing on the origins of the war garnered from the study of things other than international high politics but related to it—historical patterns of political and cultural behavior, long-term effects of the historical experience of authoritarianism, militarism, oppression, and conquest, models of challenge and response embedded in particular polities and cultures, the influence of social, racial, gendered, and religious beliefs and assumptions—all this and more gets swept under the rug or subsumed and buried beneath one portmanteau explanation: systemic breakdown.[6]

This, I wearily insist, is just what my argument does not do but tries to avoid. It concedes that these and other putative underlying historical causes and factors had something to do with the

---

6   Isabel V. Hull, *Absolute Destruction: Military Culture and the Practices of War in Imperial Germany* (Ithaca, NY, 2005); Alan Kramer, *Dynamic of Destruction: Culture and Mass Killing in the First World War* (Oxford, 2007).

outbreak of World War I, and that vital things are learned from studying them. The argument here is less about what in some deep historical sense caused World War I than about what in some practical sense might conceivably have averted it—hence the stress on the significance of an absence of systemic conflict for a century from 1815 to 1914, and what might be learned from its unprecedented non-occurrence.

Nor is my argument intended to bury the complicated, concrete story of how and why war broke out under the vague moral judgment that everyone broke the rules. It attempts instead to focus attention on one essential requirement for international peace, keeping the game of international politics going within necessary limits and restraints. If it preaches anything, it is that eternal politics is the price of peace. It does not attempt to judge which attitudes, aims, decisions, actions, and policies of various actors made for peace and which for war—questions usually impossible to resolve on any objective, intersubjectively verifiable basis. Instead it stresses the essential requirement for international politics, prudence, as the central virtue, and condemns its opposite, recklessness, as the cardinal sin. Prudence, that is, as meaning understanding the game of international politics and its rules and practices, limits and possibilities; recognizing the connection between one's own long-range interests and the system's functioning; and letting these insights serve as a guide and restraint.[7] "Recklessness" means the opposite—ignorance of the system, disdain for its rules and practices, willingness to gamble, readiness to act on inner conviction, feeling, and intuition, the belief that one must somehow succeed so long as one's cause is just.

Using prudence versus recklessness as the main criterion will not solve all the problems of assessing responsibility for World War I, but it can help clarify things. I would not presume as a historian to judge which state or states were overall more bellicose or peace-loving in the quarter century before 1914. This would involve too many varied, ill-defined, and conflicting criteria,

---

7   See the related discussion of prudence in James W. Davis, "The (Good) Person and the (Bad) Situation: Recapturing Innocence at the Expense of Responsibility?," in James W. Davis, ed., *Psychology, Strategy and Conflict: Perceptions of Insecurity in International Relations* (London, 2013).

standards, and underlying assumptions for any judgments that could satisfy me, still less others. But I think that appraising the various actors on the stage in 1914 on the score of prudence and responsibility versus recklessness and irresponsibility is possible within reason, and might be useful.

For what it may be worth, then: Of all the actors directly involved in the outbreak of war, I consider Serbia the most reckless and irresponsible, the most defiant of elemental norms of international conduct, the most hostile to the very existence of the international system, and the most eager to see it destroyed for the sacred cause of Serbian or South Slav nationalism (for most Serbs, the same thing under different names).

Among the great powers (this will surprise some and outrage others), the most reckless was not Imperial Germany but Tsarist Russia. The evidence is clear, though too vast and diverse to survey here. William Gladstone famously remarked in a campaign speech in 1879 that there was no spot on the globe where one could put his finger and say, "There Austria did good" (the remark says more about Gladstone than about Austria's record). His charge, however, could well be adapted to apply to Imperial Russia in this era. One is hard pressed to find a spot on half the globe where one could put his finger and say, "There Russia was prudent and responsible." In surveying its policies and actions from 1895 vis-à-vis East Asia, China, Manchuria, Korea, Japan, Central Asia, Persia, the Ottoman Empire, the Straits, the Balkans, the Ukraine, and Poland, one finds them virtually everywhere filled with Russia's reckless risks and imprudent challenges to other powers and the system. The Bourbon kings restored to power after the French Revolution and Napoleon in 1815 are supposed on their return to have learned nothing and forgotten nothing—perhaps true of Charles X (1824–30) but not Louis XVIII (1815–24). The last two Romanovs, however, Alexander III (1881–94) and especially Nicholas II (1894–1917) really did learn nothing and forget nothing in international politics, despite the disastrous defeat by Japan and the revolution in 1905 that nearly brought the regime down.

Among the other great powers, Germany, for reasons too well known to need rehearsing, comes next in terms of reckless conduct. Austria-Hungary's choice in 1914 was obviously an extremely reckless gamble born of desperate resolve rather than aggressive ambition, and Austrians gave hints of a dangerous recklessness earlier on. But prior to 1912 the Habsburg Monarchy had had a pretty consistent record of prudence, trying to keep the system it relied on for security and status intact and working. France's record is harder to appraise. The leaders of the government, though determined not to back down before a German threat, did not want war. But I think the rashness of France's challenges to Germany in the two Moroccan Crises, and even more the dangers of its unqualified backing for Russia's moves in the Balkans after 1912, have been underestimated.

Judging British policy on a prudence-recklessness scale is hard. Britain broke important rules and precedents and was provocative in its aggressive defense of its Empire (e.g. directly threatening France with war over a colonial issue—something unprecedented since 1815 and demanding a complete surrender with no compensations, following this with a preventive war in South Africa and the conquest and annexation of the Boer Republics in 1899–1902). The British deal with Russia in 1907 that partitioned Persia into British and Russian spheres of influence was designed to keep Germany out, and posed a real challenge to Germany, though in the context of the time this was hardly reckless conduct. Nor can one claim this about Britain's response to Germany's naval challenge or its rapprochement with France and Russia, intended, ostensibly at least, to prevent German hegemony in Europe. However, Britain's agreement to hold secret talks with Russia in the spring and summer of 1914 for naval cooperation against Germany in the Baltic seems like playing with fire in a room laden with explosives. No matter whether the British intended these talks to lead to an agreement or not, they knew that the Germans were likely to learn about them given the high level of espionage and leakage of sensitive information within the system, and that this would certainly have crucial repercussions given the already acute German fears about encirclement. The argument that Britain needed to do this to keep Russia from running amok in Persia is an explanation, not an excuse.

Still the worst one can say of Britain is that, like virtually all the other powers in 1914 and before, and less egregiously than most, it merely followed the prevailing concept of the system's rules: to defend and promote your own rights and interests by whatever means necessary, expect others to do the same, and count on the balance of power to preserve general peace. In other words: each state for itself, and God for us all—or the devil take the hindmost.

There lies the rub. Indifference and inaction in sustaining the international system as a civil association undermined it as much as reckless actions and provocations did. And this judgment, to be even minimally fair and accurate, must be made to include states that did not enter the war in 1914 and are not conventionally charged with causing it or touching it off. As system members and participants in the game they share the responsibility for the consequences. Japan's policy in East Asia, for example, was imperialist, though its sphere was too peripheral to the theater to make much difference in 1914. That would wait for World War II.

Italy and the USA are more important. One actively undermined the system as a civil association before 1914; the other made its active contribution to its decline at the turn of the century, and then remained an inactive but potent threat to it by its position and potential role in international affairs thereafter.

No power did more in the critical years of 1911 to 1913 to demonstrate a cynical recklessness and contempt for hitherto prevailing rules and restraints in international politics than Italy. First it picked a quarrel for purely domestic-political reasons with the Ottoman Empire over North African territory (Libya) that the Ottomans only nominally controlled. Then after invading and annexing Libya (again breaking a rule about how imperial acquisitions ought to be covered with at least the fig leaf of a protectorate) and finding itself unable to pacify the territory, Italy deliberately expanded the war into the most dangerous and volatile area possible, the eastern Mediterranean and the Turkish Straits, in violation of vital international agreements. This was tupenny-ha'penny Machiavellism at its worst. It encouraged the Balkan states joined in a Russian-sponsored Balkan League to attack the Ottoman Empire, promoting the Balkan Wars of 1912 to 1913 that followed, almost touching off general war then and paving the way for the war in 1914. For this, Italy suffered no sanctions or loss in alliance protection and won handsome territorial gains. But ironic, unintended consequences of Italy's imperialism on the cheap were not long in coming. In 1915 the Italian government, operating on similar principles, decided to run to the aid of

the expected victors, again for domestic-political reasons and territorial loot. This decision, plus an incompetent and ruinous war
effort and a supposedly unsatisfactory peace, contributed power-
fully to the triumph of fascism and the ultimate downfall of the
Italian monarchy and empire.

The USA's impact on the prewar international system looks
quite different, but there are deeper similarities on the score of
prudence versus recklessness vis-à-vis the system. The Spanish-
American War in 1898 had a powerful effect on the system, not so
much because it showed America's military power (not all that
impressive) but because it revealed America's attitude toward the
international system and how little any other power, or all of the
powers together, could do about it. Prevailing American views see
1898 as the entrance of the USA onto the world stage: in crushing
Spain, "liberating" Cuba, and seizing the Philippine Islands, the
war launched the USA on a new overseas, European-style course
of imperialism and a new role in world affairs. This a misleading
American perspective. From a world perspective, the great age
of American imperialist expansion was 1760 to 1850; compared
to it, 1898 and all that was no more than an episode.[8] It also
supposedly confronted Americans with a choice of the basic
principles by which the USA should conduct itself on the world
stage, whether Republican realism or Wilsonian idealism—again
a particular American perspective. Europeans then and now
might view the USA's actions in 1898 and after as simply confirming historic American attitudes and conduct toward the
international system. By casually rejecting the half-hearted but
genuine European effort to mediate the Spanish-American
quarrel and prevent a war that presented serious dangers to
Europe, by insisting on a total and immediate Spanish surrender
as the only alternative to war, and by expanding both its military
operations in the Atlantic and western Pacific and its peace terms
as it did, the USA demonstrated America's habitual disdain for
systemic rules and restraints and for any of the consequences its
actions might have for the system in general or for other members
in particular.

---

8   Walter T. K. Nugent, *Habits of Empire: A History of American Expansionism* (New York, 2009).

One might thus picture prewar Italy as an active but small loose cannon on the international ship of state, capable of being secured and bolted down had other powers decided it was necessary. By contrast, 1898 showed the USA to be in practice what Europeans had long feared it might become: a great loose cannon, for the moment fairly immobile but impossible to secure, and capable at any time of breaking loose and wrecking the ship. The contribution this perception made to the undermining and collapse of the system in the years before 1914 cannot be precisely measured (certainly not by me) but should not be ignored.

Supposing that the argument in this essay is sound, what end does it serve? It clearly supports Jervis's case for the importance of system and system effects in international politics and for the need for scholars and practitioners to pay careful attention to them.[9] It also shows and exemplifies to a certain extent how systems in international politics can grow, be nurtured, work, decay, and be undermined and overthrown.

I also hope that it might in some small measure encourage an attitude to "system" and its companion and product "order" in international politics, well expressed by a great historian of two generations ago, Herbert Butterfield, in concluding his perceptive analysis of the meanings and practical applications of the term "balance of power" in the European international system of the seventeenth century through the nineteenth:

> I should infer from all this that an international order is not a thing bestowed upon us by nature, but is a matter of refined thought, careful contrivance and elaborate artifice. At best it is a precarious thing, and though it seems so abstract it requires the same kind of loyalty, the same constant attentions, that people give to their country or to other private causes which only the international order enables them to follow.[10]

---

9 Robert Jervis, *System Effects: Complexity in Political and Social Life* (Princeton, 1997).

10 Herbert Butterfield and Martin Wright, eds., *Diplomatic Investigations: Essays in the Theory of International Politics* (London, 1966), 147.

PART III

7

World War I: A Tragedy, Not a Pity

This book, which has received a good deal of public attention, is hard to assess fairly.* The generous space allotted to this review could all be spent discussing the book's outstanding virtues: a huge, important subject; wide research and broad coverage; vast information that is well organized and clearly conveyed; an engaging style; an unmistakable mastery of some fields, especially economics and finance; provocative arguments, including many revisions and challenges to conventional views; and bold counterfactual reasoning (in principle, a good, necessary thing). Yet, an appraisal must center on what the work primarily purports to offer and what has gained for it such wide attention: a highly revisionist explanation of World War I's historical significance, including what caused it and whether it need have happened at all; what made it last so long and end as it did; and finally, why it not only could, but should, have ended differently. On these scores, this reviewer's reaction ranges from mild demurral to sweeping rejection, and his task is briefly to explain why.

Ferguson's skill and fairness in exposition are such that his main arguments, recapitulated in his concluding chapter, can be still more drastically summarized here. His first two points consist of long arguments that 1) "neither militarism, imperialism nor secret diplomacy made war inevitable"; and 2) that Germany's decision to gamble on war in 1914 derived not from hubris and a bid for world power, but from weakness and

---

*   Niall Ferguson, *The Pity of War* (New York, 1999).

perceived threats, especially from Russia (p. 442). Both points are largely true and worth emphasizing, though the former, to this reviewer's knowledge, is fairly conventional and the latter was recently advanced by many leading scholars. What keeps him from establishing that the war was avoidable is, first, that the primary threat was never war between Britain and Germany, or even France and Germany, but Russia and Germany; and second, that Ferguson virtually ignores the factor crucial for either avoiding or bringing on a Russo-German war, namely, Austria-Hungary. Austria-Hungary made the decision to gamble on war in 1914 and demanded that Germany support it. This coincidence started the war and requires explanation. Here Ferguson's lack of mastery of international history in comparison to other areas, of which telltale signs occur earlier, becomes critical. No account that centers on prewar Anglo-German relations and on the July Crisis, while covering 1908–14 in five pages; whitewashing Serbia's policy and actions; omitting such things as Russia's sponsorship of the Balkan League, the Serbian-Greek-Montenegrin efforts to partition Albania, and the defection and Russo-French wooing of Romania; and trivializing the import and impact of the assassination at Sarajevo, can possibly explain Austria-Hungary's problem and therefore say much about the war's avoidability. Serious counterfactual reasoning must start with asking whether this problem was soluble or manageable, and if so, how.

Ferguson's third argument, that the British decision to enter the war and to send the British Expeditionary Force was not foreordained, is true, but it is hardly revolutionary. The corollary, that it decisively affected the duration and outcome of the war, is unquestionable, but, to my knowledge, it is never challenged. Less clear is how contingent that decision was and how long it could have been postponed, and more dubious still is the contention that it derived from misreading German intentions as Napoleonic in their dimensions. Regardless of German aims, which quickly became fairly Napoleonic, sensible Britons could see that the *consequences* of German victory would be Napoleonic.

The rest of the book is devoted to questions of how the war was waged, what it was like experientially, why it lasted so long, and why it turned out as it did. It includes less to which one should object and more to appreciate; there are vast amounts of information and evidence, often statistical, many corrections of details in other accounts, as well as numerous sound arguments, and some unsound ones. Yet this reviewer's impression, which is intended as praise, not criticism, is that on balance the book corrects, enriches, informs, and confirms prevailing views rather than overturning them. That the war was not really greeted everywhere with popular enthusiasm is now widely recognized, as are the important but indecisive effects of war propaganda. More controversial and open to challenge are Ferguson's elaborate arguments, buttressed by arrays of statistics, on why the Allies' advantage in economic resources did not translate into earlier victory, and, conversely, why Germany's greater "killing efficiency" did not bring it victory in the West as in the East. Despite interesting and persuasive individual arguments (e.g., that Germany's economic war effort was actually more effective than the Allied one), both arguments represent specious answers to unreal problems. Neither an initial advantage in economic resources nor greater "killing efficiency" have normally been decisive in nineteenth- or twentieth-century warfare—otherwise the Confederate States of America would have swiftly lost the Civil War, Germany and Japan would have been quickly defeated in World War II, and the Third Reich would have destroyed the Soviet Union in 1941. Ferguson's evidence really helps explain what everyone knows happened: the two factors largely negated each other, a remarkable German war effort served to avert defeat, but it never quite overcame the Allies' material advantage.

In contrast, the questions raised by Ferguson as to why men fought and/or surrendered are very real, and his discussion is often penetrating and provocative (e.g., on the mortal dangers of surrender and the prevalence of shooting prisoners). Yet, perhaps inevitably, they are impressionistic and inconclusive.

In any case, throughout the book Ferguson states his case clearly, lays out his evidence, and thus allows readers to judge for themselves. Only at its end and climax, on the war's meaning for history, does his argument become slight and his conclusion arbitrary and untenable. He answers the question "Who won?" with the standard, unexceptionable verdict that everyone save the United States lost, then and later. But, he attaches another assertion. The war was less a tragedy than a pity, because it was "the greatest *error* [author's emphasis] of modern history" (p. 467). Not only could it have been avoided, but, once it did start, it should—for Europe's and the world's sake—have ended with a relatively quick German victory, as it would have done had Britain not promptly entered it. This result would have left the British Empire intact and unexhausted, while uniting Europe under a tolerable German hegemony like that of today, averting all the horrors of the intervening decades.

The problem here is not, as some critics have charged, that this counterfactual argument is illicit, but that it is superficial. Counterfactual historical reasoning must identify the critical issues and build on concrete evidence as rigorously as "normal" historical argument, and this author does not do so. Avoiding war in 1914 would not have led, as he claims, to further cold war among the five great powers, but to the acceleration of something already far advanced: an intense competition, which Austria-Hungary had already lost militarily and was rapidly losing politically, pointing to its paralysis and possible breakup. A serious counterfactual argument for avoiding World War I must explain both why Austria-Hungary and Germany would allow this process to proceed indefinitely and how, even if they did, it could have failed to end in general war.

The author's assumption that Germany's war aims would have remained relatively moderate in victory equally defies both the history of wartime politics and diplomacy, largely absent from the book, and probability. German moderation in war aims was always produced by prospective defeat or stalemate, reinforced after 1916 by desperate cries for peace from Vienna, and regularly swept aside by any prospect of victory. Many features of German society that helped restrain Germany before 1914 did not survive the actual war and would have survived victory still less. Take one example, the "philo-Semitism": which Ferguson ascribes to Imperial Germany in contrast to Russia or France. Disregarding the questions of what this "philo-Semitism" was really worth, what would have happened when the Germany of 1914, with its small, assimilated, loyal Jewish minority, gave way to a militarily triumphant Germany that expanded territorially to the East, leading a satellite Austria-Hungary with its racist and anti-Semitic Austro-Germans, and dominant over "independent" countries (Poland-Lithuania, Ukraine, Romania) containing powerful anti-Semitic traditions and millions of Eastern Jews?

Worse still are the twin assumptions that the British Empire could have survived and thrived beside a German-dominated continent and that German hegemony could have been, like the alleged German hegemony in Europe today, durable and peaceful. The first defies central facts about Britain's history and position; the second defies Germany's. Apart from the German colonial, commercial, and naval ambitions that victory would have revived and empowered, when had even the most powerful British Empire been able to ignore a clear-cut hegemony on the continent or check it without powerful continental support? As for comparing German "hegemony" in the 1990s to a supposed German unification of Europe through victory in World War I, the analogy not only breaks down at every actual point, but ignores the controlling fact and burden of Imperial Germany's position in Europe: that it was too strong and centrally located to be an ordinary, safe great power, but never populous, large, or powerful enough to impose its rule on all the others. Even a German victory would have left it facing a revisionist Russia and France; an opportunistic Italy; a chaotic, quarrelsome Eastern and Southeastern Europe; and a resentful Austria-Hungary. To conceive of this situation as somehow anticipating Europe's achievements in the late twentieth century and of German victory after 1914 as a potential shortcut to these achievements is romanticism, not history.

Yet, books can be constructively wrong, and this one is. It will compel everyone to think; even experts will learn much from it, while the lay reader will certainly be enriched and possibly entranced. But not so entranced, one hopes, as to forget some hard-won truths: that Germany can lead Europe if, but only if, it is first integrated into a larger Western community—including the United States—and renounces power politics; and that, tragic as World War I and its outcomes were, a German victory would have been worse.

8

A. J. P. Taylor's International System

To discuss A. J. P. Taylor's concept of the international system seems like discussing Samuel Beckett's concept of God (or, for that matter, Taylor's); the first thing to recognize is their denial that any such thing existed. Taylor's classic volume in the Oxford History of Modern Europe series, *The Struggle for Mastery in Europe, 1848–1918*, the main focus of this essay, certainly does not set out to discuss or analyze the international system in theoretical or systemic terms.[1] Only very rarely does he use the term "system" in connection with international politics as a whole, as distinct from the ideas and approaches of particular statesmen. The character of the book, as well as that of his other works, moreover, seems to make them resistant to systemic analysis. Like the others, this one tells a story, that of European high politics in the latter two-thirds of the nineteenth century, in chronological order, emphasizing individual contingent events, decisions, and developments, and explaining them in various ways and by means of many factors both superficial and profound, but not in terms of any system of international relations. One can find penetrating insights, bold interpretations, sweeping generalizations, and apodictic assertions galore; Taylor always offers his readers plenty to think and argue about. But

---

1 Taylor's other works, those on Prince Bismarck, the Habsburg Monarchy, the origins of the Second World War, the history of England 1914–45, and various lesser monographs and collections of essays, all contain considerable material on foreign policy and international history, and certain of them will be referred to here. But *The Struggle for Mastery in Europe, 1848–1918* (Oxford, 1954) is undoubtedly his magnum opus in this field and his only detailed account of international politics over an extended period of time, and represents the right place to look for his system, if any.

where is the system? Perhaps Taylor is precisely what he claims to be in the preface to one of his books and recommends that other historians be, a storyteller recounting what happened and leaving questions of system, overarching interpretation, and speculation as to what might or could or should have happened under different circumstances to others.[2]

This conclusion would be too simple. For one thing, one could easily show (though I shall not do so *in extenso* here) that *The Struggle for Mastery* and Taylor's other works are full of broad, sweeping views on history and of counterfactual argument and speculation.[3] One could further show (if anyone cares) that any claim to be telling a simple narrative story in history based strictly upon the facts involves very large assumptions that need at least to be articulated and examined. It would also be possible, if less easy, to show (and again, not here) that historians cannot avoid counterfactual reasoning in their work, and that the only real question is not whether to use it but how.[4] But more to the point, Taylor himself did not always profess a simple positivist view of history and the historian's task. As Kathleen Burk writes in her new biography of Taylor,

> Most interestingly, Taylor set out in his introduction [to his first book on the Italian problem, 1847–9] his approach to diplomacy and to diplomatic history. "At first sight," he wrote, "the European diplomatic system appears to proceed in the most haphazard

---

2   A. J. P. Taylor, *The Trouble Makers: Dissent over Foreign Policy, 1792–1939* (London, 1957), 17, 22–3.

3   To keep this from being a naked assertion, take just one passage, critical in Taylor's account of the origins of the First World War: "Certainly, Russia would have been a more formidable Power by 1917, if her military plans had been carried through and if she had escaped internal disturbance—two formidable hypotheses. But it is unlikely that the three-year service would have been maintained in France; and, in any case, the Russians might well have used their strength against Great Britain in Asia rather than to attack Germany, if they had been left alone. In fact, peace must have brought Germany the mastery of Europe within a few years." Here are five instances of counterfactual speculation in three sentences, each one more sweeping and more ungrounded in reasoning and evidence than the last (Taylor, *Struggle for Mastery*, 528).

4   P. E. Tetlock and A. Belkin, eds., *Counterfactual Thought Experiments in International Politics* (Princeton, 1996), chap. 1.

way. Personal likes and dislikes . . . the accidental delaying of a dispatch, the evil intentions of one diplomat or the levity of another—by these the tranquility, even the peace, of Europe seem to be determined . . . But on a closer view, there emerge more and more clearly certain broad principles, until the petty struggles of day-to-day diplomacy take on the appearance of a battle of Platonic ideas . . . [The] course of national policy is based upon a series of assumptions, with which statesmen have lived since their earliest years and which they regard as so axiomatic as hardly to be worth stating. It is the duty of the historian to clarify these assumptions and to trace their influence upon the course of every-day policy."[5]

In other words, certain broad principles, fundamental assumptions, and enduring circumstances and forces influence the day-to-day conduct of diplomacy and help to shape foreign policy, and these the historian must uncover and explain. This represents a kind of systemic approach. Nor was this notion simply one Taylor adopted under the influence of his mentor, the Viennese historian A. F. Pribram. It shows up among his premisses in *The Struggle for Mastery*, where he writes in the introduction:

Europe has known almost as much peace as war; and it has owed these periods of peace to the Balance of Power. No one state has ever been strong enough to eat up all the rest; and the mutual jealousy of the Great Powers has preserved even the small states, which could not have preserved themselves. The relations of the Great Powers have determined the history of Europe.[6]

True, shifts occurred in the nineteenth-century balance and there were potential challenges to it, as in the past, from ambitious powers and would-be hegemons, and from ideologies calling for the establishment of international relations on some ideal

---

5   K. Burk, *Troublemaker: The Life and History of A. J. P. Taylor* (New Haven, CT, 2001), 96–7. The quotations are from Taylor's *The Italian Problem in European Diplomacy, 1847–9* (Manchester, 1934), 1.

6   Taylor, *Struggle for Mastery*, xix.

universal basis, moral or other. But neither kind of challenge proved successful or even very serious in this period until the very end, when Germany's bid for the conquest of Europe, though defeated in the First World War, brought Europe's self-sufficiency in the world to a close. Nor did nineteenth-century imperialism outside Europe have any decisive effect on great-power relations. As for ideologies, they

> were a minor theme in the seventy years between 1848 and 1918; and the Balance of Power worked with calculation almost as pure as in the days before the French Revolution. It seemed to be the political equivalent of the laws of economics, both self-operating. If every man followed his own interest, all would be prosperous; and if every state followed its own interest, all would be peaceful and secure.[7]

Other forces besides the balance of power were at work in Europe, of course, forces that Taylor sketches in his intro-duction—demographic change, political and social evolution, and especially economic changes rising out of industrialization and urbanization. But until Germany's late rise and bid for Euro-pean conquest and world power these, too, were accommodated within the balance. As he sums up the story, "the European Balance of Power is the theme; and the theme ends when this theme is dwarfed. The European Balance worked untrammeled in the seventy years between the fall of Metternich and its several repudiations by Lenin and Wilson."[8] Or again, summarizing the state of affairs before German world policy and United States intervention wrecked the European balance and "overthrew all rational calculations":[9]

> The seventy years between 1848 and 1918 were the last age of the European Balance of Power, a Balance reinforced by political and economic developments which had been expected to destroy it. The first twenty-three years were a period of turmoil . . . It ended

---

7   Ibid., xx.
8   Ibid., xxi.
9   Ibid., xxxvi.

with "the lesser revision"; the new national states of Germany and Italy were fitted into the system of the Balance of Power; and Europe combined vast change with international peace for more than a generation.[10]

Taylor's concept of the international system in this period is thus clear and familiar. It consists of the balance of power among the great powers; he even refers to this as a system. He regularly capitalizes "Balance of Power" as he does the "Great Powers," and uses it as the subject of active verbs, suggesting that even if it is not formally reified in his mind, it nonetheless represents for him something real, active, powerful, having palpable effects and producing tangible results. It works untrammelled, accommodates and regulates change, provides stability and peace.

Taylor's definition of the international system, at least during this period, in terms of the existence and operation of the European balance of power entitles one to expect his history of international politics to explain how the balance of power accounts in large measure for what happened. True, many questions about the balance of power over which scholars have broken lances for centuries remain unaddressed—for example, that of definition. Exactly what does the phrase "balance of power" mean? My own study of balance-of-power language, as used by European statesmen in the nineteenth century, found eleven different definitions belonging to two separate and distinct though related strands of meaning.[11] Other scholars have found different numbers and kinds of varying definitions.[12] Taylor never confronts this problem directly or indirectly. A related question concerns the various concrete definitions of a proper balance advanced by different governments or leaders, along with their practical programs for achieving that balance, some of which (arguably most) amounted in practice to programs for achieving

---

10   Taylor, *Struggle for Mastery*, xxxv–xxxvi.

11   P. W. Schroeder, "The Nineteenth Century System: Balance of Power or Political Equilibrium?," *Review of International Studies* 15 (1989): 135–53.

12   E.g., E. B. Haas, "The Balance of Power: Prescription, Concept, or Propaganda," *World Politics* 5 (1953): 442–77; M. Wight, "The Balance of Power," in H. Butterfield and M. Wight, eds., *Diplomatic Investigations: Essays in the Theory of International Politics* (London, 1966), 149–75.

hegemony. Who decides which programs are valid or bogus, and how? What kind or kinds of distribution of power are required for a balance? Must it be roughly equal among the great powers, or will any distribution short of clear-cut preponderance by any one power do? Does it operate automatically like the invisible hand of the marketplace, or require close attention?

On this critical point, Taylor seems to come down on both sides. Much of his language suggests that the balance was self-adjusting, and he says more than once that the British often thought so; yet he also says that the events of the First World War and after discredited that notion. Does the balance require and encourage states consciously to maintain it in the interest of stability and peace, or is it compatible with an amoral Realpolitik in which each merely pursues its own selfish interests? Again the answer is unclear. Taylor's swipe at Herbert Butterfield as "that Christian exponent of the Balance of Power" who thinks that "Christian statesmen . . . should be as Machiavellian as their opponents" seems to identify balance politics with Machiavellianism,[13] and Taylor certainly finds some amoral and aggressive policies (for example, Count Cavour's in 1859–60) compatible with the balance of power and even beneficial to it.[14]

At the same time, in holding that Europe owed its long peace largely, if not solely, to the balance of power, Taylor credits its statesmen with "something like a common aim—to preserve the peace of Europe without endangering the interests or security of their country."[15] Does the balance of power require a manager? If the latter, can that managing power or statesman stand outside the balance, holding it and playing the role of arbiter over it, or must the manager be involved as part of the balance? If the former is the case, is such a position and function as arbiter compatible with a genuine balance or does it constitute hegemony? How does one define and measure the power being balanced, compare its diverse kinds and sources, weigh them against each other? How does one, either as practitioner or analyst, appraise the relations between available power and threat or vulnerability

---

13   Taylor, *Trouble Makers*, 13.
14   Taylor, *Struggle for Mastery*, 112.
15   Ibid., xxi, xxiii.

for each player, and over the system as a whole, to determine whether it is indeed balanced or not?

Taylor himself, were he here, would doubtless dismiss these questions, and so might his followers today, with the reply that he was a historian, not a theorist or social scientist. The balance-of-power idea was never intended to be precise in definition or measurement. It was an idea used by living human beings to help them understand and conduct international affairs, and while it may escape precise definition, it passes the test the US Supreme Court Justice Potter Stewart applied to pornography: "I know it when I see it." Anyway, all these problems or pseudo-problems of the definition and operation of the balance of power ought either to be solved, or dismissed as irrelevant, through history, that is, *ambulando*, in the course of relating and analyzing the historical narrative and by the process of doing so.

Fair enough. What we are thus entitled to look for in Taylor's balance-of-power system is not a contribution to balance-of-power theory or international relations theory in general, but solely a historical explanation of how the balance worked to shape international politics in one particular place and era, nineteenth-century Europe.

The difficulty, however, is that this is just what one seeks in vain, at least for the first fifty years of the era and well over half of the narrative covered in *The Struggle for Mastery*. What one finds instead, injected irregularly into a detailed account of individual events, decisions, and developments, are fairly frequent but casual references to the balance of power and some remarks on what purportedly happened *to* the balance, how it was affected, as a result of particular developments. What cannot be found is any consistent or coherent development of the narrative in terms of what the balance of power was doing to international politics or what influence it had on it. The term itself is absent from large stretches of the narrative. More important still, there is no attempt to explain or demonstrate how the balance of power brought about particular outcomes. It is almost as if someone were to say, as certain kinds of providential history used to say, that a particular period of history demonstrated the workings of the hand of God—and then on reading the story one found that the hand of God not only was not even mentioned in much of it, and was only ritually invoked in other parts, but also that no attempt was ever made to show that the hand of God actually had shaped events and just how it did so.

This is a grave charge and requires some backing, though a full demonstration would require a page-by-page analysis of the book. All one can do here is to note some of the phenomena and developments which might be presumed on the basis of Taylor's assurances to form part of the story of the balance of power and to be at least partly accounted for by its operation, that are not explained in his book by the balance of power or are at best connected with it only in a superficial way.

Examples: neither the Vienna system nor the revolutions of 1848 are discussed at all in balance-of-power terms, and the revolutionary events and developments of late 1848 to 1850 are tied to it only in ways that obscure the putative role of the balance more than they demonstrate or illustrate it, or explain anything— for example, that the Prussian and Austrian programs for Germany would have upset the balance, or that Russia intervened in Hungary to restore the German balance, or that Viscount Palmerston considered Austria essential to the European balance, or that the "new balance seemed to work exclusively for Russia."[16] (It might be thought odd that the balance of power would produce so unbalanced a result, but never mind.) On the origins of the Crimean War, there is only a remark that the British thought defeating Russia would strengthen the balance, Napoleon III that it would destroy it. On the diplomacy of the war, there is nothing on how French and British war aims or the Austrian efforts to control and end the war by diplomacy, or the Prusso-German efforts to keep Austria and Germany neutral, were in any way shaped by the balance-of-power system. On the peace of Paris in 1856 and its provision neutralizing the Black Sea, we get only a tolerably obscure remark that this represented "an attempt to perpetuate an existing Balance of Power when that balance should have been changed."[17] On the Italian crisis and war of 1859, we are told that Italy did not count for much in the balance before 1858, and that, despite unification, it counted

---

16 Ibid., 44.
17 Ibid., 85.

still less later after Germany was unified and industrialized.[18] On the actual short- and long-term balance effects of the events of 1859 or the role of the balance system in influencing policy, however, nothing is said. Nor does the balance of power appear as an explanatory factor or variable in the Polish question of 1863 or the Danish-Duchies question of 1863 or the Danish war and the Austro-Prussian victory in 1864, except for a sudden, unembellished assertion that "the Balance of Power survived Bismarck's three wars."

There are more references to the balance, though still not many, in relation to the German question and the Austro-Prussian duel for supremacy, but these only further illustrate the protean character of the phrase and the conceptual confusion bred by its offhand use. Russia, we are told, "might have counted for something in the balance of central Europe" but "both Russia and Great Britain had virtually eliminated themselves from the European balance," while a French show of force on the Rhine in July 1866 "would have tipped the Balance of Power in Germany."[19]

Much the same holds for the origins of the Franco-Prussian War in 1870. The balance of power enters into the discussion only via Taylor's claim that none of the other three great powers feared a war "or supposed that it would disturb the Balance of Power in Europe."[20] Only when we get to the Great Eastern Crisis in 1876 is there a clear statement that balance-of-power purposes governed Otto von Bismarck's policy here as they had in Germany. The passage is worth quoting for the light it sheds on Taylor's conception of that balance. Explaining Bismarck's opposition to any dismemberment of Austria-Hungary, Taylor writes:

18　Ibid., 99.

19　Ibid., 156, 167.

20　Ibid., 200. This assertion, incidentally, together with Taylor's previous one that "neither Russia, Great Britain, nor Austria-Hungary cared about South Germany," (199) is true enough regarding Britain; mainly false regarding Russia; and quite wrong regarding Austria-Hungary. For the best of several major works showing that the Austrian government cared strongly in 1867–70 about preventing a war over the German question, which was bound to arouse German nationalism in Austria and thereby threaten the state, and about trying to preserve the 1866 status quo by strengthening the independence of the south German states, see H. Lutz, *Österreichisch-Ungarn und die Gründung des Deutschen Reiches* (Frankfurt am Main, 1979).

The Habsburg Monarchy was essential to the limited Germany which Bismarck had created; and this in its turn was essential to the Balance of Power, in which Bismarck believed as the only means of preserving the peace of Europe. The Balance of Power determined everything for Bismarck; and he sacrificed to it even German national ambitions . . . Bismarck certainly thought Austria-Hungary the weaker of the two [as compared to Russia] and therefore put his weight more on her side. Nevertheless, balance between them, not the victory of either, was always his object, as for that matter he had fought two wars of 1866 and 1870 to restore a balance in Europe.[21]

In other words, Austria-Hungary's existence was necessary, in Bismarck's view, only in order to prevent Germany from becoming too large and powerful and to provide a balance of power between Austria-Hungary and Russia in East-Central Europe as part of balanced power relations elsewhere in Europe. This was what counted for him and constituted his reasons for not allying with Russia in 1876 and for allying with Austria-Hungary in 1879.

For a historian who wrote a biography of Bismarck and admired him as much as he could admire any German, this represents a remarkably narrow interpretation of Bismarck's thinking. Bismarck certainly did want to end Germany's expansion at its 1871 boundaries and, for many different reasons based on both foreign and domestic policy grounds, he did not want to add Austro-Germans and other peoples of the Monarchy (principally Czechs in Bohemia and Moravia) to the German Empire. His larger reasons for wanting the Habsburg Monarchy preserved as a major state, however, far transcend the simple balance-of-power considerations portrayed here. As Bismarck repeatedly emphasized from 1866 on, also on this occasion, any break-up of the Habsburg Monarchy could only result in a permanently revolutionary, incalculable, and uncontrollable situation in South-eastern Europe, inevitably dragging Germany into dangerous quarrels alien to its interests. Even worse, without Austria-Hungary as a third party in the German-Russian-Austrian equation, though a restrained, passive one, Germany's relations with Russia,

---

21   Taylor, *Struggle for Mastery*, 240.

always the most important in Bismarck's eyes, would become unmanageable, set on the course of a Teuton-Slav struggle for supremacy in Europe which Bismarck was determined to avoid. In other words, in Bismarck's eyes the Habsburg Monarchy, though he never liked or respected it much, was necessary for Germany and Europe because without it there could be no tolerable way to manage international politics in Southeastern and Eastern Europe and Russo-German relations in general. That Taylor was prejudiced against the Habsburg Monarchy is clear both from his history of it[22] and from various passages in *The Struggle for Mastery* (for example, p. 280). That he should have shown so little comprehension of Austria-Hungary's role and functions in the European system is more remarkable, and derives less from his bias against the Monarchy than from a superficial, purely power-political concept of how that system operated.

On other major developments of the Bismarckian era—the Great Eastern Crisis and its outcome, Bismarck's alliance system, Egypt and Anglo-French colonial quarrels, the Bulgarian crisis, and the origins of Franco-Russian rapprochement—Taylor provides occasional allusions to the balance of power, sometimes conventional, sometimes cryptic,[23] but none specifically indicates the role that the balance had in bringing them about. This pattern slowly changes, however. From 1890 on, initially gradually and then more decisively after 1905, the story of the European balance of power increasingly takes center stage—not because it changes, or because Taylor explains more precisely how the balance of power affects events and developments and they affect it, but because for the first time since Napoleon the balance of power itself comes under attack. Taylor announces it in one of his advance notices of the story to come, when, in discussing the vistas of European peace opened up by the late Bismarckian era through capitalist expansion, industrialization, and overseas imperialism, he remarks:

---

22   A. J. P. Taylor, *The Habsburg Monarchy, 1809–1918* (London, 1948).

23   An example is the remark Taylor makes about Bismarck's elaborate tangle of balanced antagonisms that emerged from the crisis-ridden year of 1887: "The balance which Bismarck had created at the beginning of 1888 was a curious one" (325). Here "balance" would seem to mean any alignment of the powers or pattern of relations between them, however strange or artificial, that does not constitute empire or hegemony.

The days of European upheaval were over; they would not come again until one of the Powers felt itself strong enough to challenge the balance which had been established at the Congress of Berlin.

That Power could only be Germany . . . The new Germany was conscious only of its strength; it saw no dangers, recognized no obstacles. German explorers, scientists, and capitalists spread over the world. Germans were everywhere—in the Balkans, in Morocco, in central Africa, in China; and where they were not, they wished to be. So long as William I lived, Bismarck could keep a hold on the reins. His system was doomed, once an emperor representative of the new Germany was on the throne. Bismarck in office had been to the Great Powers a guarantee of peace, even though a peace organized by Germany. Now the Powers had to seek other guarantees, and ultimately guarantees against Germany itself.[24]

This statement only represents an initial blast of the trumpet. Most of the events and developments of the post-Bismarck era up to 1905 are discussed without more precise reference to the balance of power and its role than before. With the Moroccan Crisis in 1905, however, we get a clear statement of how the struggle over the balance determined the course of history:

In 1905 there took place a revolution in European affairs. This was caused neither by [Théophile] Delcassé [the French foreign minister] nor by British statesmen fearful of isolation. It was caused solely by German initiative. The Germans were not in any danger . . . Though they still talked of security, this preoccupation was fraudulent; their real object, not formulated even in their own minds, was to establish peacefully their predominance over the Continent and thus be free to challenge the British empire overseas . . . Russia had ceased to exist as a Great Power; and the Germans had an opportunity without parallel to change the European Balance in their favor.[25]

As a result of the Germans' actions in the first Moroccan Crisis "when they butted into Morocco," threatening the independence

---

24   Taylor, *Struggle for Mastery*, 324.
25   Ibid., 427.

of France, the British were forced to react in defense of the balance:[26]

> Once the British envisaged entering a continental war, however remotely, they were bound to treat the independence of France, not the future of Morocco, as the determining factor. The European Balance of Power, which had been ignored for forty years, again dominated British foreign policy; and henceforth every German move was interpreted as a bid for continental hegemony . . . A vital change of emphasis followed . . . In [the marquess of] Salisbury's time, Great Britain made arrangements with European Powers in order to defend her empire; now she made concessions outside Europe in order to strengthen the Balance of Power.[27]

It would take too long, and require too tedious a rehashing of well-known stories and old controversies, to trace how Taylor crafts everything between the first Moroccan Crisis and the outbreak of the First World War—the Algeciras conference, the Anglo-German naval race, the evolution of the Anglo-French entente, the Bosnian Crisis, the second Moroccan Crisis, the Balkan League, the Tripolitanian war, the Balkan wars, the Liman von Sanders affair, and of course the July Crisis launched by Austria-Hungary at Germany's urging—into this mold of a persistent German bid for continental hegemony and world power, and a conscious British, and increasingly conscious French and Russian, effort to defend the balance of power by checking Germany. The only important point here is that Taylor leaves no doubt in every case as to who was defending and who was attempting to overthrow the balance. Speaking, for example, of the Russo-French efforts in the spring of 1914 to bring all the Balkan states including Romania, Bulgaria, and even the Ottoman Empire into a Balkan League under Russian leadership and protection and aligned against Austria-Hungary, he writes:

> His [the Russian foreign minister Sergei D. Sazonov's] purpose was encirclement [of Austria-Hungary], not aggression, so far as

---

26   Ibid., 428.
27   Ibid., 438.

the Balkans were concerned; or, to use a more respectable modern term, it was containment. Exactly the same was true of Great Britain in the west. No Power of the Triple Entente wanted a European upheaval; all three would have liked to turn their backs on Europe and to pursue their imperial expansion in Asia and Africa. Germany, on the other hand, had come to feel that she could expand her overseas empire only after she had destroyed the European Balance of Power; and Austria-Hungary wanted a Balkan War in order to survive at all.[28]

As for the war, there is equally no doubt what caused it: "It is futile to discuss whether the great navy, the Bagdad railway, or the bid for continental supremacy was the decisive factor in German policy. But the bid for continental supremacy was certainly decisive in bringing on the European war."[29]

In sum:

> As to the Balance of Power, it would be truer to say that the war was caused by its breakdown rather than by its existence. There had been a real European Balance in the first decades of the Franco-Russian alliance; and peace had followed from it. The Balance broke down when Russia was weakened by the war with Japan; and Germany got in the habit of trying to get her way by threats. This ended with the Agadir crisis. Russia began to recover her strength, France her nerve. Both insisted on being treated as equals, as they had been in Bismarck's time. The Germans resented this and resolved to end it by war, if they could end it no other way. They feared that the Balance was being re-created. Their fears were exaggerated . . . In fact, peace must have brought Germany the mastery of Europe within a few years. This was prevented by the habit of her diplomacy and, still more, by the mental outlook of her people. They had trained themselves psychologically for aggression.[30]

The reason for quoting these passages is not to dispute Taylor's interpretation of the origins of the First World War (though I

---

28 Ibid., 518.
29 Ibid., 519–20.
30 Ibid., 528.

do), but to illustrate how the balance of power figures in it. Here it occupies center stage, as it never really did before 1905 or at least 1890. But its role in international politics and the international system is exactly the same as earlier: passive rather than active, the object rather than the subject of policy, affected and molded by actions and events rather than causing or influencing them.

The story of European international history as the story of the workings of the European balance of power implicitly promised by Taylor thus reduces to something very simple. There was a balance of power in the nineteenth century, consisting of five great powers more or less equal in power and competing with one another. As long as some sort of balance among them persisted, no matter what shifts or changes occurred, the system persisted. But when one power decided to overthrow the balance, the system was destroyed, even though others tried to defend it. The scheme is circular and empty. "System" and "balance" are co-extensive and synonymous, and neither signifies anything concrete or explains anything that happened. The "balance of power" never caused or influenced anything; it merely existed for a long time and then was destroyed. In short, Taylor does operate with a concept of an international system, but one that is superficial, crude, and above all otiose.

The reply to this from a weary and impatient critic might be that, while Taylor perhaps alludes to the balance-of-power idea too loosely, thus giving the impression that it is some sort of agent that accounts for outcomes when his own narrative fails to show any such thing, this is unimportant, a minor fault at most, that only a misplaced literalist reading would take seriously. The balance of power for Taylor is an organizing theme to tie his story together, often a figure of speech, a rhetorical embellishment or literary device for making it more graphic and understandable. He does not really mean that the balance is an entity doing this or that, any more than an economist thinks the stock market is a thinking, active being when he talks of the market hesitating or deciding that interest rates will go up. What Taylor does mean is that the balance idea was important in men's minds and therefore in their actions; that statesmen thought about the balance of power, that governments acted in ways intended in their lights to defend or change or overthrow it, and that this made a great difference in outcomes. In this he is plainly right. The problem with this critique is that, besides taking Taylor's language too literally, its author simply disagrees with the story Taylor tells, and keeps insisting, for reasons unspecified here and best known to himself, that there must be something deeper and more systemic, whatever that means, behind it.

The reply is a plausible one. A possible response would be that language tending to reify concepts such as the balance of power is not harmless, but serves to obfuscate issues and get in the way of useful analysis of causes and instrumentalities in history. One could readily show that both historians and political scientists have frequently thought of the balance of power as a kind of automatic self-adjusting mechanism or a rule that states were bound to follow, and that this can lead to serious misconceptions.[31] There are times when Taylor himself seems to have thought of it as such, despite his ironic remarks about the British tendency to do so. Yet a major part of the reply is doubtless sound. One can indeed separate the story Taylor recounts from the balance-of-power system implied by his language (in fact, the two *are* largely separate and unconnected), without diminishing the value of the book, still remarkably readable after fifty years. Therefore, if this essay's only purpose and contribution were to

---

31   An example: D. C. B. Lieven in his excellent work on *Russia and the Origins of the First World War* (London, 1983) argues that German fears before 1914 of Russia's armaments program and of growing Pan-Slav and anti-German and anti-Austrian sentiment in Russia help explain Germany's decision for war, but do not justify it because the Germans "should have realized both that Russia was still ill-placed to follow Prussia's example [of 1866–71] and that should she attempt to do so the self-regulating mechanism of the Balance of Power would turn against her." Since German fears of Russia centered, just like Russian, French, and British fears of Germany, not mainly on the danger of sudden attack, but on being ultimately dominated by militarily superior foes and thus losing one's great-power independence, and since containing Germany and achieving a margin of military superiority over it in order to prevent this was precisely the shared goal (and the only shared one) of British, French, and Russian policy, and constituted their common definition of a satisfactory balance of power, the suggestion that Germany should have trusted in the self-regulating mechanism of the balance of power to prevent the Triple Entente powers from pursuing the very "balance of power" they were bent on achieving seems almost bizarre.

show that Taylor's balance-of-power system is worth little as an explanatory or heuristic device for understanding or analyzing the course of international politics, the essay would hardly be worth writing or reading, particularly since it must appear to many a gratuitous post-mortem execution written in a spirit of *de mortuis nil nisi malum*. For my part (if allowed a personal observation), if this were all I had to say, I would have persisted in declining to write it, leaving my verdict on Taylor's work the one published some years ago: "a masterly work, though starting from premisses different from my own."[32]

There is another, more constructive, point to this essay. It is that beneath the balance-of-power "system" lying on the surface of Taylor's narrative is another one struggling to get out. Though it is doubtful that Taylor recognized it, and even more doubtful that he would have accepted or endorsed it, this system is implicit in the narrative and strongly suggested by much of what Taylor says. It, unlike the balance-of-power system, has real explanatory and heuristic value, helps explain why things happened as they did, and points the way to discovering further, deeper causes. What follows is an attempt to indicate what this "system" is and tie *The Struggle for Mastery* to it. It goes without saying that this will be a sketch that leaves many questions that could and should be raised about it unanswered.

First of all, a European balance of power did exist throughout the nineteenth century in one precise, limited sense. Five great powers of at least comparable if widely unequal strength and capability coexisted in Europe. (After 1861, with the creation of the kingdom of Italy, one could claim, as Italians did, that there were six great powers. But Italy was never more than a would-be great power whose efforts to achieve genuine great-power status were always futile and frequently counter-productive and faintly absurd.[33]) These powers maintained constant contact and relations with one another, and a prime goal for each, just as important

---

32   P. W. Schroeder, *The Transformation of International Politics, 1763–1848* (Oxford, 1994), 800n.

33   See R. J. B. Bosworth, *Italy: The Least of the Great Powers* (Cambridge, UK, 1979).

as its strategic and military security and closely tied to it, and usually more important than any particular ambitions or acquisitive aims, was to preserve its status as an independent great power. This balance of power was thus important both as a fundamental condition of international politics and as a sort of ideal—as a condition in the sense that, in the absence of any balance, the system would not be international but imperial, and as an ideal because it was widely and plausibly believed that excessive power held by any one power or combination of them could tempt them to threaten the independence of the others, and that a relatively even distribution of power helped to safeguard against domination or aggression and should be maintained.

So far this is standard fare and compatible with Taylor's views. Here begins the divergence, however: this balance of power was a condition and an ideal only in a vague, protean, highly manipulable sense. Almost any combination or distribution of power within the system, so long as it did not represent clear-cut empire or unmistakable domination by one power over all the others, could plausibly be represented as a good balance of power, and many such actually were. Almost any policy or action, however threatening, aggressive, or revolutionary in power-political terms, could claim to be a step towards maintaining or establishing a just balance of power, and almost all such policies and actions were, in fact, so justified. In other words, the idea of balance of power was not in any useful, concrete sense a guide to policy, and could not be, and as an ideal goal it did not extend further than a vague, general, non-binding acceptance of the right of other great powers to continue to exist and to be recognized and treated as such, and perhaps a recognition that it was useful to one's own existence as a great power that this state of affairs continue. No state ever took any particular action or followed any particular policy primarily for the sake of maintaining or defending the balance of power; nor, if any state wished to, would the simple idea of the balance of power give that state any clear direction on just what to do (though it might, and often did, provide them plausible pretexts and justifications for what they wished and chose to do).

Thus, the notion that the balance of power ever was or could be a self-sustaining, self-adjusting mechanism, resulting naturally in a balanced distribution of power among the major states preserving the independence and status of all, is, empirically speaking, nonsense. The very fact that a sort of balance of power within the European great-power system emerged in the eighteenth and nineteenth centuries was the result of long historic evolution, partly accident, partly design. The balance did not produce or sustain itself; preserving it and managing it required special institutions and practices. No matter what neo-realist international relations theorists may say, balancing against growing or threatening power is not a natural or necessary response for either small or great powers in international politics, an unchanging bedrock rule for survival in international politics over the centuries.[34] It is instead, like the nineteenth-century system itself, a product of a particular, time-bound historical development, always contingent and conditioned by circumstances and open to alternatives.

Therefore, if one wants to explain the nineteenth-century European international system with its special durability, stability, and peace (on which Taylor often remarks), the place to look is *outside* the balance of power itself to those ideas, practices, policies, institutions, and mechanisms that actually worked in the nineteenth century to produce stability and peace and thus to preserve the balance of power. The problem and task is not to explain how the balance of power produced peace and stability (which, as earlier argued, Taylor's account proposes but fails to do), but to determine which particular practices, rules, norms, and institutions, or combination of them, actually produced peace and stability within an overall broad and general condition and framework of a shifting balance of power.

There are three likely candidates for the leading role in thus sustaining the nineteenth-century system, each of which did make a substantial contribution to its peace and stability. The first is hegemony, that is, regional hegemonies or spheres of influence enjoyed by various great powers, occasionally exercised exclusively and individually but in most cases shared. There is no contradiction between such spheres of influence and a general balance of power among the major powers in the minimal sense stated above.

---

34   K. N. Waltz, *Theory of International Politics* (New York, 1979); S. M. Walt, *The Origins of Alliances* (Ithaca, NY, 1987).

In fact, exercising some influence over affairs beyond one's own boundaries, particularly in one's immediate neighborhood, was part of the tacitly accepted definition of a great power in the nineteenth century (the other main defining element being the ability to assume the main burden of one's own defense against any enemy); and the mutual recognition and management of great-power spheres of influence was a constant, vital part of minimizing and managing great-power rivalries. In any case, one could readily illustrate the stabilizing role of this particular kind of hegemony from the story Taylor tells, though reconciling it with his understanding of the balance of power might present a problem. British hegemony on the seas and in its overseas colonies contributed generally to peace in Europe. Britain's industrial and commercial leadership also enhanced its ability to preserve peace in Europe. Austro-Prussian joint hegemony in Germany after 1815 preserved peace between them and in Germany for almost fifty years; Austrian hegemony did so in Italy for over thirty despite the challenges from France and revolutionary movements. Russian hegemony in Eastern Europe made it possible for Russia to preserve peace between Austria and Prussia in 1849–50 (Taylor calls this preserving the German balance). Germany's labile half-hegemony (to use Andreas Hillgruber's phrase[35]) in Europe after 1871 enabled Bismarck to manage European politics to preserve peace, as Taylor recounts. Other examples are available.

Yet regional hegemony and exclusive or overlapping great-power spheres of influence cannot be the main answer to how peace was preserved under conditions of balance of power. For often these were a prime focus of great-power rivalry; they were subject to breakdown or decay; smaller powers within them grew restive and rebelled, or drew the hegemon or hegemons into their quarrels. In principle, moreover, just as no particular kind of distribution of power itself produces peace and stability, neither does any scheme of hegemonies or spheres of influence; all are at best insufficient enabling conditions, and all can under some circumstances become destabilizing.

Another obvious candidate is the Concert of Europe—the understanding and rules whereby all the great powers as equal

---

35 A. Hillgruber, *Bismarcks Aussenpolitik* (Freiburg, 1972).

members constitute a kind of directory of Europe, settling major international questions, enforcing certain norms, and sanctioning changes in the system together in conference or by normal diplomacy. Though Taylor only occasionally mentions the Concert and does not define or emphasize it, it certainly figures prominently enough in his story. The story of the Crimean War concerns, among other things, the failure of Concert diplomacy either to prevent the war or to control and end it short of military victory. The career of Napoleon III, which Taylor portrays quite fairly and perceptively, can be seen as one long story of Napoleon's launching adventures in defiance of any Concert rules and then trying to invoke the Concert to rescue him. The Great Eastern Crisis is another long story of Concert politics, both in its failure to contain the crisis and the fairly successful effort at the congress of Berlin to resolve it. The London conference of 1912–13 shows the reverse—apparent short-term success, long-term failure. But Concert politics cannot provide the key either, important though they were at particular periods, for the Concert's record in this era is mainly one of failure and ultimate breakdown. The most successful statesmen of this era, Bismarck and Cavour, made their name by defying and wrecking the Concert; the gains they made were never sanctioned by it. The most important movement of the last half of this era, European imperialism in Africa and Asia, went entirely uncontrolled by Concert rules and norms or any other save the survival of the fittest. The one feeble effort to impose some order on the process, the Berlin West Africa conference of 1884–5, had mainly ironic results.[36] And Austria-Hungary's fatal initiative in 1914 represented a rebellion against a Concert that in Habsburg eyes worked to isolate the Monarchy and condemn it to inactivity and slow death. Thus, while the Concert was important, it too cannot be the main factor explaining outcomes.

The best choice is fairly obvious—the pattern of alliances and alignments among the great powers ("alliance" being understood in the common nineteenth-century way to include informal ties for common action—ententes, partnerships, traditional friendships—

---

36   S. Förster et al., eds., *Bismarck, Europe, and Africa: The Berlin Africa Conference, 1884–5 and the Onset of Partition* (New York, 1988).

as well as formal alliances sealed by treaties). Taylor certainly does not neglect these. His whole account centers around European alliances and alignments, which he analyzes for the most part accurately and penetratingly. The problem is that, in line with his general balance-of-power views, Taylor regards alliances and alignments in the conventional way, as weapons of power politics: instruments for security and capability aggregation intended to help powers defend what they have, gain what they want, and secure advantage relative to their rivals. This represents only one side of the purposes and functions of alliances, especially in the nineteenth century. At least as important as their uses as weapons of power are their uses as tools of management; a means of managing crises, preventing conflict, and in general managing the policies of other powers, including especially those of one's ally.[37] While this holds for alliances in every age (one reason being the need when entering an alliance to consider how it might be exploited by one's ally and therefore how to manage its policy), it is particularly true for nineteenth-century Europe. Unlike the eighteenth and earlier centuries, most nineteenth-century alliances, both formal and informal, were designed and used more as alliances of mutual restraint and management than as weapons of power, security, and capability aggregation. This fact more than anything else accounts for the greater stability and the more extensive peace of the nineteenth as compared to earlier centuries.

This sweeping generalization cannot for reasons of space be developed and substantiated here. If I were claiming that Taylor was blind to this consideration, that he simply failed to understand and take account of the differing nature, functions, and results of alliances and thus got his story wrong, then I would of course be obliged here to back up both the generalization about the nature and uses of nineteenth-century alliances and the allegation that Taylor missed it. But the contention here is rather that Taylor *was* aware of the difference between alliances as weapons of power and as tools of management, though he never

---

37   See P. W. Schroeder, "Alliances, 1815–1945: Weapons of Power and Tools of Management," in K. Knorr, ed., *Historical Problems of National Security* (Lawrence, KS, 1976), 247–86.

makes that distinction explicit or draws out its implications; that the distinction is implicit in most of the story Taylor recounts, though obscured by the balance-of-power rhetoric he employs; and that here, rather than in the simple notion of balance of power, lies the real international system in Taylor's narrative. I contend, in other words, that the interplay between alliances for restraint and alliances for gain, the ways in which the two purposes can compete for supremacy within the same alliance or that alliances formed mainly for one purpose can turn out to be used primarily for the other, and the shifts between the one kind and the other as the dominant form and function of alliances over the whole system are not merely detectable as a constant undertone in Taylor's narrative, but that this distinction and these themes repeatedly help to explain the outcomes that his ritual references to the balance of power only pretend to explain, or at least they indicate where a deeper explanation is to be found.

In short, this is an argument that Taylor's real international system, whether he knew it or not, centers around the interplay between alliances for purposes of competitive and acquisitive power politics and alliances for political management and restraint. Still further, I argue that the real story he tells is not how the European system proved stable and provided peace so long as the balance of power was maintained, and broke down when it was challenged and overthrown. It is rather how the European system proved stable and provided peace when the alliances of restraint and management were dominant, and that the periods of instability, major change, conflict, and ultimate breakdown were those where alliances of restraint and management broke down or were abandoned and alliances for power predominated. This contention can at least be illustrated if not proved here.

A preliminary point: there is no contradiction between believing, first, that there was a balance of power within the nineteenth-century European states system and believing, second, that the international system was sustained primarily by alliances of restraint and management. In fact, the former logically implies the latter. The bedrock presupposition of a balance of power is that no one power be strong enough to defy all the others or force them to do its bidding. This means that even the strongest power, if it wants to achieve anything important within the system, must work with a partner or partners, and if that partnership is to be durable, and particularly if its general aim is to preserve peace and stability, it must be one of mutual restraint. The second principle, however, does rule out two notions often connected with the balance of power. The first is that a balance-of-power system can work automatically or be self-adjusting. As noted earlier, that idea, common among nineteenth-century Britons, is an illusion, and Taylor seems at least at times to recognize this. The other wrong notion is that a balance of power works and is sustained primarily through the deliberate, overt use of countervailing power, that is, by deterrence, confronting either excessive power or a threat of aggression with sufficient deterrent power. If the system is to remain stable, that kind of balancing technique has to be a last resort or latent possibility generally held in reserve. Overt threats or displays of power as deterrents, even where apparently successful, are inherently destabilizing in many ways.[38] One major argument in favor of alliances of restraint is the insight, common to many conservative nineteenth-century statesmen, that the best and safest way to curb a potential hegemon or aggressor is, wherever possible, to do what Prince Metternich and others referred to as "grouping," that is, to confine the potentially dangerous power within a group in a formal or informal alliance of restraint and thereby induce it to conform to group norms. This is, of course, the essential idea behind the European Concert.

This merely says, to be sure, that this idea does not contradict the general balance-of-power view Taylor espouses. It is harder to show that this notion is actually implicit in his account, is in a general way consistent with it, and offers a better explanation of many of the outcomes Taylor attributes simply to the balance of power. The claim, however, can be illustrated if not demonstrated here, first in a broad general way. The story of European great-power alignments Taylor tells is not really one of constant kaleidoscopic shifts within a balance-of-power framework, but of changes within two main alliance systems which persisted in

---

38   See R. Jervis, J. Gross Stein, and R. N. Lebow, *Psychology and Deterrence* (Baltimore, 1985).

different forms over the century—the liberal alliance between Britain and France, with some other states (Italy, Spain, Portugal) at times associated with it, and the conservative eastern alliance of Prussia (later Germany), Austria (later Austria-Hungary), and Russia with their satellites. Most of the time these two alliance groupings, especially the latter, functioned until 1890 mainly as alliances of management and restraint. The great change Taylor describes as setting in around 1890 and accelerating from 1905 can be summed up as a shift both in alliance alignments and in their dominant purposes and functions. This shift was manifested principally in, first, the breakdown of the conservative eastern alliance into direct German-Russian and Austro-Hungarian-Russian rivalry; second, the evolution of the Dual and Triple Alliances, originally alliances of restraint by which Bismarck managed Austrian and Italian policy and compelled them to be allies even though they were rivals, into alliances which on the one hand encouraged Italian adventures and on the other, according to Taylor, became an instrument for Germany's bid for continental supremacy; third, a similar evolution in the Franco-Russian Alliance which, though always primarily a security instrument, changed from a purely defensive pact restraining each partner from dangerous moves in Europe to one which tied the two together through thick and thin; fourth, the evolution of the Anglo-French entente from (according to Taylor) a purely colonial arrangement for settling extra-European affairs into a quasi-alliance with major European power-political implications; and fifth, the replacement of Anglo-Russian world rivalry by a new entente for purposes of mutual management and restraint of their respective imperial possessions and programs, freeing Russia for greater activity in Europe, especially the Balkans. In short, the whole broad story can be conceived far better in terms of shifts in the nature and functions of alliances and alignments than in terms of the maintenance or destruction of the balance of power.

The same holds for the story's individual chapters. When Taylor speaks of Russia's intervening between Austria and Prussia in 1849–50 to preserve the German balance, he in fact portrays how the leader of a conservative alliance of restraint (the Holy Alliance) acted to manage both of the other partners within the alliance and keep it intact. The story of the origins and diplomacy of the Crimean War is one of how an informal alliance between England and France intended originally to prevent war by restraining and managing both rival powers, Russia directly and France indirectly, was turned partly by accident and partly by design into a formal alliance designed for power politics and war, used to defeat Russia and throw it back and to gain France new power and freedom in Europe. The Crimean War is equally a story of the breakdown of the Holy Alliance as a pact for mutual management and restraint; of Austria's unsuccessful attempt to create a new restraining alliance with Britain and France that would at once check Russia and enable Austria to manage its new partners, especially France; and finally of a successful Prusso-German effort to hold Austria back through their common alliance. Romania's unification up to 1858 illustrates that the Anglo-French alliance of restraint still worked; the unification of Italy shows what could happen when it broke down, liberating Napoleon for adventure, and when Britain tried to restrain Napoleon without restraining Cavour. The Italian war of 1859 had its specific origins in two failures: Austria's inability to reach a conservative restraining alliance with France, so that using force against Sardinia-Piedmont seemed the only alternative, and the failure of Britain and Prussia to restrain the other powers, especially Austria, by joint mediation. Further Italian unification in 1860 depended wholly, as Taylor makes clear, on whether or not the Holy Alliance would be revived. The further breakdown of the Anglo-French restraining alliance, as Taylor again sees, paved the way for Bismarck's intervention in the Danish-German conflict and ultimately for his further wars of German unification. The key to the decisive Austro-Prussian War of 1866 lies in the Austrian foreign minister Count Rechberg's failed attempt to contain Prussia in an alliance of restraint, which Bismarck succeeded in turning first into an alliance for conquest and then into a trap for Austria and weapon against it.

Even the Franco-Prussian War of 1870, on the surface a head-on clash between two equally aggressive great powers, cannot be explained without recognizing the role of restraining alliances. Ever since 1867, the Austrian foreign minister and chancellor,

Count Beust, had sought an alliance with France that would restrain both France and Prussia in the west and Russia in the east while helping preserve the status quo of 1866 in Germany. Beust's tactic in trying to reach the latter goal was to encourage the south German states to change their offensive alliances with Prussia into purely defensive, restraining ones. This (in my view at least) was the development Bismarck most feared, and which his own reckless gamble in the Hohenzollern candidature and the still more reckless French response prevented.

One need not trace this pattern through the rest of the period Taylor covers; its outlines are plain to see. All Bismarck's alliances from the Three Emperors' League of 1872–3 to the Reinsurance Treaty of 1887 were first and foremost pacts of restraint and management designed principally to enable him to control the policies of his allies. All the serious crises were the results of pacts of restraint breaking down—the Great Eastern and Bulgarian crises arose out of the breakdowns of the Three Emperors' League and the Three Emperors' Alliance, the Egyptian Crisis and Anglo-French alienation out of the breakdown of Dual Control. The most seminal of the pre-war crises, the Bosnian crises of 1908–9, grew directly out of the breakdown of the Austro-Russian restraining partnership in the Balkans that had kept the region on ice since 1897 and (though Taylor fails to see this) the failure (or deliberate frustration) of Austria's attempt to restore that partnership and revive the conservative Three Emperors' League through a deal with Russia. What temporarily postponed the war in 1912–13 was the fact that Germany genuinely used its alliance with Austria-Hungary to hold the latter back, and that Britain at least pretended to hold back Russia. What pushed the war forward was France's unconditional support for Russia's drive to isolate Austria-Hungary in the Balkans, where formerly France had restrained Russia, and what set it off was Austria-Hungary's despairing determination to break out of isolation by turning the Dual Alliance, in which until now it had usually been a restraining partner, into an offensive weapon.

I do not claim that Taylor would agree with all of this; obviously, he would violently reject parts of it. But I do claim that this overall scheme is implicit in his narrative and in much of the analysis found in that narrative. Time and again he makes clear that the crucial question was whether a conservative (in my terms restraining) alliance would be revived or not, or which kind of alliance for which kind of purposes various powers would choose. Consider his remarks on Napoleon III, Britain, and Russia after the peace of Paris in 1856:

> Napoleon III had accomplished something beyond the reach of Napoleon I: he had achieved alliance with Great Britain. But it had been accomplished at the price of abandoning Napoleonic designs in Europe; he had failed to extend the war from the Near East to Italy and the Rhine. Napoleon III was aware of his failure; and he had thought too of a solution. While retaining the British alliance, he would escape from its control by building an alliance with Russia.[39]

This is the scheme of restraining versus power-political alliances in everything but name. Taylor goes on to describe the mutual deception involved in the Franco-Russian courtship as follows:

> Besides, the project of alliance between France and Russia rested on pretense towards each other. Napoleon expected that the Russians would treat their defeat in the Near East as permanent and yet would acquiesce in his overthrowing the *status quo* in western Europe; the Russians hoped that Napoleon would remain conservative in western Europe and would yet acquiesce in their destroying the peace settlement in the Near East.[40]

This is a perceptive description of how states can try to pursue both aggressive and conservative-managerial purposes at the same time within the same alliance.

This scheme is not proposed as the secret to the whole nineteenth-century system, the "open sesame" that answers all questions. I would contend, however, that it works much better than "balance of power" as a concept useful for integrating the *forces profondes* of international society into the analysis of

---

39 Taylor, *Struggle for Mastery*, 89–90.
40 Ibid., 90.

international politics. In fact, this scheme compels us to do so—
to consider how such developments as demographic change,
economic change, industrialization and urbanization, the rise of
mass politics, the advance of liberalism, secularism, and democracy, and the emergence of different kinds of nationalism are
connected with this interplay between alliances of restraint and
alliances for power, and to what extent they explain the rise and
fall of each. I would also contend that it is a better scheme for
integrating some elements of international politics neglected in
Taylor's account into the story. Some examples: the German
Confederation, which he almost entirely ignores because it was
not much of a factor in the European great-power balance, was
an important component of the alliances of restraint and management governing Central Europe through the first half of the
century. Taylor consciously downplays the expansionist movement of New Imperialism because it was seldom in his view a
crucial factor in the power relationships among the great powers.
Perhaps not; yet hardly anything was more decisive in giving a
new tone to European politics and imbuing it with a new all-out
competitive ethos, and this had a tremendous impact on the rise
of alliances for power and the decline of alliances of restraint.

Nor is there very much in Taylor's interpretations (even those
with which I disagree) that would have to be changed if this
scheme were highlighted. The anti-German stance, for example,
could stay. There is no reason in principle why Germany's growth
in power and its supposedly aggressive behavior and aims could
not be the main reason for the shift in the dominant nature and
purposes of alliances, as Taylor makes it the cause of the breakdown of the balance of power. One thing, however, would have
to change if this system were recognized as valid; indeed, it is
incompatible even with the balance-of-power views Taylor
espouses. This is the picture he gives of the role and functions of
Austria in the nineteenth-century system. The problem is not that
he regularly gives a distorted and unfair picture of Austrian
policy, most of all in 1908–14, though in my view this is the case.
It is rather that Taylor, as earlier mentioned, has no apparent
concept of what Austria's existence as a great power meant to the
system, what it was doing simply by being where it was and doing
what it had to do to remain a great power. He seems not to

have understood that Austria, though undeniably a great power in status and systemic functions, had never been a great power in ordinary power-political terms and could never be one. Its exposed geopolitical position, surrounded by powerful opponents and other security threats, plus its multinational composition and decentralized governmental structure, meant that, though a great power in size, population, and resources, it never could meet all the likely threats against it mainly from its own resources. Nor was it supposed to. The functions it was given in the Vienna system founded in 1815 were primarily defensive—to defend itself, Germany, Italy, and Southeastern Europe against France and revolution with the aid of conservative partners. It was not expected to rest its existence primarily on force like a normal great power and did not normally act as one, and when out of folly or desperation it tried to act simply as one, as in 1859 and 1914, the disastrous effects for itself and the system became apparent.

Taylor does not even seem to understand what its disappearance would mean for Europe and the international system. Twice he specifically discusses the question of Austria's possible demise or partition, the first in connection with Napoleon III's and Prince Jerome's plans for the partition of Austria with the aid of Russia and Sardinia, the second in conjunction with Delcassé's plans in 1899 to mobilize the Franco-Russian Alliance and join with Italy in controlling the division of spoils following the break-up of the Monarchy to prevent Germany from gaining an outlet to the Mediterranean at Trieste.[41] In neither case does he say a word about the potential effects of this threatened disappearance of Austria on the European balance. His account of the origins of the war makes Germany's alleged threat to the independence of France as a great power the heart of Germany's bid to destroy the balance of power. But Russia's attempt from 1909 on, aided by France after 1912, to construct a Balkan League under its leadership intended to paralyze Austria (in Taylor's own words, to encircle it) and cut it off from its one remaining zone of great-power influence, the western Balkans, is portrayed in contrast as a peaceful, defensive move against Austro-German

---

41   Ibid., 105, 385.

aggression that did not threaten Austria or the balance in the least.[42] Clearly, so far as Taylor is concerned, it made no essential difference to the European system by 1914 whether Austria-Hungary survived or disappeared. So long as it did not disturb the peace itself, or become an instrument of German expansion, the European system would continue to function perfectly well.

If the real European system required alliances of restraint and management (and where more than in Eastern and Southeastern Europe?) that view is obviously untenable. Austria, the great power relatively the weakest and most vulnerable in terms of strategic overcommitment, had always naturally depended most upon alliances of restraint and management and had most consistently practiced them, so that one simply cannot conceive of the actual history of European peace in the nineteenth-century without the conservative alliances to which Austria was vital—the Holy Alliance, the Austro-Prussian partnership, Austrian leadership of the German Confederation, the Three Emperors' League and Alliance, the Triple Alliance, the Russo-Austrian entente in the Balkans, and more. This indifference to Austria's fate and role by 1914 is not peculiar to Taylor. In fact, it is here, rather than on more publicized issues such as his controversial views on the origins of the Second World War, that the Taylor legacy remains most apparent, and is still encountered in recent historiography.[43]

The strangest aspect of this indifference is that it also clashes with any conventional balance-of-power interpretation of international politics such as Taylor's own. One area of universal

---

42   Taylor's account, incidentally, contains clearly incorrect statements on important points. For instance, he claims that Russia only wanted Serbia and Romania as neutral buffer states between it and Austria-Hungary. The facts are that Serbia had been Russia's ally since 1912, that Russia and France were working hard to win Romania over to their alliance, and that Bulgaria and the Ottoman Empire were also being wooed to join the anti-Austrian coalition.

43   E.g., N. Ferguson's *The Pity of War* (London, 1999) has made a considerable stir by challenging prevailing views (including Taylor's) on British prewar policy and on German responsibility for the First World War and by arguing that a German victory would have been better than the actual outcome. Virtually every critic has fastened on these arguments, mainly denouncing them and reaffirming the standard views about Germany. Few noticed that Ferguson largely ignores Austria-Hungary in his account and that what he does write closely follows Taylor.

agreement in balance-of-power thought is that a balance is supposed to protect the independent existence of, if not all actors,
at least all essential ones, and no one, then or now, can make a
case that Austria-Hungary was not an essential member of the
nineteenth-century system. This is not a question of Austria-
Hungary's character as a state or of the wisdom or folly of its
policy; it is simply a question of where it was and what it did by
being there, and what was bound to happen if it disappeared.
Anyone who contends that the nineteenth-century European
international system could and would have continued to function
reasonably well if Austria-Hungary had ceased to be a great
power or to exist, must explain how an ongoing bridge game can
continue if one partner is eliminated and a large number of cards
are removed from the deck and replaced by different ones. Anyone
who suggests that Germany and Russia could have lived in amicable harmony without Austria-Hungary being where it was,
provided only that Germany not be aggressive, has to explain
how one can sit durably and comfortably on a two-legged stool.
In apparently failing even to ask these questions, much less
answer them, Taylor proved that, in this respect at least, his
concept of the nineteenth-century international system and how
it worked was sadly deficient.

PART IV

9

World War I and the Vienna System:
The Last Eighteenth-Century War
and the First Modern Peace

This paper lays out my main ideas and arguments for a book reinterpreting the history of international politics and the international system over two centuries (1689–1919). It focuses on two seminal events of this era: World War I (1914–19) and the Vienna system, the peace settlement reached at the Vienna Congress (1814–15) ending the Napoleonic Wars and promoting general peace till the early 1850s. By comparing their respective causes, courses and consequences I hope to build a plausible case for a different interpretation of their roles in the overall development of the European/world international system.

As every historian knows, this is an extremely ambitious aim. Both eras, especially World War I, have been intensively studied and fought over in great detail from almost every conceivable angle. I cannot claim to bring new facts or evidence to bear on them. Nonetheless, I think something different and useful can still be gained particularly by comparing and contrasting them on their roles and impact in three distinct historical master narratives. The first two narratives are obvious, familiar, and highly developed: the general history of society, and the history of international politics in the conventional sense (interstate relations, diplomacy, foreign policy, strategy and security, peace and war, international commerce, international organizations and institutions, etc.). The third narrative specifically concerns the development and evolution of the international system since the late fifteenth century. No one questions that the first two narratives are important for history in general, and that the second is a history of change and development over time, like all history—though here too I will propose some changes in perspective and interpretation. The third narrative, the long history of the development of the international system, I believe, though widely discussed and debated, remains too little recognized and too often underrated and misunderstood.

The meanings and importance we attach to the Vienna Congress and World War I depend to a considerable degree on the context and narrative within which they are placed. Any general history of society, no matter how current and global its perspective, recognizes World War I as a major turning point, while the Vienna system in this context is more an episode or footnote. Both represent important chapters in the general history of European and global international politics in the early-modern and modern eras, but World War I must again be seen as far more significant in terms of the forces and causes leading to it, its immediate impact and results, and its long-range consequences. Within the third historical narrative and context, however, the development and evolution of the European/world international system, I contend that the Vienna system is as significant as World War I in explaining in systemic terms what really happened in international politics over the whole long nineteenth century (1787–1919), and in indicating the kind of history this is—a history not cyclical and characterized by an unchanging structure of competition for strategic security and advantage, but directional, showing change, evolution, and dialectical progress and regress, governed in systemic terms both by an ongoing competition for strategic advantage and a changing and evolving search for durable order.

The book will close with reflections on why this insight into the nature and history of the international system is in my view important and instructive in today's world situation. To put the argument in drastically oversimplified and overstated form: if you want to understand the politics that ultimately helps make wars occur and international systems break down, study World War I. If you want to understand better how a durable system of general relative peace and order can emerge, survive, and solve major problems for a considerable time, examine the Vienna system. The book will conclude with thoughts on why the American government and people especially need to learn this lesson and gain these insights, and why America's history, political culture, and institutions are not ideally suited to equip and dispose them to do so.

A minor editorial note: Material in this outline that is enclosed in square brackets involves subject matter I consider relevant to the theme being discussed, but that could well be omitted or consigned to a footnote or appendix in the book.

The book's goals, intended audiences, and the problems they present

One major challenge for me is that the main argument just outlined and the connected ones, oversimplified and overstated here for purposes of brevity and clarity, obviously need to be developed, nuanced, and backed with sufficient evidence, argument, and attention to other divergent views for them to be worth being considered by scholars in the field, mainly historians and political scientists. In addition, the ideas and arguments offered here are still to some extent provisional; I will doubtless have to revise them in the light of further reading on my part and critiques and suggestions I am seeking from others. That minimal scholarly goal in itself presents a huge challenge given the size, complexity, and controversial nature of the subject.

The challenge is made worse by a conflict between this scholarly goal and another important one: to keep the book simple, clear and brief enough to be accessible and appealing to a wider audience of educated lay readers, serving as a high-level popularization of a difficult, complicated, and controversial subject and story. This task of combination and compromise, obviously difficult at best, must impose limits, first of all on what material the book can and must include and exclude. It can attempt to present a different interpretation of the whole story and back it up in some fashion, but cannot tell the story in detail or explain it by a detached, balanced narrative. For that reason alone its assertions and judgments may often appear to be biased and apodictic or dogmatic. It will have to omit or merely summarize far more facts and material relevant to the theme than it can include, and not claim to present new research, facts or material. It may therefore read (as this outline surely will) more like a lawyer's brief or a prosecuting attorney's argument before a grand jury than a supposedly objective work of history.

Given these risks and limitations, why try for both aims and target audiences at once? Why not reach out to the desired wider audience with a simplified thesis and exposition without worrying about what scholars in the field may think, or write the book mainly for scholars and hope that its ideas may filter down to the broader public? Both approaches are certainly valid; many good examples of both can be found. Nonetheless, the attempt to combine them, awkward though the combination may be, seems to me necessary both for practical reasons and on principle. I have no reason or desire to write this book mainly in order to try to convert other scholars to my views, but do consider it important to show that it rests on serious scholarship and contains ideas and arguments worth consideration. On this score scholars are legitimate gatekeepers; anyone aspiring to address the wider audience within the gates ought to try to pass this test, even if he feels as I do that professional scholars ought not be the sole judges of what the wider public should know and think about in this arena. History is too important to be left solely to historians. In any case, my main reason and motive for trying to write the book at this late stage in my life is not the usual academic one. It derives instead from a conviction that certain things on this subject need saying, above all to a wider public and especially in America. The reasons, I hope, will become clearer in the course of this outline, and be summed up in the conclusion.

The basic thesis

The title is intentionally provocative. Our overwhelming impression about World War I is that it was a modern, forward-pointing war—the first great modern, industrialized, mechanized, mass, total war. By common consent (with which I agree) it grew out of worldwide movements, changes, and forces in the late nineteenth- and early twentieth-century world that are still alive today, that for better or worse shaped and transformed that world and connect World War I to our present one. To call World War I an eighteenth-century war and to link its causes, course, and effects to a bygone, profoundly different era therefore seems clearly anachronistic.

Something like the reverse could be said about the Vienna system, the European international system and settlement that, conceived in 1813–14 during the last of the Revolutionary-Napoleonic Wars and born and baptized at the Vienna Congress in 1814–15, lived and worked through adolescence, maturity, and old age into the mid-1850s. Despite major shifts in some of the recent scholarship, the historical consensus on the Vienna system remains that it pointed backward, was a product of an earlier eighteenth-century era of which it remained a part and which it at least partly restored. Though its success in achieving and maintaining international peace and stability is now widely acknowledged, and negative judgments about its repressive character and effects have at least been modified, for most observers it still remains an old-fashioned peace—one imposed from above by authoritarian governments exhausted by war, fearful of revolution and change, and concerned mainly with reviving and preserving the political, social, cultural, religious, and economic order of a bygone era.

Overall, as I noted earlier, in terms of the general evolution of European and world history and society, I agree. World War I was modern and forward-pointing in many ways, for better and worse, and the Vienna system was not. But in regard to the questions most important for international history, the evolution of European international politics and the European international system, I argue that the reverse is mainly true. The dominant practice and style of European/world politics during the latter half of the nineteenth century and the first quarter of the twentieth represented a return to a pattern and system of international politics and the international system characteristic of the later eighteenth century. This perspective and insight, I contend, justifies terming World War I the last eighteenth-century war, not simply for giving it a new tag and different description, but for explaining its causes, character, and consequences in a different systemic context and fashion. In similar fashion the Vienna system constituted an advance or breakthrough toward a new, changed brand of international politics and international system, so that even though it was created under early nineteenth-century conditions by early nineteenth-century states and leaders, it represented the first forward-looking, modern peace settlement.

The character of eighteenth-century international politics, war, and peace

The case begins with a brief examination of eighteenth-century international politics, emphasizing two broad characteristics in it. First, eighteenth-century international politics was highly bellicist. The term "bellicist" (apparently not yet standard in English but commonly used in French and German) does not mean bellicose—aggressive, warlike, spoiling for a fight. The major European state actors in this era were not especially bellicose—certainly not so in comparison to previous centuries. "Bellicist" instead means "war-prone." It means in this instance that European international politics in the eighteenth century was inherently prone to war, inclined toward war, that it constantly spawned conflicts and crises difficult to settle peacefully and led to wars that often grew out of control and proved hard to end. The evidence for this assertion seems abundantly clear to me and other scholars today (more on that later). A second related point, however, is less clear and needs more argument and proof—that this bellicist character of eighteenth-century international politics was not primarily a result of the general nature of Europe's society, politics, economics, and culture in that particular era and of the competitive forces and conflicts engendered in international politics by these factors, but derived mainly from its own particular structure and character, the nature of the eighteenth-century system itself.

Here I must define key terms and concepts. By "system" and "structure" I mean the principles, assumptions, rules, norms, and reigning practices governing the game of international politics in particular eras and times, and I will try to adhere to this definition consistently throughout the book. One reason for this is practical—to clarify these terms and concepts and keep them from becoming otiose through careless and indiscriminate use, as has happened and still happens with other important terms such as "balance of power" and "reason of state." Another reason is even more important for this book in particular—my conviction, mentioned earlier, that the history of international politics should not be conceived primarily in cyclical terms as one simply of events, the history of foreign policy, the rise and fall of great powers, the story of how wars and peace settlements come and go, or as the varied results of some unchanging underlying structure, the operation of the balance of power or some other putative unifying mechanism or force. It needs to be seen and recognized first and foremost as like the rest of history—a linear, directional story of change, development, evolution, and even progress within the international system. In this connection I will stress the importance of system and systemic effects in foreign policy decision-making and outcomes and changes in outlook and collective mentalities among actors as important elements within a particular international system and often decisive factors in change. (Cf. Robert Jervis's *System Effects*, 1997).

The view that the eighteenth century was a highly war-prone era is still a bit controversial; it clashes with an older picture of it as relatively peaceful. According to it, eighteenth-century wars were relatively small, short, more limited, more rationally calculated, and better controlled politically than heretofore. They supposedly aimed at more limited goals and ends and were accompanied by diplomatic negotiations leading to compromise or indecisive peace settlements, with the result that despite frequent wars an overall working balance of power was preserved. A linked thesis sees the French Revolution with its revolutionary passions and mass popular armies as breaking in on this system like a snowstorm in springtime, bringing its downfall.

Unquestionably eighteenth-century international politics was on balance more peaceful and controlled than in the seventeenth or sixteenth century, which were both extraordinarily violent, bellicose, and chaotic centuries (see Geoffrey Parker and others). That fact, however, did not at all make international politics in the long eighteenth century (1689–1815) peaceful or stable. A look at the incidence of wars suffices to show this. Four long general systemic wars (meaning conflicts involving all or most of the European Great Powers, that either drastically altered the structure of politics or threatened to do so) were waged in 1689–97, 1702–13, 1740–8, and 1756–63. Each of these in a certain sense was a world war, fought both on the European continent and in important theaters of the wider non-European world. Every one entailed major changes in both arenas; none was followed by durable peace (the period after the Peace of Utrecht in 1713 representing a partial exception); and all led up finally to the greatest systemic war since the Thirty Years War in 1618–48: the French-Revolutionary-Napoleonic Wars from 1787 to 1815. These were not the only major eighteenth-century wars; other long conflicts had profound systemic effects. The War of the American Revolution (1775–83) almost became a general systemic war and produced major changes in the world system. The Great Northern War (1702–21) destroyed the Swedish empire in the Baltic and Northern Europe and made Russia a major European power. Austro-Ottoman wars between 1689 and 1739 did the same for the Habsburg Monarchy and started the Ottoman Empire's long slide toward retreat and decline. The Russo-Turkish War in 1768–74 brought Russia its greatest territorial gains in Europe ever. Even smaller wars made important changes in the system or represented attempts to do so. The Polish Succession War of 1733–5 pretty well settled Poland's fate as a once-independent major power; the Prusso-Austrian War of the Bavarian Succession in 1778–9, almost bloodless and now virtually forgotten, was started by Prussia to bring Austria down as a major power and replace the Habsburg dynasty as Holy Roman Emperors and leaders of Germany with the Hohenzollerns.

Nor were these wars militarily mainly small, limited wars of position, fought for limited goals and easily ended by negotiations and a compromise peace. They were instead mostly long hard struggles fought in serious battles at heavy material and human cost, usually to the point of exhaustion, ending either in a decisive victory for one side that promoted drives for revision or revenge among the losers or by an indecisive truce that everyone expected would be followed soon by the resumption of war.

This is not a general indictment of the eighteenth century as an especially lawless, violent century in international affairs—certainly not in comparison to its fourteenth- to seventeenth-century predecessors. The eighteenth century as a whole was marked by many major achievements and advances in Europe, some of which altered the conduct of international affairs in important, progressive ways. These include the formation and strengthening of more impersonal, efficient, rational states, the development of better bureaucracies and tax and financial systems, improvements in the recruitment, training, and discipline of armies, advances in weaponry, the development of a more professional diplomatic corps, and better, more permanent diplomatic representation and communication. Wars did become somewhat more humane for civilian populations. In short, real change, evolution, and progress came about even in international politics in the eighteenth century. But this did not make the international system less war-prone, and in some ways probably made it more so. More efficient, rational states with better administrative, tax and financial systems, more productive economies, and larger, better-trained armies were able to fight wars harder and sustain them longer, and mostly did. Eighteenth-century bellicism arose rather from the structure of eighteenth-century politics, from its prevailing rules, practices, norms, and incentives structure. Showing in a little more detail just what this structure was and how it worked will be a task for the book, but this is the basic thesis.

Why this apparently clashes with the view of World War I as an eighteenth-century war

This portrait of the eighteenth century as being bellicist for systemic reasons, however, seems hard to reconcile with the claim that World War I in systemic terms was an eighteenth-century-style war. The differences between the two eras in general societal, intellectual-cultural, socioeconomic, and above all domestic-political conditions and developments in each, the soil out of which international politics supposedly grows and within which it operates, seem too clear and sharp. Despite major changes and progress, Europe at the end of the eighteenth century was by and large still emerging out of the medieval and early modern world into modernity, and more than half of it in territory and population remained mired in the older one. Its overall economy remained overwhelmingly agrarian, and most of its agriculture, especially in the center, east, and south, was of a fairly primitive kind. Commercial capitalism had evolved especially in the Dutch

Republic and England, but only the beginnings of an industrial revolution had emerged anywhere, even in Great Britain. Trade and communications were increasing and improving fairly rapidly, but the vast majority of people still lived local, even isolated lives. The social order was still based on orders and classes and dominantly monarchial-aristocratic. The great majority of Europe's peoples were unfree serfs or small peasants and laborers excluded from any role in the political process. Some states were becoming more rational, impersonal, efficient, and bureaucratic, but many units remained old-fashioned patrimonial and feudal entities, the most important were composite monarchies and empires rather than nation-states, and only a few small city-states and tiny republics could be called free or democratic in any sense. A real widespread revolution was underway at the top in intellectual and cultural life (various forms of enlightenment in religion, philosophy, and science, major movements in literature, music, arts, architecture, and education, considerable development in technology) but most people were still unschooled and both the geographical extent and the societal depth of penetration of educational and cultural development was limited and characterized by a sharp downward slope from northwest Europe toward the east and southeast.

By the time World War I broke out in Europe all this had decisively changed. Without going into details, in all the general societal aspects noted above, while marked regional differences and contrasts remained, Europe as a whole had become a different place—one of a bourgeois world and strong states (Thomas Nipperdey). It had risen to world hegemony and remarkable power and prosperity over a century of general peace and stability in Europe, one in which the international system, moreover, had repeatedly managed to handle crises without major or general war.

This suggests an opposite argument on war-proneness in these two centuries: that general progress in society over the course of the nineteenth century made international politics and the international system, in Europe at least, as war-averse as the eighteenth century had made them war-prone, and that this difference in bellicism derived not from the nature and rules of the prevailing international system in each but from the different wider political, economic, and social systems underlying international politics and the international system in the two cases. According to this view, wars in the eighteenth century arose naturally, almost inevitably, out of the broad political character of the old regime. It was one in which monarchs and narrow aristocratic elites made all the important foreign policy decisions, encountering in most instances and most countries little or no interference or restraint from constitutions, parliaments, political parties, the press, and other domestic pressures. This more or less arbitrary decision-making power accustomed decision-makers to using war to solve their domestic and foreign problems and to enhance their power in various ways—e.g., seizing foreign territory to gain more subjects and revenues—or to defend their rights, avenge wrongs, satisfy their personal honor and ambition or enhance their positions and glory. Thus war in the eighteenth century became or remained the normal default option in international politics. By the time World War I arose, in contrast, major transformations of European society—great economic expansion and the growth of intra-European and global interdependence, the rise of constitutional, representative, and even democratic governments, the development of an active and extensive public sphere, the growth of powerful political parties, widespread literacy, class and ideological conflict, a wider politically aware press and citizenry, and other powerful new influences, restraints, and pressures on governments and their foreign policies—all combined to make war no longer the last resort of kings or the normal option in international politics. Instead they promoted a more rational purpose and structure for the international system in providing at least the possibility of popular participation in foreign policy and control over it, helping make it one in which nation-states, so long as their governments prudently assessed the foreign policy options which the existing balance of power made available to them, could reasonably hope to defend their security and advance their own particular state interests within that balance-of-power framework while avoiding general war. The expansion of international and world commerce and industry and the rise of economic interdependence among European states enhanced this tendency.

This interpretation of the overall course of international politics in the nineteenth century goes along with the standard explanation of why the nineteenth-century international system, apparently successful for a long time in handling international crises and problems, eventually ended in total war. The core answer is overall uneven development. The breakdown occurred fundamentally because certain governments, notably Germany, Austria-Hungary, and by some accounts Russia, supposedly regarded these broad societal, political, economic, and ideological developments in nineteenth- and twentieth-century Europe as threats to their regimes and domestic governance, social order, and internal security, and/or as dangerous changes in the strategic balance of forces, and therefore took actions that turned a particular crisis into an occasion to meet these perceived threats, if necessary by war.

As most will recognize, this is a very bare-boned version of a common, probably still-reigning explanation of the origins of World War I. It means that even before trying to make a positive case based on historical evidence showing World War I as an eighteenth-century war, I face two problems and tasks. The first involves indicating why the apparently sharp contrast in Europe between eighteenth-century international politics, war-prone and war-filled throughout, and that of nineteenth-century Europe, apparently war-averse and outwardly more peaceful *in toto* up to 1914, should not be explained, as it often is, primarily by the differences between the pre-modern political and civil society of eighteenth-century Europe and the more modern, rational development of nineteenth-century Europe generally, and the ways in which these changes influenced governments to play the game of power politics differently in the two centuries. Conversely, I need to show how and why the main cause lay elsewhere.

My answer (here very much oversimplified, but developed somewhat more later in the outline) will be to concede—in fact, emphasize—that the kind of power-political game Europe played pretty consistently throughout the eighteenth century also operated over the latter half of the nineteenth and early twentieth centuries, and that the same general rules, norms, principles, and practices came to dominate international politics. What accounts for the marked difference overall between the two centuries in terms of war-proneness and the incidence of major wars,

however, is a fact often underrated, unappreciated, even sometimes flatly denied. The nineteenth century did not represent one
single era in the long history of international politics and the
international system, but two. The early nineteenth century saw
a sudden major change, a move from one kind of international
system to a distinctly different one. That newer kind, to be sure,
was over time abandoned and ultimately destroyed, but it took a
long time to die. Elements of it hung on even through the gradual
reversion to the old international system, revived this time in the
latter nineteenth- and twentieth-century context of the rise of a
new mass industrialized, globalized world. This great regression
in international politics and the international system, I hold,
ultimately led to an outcome similar to that in the late eighteenth
century, only worse—an even more destructive general war and
more disastrous systemic breakdown. This makes World War I
systemically a last eighteenth-century war.

Even if I succeed in making this broad scenario at least prima
facie plausible, a second serious challenge remains: providing
another narrative concretely explaining the longer-range and
immediate origins and outbreak of World War I in accord with
this proposed overall hypothesis, thereby providing an alternative
to the reigning one.

Differences and similarities between the two eras in international politics

The first challenge, showing that the apparently more peaceful,
controlled character of European international politics in general
over the whole nineteenth century cannot be adequately explained
by Europe's general change and progress in its society, politics,
and culture, is not really difficult. I indicated earlier why the
progress achieved in many aspects of European civilization in the
eighteenth century did not make the European community of
states more inclined to establish stable peace or capable of doing
so, but in important respects reinforced its proneness to war.
Allowing for the inevitable differences, nuances, and qualifications involved, the same argument can be made for the
nineteenth century, in certain respects more easily and convincingly. Nineteenth-century Europe unquestionably changed even

more rapidly than in the eighteenth century and achieved far greater progress toward modernity in many realms, including international affairs. Yet if one compares the course of overall nineteenth-century progress in Europe with the general course of international politics in terms of bellicism and conflict over the whole century, it becomes even more clear here than in the eighteenth century that this general progress did not make Europe become less war-prone, but more so.

Even a superficial overview can illustrate this. If one tried to draw graphic charts depicting the overall course of European change and progress from 1815 to 1914 in various respects and areas (population, wealth, industrial and agricultural production, rate of invention and technological change, advances in science and culture, levels of literacy and general education, life expectancy, volume of trade, speed and volume of travel and communication, construction of roads and railroads, growth of cities and towns, etc.) all the graphs, allowing for periodic and individual and regional variations, would show an overall trend upwards over most of the entire subcontinent, beginning slowly, accelerating in mid-century, and climbing most steeply from about 1890 on— trends different from those in most of the rest of the world except for North America.

If, however, one were to draw a similar graph portraying war-proneness in Europe in the nineteenth-century international system (overall attitudes toward war and military force among governments, elites, and broader publics, willingness to resort to war to solve problems, the incidence of serious crises and threats, the number of outbreaks and the duration and intensity of important wars), the entire pattern would differ dramatically from those depicting general societal progress. Instead of one fairly simple overall pattern of steady and accelerating growth in the same general direction, it would show markedly different shifts in direction and different patterns—in fact, require a different graph—in each of four distinct periods.

The first graph covering 1815–48 would show a period of historically unprecedented general peace. No wars at all broke out between the great powers. Only minor armed conflicts of any kind occurred; most of these were quickly settled by negotiation under international supervision; and the numerous disputes and occasions for conflict that did arise, resembling ones that in previous centuries had repeatedly led to major war, were settled or managed by diplomacy without any war at all.

The second graph, from the 1848 revolutions to the end of the Franco-German War in 1871, would show an abrupt steep rise in bellicism and major conflict. Besides several smaller armed conflicts, five major wars would occur involving all the great powers in one or more of them. The first, the Crimean War (1853–6) was the bloodiest in Europe between 1815 and 1914, and the only reason it failed to escalate into all-out systemic war was that persistent efforts made by Britain and France to pull Austria, Prussia, the German Confederation, and Sweden into their war against Russia narrowly failed. The other four main contests in 1859–71, the so-called wars of Italian and German unification, though more limited in length and military action, were nonetheless major conflicts raising serious threats of wider wars that were only narrowly avoided. The systemic effects of these wars, concrete and subterranean, immediate and long-range, moreover, were even more profound than those arising out of the Crimean War. They drastically changed the territorial and political map of Europe, wrecked the treaty system established in 1815, eliminated many important independent states and units, and significantly altered the ideological and strategic bases of international politics and the international system not only in Europe but also in parts of Asia and the Near and Middle East. Other crises and threats of war also arose in this period that, though apparently successfully handled (e.g., crises over Crete, neutralization of the Black Sea, the Polish Revolt of 1863, Schleswig-Holstein, the independence and union of Romania, and the neutralization of Luxemburg) left behind scars and seeds of future trouble.

The next graph for 1871–90 would start with a brief but deceptive return to general peace. A so-called "War in Sight" crisis in 1875, however, quickly demonstrated that this would be peace of a very different kind. Its basis was a labile German half-hegemony in Europe (Andreas Hillgruber and many others); its manager was Prince Bismarck, the century's most brilliant and effective foreign policy statesman. Having achieved his own maximal goals for Prussia-Germany through the deliberate

destruction of the Vienna system, achieved by consciously adopting Frederick the Great's methods of Realpolitik and war,
Bismarck after 1871 set out to defend these gains and avoid the
two-front war against France and Russia he dreaded by steering
and manipulating the continent through a long succession of
tensions and dangerous crises. One biographer (Lothar Gall)
aptly characterizes his policies as the efforts of a statesman who,
after brilliant success in 1862–71 as a white revolutionary, turned
sorcerer's apprentice in order to control the spirits he had sum-
moned and now could not dismiss. It was a remarkable, almost
heroic juggling act, carried off partly by diverting European
quarrels and energies to imperialist expansion overseas, mainly
by means of ever more elaborate, risky, and fragile diplomatic
expedients. Without Bismarck's devices and pressures Europe
would almost certainly have fallen much earlier into a wider war,
especially during the Great Eastern Crisis and Russo-Turkish war
of 1875–8. By 1890, however, when he fell from power, even his
vast store of diplomatic resources had been exhausted. Unable
any longer to isolate France, appease Russia, or at the last minute
obtain an alliance with Britain, Bismarck was reduced to threatening a preventive war against France as a device to keep Russia
and Austria from coming to blows, or, if that proved impossible,
to eliminate the French danger to Germany first and then turn to
settle things between Russia and Austria. At this same time he
planned anti-constitutional action in Germany to maintain
control against his opponents at home.

During this same period European tensions and rivalry built
up also in other areas and over other issues in Europe, especially
the Balkans, and outside it. European imperialism abroad, after
subsiding somewhat in the Vienna era, had reawakened after 1848,
spurred especially by the Crimean War, but did not become a
major source of European conflict so long as attention was centered on more important continental wars and realignments.
After 1871, however, renewed colonial rivalry blossomed into a
general scramble for Africa and led to serious quarrels there,
along with even more dangerous crises and threats of European
war over the Near and Middle East and Central Asia. By 1890, in
short, Bismarck's efforts to preserve European peace by diverting
European energies and quarrels overseas had also run aground.

The graph for the last era, 1890–1914, would display almost uniformly the most frequent and steep spikes in bellicism and general trajectory of all. One dangerous crisis and threat of general war after another rose concurrently or in succession, over issues and rivalries centered mainly on imperial and world competition from 1890 to 1906, but focused even more narrowly and dangerously thereafter on continental ones that involved all of Europe—west, north, and especially east and south, as well as the adjoining seas.

In sum, any graph trying to trace Europe's war-proneness throughout the nineteenth-century international system would show no resemblance at all to one depicting the remarkable overall gains in Europe's political, social, economic, and cultural development. Starting from a peak of war-proneness and actual conflict in 1812 higher than any reached earlier even in the consistently bellicist previous century, it would drop suddenly in three years to a low level of stable peace never before seen, and remain essentially steady there for the next three decades, marred only by brief minor spurts upward and a gradual rise just before 1848. This would suddenly be followed by an abrupt, broad rise in bellicism leading to major wars over the next two decades. A very brief pause thereafter would give way to another jagged, fairly sharp rise from the mid-1870s to 1890, and the whole graph would end with a still steeper, almost unbroken rise in frequent, dangerous crises, conflicts, and actual wars from 1890 to 1914. Scholars will doubtless disagree on many details and over broad explanations. The overall pattern, however, is too clear to allow any argument that societal change and progress in the nineteenth century can supply the broad explanation of why general war and systemic breakdown were for a long time avoided or postponed.

A natural rejoinder would be, "All right, what does explain this? Your overall trajectory of rising bellicism and increasing difficulty in maintaining general peace from the 1850s on would seem to make World War I the natural, quasi-inevitable outcome of prolonged systemic degeneration. What then delayed the war so long? Was it mere accident or muddling through? Does not the fact that general peace survived in Europe until 1914, if uneasily and perilously, show at least that the reigning competitive balance-of-power system was still working until 1914, and indicate that overall progress in Europe, particularly in economic development, trade, and global interdependence, perhaps helped it work, and was an important part of the answer? Did not these progressive developments plainly raise the costs and risks of war and sharpen the actors' perceptions of them sufficiently to induce the great powers in particular time and again to stop short of the brink and end crises peacefully?"

There is some substance to this argument, especially in showing a connection between economic growth and interdependence and the fear of the costs, dangers, and effects of general war (though in the book I will try to show how this connection was complicated and paradoxical, and could under certain conditions promote war rather than inhibit it—that powerful leaders, groups, and whole countries could easily and rationally become more afraid of this particular kind of "peace" than of the outbreak of war). The argument, moreover, does apparently strengthen the case for seeking the concrete cause of this specific war in particular circumstances and events in 1914. The usual account of the origins of the war provides just this kind of answer in a coherent, plausible narrative form, focused on the July Crisis and on particular decisions taken at that time and in most versions seeing the Austro-German decision in July 1914 to provoke a preventive war with Serbia as the crucial ingredient. It seems thus both to explain the immediate origins of the war and indicate longer-range causes behind the decision—in particular, Germany's drive for world power and position and Austria-Hungary's reaction to its worsening internal and external security problems and challenges.

This widely held approach and argument is also not simply wrong, to be rejected outright. One point in it always has been incontrovertible: this Austro-German decision, regardless of what prompted it and who bears the major responsibility for it, triggered the war. The controversy over it, moreover, has served important uses, both in promoting research and uncovering important facts and in refuting some clearly untenable and harmful arguments. What the Fritz Fischer controversy of the 1960s in Germany and elsewhere, for example, accomplished was to discredit the most dangerous myth that arose during and after

World War I over the war-guilt question—not what Germans termed the Allied war guilt lie (*Kriegsschuldlüge*) against Germany, but the German war innocence lie (*Kriegsunschuldlüge*) directed by the German right against the Allies, the Weimar Republic, and the alleged betrayers of the German army and people (Socialists, Communists, and Jews). This German war innocence lie, far more than the Allied war guilt charge or the Versailles Treaty, helped undermine the Weimar Republic and enable German militarism to survive the lost war and revive under Hitler.

Nevertheless, I consider the standard version one-sided, missing or obscuring the main point. Anyone, however, who proposes a supposedly different long-term and deeper explanation faces the formidable task of not only challenging the standard narrative on particular points but providing a convincing alternative one. I have learned this myself in publishing various articles since 1972 critical of the reigning view on various counts. One needs not only to counter the standard account's individual arguments, but also present a convincing alternative narrative explaining in concrete detail what actually happened. Absent this, individual assaults, like isolated artillery barrages against a formidable fortress, may breach a wall or two, but not destroy or capture it.

That requirement has now substantially been met. Christopher Clark's recent work on the origins of the war, *The Sleepwalkers* (2012), a bestseller here and abroad and the recipient of various awards and honors, provides the convincing alternative narrative needed, and is complemented, by and large and to various degrees, by other important recent scholarship (e.g., Stefan Schmidt, Stephen Schröder, Sean McMeekin, Dominic Lieven and others). Clark's argument is too rich and complex to summarize here, but I can try to indicate important aspects in which, as I see it, it differs broadly from the reigning paradigm. He shows how competition and conflict rose considerably more steeply and dangerously in intensity over the prewar quarter century than before, especially in the last decade. On the question of whether this competition between the two camps was approaching endgame, i.e., a point at which one side or another would predictably reach a dominant hegemonic position or be expected to do so, or whether it could have continued indefinitely without reaching such a tipping point, Clark indicates not only that the rivalry was approaching endpoint, but that the great powers were seeking it, aiming for decisive superiority, and that the Entente powers had more hopes of attaining it in the foreseeable future than the Central Powers did. Finally, while everyone to some extent recognizes the high-stakes gambling character of the prewar diplomatic and foreign policy game—intensified arms races, a succession of dangerous crises narrowly surmounted and quickly followed by even more open confrontations, dangerous wagers made by greater and lesser powers alike, and major armed conflicts only barely and provisionally kept from touching off a general war—where the standard version depicts this gambling game as going out of control only in the July Crisis and doing so then because the Central Powers opted for preventive war rather than pursuing real possibilities still open for a negotiated settlement, Clark challenges this at critical points. First of all, the proposed negotiated settlement represented a Russo-Serbian ploy and trap set for Austria-Hungary; furthermore, Britain, France, and especially Italy were not really interested in settling the Austro-Serbian-Russian confrontation or facing the basic issues involved in it. They wanted only to avoid general war at this time, provided that they could do so without harming their current positions in the ongoing power struggle and their chances of winning that game without war.

This does not imply either to me or, I believe, to Clark that the main responsibility for the war should be shifted from the Central Powers to the Entente, above all Serbia and Russia (though the leading role they played in 1914 emerges clearly enough from his narrative). My own conclusion, as consistently stated since 1972, is that the final outcome was a natural and predictable, though not strictly inevitable, outcome of the kind of international game then being played by almost every power involved, large, middle, and small. The one main exception until the very end was Austria-Hungary, primarily because up to 1914 its government recognized that it was too threatened externally and challenged internally to compete successfully or even to survive as a great power in this kind of game. (I will return to this point later.) The game was a particular version of poker that permitted and incentivized players not only to make risky bids for huge prizes, but also to join secretly or openly with as many other players as possible, coordinating their strategies for maximizing their gains and compelling their opponents to accept losses. The game was thus designed and to a large degree intended to end either in driving opponents out of the game entirely or compelling them to play it by rules, in roles, and under conditions set by the dominant players.

This is not to claim that this strategy was consciously conceived and coordinated between players fully aware of what they were doing and determined to pursue it toward this final goal. In fact, they constantly denied this both to outsiders and among themselves, claiming that they were only playing the game by standard balance-of-power rules, that it was the only game in town, and that they were forced to play it as they did because others were doing the same or worse to them, or would certainly do so if they failed to stop them. Their own aims, in contrast to those of their rivals, were legitimate, justified in terms of their particular rights and vital interests and the importance of these rights and values to the international community. It means merely that, despite denials and protestations made with various degrees of subjectively genuine sincerity, this game was headed toward endgame; that all the major players at some level knew or sensed this; and that some or most of the leading actors were seeking some version of that outcome. It follows that the mere prospect of such an outcome giving one side or the other a decisive, insurmountable superiority (a result to a considerable extent actually foreseen and aimed for) would with high probability lead sooner or later to general systemic war. The reasons are obvious. Potential losers could not be expected to accept such an outcome if they sensed it was imminent and could envision any serious chance or opportunity to prevent it, and the potential winners could not be expected to abandon a winning strategy.

This means further that any serious hope of maintaining durable peace by 1914 required that this game not be allowed to continue further, but be stopped and changed in its structure, rules, and goals. None of the players, great and small (except arguably Austria-Hungary until the very end—on this score, more later) were willing to do this or even seriously to consider the possibility or desirability of trying to.

Again, this is my interpretation, not necessarily Clark's, though I think his work portrays the war as I do—the natural outcome of the particular set of practices, rules, and goals then dominant in international politics, practices and rules that fostered, incentivized, and to an extent mandated a tide of reckless policies and actions headed toward endgame, a tide ridden in different fashions and degrees by almost all the great powers until very near the end, and eagerly joined and exploited still more recklessly by middle and smaller powers (Italy, Serbia, Bulgaria, Greece, Romania, even the Ottoman Empire). This collective tide of recklessness swept the European ship of state onto the reef.

This broad explanation helps make the case for World War I as an eighteenth-century war. As I suggested earlier and will argue later, it was this same kind of game pursued in similar ways in the eighteenth century that led to the great systemic wars from 1689 to 1713 and, after a somewhat quieter interlude, from 1740 to the Great War of 1787–1815. I have spent some time comparing the origins of these, especially the last and greatest, with the origins of World War I, something not often done—every detail of the July Crisis has been investigated more often and carefully than this question. What has struck me repeatedly are the broad similarities between them, both in the overall process and in individual strategies, decisions, and actions involved, and most importantly in the final outcomes. More on this later.

To make this claim, however, is to raise new questions while leaving important ones unanswered. What can such a putative similarity in the dominant strategies, aims, and game plans of actors in both these centuries really mean, given the obvious ways in which the two centuries differed in terms of the various players, their particular goals, their belief systems and motives, the circumstances, influences, and pressures that weighed on their decisions and actions—in short, the whole concrete setting, ground, and basis for international politics? What are the implications? Does it mean that some deep unchanging structure of the international system simply cancels these out or overrides them? Does it mean that we need to return to something like the old Rankean doctrine of the primacy of foreign policy? These may seem like purely technical academic questions, but even a layman can perceive them and see their relevance. Can the world change so much and the basic rules of international competition remain unchanged?

More important, merely asserting that this alleged tide of reckless behavior basically caused the wars does not explain the behavior. What lay behind it, caused it, how and why? Clark, after all, does not portray the statesmen before 1914 as especially warlike, aggressive, or lustful for military glory, nor would I in either era. I would even argue that in both cases, especially before 1914, most governments and individual decision-makers involved would have preferred to avoid war and were trying to reach their goals without it. What then accounts for an apparent widespread refusal or inability to resist this tide of reckless behavior?

Once again, plausible objections. I start with the second as key to answering the first and touching a point on which I disagree somewhat with Clark—the answer not specifically stated in his narrative but implied in the title *The Sleepwalkers*. Sleepwalking as a metaphor for the risk-taking behavior he depicts suggests—correctly in my view—that the actors stumbled into something they did not deliberately plan, expect, or wish at that time. Sleepwalking, however, is unconscious behavior—that of a person who wakes up at night to find himself out in the street, not knowing how he had got out of his bed or why. This is certainly not how actors played the international game before World War I. Ever since the modern game emerged, it has always been played in a highly conscious, calculated, purposive way, and was so conducted to a special degree before World War I, as Clark's narrative makes clear. Sleepwalking, moreover, is rare; the reckless conduct to which I refer was certainly widespread if not quite universal.

How then can one reconcile two apparently contradictory propositions: (1) Europe stumbled into a war its members had not deliberately sought or desired, though its possibly disastrous consequences could have been foreseen and to some extent were foreseen; (2) the players, experienced rational actors, stumbled into that unintended and undesired general war through playing a supposedly rational, calculated game in a highly conscious, purposive fashion?

My answer, in a nutshell, is to substitute for the sleepwalker metaphor a phrase familiar to Americans: doing something, pursuing one's goal, "with eyes wide shut." This means acting with eyes wide open and steadily fixed on one's goals, being highly purposive about one's aims, strategy, and tactics and remaining alert to responses and reactions insofar as they might affect attaining one's goals, but keeping one's eyes firmly shut to the broader implications and consequences of one's course of action for the wider community of which one is part and the general system and practice in which one is engaged. That, I argue, is a better metaphor for the way Europe stumbled into World War I.

"Well, yes," one might reply, "this might describe or characterize the process better, but that means little. It remains just another metaphor, a description or characterization that gets us no further in understanding what caused this kind of approach to international politics, or why it was as prevalent as you claim in the run-up to both the eighteenth-century wars and World War I."

Correct on both counts. It is only a description and characterization, not a deeper explanation of the roots and causes of this behavior. This kind of behavior, however, does not really need any such explanation. It is not a puzzle, a strange or inexplicable quirk in ordinary human conduct, but a normal aspect of individual and collective action encountered in all sorts and arenas of activity, one found present, often dominant, in many fundamental organized practices and undertakings in life. Walking with eyes wide shut is a large part of what we do as human beings, something we can often recognize even in ourselves and should expect and guard against. If one wants theoretical explanations and explorations of it, in particular for international politics, they are offered in abundance, almost in excess, by various scholarly disciplines and from different directions— epistemic theory, group-thinking theory, prospect theory, political psychology, behavioral psychology, rational actor theory and anti-rational actor theory, probably neurological science and evolutionary theory, etc. All this theory and investigation is valuable for purposes of scholarly inquiry. But we do not need it to understand the causes of the Great Wars in these two centuries; we need only recognize this aspect of human conduct as an integral part of who we are and what we do.

Even so, this could be written off as a catchphrase posing as an explanation—an attempt to blame everything on human nature, a way of saying "*Geschichte* happens." It is certainly not in this case. The argument I am trying to advance (the main purpose of advancing it) holds that *Geschichte* of this kind does not always happen; that it can under certain circumstances be kept from happening; that it sometimes is actually prevented from happening for considerable periods of time; and that the right kind of *Geschichte,* learned and taught well, can help us do so. Recognizing the prevalence and importance of the "eyes wide shut" phenomenon in the arena of international affairs helps us see where a possible answer or remedy or prophylactic lies and how it must be sought. It lies not in trying to change human nature, or the fundamental beliefs and ideologies people hold and follow, or the kinds of governments and institutions that may be allowed to operate in international politics, or the aims the actors seek in it, but in changing the international system itself. This means changing it, to be sure, in a sensible direction, not toward Utopian cul-de-sacs (world government, world federation, anarchism, libertarianism) but in a pessimistic-realistic non-Utopian direction. It involves recognizing and accepting that anarchy (which means neither a state of chaos nor the absence or total breakdown of rules and norms, but the absence of a single lawgiver and enforcer) is a necessary and unavoidable condition in international politics, and therefore accepting and dealing with some degree of serious international competition and conflict as integral to it and unavoidable, and recognizing that controlling this requires, among other things, some sort of suitable balance in the distribution of power and autonomy. But at the same time it calls for firmly rejecting two widespread assumptions: first, that anarchy and the resultant competition make Realpolitik the only rational principle by which to conduct foreign policy over the long term, and second, that a so-called balance of power does act and can serve as an invisible hand to regulate and control it, that over the long term a so-called "spontaneous order" is possible in international politics.

Balance of some kind in international politics and the international system is unquestionably of critical importance. The requirement is in fact definitional; a system of units in which decisive final authority over all important actions is not balanced or distributed in some fashion but concentrated in one member constitutes not an international community but an empire. But stable balance or equilibrium in the international system calls for far more than a balance simply of power, and can exist even under very different and unequal distributions of power, including hegemony. (I will say more about this point also later.)

If one accepts these premises about international politics and takes the tendency toward "eyes wide shut" behavior seriously, it leads to a broad conclusion that seems at first highly unlikely, even Utopian: achieving durable general peace requires enough important actors to agree on and act collectively to construct an international system with rules and restraints expressly intended to limit, manage, and control competition and conflict within tolerable bounds and to promote enough mutual cooperation and trust to operate and maintain the system.

This indicates the other half of my argument: the reason the Vienna system should be termed the world's first forward-looking peace is that for the first time it established that sort of system, designed for restraining, controlling, and limiting international competition. All the previous schemes for durable peace were Utopian, some consciously and deliberately so. This one was for real. Before making that side of my case, however, I need at least to acknowledge some additional challenges to the earlier argument and indicate my replies.

The challenges

The first is that even if one conceded that a general tide of "eyes wide shut" recklessness was the central cause of World War I, this explanation of its origins does not make World War I an eighteenth-century war. The pre–World War I recklessness can be explained more naturally and more plausibly as the result of many specific developments that profoundly changed European society over the nineteenth century—the rise of nationalism and racialism, economic competition and an intensified struggle for markets, industrialization and heightened competition and conflict over scarce resources, globalization and drives by various states for world power and position, shifts in domestic politics and the rise of mass movements and parties, European imperialism and the beginnings of anti-imperialist resistance, the clash of ideologies, growth and shifts in population, developments in armaments and the size and character of armed forces, etc.—all combining to raise international tensions and promote conflict. A critic might well point to these factors and their results cited as the underlying cause of the war in some of my articles—for instance, the fact that the Bismarckian type of balance-of-power politics based on an ethos of pure Realpolitik was supplanted after 1890 by a system dominated by a still more reckless ethos of imperialism.

Another similar question and challenge arises at the other end of the nineteenth century: how does your explanation of the origins of World War I make the Vienna system really forward-looking? Does not the mere fact that general war was so long delayed until after so much societal change had occurred make it more natural and plausible to see it in its special context as unique and temporary, the product of special circumstances—a pause between storms, an interval in which the major powers found themselves temporarily sated, war-weary, and fearful of change and revolution, had less to fight about, more to preserve, and more reason for caution and avoidance of conflict than they had earlier or would have later?

Once again, reasonable challenges. I will reply to the second later in discussing how the Vienna system emerged and worked, basically arguing that those who fashioned it were not simply responding to different conditions and circumstances, but actively learning from experience how to make peace better and more durably. The first challenge is more difficult and complicated, partly because in one sense it is correct. Clearly many broad, deep changes, conditions and trends in the late nineteenth century helped drive Europe toward World War I. The more important question, however, lies not in what drives, motives, incentives, etc. tended to push Europe toward war—here one confronts an *embarras de richesse* in choices—but what failed to prevent it, what rules, practices and restraints disappeared or proved insufficient to hold Europe back from general war any longer, and why.

To indicate my answer to this question even in a general fashion requires stating distinctions that may seem at once too abstract and theoretical to be of practical use and too basic and obvious to need discussion at all. Citing them to other scholars may seem almost insulting, like talking about the alphabet to professors of linguistics. Yet here, I think, some root problems lie in much historical and social scientific analysis of the central themes dealt with in this book. Inadequate or misleading distinctions are made at several key points: within the history of society generally, between (to use a nineteenth-century catchphrase) the forces of movement and the forces of order; in international history, between the history of foreign policy and diplomacy and the wider history of international politics and the international system; and in both these aspects of international history, between two broad meanings and definitions of that much used and abused but inescapable and indispensable concept, the "balance of power." As always, what I say here about these three distinctions will be sketchy, only enough to make the answer more than a mere promissory note.

On the first: historical and societal changes and developments, including those in domestic politics, foreign policy, international affairs, and the historical and current international systems, are by and large the products of forces of movement. Studying and analyzing these forces is what historians and many political and social scientists mainly do—the study of the changes of things that change (Herbert Butterfield). But the international system as it has historically developed in the West since the late fifteenth century has always had a different central task, function, and target: the creation and preservation of order. This task puts the history of the international system mainly into another domain, that of the forces of order.

To illustrate: consider automobile travel. Everything that directly and indirectly contributes to making automobile travel today possible in general terms (scientific, engineering, and technological progress, the industrial revolution, the modern corporation, etc.) and everything belonging to the development of the automobile itself as a vehicle belong to the forces of movement. So do the needs, wants, and demands for improved transportation in a changing world and the livelihoods and wishes of people living and working in it. Therefore most aspects of automobile travel today, including its origins and causal forces, means and institutions, actions and interactions with other institutions, and the societal changes it generates or is part of, can quite properly and usefully be portrayed and explained in broad terms by these forces of movement, as histories of the automobile generally do. Yet automobile travel today cannot really be explained without equal and in some aspects separate attention also to the forces of order that make it possible and sustainable. Some of these are embedded within the automobile itself, part of its manufacture and use—everything enabling the vehicle to be controlled and used with reasonable safety, comfort, and convenience such as steering, suspension, brakes, shock absorbers, controls and warning devices, lights and signals, chassis, body, seating, etc. But the forces of order are far vaster and more complex than this and lie mainly outside the vehicle and its particular capabilities and purposes. They include everything that underlies, controls, and makes possible vehicular automotive travel on a massive scale throughout the world—roads, bridges, other infrastructure, regulations, taxes, police, courts, various governmental agencies, licenses, a vast body of traffic rules, laws and systems, schools and rules for driver education, and the development and cultivation in both governments and citizens of a shared responsibility to respect, maintain, and improve these means of order. Only such an elaborate, carefully contrived and steadily maintained balance between the forces of movement and of order makes the current system of automotive vehicular travel possible.

Furthermore, placing this systemic view of automotive travel into a wider picture of the overall systems of transportation and its governance in modern society requires attention to all the additional measures and steps necessary to make automotive travel a net benefit to society and keep it from becoming a detriment and menace—discriminatory taxes on some models and kinds, restrictions and bans on its use in particular areas or times, encouragement and direct support of alternate means of transportation, regulations on types of vehicles and fuels allowed, governmental restrictions on size and fuel consumption, etc.—all these inescapably involving competition within the whole transportation system between automotive travel and other forms of transportation and within automotive travel itself between its own forces of movement and of order.

As the German saying has it, every analogy limps. This one, though doubtless imperfect and arguably anodyne, may, however, help illustrate why histories of diplomacy and foreign policy may naturally and legitimately concentrate on the forces of movement in international history, but why a systemic history of international politics and the international system must focus at least as much on the forces and requirements of order.

This is not a cliché or truism. It makes a difference that shows up in histories of modern society themselves (I may give examples in the book) and implies a different view of the history of international politics itself, one often overlooked or denied. It suggests for example that any "structural" view of the historical development of the international system that sees and focuses mainly on a supposed succession of hegemonic challenges or bids for outright empire by certain actors evoking resistance from others determined to maintain their independence through a balance of power is too reductionist. It not merely ignores far too many nuances, variations, and qualifications evident from the historical record, but ignores a central element: these were per se struggles not just over power and its distribution, but between different concepts of order and divergent quests for various kinds and systems of order. This is not theory but the concrete stuff of history. All the chief actors conventionally charged with bids for system-wide supremacy in the Western world—Charles I of Spain and his son Philip II, Louis XIV, Napoleon, William II, even in their fashion Lenin, Hitler, and Stalin—primarily claimed and probably at some level believed that they were defending or founding systems of durable order. Again I intend to back this up in the book. Their leading opponents did the same. (A possible exception is Napoleon; he claimed this and was good at leading others to believe him, but in my view never believed in or aimed at it himself.) The slogans attached to the forces of movement and of order reflect their differences and the inescapable linkage between the two: durable order derived from God and based on throne and altar versus order based on rights to life, liberty, and property (or substitutes for property, e.g., the pursuit of happiness or equality and fraternity); order resting on monarchical sovereignty and rights and privileges derived from hereditary possession and tradition versus order derived from popular sovereignty based on race, nationality, and community, and so on. All these can be subsumed into a formula that embraces all the goals and goods actually sought in international politics and the international system and their inherent contradictions as elements in a broad quest for OWL—order, welfare, and legitimacy (Edward Kolodziej).

This further suggests why one general conception of that protean, portmanteau phrase "balance of power" is unhelpful in analyzing international relations while another one, less common, is better—but that discussion fits better later. First I must address more directly the question raised earlier: why and how does my argument about a general tide of recklessness as the root cause of World War I help show it as an eighteenth-century war? It involves giving more concrete evidence about the origins of the first Great War (1787–1815) to indicate more specifically why World War I, forward-looking in that it unleashed an era of total war, violence, and systemic breakdown in the twentieth century, can also be viewed as the result of a regression to the reigning style and system of international politics in the eighteenth century.

I will point first to some striking analogies in the origins of the two crises: the strategies pursued by particular leading actors in both (notably Great Britain and Russia); the greater and more dangerous threats other great powers faced—France and the Habsburg Monarchy in 1787–92, France, Imperial Germany, and Austria-Hungary in 1906–14; the intertwined dangers and opportunities other smaller intermediary powers were confronted by in both cases (Italy, the Holy Roman Empire, Poland, the Ottoman Empire, the Low Countries, certain Balkan and Baltic states). These at least hint at a broad similarity in both situations in Europe overall—dominant flanks, vulnerable center, threatened intermediaries. My case, however, will not rest primarily on analogies and resemblances of this kind, at best suggestive and often misleading. The main evidence will be an effort instead to show how decades before the Revolutionary-Napoleonic Wars began, as early as 1740, the main European actors became involved in playing an international game by essentially the same playbook and rules for much the same basic stakes as that of the European powers from 1890 to 1914, and that this produced over time a similar rise in recklessness and loss of control and led to similar ultimate results.

This is not a claim that the paths to both great wars were identical or anywhere close to it. There were important differences in respect to contingent events, decisions, and developments. For example, full-scale war broke out rapidly in 1914 and quickly expanded beyond Europe into Africa and Asia, whereas the war broke out and spread over Europe and into the New World, Asia, and Africa after 1787 only relatively slowly, gradually and incrementally. Contrary to much conventional opinion, furthermore, the various actors who marched or stumbled by and large into the Revolutionary Wars were emboldened by more confidence in a relatively easy military victory and a quick favorable peace than their counterparts in 1914 were. These and other differences, however, do not change the main point: in the main, both sets of actors got into the war by playing the same general game with similar general rules, assumptions, and norms, and in both cases the expedients, devices and strategies that were supposed to control competition and conflict, solve crises, and prevent war actually accelerated the descent into the maelstrom. If I can make this reading of the facts for 1787–1812 convincing, it helps again to justify calling World War I an eighteenth-century war. More important, it helps demonstrate how both were systemic in their origins and results and why only a different system capable of limiting, controlling, and managing international competition and conflict could have durably prevented either Great War, and in so doing supports the view of the Vienna system as a contrasting early instance of a modern, forward-looking peace.

How the Vienna system managed international competition

This is discussed at some length in my book *The Transformation of European Politics 1763–1848* (Oxford, 1994, 1996) and in other related work, though not in exactly these terms. I will therefore mainly summarize some of that material in this one, with additional points, revisions, and corrections. The first correction involves a bad metaphor of my own.

Having criticized Clark's "sleepwalkers" metaphor of the road to World War I as misleading, I have to confess to using a worse one to encapsulate what the Vienna system was and how it worked. I wrote that the great powers had played the game of international politics in the eighteenth century as high-stakes poker, discovered that with Napoleon the game turned into Russian roulette, and abandoned both and turned to contract bridge. This metaphor became widely quoted and taken literally. I hereby renounce it—at least the last part.

Its first two parts can be defended. Eighteenth-century high politics, especially from 1740 on, did resemble high-stakes poker and led to major wars, and various powers great and smaller did indeed learn at their cost in the course of the Revolutionary-Napoleonic Wars that playing that game with France, especially under Napoleon, helped turn it into Russian roulette. The Revolutionary-Napoleonic Wars demonstrate this concretely. They mostly began in fact not from direct attacks by Revolutionary or Napoleonic France or one of its satellites on one or more of the opposing powers, but because one or more of France's opponents, especially after Napoleon gained power, felt compelled by France's general policy, actions and pressures to resort to arms in order to survive as independent players in the international game. In other words, formally at least these started (as very many scholars say, in certain respects correctly, World War I did) as preventive wars launched by endangered powers in response to perceived intolerable threats to their honor, security and status. What happened, however, in every case between 1794 and 1812 was that these same major continental powers learned at their cost that this preventive or preemptive action led either to putting their independent existence as great powers at grave risk or actually ending it, while in the process many smaller ones were either destroyed or forced or induced to become part of a French-run continental empire. By 1812, in other words, a series of wars mainly started and in general fought to preserve Europe as a community of independent states not controlled by a single power had led to the creation of a European empire far greater and more formidable than any previous one, posing a worse danger to the so-called "liberties of Europe" (i.e., the existence of a community of independent states in permanent, constant interaction with one another, the bedrock definition of a balance-of-power system), than any that Philip II's Spain or Louis XIV's France had ever posed.

This is part of the central thesis I put forward in that earlier book and other publications, and I still hold to it. In suggesting, however, that following the final defeat of the Revolutionary-Napoleonic challenge the powers turned to something like contract bridge as a model for a new game, I was simply wrong—seduced by an inappropriate metaphor. It implies that international politics as constituted by the Vienna treaties and conducted thereafter was strictly governed by law and played by clear, unbreakable rules, so that—as in serious tournament bridge—if a player breaks a rules (say, tries to trump an opponent's ace with a card from a non-trump suit) that player will not only lose the trick, but be out of the game, out of the tournament, and lucky ever to be allowed into a serious bridge tournament again.

Everyone knows that the Vienna system did not work like this. It was not intended or designed to abolish all major competition and conflict, including conflict over the rules, or to place strict, inflexible limits on the size of the wagers, risks, and possible gains and losses in international actions, or to govern narrowly what decisions the actors could make, or in other ways to subject all important actions and changes within the international community to the rule of law. The system, as I will discuss later, was neither inspired by this spirit in 1812–15 nor operated thereafter in this way. Throughout the life of the Vienna system, even in its heyday, there was real, serious competition almost everywhere over various issues and for certain kinds of competitive advantages among all the great powers as well as the smaller ones, both in Europe and in some areas outside it—Austro–Prussian–Third German competition in Germany, Austro-French in Italy, Austro-Russian in the Balkans, Anglo-Russian in the Near East, the Ottoman Empire, Persia, and the approaches to India, and Anglo-French over the Mediterranean (Spain, Algeria, Egypt and Syria, Greece) as well as potentially and underground in the Low Countries, their respective empires, and at sea. Even this list is incomplete; the roster has to include competition and potential or actual conflict between smaller powers and peoples within the Third Germany, Italy, the Low Countries, Spain and Portugal, and the Balkans. The issues and arenas of competition were broad and comprehensive—spheres of political and religious influence, trade and commerce, ideology and nationalism, religion, modes of government, rights of intervention versus non-intervention, and often the systemic rules, norms, rights, and institutions themselves. Despite this—or better, precisely *because* of the known, recognized existence of competition and trouble zones and the persistent danger of open conflict and systemic break-down into revolution and war—the Vienna system by intent and mutual understanding operated as a system of, by, and for the management, limitation, and control of competition and conflict in all these arenas and aspects, for the prime purposes of protect-ing the vital rights and interests of all the members, especially the essential actors, and the main goal of deterring the worst evils and dangers then faced in international politics—more war, rev-olution, and resultant systemic collapse.

The Vienna system's record for managing and controlling competition, and what explains it

The record is one of unparalleled success. It preserved general peace and stability in Europe for an unprecedentedly long period, in an era characterized in general societal terms not by quiet tranquility but by widespread social, economic, and political unrest, upheaval, and change. Between 1815 and 1852 three waves of revolution swept over Europe (1820–3, 1830–2, and 1848–9), each broader and deeper than the previous one, each one spark-ing minor but dangerous international crises and conflicts that threatened to spread into wider conflagrations in all the tradi-tional tinderboxes of the continent—the Low Countries, Iberia, Italy, Germany, the Rhineland, Poland, the Baltic, the Mediter-ranean and Levant, the Balkans and the Turkish Straits.[1] The waves of revolution in the Vienna system era were accompanied

---

1 Here again one might note a contrast between this and that of the eight-eenth century prior to 1787, where many local disturbances and risings occurred but developed into major outbreaks of rebellion in particular countries—the Pugachev revolt in Russia, the Rákóczi rising in the Habsburg Monarchy, Serb insurrections in the Ottoman Empire, the movements partly revolutionary and partly traditional-patriotic in Holland, Poland, and Belgium, Irish revolt in Great Britain—only as connected to and in good part produced by inter-national wars. In other words (another oversimplification), in the eighteenth century the serious rebellions and revolution grew mostly out of wars and international conflict, while during the Vienna system, serious rebellions and revolution grew spontaneously but failed to produce wars.

and partly produced by international movements old and new, political, national, ethnic, and socio-economic in nature, all calling for change and capable of producing armed conflict. Not one of these led to a war between any of the great powers, or even came as close to causing a major war as similar crises and occasions for war had repeatedly done before and would do later.

This unprecedented record of success in crisis and conflict management has been noted but not always explained, and then often in inadequate and misleading ways. It was not in the main achieved simply by repressing conflict and preserving the status quo, but more by fashioning and following a systemic process for limiting, controlling and managing international competition and conflict as occasions arose—a process that simultaneously induced friends, neutrals, and rival powers to cooperate to the degree necessary to preserve overall peace and stability in the general community, while also helping in various ways to create and preserve the needed framework and structure for cooperation and mutual restraint. The book will briefly discuss various examples and instances of this, concentrating especially on the means and instruments of control, limitation, and management of conflict and competition involved. These include alliances designed and used for mutual restraint and management more than for capability aggregation; an expanded and strengthened Concert of Europe; various rules and conventions for the conduct of diplomacy and international politics; various elements of binding international law, coupled to different kinds of sanctions to impose for breaching them; ambassadors' conferences and general congresses for working out agreements on knotty problems; arrangements for interlocking rights and guarantees with responsibilities, and more.

These institutionalized means and practices for controlling competition have all been discussed and are well known, or should be. A vital element enabling the system to survive and work, however, is more subtle, subterranean, and easily overlooked: a collective mentality shared among most European governments most of the time, a common disposition toward mutual restraint, a willingness not to raise or attempt to solve issues inherently insoluble by peaceable means or beyond the scope of the system's capacity to handle and likely if pressed to break it down, a joint recognition that righting one wrong or correcting one imbalance can easily produce a greater wrong, imbalance, and danger—that in international politics, in other words, the road to hell is paved not merely or even mainly with good intentions, but above all with Utopian expectations and ambitions. The most important principle and rule of action derived from this collective understanding was that disputes which affected the vital interests of the whole community (meaning usually all the great powers) had to be settled in concert, not singly. I will cite examples in which that disposition proved critical.

Why the undeniable defects and abuses in the system do not negate its success

To defend the system in this way does not mean denying or minimizing its limitations, dangers, and vulnerability to abuse. I intend to discuss the usual complaints—denial or restriction of national wishes, especially on the Polish Question; repression of popular risings, reform movements, and liberal constitutionalism; the control exercised over smaller powers by greater ones, often necessary but sometimes excessive; the flat denial of many historic rights and claims while others were rigidly enforced, and the like. While these charges need weighing and qualification, I intend not to excuse or minimize them but to stress their significance. At their worst and to a considerable degree they led to a perversion of the Vienna system into something I term the Metternich System—a more or less deliberate and successful effort to convert an international system intended for the limitation and management of international competition and conflict into an instrument, in Prince Metternich's words, for "the preservation of every legally existing thing," to remake a design for maintaining general peace into an ideology and justification for resisting change and preserving the political and social status quo. This unquestionably succeeded to a considerable degree in major parts of Europe—the Habsburg Monarchy, parts of Germany and Italy, Iberia, and Russia—and had serious negative consequences for Europe's domestic development and the system's reputation then and since.

This fact, however, does not contradict or weaken the main

point, that the system worked for its essential purposes of conflict management and general international peace as none has done before or since. Moreover, the same powers that can rightly be charged with distorting it into an ideological instrument for absolutist governance at home—Austria, Russia, to a lesser extent Prussia and at certain times France, along with a number of smaller states—were also frequently leaders in using it for its main purpose of international peace and stability. These two sides of the coin must both be recognized. The famous sexist remark by Dr. Samuel Johnson about dogs dancing and women preaching applies here to the Vienna system: the wonder is not that this task of preserving peace and international order was done well, but that it could be done at all. That may be a low bar, but it is a correct, necessary one for international politics in this era, and perhaps any.

If the Vienna system was so successful, why did it fall?

Another good question. The answer to it and the process involved will have to be oversimplified brutally in the book. Here I will say only that if the question asks whether ultimately the main cause was neglect, or lack of reform and development, or misuse, or a failure to meet changed conditions and new needs, or deliberate repudiation and overthrow, my short answer would be "All of the above, but especially the last—deliberate repudiation and overthrow." Behind them all, moreover, lies a still broader cause and answer, a factor as important in history as growth and change—entropy. It seems often to be assumed that human beings by nature prefer peace and abhor war, so that peace should be seen as natural and war artificial and contrived. No assumption is more simplistic and distorting in international politics than this one. In certain real, profound senses, war in international politics is natural; peace is artificial, the product of effort, reason, and artifice. Making a system like this work and endure is always an uphill task requiring shared commitment, prudence, and responsibility. These qualities and dispositions ran out or failed or were defeated in the decades after 1848. That assertion also of course needs a fuller though still compressed discussion in the book.

How did the system emerge, and why?

This question is more important and relevant to my case, and more difficult to answer, requiring more explanation: how did this system emerge and develop out of a very different eighteenth-century one? Again I offer here only an oversimplified answer. If, as argued earlier, the European powers walked or stumbled into both Great Wars with their eyes wide shut, in the course of the first in 1787–1812 the great powers in particular had their eyes forced wide open by events and outcomes, making it possible, though not easy or natural, for them to adopt a different outlook, approach and collective will needed to do things differently in 1812–15.

Traditionally the story of how peace was achieved in 1814–15 unfolds along two lines, overlapping and intertwined but substantively distinct. The most important component in this narrative is the essentially military account of how the Allies finally defeated Napoleon's army and ended his rule. It begins in Russia in 1812 and ends at Paris in March 1814, with military victory then having to be confirmed at Waterloo in June 1815. The second subordinate strand is the political story—how the Allies negotiated the terms of peace among themselves and with France under the restored Bourbon monarchy, chiefly at the Congress of Vienna between September 1814 and June 1815. This view thus sees military victory as being first and foremost, establishing the conditions essential for the subsequent peace settlement.

It is a natural, plausible view, but seriously misleading. The whole process of building peace was always primarily political; the Allies' focus was always on a durable peace, not a final decisive victory to be followed by peace. Clausewitz's famous dictum that war is the continuation of policy by other means applies here in a special sense. Of course the Allies understood from 1812 on that a measure of military success against France was essential, though they frequently disagreed on how much victory was needed and how it should be attained. At the same time they consistently viewed military victory not as the goal in itself but as one necessary means to achieve a durable peace, and never considered a final military victory so decisive as to compel the common enemy to surrender and accept whatever terms the Allies wanted. From early on, even while differing on emphases, priorities, and details, they pursued the same central target and goal: to construct a European state system within which all essential actors, above all the great powers *including* France, along with many lesser powers, would be able jointly to enjoy stable peace, order, legitimacy and security through recognizing and respecting everyone's legitimate rights, accepting limits and obligations, following rules, and assuming shared responsibilities.

Naturally many self-interested and conflicting individual aims were involved in this, so that the whole peace process frequently threatened to break down. Nonetheless, this collective focus on the pursuit and construction of peace constituted a different approach and marked a significant change in international politics. It was not simply the product of anti-revolutionary monarchical conservatism, war-weariness, and the desire to return to normalcy, though these motives were naturally present and important. It added up to something new: a collective will to form and sustain an international security community.

Another even more important point: this new collective mindset was not mainly a product of idealism or moral principle, but of necessity and practical learning. What led the continental allies, above all the great powers but also eventually some smaller ones, to fight for general durable peace more than for victory was precisely the hard lessons they learned in twenty-five years of wars waged both against France and among themselves from 1787 to 1812.

To see this, one has to recognize some important differences between this long general war and earlier eighteenth-century ones. All the other major wars (1689–1713, 1702–21, 1740–8, 1756–63, 1775–83), though fought in various theaters and often in distinct phases in which some participants entered the war late or dropped out early, still can be seen as representing one central contest between particular leading powers ending with definite winners and losers. In this respect they resembled World War I, and like it they also ended, at least in Europe and adjacent areas, at particular times with major peace treaties ostensibly designed to produce lasting peace under a new settlement. All these eighteenth-century peace settlements, except to a degree the Treaty of Utrecht in 1713, failed in this, breaking down after a few years and leading to new war, but they did provide at least an interval of relative peace—another way in which they resembled World War I.

The Revolutionary-Napoleonic Wars were different on both counts in important respects. They included seven distinct continental wars from 1787 to 1812, the earliest of which, in the Balkans and Poland, did not even involve France directly. After 1792, however, general conflict quickly spread over most of the continent and well beyond, becoming especially concentrated in a series of distinct wars conventionally (in some cases misleadingly) termed coalition wars against France. There were important conflicts above all in Western and Central Europe, but also in the Balkans, Egypt and the Mediterranean, Switzerland, Spain and Portugal, southern Italy, Scandinavia and the Baltic, the West Indies, India, and the global high seas. In two of these France did not even take part militarily, though it was always a main political player. Some wars were launched or provoked by France on its own against neutral powers and even against an ally, Spain, and in several of them the French-led coalition was larger and more coherent than the opposing one. This was true especially for the biggest and most important war of all, in which in June 1812 Napoleon invaded a virtually isolated Russia at the head of a massive imperial army gathered from most of the continent.

Thus the Revolutionary-Napoleonic Wars should be seen as a series of separate wars, so closely connected in time and impact, however, as to be experienced and seen as an era of almost continuous war and threat of war, and to drive home the same main lesson. All the continental ones before 1812 except three—the two in which France was not directly involved, plus the Peninsular War launched by Napoleon's attempted takeover in Spain—led to decisive military victory for France and ended with treaties that were accepted by the defeated powers in the expectation or hope of gaining at least a tolerable peace. Each one of these treaty settlements broke down, however, even more quickly than their earlier counterparts had in the eighteenth century, and all for the same basic reason. In every instance the major states which had lost militarily and made peace in the hope of escaping more war in order to survive discovered instead that even if they tried to come to terms and live with France, the French government, especially after Napoleon took control, exploited the treaties and peace settlements in so humiliating and dangerous a fashion as to lead one or more of them to decide that war was better than such a peace, and either to accept a new war or actually launch it.

This differs from the widely held perception of these conflicts as one long struggle by the opponents of France to overthrow French hegemony and restore a balance of power in Europe. Some historical interpretations, especially those that view the war primarily from the perspective of Anglo-French conflict, the final chapter in their so-called Second Hundred Years' War of 1688–1815, as well as a major version of international relations theory (neo-realism or structural realism) see this almost as a truism, something reflecting the essential nature and structure of international politics. The other major powers in Europe, especially Great Britain, could not accept and live with France's military superiority and political hegemony; it represented an existential challenge to their great-power status and autonomy and led them repeatedly to form new coalitions to overthrow it and restore a balance of power. This constitutes another major example of repeated European reactions to bids for hegemony throughout modern history, like those of Charles I/V, Philip II, Louis XIV, Napoleon, Wilhelm II, Hitler, and Stalin.

Leaving aside the question of whether this line of explanation is satisfactory in these earlier instances (I do not think it is), it does not work for this Revolutionary-Napoleonic one. Here, rather than say that new war repeatedly broke out because France's opponents could not tolerate French hegemony and resorted to war to restore a balance of power, one needs in general to say that the reason war was reignited was that France's opponents discovered that their efforts to attain real peace with France even by accepting French hegemony and attempting to live with it or to join it and benefit from it repeatedly failed, proved futile and counterproductive. One by one they learned that neither their military efforts, alone or in coalition, or various other political strategies they tried—negotiation, accommodation, appeasement, neutrality, hiding, bandwagoning, even joining the French Empire as a satrapy or satellite—enabled them to reach durable peace with France. The attempts all ended instead in more threats, humiliation, destruction, and subjugation. Napoleon's insatiable pursuit of power, conquest, and glory led them gradually, unevenly and by different paths at different times to the conviction that peace had to be attained by a different route. Part of the answer of course had to be military—France had to be reduced in power and brought to agree to terms—but this did not require eliminating the French threat through destroying it as a great power or even necessarily displacing it as the leading power in Western Europe, provided they could fashion adequate safeguards against France's abuse of its power. More important still, they came gradually to see that they themselves could not make the kind of persistent, united military effort necessary to gain even this more limited goal unless that military effort was based from the outset on prior agreement among themselves on just what they were fighting for—a concrete political definition of peace reached before forming the coalition and maintained while fighting France. That required negotiating and reaching consensus on specific conditions needed to constitute peace in the whole European system, and then fighting essentially only for that goal, and only until they could bring France itself, under whatever regime or ruler it had, also to accept, belong to, and help maintain this kind of peace settlement. In other words, they had to conceive and create an international security community and then act as members of it.

All this applies mainly to the process by which the continental great powers gradually developed and worked out a collective mentality among themselves, a process in which Napoleon's satellites and conquests also became involved. The British government came to a similar outlook by a different path. By 1812 Britain had fought France not just longer and more continuously than any other power, but also with greater success. Despite many individual failures and setbacks in battle and serious French challenges on various fronts, the British (aided of course by geography) never decisively lost any of their contests with France, nor except for brief threats of French invasion in 1798 and 1803–5 faced any grave danger of being conquered or compelled to accept French terms. By 1811 the British had gained decisive victories over France and its allies and satellites on the high seas, in Egypt, the Mediterranean, the Iberian Peninsula, the commercial struggle against Napoleon's Continental System, India, and the West and East Indies, driving Napoleon into a Fortress Europe military stance and to the sideline in worldwide empire and control of all the world's sea lanes.

These successes, however, did not lead the British government to conclude that it could or should simply hold out in its war with France until the continental powers rebelled against Napoleon's domination and joined Britain for final victory. In fact, throughout the long struggle against France the British government never formally adopted a policy of uncompromising resistance as it did in 1940 against Germany. Napoleon's intransigence forced them into it. Britain actually made peace with Napoleon in 1802 and would have kept it had Napoleon not persistently challenged and humiliated them in the aftermath. Even in early 1808, with Britain isolated and the continent alienated from Britain and at Napoleon's feet, the British government, though still unbowed, was ready in principle to consider a peace on the basis of *uti possedetis* (each side keeping its conquests). Napoleon, incapable of making peace even on this basis, occupied himself at this time with reorganizing his Grand Army for more war and pursuing his takeover of his erstwhile ally Spain.

What British leaders instead primarily had learned by 1811 from experience was that victories like theirs, though enabling them to survive and sustain a remarkable war effort, could not bring real peace. Ending the heavy burdens of war and securing Britain's future security and prosperity at home and abroad required not just military victory over France on the continent, but also a durable structure for peace in Europe as a whole, and that demanded serious attention to the needs and concerns of all Europe's major powers and all its areas of conflict.

This represents a significant shift from the outlook toward Europe Britain had shown in its earlier great contests with France (1702–13, 1740–8, and 1756–63) and its policy during the approach of war from 1787 to 1793 and in the earlier war years up to 1805 or 1809. During that era, despite real differences in policy and attitudes between the "blue water" and "continental commitment" schools of thought in Britain, one can see in general that so long as the British government's central strategic concerns in regard to Europe were met (the containment of France, security for the Low Countries and Hanover, some sort of balance of power, and British control of the Atlantic and of its imperial possessions and outposts), it was not particularly concerned how the rest of Europe was organized. There were particular British interests to be protected, of course—Hanover, trade interests, a European balance that did not over-commit Britain and that the British could manipulate from their favorable geographic position—but these were ancillary to its main aims and strategy. This British attitude informed its policy throughout the first and second coalition wars against France and persisted into the third despite some shifts in emphasis and tactics, only to change decisively after 1810.[2] One can see the change clearly in the stances Britain took toward Russia in 1812, toward the rest of Europe, especially Prussia, Austria, and the rest of Germany, in 1813–14, and toward the USA in 1812–14. They show how British leaders, especially Castlereagh, Liverpool, and Wellington, also had their eyes opened by decades of war and possessed to an uncommon degree the rare kind of common sense sufficient to see what needed doing.

How this learning turned into action

This collective learning experience was behind the course pursued by the Allies in coalition-building, war, and negotiation from the end of 1812 to March 1814. Starting with the Russo-Prussian alliance in early 1813, the Allies at each step worked out between themselves what minimum concrete conditions and status in Europe each required for peace, agreed to fight together until these were achieved, and then fought on that basis and to that end. They recruited further members to the coalition from

---

2   I will discuss in the book the contingent changes involved in this, as they always do, above all changes in leadership. For example, had Canning remained foreign secretary instead of being replaced by Castlereagh, it is hard to imagine how much of the evolution in British policy and attitudes could have happened.

Napoleon's allies and satellites by the same methods. At the same time, they pursued negotiations with France until very late in the game (though Napoleon remained in charge of France until the bitter end) in an attempt to persuade the French government to agree to terms as well. They offered France surprisingly generous terms, even after the decisive Allied victory at Leipzig in October 1813, and by no means limited their flexibility, realism and moderation to their dealings with France. Austria, after it suffered its fourth crushing defeat at Napoleon's hands in 1809, tried seriously thereafter to come to terms with that defeat and find a respectable place and role in Europe as a junior partner at Napoleon's side. It even reluctantly and within limits joined the French assault on Russia in 1812. The destruction of Napoleon's Grand Army in Russia made Austria cautiously back off and look for a safe and favorable position between the two sides, but the Austrian government refused to join Russia and Prussia to fight Napoleon in the spring 1813 campaign, in which the two allies suffered a narrow but decisive defeat that came close to driving them out of the war. Following this defeat, Russia and Prussia, though naturally suspicious of Austria and especially of its chancellor and foreign minister Prince Metternich, agreed to a truce with Napoleon mediated by Metternich and authorized him to negotiate with Napoleon on their behalf for a general continental peace in the summer of 1813. There is good ground to believe that Metternich really tried hard at that time to reach a compromise settlement in which Austria and much of Germany under Austrian hegemony would constitute a neutral bloc separating Russia and Prussia in the east from a Napoleonic France still in control of all of Western Europe and leaving Britain out in the cold. Once more Napoleon's intransigence rendered Metternich's efforts futile, leaving Austria no option but to go over to the side of Russia and Prussia. Knowing pretty well what had happened, they nonetheless welcomed Austria into the alliance essentially on Austria's terms and put an Austrian general in charge of Allied military strategy.

The same shrewd, realistic moderation and generosity characterized Allied diplomacy toward lesser powers as well. Longtime loyal Napoleonic satellite states such as Bavaria and Wuerttemberg and satrapies such as Joachim Murat's Kingdom of Naples were brought into the Allied coalition, retaining the independence, constitutions, and territorial gains they had acquired in Napoleon's camp. A renegade from Napoleon's Grand Army, Marshal Bernadotte, was accepted as Crown Prince and later King of Sweden as a full ally, and was allowed to fight Sweden's separate war against Denmark in his own self-centered way, using only the German troops fighting under Swedish command in the main theater of war. The same moderation and good sense was shown Spain. It had survived Napoleon's bid for takeover by long, cruel regular and guerilla warfare and major British help, but once Spanish soil was cleared of the invader it was allowed to drop out of the war. The former British colonies in North America who had gained their independence in 1783 only with indispensable help from French and Spanish allies and had then conveniently ignored that debt in order to gain a favorable separate peace with Britain, and later exploited the opportunity offered by Napoleon's invasion of Russia and Britain's peril in mid-1812 to try to conquer British Canada, and who then failed miserably in this effort, suffered no punishment for all this after the British and Allies had defeated France in 1814.

As for their dealings with the main longtime foe, not only did the Allies after victory fully honor their wartime promises to France that if it would make peace, it would remain larger and stronger than it had ever been in the old regime. They also, before and during the military struggle, encouraged Frenchmen themselves—leaders of Napoleon's Army and Senate including Napoleon's former foreign minister Talleyrand—to make the actual decision for peace, to depose Napoleon when he refused to go along, and to draw up France's new constitution preserving some of the most important national achievements of the early Revolution. They then proceeded almost immediately to bring France to the negotiating table at Vienna as a sovereign great power and equal, and to let it help decide on the general terms of European peace. By the late summer of 1814, Talleyrand (who had as always turned his coat in a shrewd self-interested direction but, as he claimed, in the best interests of France) became France's leading negotiator and Britain's chief partner in handling the problems emerging in the negotiations at Vienna. Even after the French ruined this remarkable success themselves by accepting

Napoleon's renewed takeover of power, thus provoking a new war ending in total defeat at Waterloo, the Allies in the second peace treaty imposed no serious long-range punishment on France either for its previous decades of conquest and imperialism or for its latest folly and betrayal of its treaty commitments. Within three years France was formally re-admitted to the general alliance and Concert of Powers. One must no doubt pay tribute to the way the Allies hung together militarily so as finally to win the war, but what was truly new and different is the way in which they worked together to construct and save the peace.

Balance-of-power politics? Yes, but of a different kind

All this, of course, can be accounted for as simply prudent balance-of-power politics, responses to its obvious demands and pressures, and often is so explained. The needs and pressures were clear enough: to reduce French power and domination without promoting its replacement with Russian or British hegemony; to prevent another eighteenth-century-style Austro-Prussian struggle for mastery in Germany, while at the same time balancing their respective influence and promoting their cooperation there; to realize that a quarter-century of war and revolution had made a number of irreversible changes in Europe (e.g., the end of absolute monarchy in France, the demise of the old Holy Roman Empire in Germany and many of its constituent units, the transformation of Italy, the awakening of some national movements, the creation of larger middle states with constitutions)—facts that had to be recognized and dealt with; the need to organize Europe's vulnerable center from the Baltic to the Mediterranean into a loose defensive confederation separating the more powerful French and Russian flanks; and to make particular arrangements for security and stability in other trouble zones—Italy, Iberia, Switzerland, the Low Countries, Poland, the Baltic and Scandinavia. The worst trouble spot, the Balkans and Near East, was recognized as too difficult and risky for the Congress to handle and by tacit agreement reserved it for future handling by the great powers in concert—another prudent decision. As for another great area of potential conflict, the world beyond Europe, where according to some historians the great game between Britain and

Russia in Asia had already begun, this was by common unspoken consent and implicit British veto declared off limits for the sake of European peace.

In other words, as critics may argue and will, even if the states-men in 1812–15 and the succeeding decades showed considerable skill, moderation, and common sense, this does not demonstrate a change in their basic goals and collective outlook or a break-through to a new concept of international order and security. The Vienna system in both its territorial and political arrange-ments and its institutional and legal features should be seen more simply and naturally as the product of classical balance-of-power politics. Each state was still aiming primarily to improve its own security in a prudent but self-interested fashion, balancing one power against another to ensure that no actor would become so powerful as to dominate all the others.

The short answer to this interpretation is that one can indeed make such a case and fit all the evidence into it, after a fashion, but that there are good reasons why this is not the best way to look at the Vienna system, or at history in general. Some of these I can only mention here, reserving discussion of them for the book. They include points such as this: (1) that this interpretation is unacceptably reductionist. It argues essentially that under-standing human conduct reduces to determining what particular contingent circumstances and needs motivated it, what can be demonstrated or inferred from evidence as driving particular actions, decisions, or policy, whereas any real understanding includes determining what it all led to, how it changed things, and what it amounted to. (2) It ignores the fact, demonstrated by this case in particular, that what is considered normal prudence and common sense in international politics is precisely abnormal, uncommon, requires explanation, and makes a vital difference. (3) It assumes what is really in question, the nature of what actu-ally drives conduct in international politics. It seems to suppose that the driving force for actors is necessity, and that all that is necessary in actors is sufficient nous to recognize necessity and draw the appropriate conclusion. Those who do so, it suggests, are not really different from or better than those who do not, only perhaps luckier or smarter. This also is too simple. Not only does it fail to recognize the power and influence of systemic rules and effects on actions, but it misunderstands what "being smarter" and "being better" mean in foreign policy and international politics. They are not opposites or even contraries, but two sides of the same coin. Being better requires and means being smarter in a particular way, and vice versa, and in combination they add up to being wiser. The central puzzle that needs to be addressed in so much of the history of international politics, including this era, is why recurrently actors who are individually not stupid or evil and are, or claim to be, bent on rational decisions and responsible policies do so many stupid, irresponsible things that lead to disastrous, evil consequences. The broad answer, I suggest, is collective institutionalized systemic irrationality and stupidity—and the practical response to it is the construction of an international system to counter this profound systemic tendency. Of this, the Vienna system stands as a rare example.

Fuller argument on these assertions must wait for the book. The narrower question, whether the Vienna system merely represents one version of normal balance-of-power politics, can be answered here a little more concretely. The answer is that this is true in a way and to some extent, but to the extent it is true, with the needed reservations, it supports my case rather than undermines it.

The key issue here is what constitutes so-called normal balance-of-power politics in theory and practice. Here I have to confess to another error or overstatement. In writing in my book and other publications that international politics could operate without a balance of power, or that the Vienna settlement did not rest on a balance of power, or that "political equilibrium" was a more accurate and standard term for the political conditions nineteenth-century statesmen envisioned and aimed for, I was then trying to make certain points and stating positions I would still defend. The language I used, however, was imprecise and sweeping enough to give the impression that I considered the balance-of-power principle of no practical or theoretical importance or value in international politics and the actual distribution of power within the system inconsequential.

Such a view is untenable. A balance of power of some kind is not merely necessary for a durable international system, but defines what an international system is: a system in which final decisive power is not held by one member—in other words, an international system, not an imperial one.[3] In any case, regardless of formal definitions, achieving a sound balance in international relations is not merely one goal among others in international politics but a central requirement for a stable international system, and achieving it by balancing power with countervailing power is obviously a necessary part of that effort. These are truisms. But other equally important truisms are often denied, ignored, or slighted. To be a durable and stable or general peace, a system requires much more than just some putatively correct distribution of state power, and what is a correct distribution is highly debatable, controversial, and dependent on individual perceptions, motivations, and interests. Most definitions of "balance of power" as actually held and pursued by different governments, furthermore, turn out on concrete examination to be thinly disguised euphemisms for schemes of imbalance, domination, and hegemony—witness, for example, the grotesque oxymoron in which former Secretary of State Condoleezza Rice defined the Bush Doctrine with its unabashed assertion of America's unilateral global military and political supremacy as "a balance of power that favors freedom." Measuring power for purposes of balancing it, moreover, is far more complicated and inexact than just calculating the relative distribution of some elements of hard power (military, economic, and strategic-geographic ones), itself a delicate, uncertain undertaking. If one adds the elements of so-called soft power (a state's influence, values, reputation, credibility, systemic functions, etc.) and the historical, legal, cultural, moral, and ideational elements related to state power (norms, shared practices, existing treaties and conventions, concerns about honor, reputation, and tradition, and the presence or absence of a shared sense of membership in an international community with common interests and

---

3 For example, Napoleon's system for Europe, though never defined because Napoleon could not do it himself or confine his goals, was imperial in precisely this sense. His only real goal in invading Russia in 1812 was to impose his will on Russia as the last major independent power on the continent, not to acquire territory or other concrete performances and commitments.

responsibilities) to the calculation, the task becomes even harder. These are elements that can be considered tools of power only with difficulty or not at all, yet they are important restraints, limits, and tools in its exercise. Thus without first carefully analyzing the power-political aspects of a system and then determining how, whether, and to what extent they are themselves balanced and complemented by other systemic factors, one cannot even say what a real balance-of-power system is, let alone whether one exists in a particular situation, or of what kind, or what kind is needed to promote international stability.

This sounds like a declaration of analytical bankruptcy. A "balance of power" of some kind is crucial in international politics, but it cannot be precisely defined, described, or prescribed. This admission is clearly true in part; the term is highly protean. Scholars list somewhere between nine and thirteen meanings in common usage, some contradictory to others or empty of concrete meaning. As the historian M. S. Anderson remarks, for the British in the eighteenth century the phrase often served as a substitute for thought, and the same judgment could be applied to other people and eras. Yet one can think about the term usefully and discuss it. It requires distinguishing two broad currents in the meaning and application of the phrase "balance-of-power politics"—strands that are neither harmonious nor flatly contradictory but linked in dialectical tension and potential contradiction with each other. It calls further for seeing how a similar tension arises between the basic rules and practices each calls for in playing the game of international politics and how this affects the game and its outcomes.

The first strand of meaning, that of a broad diverse school of realism and Realpolitik, is mainly descriptive. It concentrates on the actual distribution of power, above all applicable military power, asking whether and how this is balanced within the system, and operates on the assumption that in the final analysis, in times of real crisis and war, power and its uses and application determines the outcome. It is in general prescriptive only in the sense that it urges a realistic appreciation of the primacy of power and security concerns in international politics, while also recommending prudence and rational choice in the use of power and the quest for security as a way to improve the overall chances for systemic stability and durable peace. [Any discussion here of historical roots of this—allegedly going back to Thucydides (Lebow)? Its dominance above all in American IR scholarship? Or of the assumption that this is really the only possible way international politics can operate—any alternative is illusory?]

The second strand accepts the obvious truths in the first realist one, but insists that these are penultimate, incomplete truths and therefore misleading and potentially dangerous, even disastrous, unless complemented and controlled by a further moral element or dimension: a recognition and appreciation of the existence and importance of the international community and its collective interests in international politics, of the need for this community to be preserved and reformed when necessary, and the responsibility of individual members of the community to obey the rules, norms, and requirements vital to this end. [Seymour Kaplan on the two primary rules for balance-of-power thought and practice: (1) Preserve all essential actors. (2) Exploit opportunities to maximize one's own security and advantage. How these are both clearly true, but also in tension and often in contradiction in both peacetime and war, and how much depends on which of the two mandates have priority.]

The question then is which of these two schools of thought on the balance of power, the realist/realpolitical or the moral/normative—both of which have long historical traditions behind them and strong current exponents (in the latter case especially the so-called English school of historians and political analysts today)—is more sound, theoretically and in practice. My answer is obviously the latter, the "English School" moral/normative concept of the balance of power in theory and practice. The historical argument I have offered for this conclusion, oversimplified, essentially amounts to an attempt to show how the realist approach carried to its logical conclusions leads naturally to great wars and systemic breakdown. It did so in the late eighteenth century without much resistance mainly because at that time a viable alternative could hardly be conceived, much less put into practice. The eighteenth-century international community had only recently and incompletely been developed and filled out, there was little real sense of any collective responsibility to it or for its survival, and it still operated on reckless competitive norms. These deficits were overcome in the final stages of the Napoleonic Wars and a new community-based system established in 1812–15 that operated successfully until about 1850, only to be gradually abandoned, undermined, and destroyed thereafter and replaced by the previous kind of balance-of-power system in an even worse, more disastrous form.

Some concrete historical argument to illustrate and support this claim

Even a patient reader may now be muttering, "This is all too abstract and aery-fairy. Even if your scheme throws some light on international politics generally and on what the balance-of-power principle means and how it fits in, it give us no real basis for calling the Vienna system forward-looking simply because it allegedly met certain standards you set up, and condemning European diplomacy before World War I as a reversion to the past because it did not. That verdict requires more than generalities and assertions; it calls for specific evidence showing how the claims advanced here about each era and their respective systems explain and illuminate the real, down-to-earth, complex, contingent course of international history. Systems, rules, norms, collective mentalities, structures, tides of recklessness, eyes-wide-shut or eyes-wide-open patterns of conduct do not make peace or wage war. Individual historical actors do, in a process full of concrete decisions and choices, moves and countermoves, challenges and responses involving much uncertainty, contingency, and chance—the process historians and other scholars trace by careful search for evidence and conscientious effort to reconstruct the thoughts of past actors after them. You need to show concretely how this 'systems' jargon applies to this process and makes us see it differently.

"You claim to have done it already in some detail for the Vienna system in your earlier works. Very well; if we accept that *ex hypothesi*, now show us how you do it for World War I. Show us, for example, just how, had the Vienna system or something like it then prevailed, the July Crisis could have been successfully managed and war avoided in 1914. Or explain to us why, if this general tide of eyes-wide-shut reckless behavior was sweeping

Europe toward general war, at least some of the current statesmen did not recognize this and propose something out of the
Vienna system playbook to stop it. Or if some did, and even
proposed using Vienna system–style remedies, show us why these
attempts failed."

Good questions and legitimate demands. Often when someone
says, "That's a good question" it means, "I don't know the answer."
Here I think I do. The reply involves some counterfactual reasoning, but that is not a problem. The question itself calls for it, and
done correctly it is legitimate. Historians use such reasoning all
the time, sometimes without knowing it. The quick answer, of
course, is that had anything like the Vienna system prevailed
before 1914, no July Crisis would ever have arisen, nor would
some of the preceding crises. At no time in the Vienna era or even
up to about 1900 could any small power in Europe have waged
against a neighboring great power anything like the campaign of
hostile propaganda, revolutionary subversion, diplomatic and
military challenge, and finally state-supported terrorism like that
which Serbia waged against Austria from 1903 on, without being
met with a strong response both from that great power and from
the international community. The only previous time in the nineteenth century when a small power tried such a strategy against
a neighboring great one was when Sardinia-Piedmont did so
against Austria in the late 1840s and 1850s (a campaign, incidentally, supported by Serbian nationalist revolutionaries at the time
and adopted explicitly as a model by the Serbian revolutionary-
nationalist ideology early on and by the Serbian government
after 1903). It culminated in an agreement secretly worked out
between France's Emperor Napoleon III and the Sardinian
premier Count Cavour to provoke Austria into war in 1858–9.
That conspiracy and the resultant crisis, however, led to a European Concert intervention headed by Britain and Prussia, with
the German Confederation supporting it and Russia despite its
hostility toward Austria abstaining. This Concert action effectively derailed the Franco-Piedmontese plans, forcing France to
back out and call on Sardinia-Piedmont to back down. The result
would have handed Austria a diplomatic triumph and forced
Cavour to resign, had not Austria foolishly tried for a more decisive military victory and thereby precipitated a war.

This reply, that under the Vienna system Serbia could never have got away with its campaign of overt challenges to Austria-Hungary, however, is not the most direct and convincing one to the main question, which, to repeat, is: Could Vienna-style methods and devices have served to defuse the July Crisis and deter a general war of the sort likely to arise, as actually happened, when Austria decided on its own punitive-preventive military measures against Serbia? The better answer is that the Vienna system actually included effective measures and procedures for preventing a general war under similar circumstances and that these were used successfully in that era and even after it (as the instance of the Italian Crisis of 1858–9 illustrates). Unfortunately, such measures, though well-known and theoretically still available to the powers in 1914, could not even be considered under the prevailing system and its rules.

A serious answer to the question posed above—"What Vienna system–style methods and devices could have prevented the July Crisis from leading to war?"—must specify concretely what had to happen to change the decade-long pattern of relations between Austria and Serbia in particular and among Russia, Austria, and the smaller Balkan powers in general sufficiently to avert this outcome. As Clark and other scholars show convincingly, the actual European diplomatic effort, launched tardily more than three weeks after the assassination and only after the Austrian ultimatum of July 23 had revealed how serious the immediate danger was, had little chance of doing so. Russia's efforts were devoted to encouraging Serbian resistance to the ultimatum and helping Serbia find ways to deflect Austria's demands while Russia itself tried to stop Austria from acting by a partial military mobilization against Austria—a mobilization that however intended could not long remain partial for both political and technical military reasons and also was bound to threaten Germany and tend to draw it into the conflict. The French government meanwhile stood firm in its alliance with Russia and awaited German action, while Germany, ostensibly at least, wavered between urging Austria forward and advising it not to go too far while at the same time trying to warn off Russia, prepare for an offensive of its own in the West, and hold Britain out of any resultant war at least for a time. As for the diplomatic effort led by Britain and Lord Grey, it not only revealed deep divisions over political and military policy within the British government and military circles and within the ruling Liberal party, but in addition that the central aim for Grey and the Foreign Office was not to solve the basic crisis between Austria, Serbia, and Russia, but rather to avoid general war by delay and prolonged inaction (provided that this could be done without alienating France or Russia, its vital friends) in the hope that somehow an international conference would make the crisis pass over. British diplomacy, in other words, did not try more than did other powers to address the real problem, and with British attention focused on more fundamental problems at the time—Persia, India, the empire, the Irish crisis and its attendant political-military problems, the potential German threat in Europe, and Britain's friendships with France and Russia—the British had no critical interest in doing so.

To defuse the crisis and open the way toward further solving or managing the basic problem, two main things needed to happen. First, Serbia had to be brought under effective international control, i.e., compelled to stop its anti-Austrian campaign, find the persons in its own ranks complicit in the assassination plot and deal with them, accept appropriate internationally enforced sanctions for its role, and give serious guarantees for its future behavior. I could give a lengthy argument on how and why all these anti-Serbian measures were both necessary, especially given the record of Serbian actions toward all its neighbors and the aims and claims of its ideology of romantic-ethnic-integral nationalism, and how these also would have accorded with nineteenth-century precedents for international action in the Vienna era and well after it. Some of this argument will be included in the book, but I think it unnecessary here.

A second requirement for effective international action, however, is just as vital: that the other great powers hold Austria back—persuade or compel the government to turn the task of bringing Serbia under control over to them, to be handled by the Concert of Europe. Again the reasons are obvious, or should be. Not only would a unilateral Austrian intervention, whether or not it was primarily proposed or supported by Germany, almost certainly set off a general explosion; the Austrians themselves had no idea of how they could even by using overwhelming military force bring Serbia under control or deal on their own with the long-term, deep-rooted challenge of a Greater-Serbian ethnic-romantic terrorist-revolutionary nationalism now directed primarily not against Turks, Bulgarians, Macedonians, and Albanians (and indirectly even Italians) but against Austrian territories, peoples, and the regime itself. Even after the Austrian government had resolved on war with Serbia, it did not know what it should do with Serbia after conquering it—annex all or parts of it, or overthrow the dynasty, or divide Serbia into various parts and give some to its neighbors—and concealed the absence of a concrete policy under the meaningless slogan of "eliminating Serbia as a political factor in the Balkans."

The response to this idea for a two-pronged diplomatic approach capable of preventing a war in 1914 is obvious: the whole proposal is absurd, totally unrealistic in the context of that time. No power would have given this sort of international action in July 1914 serious consideration. To expect Russia to force its dependent ally Serbia to accept international controls and sanctions and thereby destroy the Balkan alliance Russia had promoted and now led, to risk having its own role in encouraging Serbia's anti-Austrian campaign revealed, to bid farewell to the other major political and strategic gains it wanted and expected to make soon in the Near East and elsewhere, to alienate its Pan-Slav supporters at home and abroad, to forfeit its claim to be the protector of the Slav world, and to undermine its prestige as a great world power, all to defend the interests and honor of a rival whom Russia did not fear or respect and from whose anticipated dissolution Russia expected and intended to gain handsomely—this is ridiculous. For France to support these steps would mean to alienate its main ally and promote a Russo-German rapprochement, and for Britain, to risk losing Russia as a check on Germany and encourage more Russian expansion in Persia and a greater threat to India—on behalf of a power neither Western power had any desire or obligation to assist. Even Germany would have risked undermining and losing its only reliable ally while gambling on cooperation from its worst rivals. For Italy it would mean aiding and strengthening its arch-rival in the Adriatic and western Balkans. Even the Austrians themselves would have strongly resisted placing their cause, honor, interests, and fate into other hands, mainly unfriendly ones. And of course the Serbs would have risen as one man against the international pressure.

My point exactly. This shows the position to which normal unchecked realpolitical foreign policy with its entrenched zero-sum balance-of-power competitive-advantage rules for international conduct had brought Europe by 1914. It had rendered this sort of joint diplomatic intervention to prevent a general war out of the question, rationally and subrationally unthinkable.

Under the Vienna system, however, this kind of intervention had not merely been possible but readily available, and was actually employed fairly frequently to prevent major war—successfully over the Greek Revolt from 1821–5 and in 1829–32 and in the Near East in the Mehmet Ali crises of the 1830s, with near-success in the Russo-Turkish quarrel in 1853–4, successfully in the Danish-German conflict in 1849–52, in the Low Countries in 1832–9, and in some other less critical instances. If the reply is, "Yes, but all these crises arose in a more peace-oriented age where the atmosphere was different and the stakes not nearly so high," the rejoinder is that this also is part of my case and a further reason for emphasizing the priority of systemic requirements and rules. While the chicken-and-egg question of course arises here, as it always does given the inescapable intertwining of cause and effect in history—in this case, the question of the extent to which the system made the era less war-prone and/or general conditions in the era made the system more peaceful—the cardinal point remains clear. The Vienna system developed and made available to the powers workable devices and strategies for peacemaking and crisis management that could be and actually were successfully employed in its time, and that became unthinkable once that system and its rules were finally abandoned or destroyed.

One can also illustrate further how a change in the system and its prevailing rules and norms can make a decisive difference between peace and war in short order, not merely as a result of decades of long-range deep-seated changes, as happened in the latter nineteenth century. To see this, one need only look at a crisis that arose in the early heyday of the Vienna system, arguably the most dangerous such crisis prior to the similar one leading to the Crimean War, in the same critical arena—the general Near Eastern crisis arising from the outbreak of revolt in Greece and savage Greek-Ottoman conflict there and in western Anatolia beginning in 1821. This was no local revolt like so many others in this region, but a deep-rooted ethnic, territorial, religious, and tribal conflict that, though settled temporarily by a Concert-engineered action in 1832, would flare up repeatedly afterwards until late in the twentieth century. The following sketch is intended only to draw attention to the contrast between two directly adjacent stages within it.

By March 1821 the revolt started in January in the Greek homeland against Turkish rule, its prompt and inevitable spread to the large Greek population in Constantinople and western Anatolia, the savage nature of warfare between Greeks and Turks, the Ottoman government's response to the atrocities, and Russia's reaction to the Turkish actions had spawned a grave threat of war. Russia at the time had clear legal grounds for declaring war on the Ottoman Empire—deliberate, outrageous provocations of Russia in direct violation of Russo-Turkish treaties signed in 1774 and 1812. It is hard to imagine Russia under Catherine II (1762–96) passing up such a golden opportunity for a war that Russia could expect to win easily and to yield handsome profits in territory, prestige, and strategic security and advantage in an area of vital Russian interests and ambitions. The region in question was not even covered by the Vienna territorial settlements, and could be claimed to be outside its purview. Many Russian leaders as well as the Russian political public and Orthodox church favored war.

Nonetheless, the intervention of the other powers successfully averted war, mainly by Austria and Britain working as "good cop–bad cop" partners with French and Prussian consent and using only the then-normal Concert methods, without threats against Russia and only diplomatic pressure on the Ottoman Empire, and doing no damage to the general European alliance—all this though after the initial crisis and danger of great-power war had passed, the Greek revolt still persisted, the general Near Eastern problem remained unsolved, Russia's prestige concerns were not satisfied, and widespread public sympathies and agitation for the Greek cause in Europe and Russia continued to grow.

Contrast this example of crisis management with what closely followed it. In 1825, George Canning, Castlereagh's successor as British foreign secretary, decided to abandon the reigning system and return, as he put it, to the good old eighteenth-century system of "Every man for himself and God for us all." In this spirit and for purposes of enhancing his own position and reputation at home by breaking up the Holy Alliance and dishing Austria's Chancellor Metternich, he proposed to Russia a separate alliance with Britain to solve the Greek crisis on their own, by their peaceful pressure on the Sultan. The Russian government under its new Tsar Nicholas I, who resented the way Metternich had exploited Tsar Alexander I's desire for peace, decided to use this opportunity not to save the Greeks, for whom neither he nor Canning had any real sympathy, but to enhance his own prestige and authority, severely damaged by the uncertainty created in Russia by Tsar Alexander's sudden and mysterious death, confusion over Nicholas's succession, and a revolt by elements in the Russian army in 1825 against autocratic rule.

Omitting many intervening developments and details, what this separate Anglo-Russian alliance (concluded in 1826, protested by Austria and Prussia, but joined in 1827 by France for its own revisionist purposes) actually accomplished was open war between the Ottoman Empire and Russia in this worst, most dangerous arena for Europe, the Balkans and the Turkish Straits—a war that by 1829 had almost brought the Ottoman Empire down, strained Russia's resources, carried a Russian army through the Balkans to the gates of Constantinople, awakened the slumbering fires of Russian expansionism, encouraged a revival of French chauvinism and revisionism under the last Bourbon monarch, the reckless Ultra-Royalist Charles X, nearly wrecked the Holy Alliance, and put the whole general European alliance and territorial settlement at grave risk. The potentially disastrous outcomes of this venture were only narrowly averted by a combination of good fortune (including Canning's unexpected death) and restraint and common sense shown by the other leading actors, particularly Metternich in Austria, the Duke of Wellington and Lord Aberdeen as successors to Canning and Prime Minister Lord Liverpool in Britain, and in Russia Tsar Nicholas I himself and his conservative foreign minister Count Nesselrode. In the end, diplomatic compromises reached by Concert diplomacy, accepted willingly by Russia and with combined relief and resignation by the Ottoman Sultan and the German powers, ended the war and promoted a general return to Concert methods. Ultimately in the London Conference of 1832 a settlement was reached of precisely those issues that Canning and Russia had supposed they could settle peacefully by separate Anglo-Russian intervention. It ended the Ottoman-Greek war, recognized a smaller Greece independent of Turkish rule, and decided the questions of its territorial boundaries, constitution and monarch. This of course did not resolve the broader Eastern Question or even its Graeco-Turkish aspect. Both were rooted in wider and deeper ethnic, religious, cultural, and politico-economic differences and rivalries among the intermingled peoples of the Balkans and the Levant. Greece, which took years after 1832 to gain real independence from great-power (mainly Anglo-French) supervision and competition for influence, continued to be a major source and center of turbulence, crisis and war throughout the nineteenth century, as through most of the twentieth, while the whole region remained plagued by great-power rivalries and conflicts over strategic and political interests. The decisive difference between the Vienna system era and the succeeding ones after 1850, however, was that in the Vienna system era Europe did not ever go to war over them. The competition among the great powers was always ultimately by common consent confined to a competition for influence that allowed enough cooperation between rivals to keep the general situation under control and prevent lesser states or events from dragging the great powers into war.

This story in 1821–32 is only the most striking instance between 1820 and 1850 in which this happened—peace being threatened by a potential revival of eighteenth-century-style Realpolitik and saved by a return to the Vienna system. The same essential danger arose in the revolutions of 1830–2 and their repercussions in the Low Countries, Italy, and Germany, in 1832–9 over the Low Countries and Spain, in the 1830s over the Mehmet Ali crises, in the run-up to the revolutions of 1848–9, and in crises arising during and after these revolutions in Italy, Germany, the Baltic, and the Near East. When this great-power consensus on limiting their competition sufficiently to exclude great-power war finally did break down in 1853–4, despite serious and nearly successful Concert efforts to save it, the result was the Crimean War. More discussion of these points has to be reserved for the book.

A second plausible question raised earlier asks why, if this system had really worked tolerably well earlier in the nineteenth century and if the threat of general war had become apparent well before 1914, no leading government or statesmen then tried seriously to avert war by attempting to revive the Vienna system and return to an earlier less reckless and dangerous brand of politics—or, if such efforts were made, why they failed. The answer, in short, is that certain individuals, groups, and governments at different points did try to do this. The basic reason they failed was that an eighteenth-century-style system of Realpolitik revived after 1848 that had already largely supplanted and discredited the Vienna system in 1859–71 and came to reign virtually unchecked and unchallenged after 1890. The idea of returning to a Vienna system–style of international politics in practical terms therefore over time became unthinkable not merely for those opposed to such a course on grounds of their particular interests or general principles, but also ultimately for those who wanted and advocated it, when it became abundantly clear to them that pursuing such a strategy and goal under the prevailing conditions and rules only made them the sheep in a society of wolves.

This is probably the most controversial thesis in my argument, and will require the most detailed exposition. I believe there is sufficient evidence to back this in broader terms, but here I will have to be selective, concentrating on the one group that most clearly tried to revive a particular central element of the Vienna system. It was the peace party in Austria-Hungary, which was in control of Austrian foreign policy from roughly 1895 to 1914. Its leaders were Emperor Franz Joseph, his successor-in-waiting Archduke Franz Ferdinand, Count Aehrenthal, Austria's ambassador to Russia in 1900–6 and foreign minister in 1906–11, and Count Berchtold, who succeeded Aehrenthal at both posts, along with their advisers and subordinates. Aehrenthal, the main leader and advocate of the policy initiative, developed a specific program for reaching his prime foreign policy goal, thereby saving Austria, Russia, and Europe from war and revolution: to restore good, stable relations between Austria and Russia by reviving the Three Emperors' League. How this was supposed to do so, and why it ultimately failed, needs explanation.

The original league had been formed by Austria and Russia in 1872 for similar purposes—more explicitly, to end the Austro-Russian alienation and crisis since the early 1850s that had led to serious losses and dangers for both, including the rise of a powerful united Germany on their frontiers. Bismarck, interested in preserving Germany's gains and restoring stability in Europe, approved their rapprochement and joined the league in 1873. It quickly encountered new problems, however, from another Eastern Crisis created in 1875 by a Serb insurrection in Bosnia-Herzegovina, nominally against the rule of the Ottoman Sultan but actually against control and exploitation by local potentates, mostly ethnic Serbs who had converted to Islam. Initially Austria and Russia, despite mutual suspicions, worked together to end the conflict by forcing reforms on the Sultan, with Bismarck, who had no interest in the Balkans and would support any policy the other two agreed on, urging them on. But the revolt continued, spreading into neighboring Bulgaria, where it flamed into a major rising repressed by Turkish irregulars with fighting marked by widespread atrocities on both sides. This had the effect as usual of arousing widespread horror and anti-Turkish sentiment in Europe, especially among liberals and evangelical Christians in Britain, while its Conservative government, though internally divided, pursued a pro-Turkish policy, alarmed at the threat of Ottoman collapse or submission to Russia and Russian control of the Straits, and tried to stop Russia both by its own pressure and by urging Austria to take the lead in doing so, if necessary by force, promising British support. Thus domestic and foreign policy divisions in Europe combined with Balkan revolts and Turkish resentments and resistance contributed to the breakdown of several Austro-Russian and European Concert efforts to settle the crisis. Finally the Russian government out of frustration decided to act, paid Austria a price for its neutrality, and declared war on Turkey in 1877. The war proved unexpectedly difficult and costly for Russia and despite ending in decisive Russian victory in early 1878 worsened the crisis and threat of general war and further weakened the Three Emperors' League (more on the reasons later). The European crisis was surmounted in the spring and a general settlement reached in the Congress and Treaty of Berlin in 1878. This apparently successful outcome, however, only delivered a final blow to the Three Emperors' League. Russian diplomats had helped prepare the agreement in negotiations with Bismarck and British diplomats, and the Russian government had accepted its main provisions in advance; the settlement included important territorial and political gains for Russia in the Caucasus and the Balkans, and above all provided Russia an escape route from the potentially disastrous military and political isolation it faced in early 1878. Nonetheless, political circles in Russia, especially Pan-Slavs, and most importantly Tsar Alexander II, saw the settlement as humiliating and blamed it on a betrayal by its supposed friends Germany and Austria-Hungary (a general scenario that would be replayed later).

Despite this breakdown, the league was soon revived in a more concrete form in the Three Emperors' Alliance of 1881. The same rationale lay behind both versions—the realization by at least the policymakers of all three powers that to maintain peace between themselves and generally in Europe they had to restore in some form the so-called Holy Alliance, forged in 1813–14 and formally signed by them in September 1815. This is usually depicted especially in Anglophone historiography as a reactionary pseudo-religious instrument uniting the three absolutist monarchies in preserving their regimes by crushing revolution and repressing liberal reform at home and everywhere in Europe. No doubt it frequently served that purpose. The main purpose, function, and effect it had in international politics, however, was promoting mutual restraint and management of international conflict among these three powers themselves.

The longer historical background to the alliance was the climax and fruit of a long period full of rivalry and warfare between them. They had been principals as both enemies and allies in two long and bitter eighteenth-century wars, the War of the Austrian Succession (1740–8) and the Seven Years War (1756–63). After the latter ended in mutual exhaustion and a

draw, their rivalries and lesser conflicts and crises persisted thereafter; neither various cross-cutting alliances between them nor
joint action served to end or durably control them. In the most
striking example of this, the three powers joined (Russia and
Prussia in the lead, Austria more reluctantly) in the three partitions of Poland between 1772 and 1795 which, while narrowly
preserving a tenuous peace between them, destroyed Poland as a
state, leaving it a deeply discontented, potentially revolutionary
nationality and bone of contention between them. At the same
time the partitions helped make Russia's wars with the Ottoman
Empire in 1768–74 and 1787–92 harder to control or end and kept
the three powers from any genuine cooperation in the war against
Revolutionary France in 1792–5, without settling the three powers'
own rivalries over Poland, the Near East, and Germany.

If these results of the all-out eighteenth-century Realpolitik
practiced by all three powers, Russia relentlessly and skillfully,
Prussia with alternate hesitation and recklessness, Austria more
reluctantly, were not enough to show that Realpolitik can work
for a considerable time and bring rewards—until it doesn't—
what followed would drive the lesson home with a vengeance.
With these three great powers locked in rivalry by geography
and conflicting interests and aims—all three in Poland, Austria
and Prussia in Germany, Austria and Russia in the Balkans—and
with both German powers directly threatened by a revolutionized and mobilized France in Germany and Italy, leaving a
victorious Russia with Britain's help free to expand and manipulate them, it is easy to understand why they did not unite
effectively against France and the still worse threat rising from
Napoleon and his empire. Rivalries, tensions, and cross-purposes
hampered all the attempts at alliances and coalitions between
them from 1792 to 1812. It required a succession of lost wars,
near-disasters and epic struggles culminating in Napoleon's invasion of Russia in 1812, an unexpected Russian victory, the defeat
of Russia and Prussia in the spring of 1813 followed by the ultimate Russo-Prussian-Austrian victory in Germany the next year,
to enable the three powers to overcome their inherent conflicts in
Central and Eastern Europe (more on just how this came about
later) and achieve victory in 1814. Even then during the negotiations for peace the old conflicts simmered below the surface

and threatened to explode, giving reason to fear that with France defeated the paralysis in Central and Eastern Europe would re-emerge.

The Holy Alliance from 1815 on more than anything else kept this from happening. It enabled them to handle the central problem, that of limiting, managing, and controlling their various rivalries and conflicting interests, and thus to cooperate in promoting their shared interests: restraining France, managing various Eastern crises, preventing Britain from interfering in their spheres, avoiding the Siamese twins of war and revolution in Europe, preserving the existing territorial settlement, and strengthening their domestic regimes and tranquility. The two Three Emperors' Leagues were real, if limited and flawed, efforts made under unfavorable conditions to revive this arrangement. Aehrenthal's attempt to revive the Three Emperors' League was another.

My general argument will be that this scheme was a practical conservative policy for peace, but had little or no chance of success under the prevailing system and instead was inherently likely for systemic reasons to end in promoting worse rivalry and more dangerous threats to the general peace. To understand this calls for a look at the Bosnian Crisis arising from Austria-Hungary's annexation of Bosnia-Herzegovina in 1908. Historians agree that this crisis more than any other event before 1914 set Austria and Russia at odds and on a path toward war. I concur, but disagree with the standard explanations of why it did. Certain other chapters in the prewar history of European international politics might still be revisited even after the valuable recent revisionist work by Clark and others, but the conventional interpretation of the Bosnian Crisis needs to some degree to be overturned, the story understood from a different angle.

Since this may be the most controversial part of the book, I will explain it here in more detail. To start: Austria's annexation of Bosnia-Herzegovina should never have caused a crisis at all. Unlike other prewar European crises going back to the 1880s, it was not really a conflict over power or territory, winning or losing in a test of strength and resolve, strategic security or insecurity. The actual Austro-Russian deal, originally proposed by Russia's foreign minister Count Izvolski and agreed to by Aehrenthal at their conference at Buchlau in Austrian Moravia in September 1908 represented a normal *"Do ut des"* bargain between the two parties, giving Russia's consent to Austria's intended annexation (something, as Izvolski's second-in-command Charykov reminded him, Russia had already consented to and been paid for in treaties of 1881 and 1894) in exchange for Austria's support of Russia's desired change in the international status of the Turkish Straits. The transaction was aimed (ostensibly by Russia, genuinely by Austria) not at altering the territorial, strategic, and political status quo in the Balkans or Europe generally but consolidating it peacefully by mutual agreement, thereby helping them patch up the tangled and faintly absurd quarrel over trans-Balkan railway schemes that had recently risen between them and give both powers a better chance to solve or manage their other domestic and foreign policy problems. Aehrenthal in particular hoped to revive the joint policy of mutual restraint and cooperation in the Balkans they had agreed on and practiced in 1897–1906—one as already noted of keeping the region on ice by joint management of the dangerous Macedonian question. The one way the Buchlau agreement would have affected the European strategic and political status quo was the strategic boon given Russia in changing the international status of the Turkish Straits.

Nor did the bargain fail because of mismanagement or deception in the negotiation of the agreement at Buchlau or its subsequent execution—at least not by Aehrenthal's doing or desire—or the fact that protests were lodged against Austrian annexation by the Ottoman Empire, Serbia, the Russian government, and circles in the West. Other factors were really more responsible—the hidden agenda Izvolski had pursued in the negotiations from the outset and the mendacious self-defense he mounted when his plans backfired (more on this further on); the French and British rejection of that part of the bargain Izvolski and Tsar Nicholas II had most wanted and counted on, the changed international status of the Turkish Straits; the Russian government's disapproval of the scheme which Izvolski had kept secret from its leaders; the Tsar's abandonment of it when it turned sour; and finally, encouraged by these Russian and Western reactions, the protests against the annexation raised by the Ottoman government on grounds that were technically legal but in practical terms obsolete and impractical, reinforced by Ottoman economic sanctions against Austria, and Serbia's protests and demands for compensation on revolutionary nationalist grounds, backed by an overt Serbian military and political challenge to Austria.

In short, the Bosnian Crisis did not arise out of Austro-Russian rivalry in the Balkans (still less from an Austro-German trick or power play against Russia, a Habsburg land grab, or Austria's betrayal of its commitments, among many other charges that have been levelled) but because of a more general systemic condition and cause: the fact that the prevailing European alliances and alignments among various powers great and small and the various foreign policies and domestic political interests attached to these alliances and alignments were almost automatically and as a matter of course permitted and used to wreck a potentially useful bargain over a sensitive issue between the two principals, knowing that these two great powers, without such an agreement, might well clash openly in this most explosive area in Europe and thereby endanger the general peace. The Bosnian Crisis, in sum, was a result and an integral part of that tide of reckless conduct that, I contend, swept Europe into World War I.

Even if this interpretation of its origins is granted, however, it would not seem to alter the conventional verdict on the most important, proximate cause of its major effects: the fact that Germany flatly rejected Russia's request in early 1909 that Germany restrain Austria from compelling Serbia to back down and to apologize to Austria for its challenge under threat of war. Germany supposedly decided to reject this request in blunt terms so as to demonstrate to Russia, still militarily weakened by the 1905 Revolution, that it could not stand up to the Central Powers, as well as to signal to Austria that it must not make deals with Russia behind Germany's back. This so-called German ultimatum to Russia did end the crisis by forcing Russia to tell the Serbs to back down. But it also turned the confrontation into a power play between alliances, and still worse, the Russian government and political public took the outcome as a profound humiliation never to be tolerated again.

Once more, this is correct on its systemic consequences and on Russia's perceptions, attitudes, and policy, but one-sided as a view of the whole matter. It emphasizes only the systemic impact of the German response and the hard choice Germany's reply gave Russia—either back down or risk a hopeless war—but ignores what Russia's request if granted would mean for Austria-Hungary, that it would have to swallow a direct challenge from a small enemy power on its frontiers, and what the Russian request explicitly demanded of Germany—that it humiliate and alienate its own ally Austria simply to avoid offending Russia, France's ally against Germany. Germany's language may have been blunt, but the Russians ought to have seen what kind of answer Germany was bound to give, and no conciliatory language from Germany could have made it palatable. To put it bluntly, Russia's "humiliation" arose mainly from faulty Russian calculations, unreasonable expectations, and reckless diplomacy (something to which Russian foreign policy under Tsar Nicholas was notoriously prone), and represented at least in part a self-inflicted wound.

Still, one might argue, this re-interpretation of the origins and course of the Bosnian Crisis does not change its overall significance for the origins of the war. Even if Russia was partly or mainly responsible for the crisis, the Russian perceptions of what had happened and reactions to it were decisive factors in shaping Russia's future policy, above all in the Balkans and vis-à-vis Austria, and paved the way to the eventual crisis in 1914. Austria and Germany should have foreseen this and avoided it.

One may indeed argue this in regard to Russian attitudes and it may hold true to a degree for the Central Powers. What one cannot do, however, is treat this as simply a problem for the Central Powers and a crisis they caused, rather than as a European one in which the roles, feelings, policies, and reactions of other powers, not merely Russia, Serbia, and the Ottoman Empire but including especially France, Britain, and Italy, also figured heavily. Put simply, all three governments chose to exploit the crisis to their advantage rather than try to manage or reduce it. France did not want any part of a Balkan quarrel, but did wish to make Russia more aware that it needed French support and must not take it for granted, and also was glad to have German attention distracted from what France was doing in Morocco. Britain acted from like motives vis-à-vis Russia. Except for certain periods and some occasions before 1848, the British aim had always been to keep the German powers and Russia at odds as part of its strategy in the Great Game in Asia against Russia (witness Lord Salisbury's welcoming the Austro-German defensive alliance of 1879 as "good tidings of great joy"). The British desire at this time to tie Russia more closely to cooperation over the Straits, Persia, and India was especially strong. Italy's response to this crisis was less important, given Italy's well-known weaknesses and vulnerability and its reputation as only a would-be great power, but also reckless and opportunistic, a mixture of fear of entanglement in a serious crisis and unrealistic ambitions for exploiting the Russo-Austrian quarrel in the Balkans and Mediterranean for its own purposes. If the rejoinder to this is, "All this was a normal part of the balance-of-power game," my reply is, "Yes—*that* is the problem."

In addition, besides examining developments and outcomes that actually flowed from the crisis, one needs to include the possible outcomes and developments it foreclosed, the doors still open that it slammed shut. Here one must return to Aehrenthal's wider foreign policy aims at the time he accepted Izvolski's proposal for a deal on Bosnia, looking at what their breakdown signifies about the past and the future. Aehrenthal, as noted, had two major closely intertwined aims in mind in trying to revive the Three Emperors' League: to help the regime reorganize and strengthen the Monarchy internally, and to stabilize Austro-Russian relations and limit and manage their competition and conflicts, mainly though not solely in the Balkans. (The so-called Ruthene question concerning Ukrainian nationalism in Austrian Galicia and Russian Ukraine was almost as critical a problem.) His further goal, important but subsidiary, was to make both powers more independent of German pressure and help them exert more influence on German policy.

All these facts are well known and have been carefully examined— too often, however, through the prism of Austrian domestic politics, as one aspect of Aehrenthal's so-called Action Plan, the ideas he and others had for reforming and rejuvenating the Habsburg Monarchy by various administrative, electoral, and political changes so as to meet its various nationalities problems, in particular those involving Hungary and the South Slavs, and thereby prove the central government to be still strong and effective as a great power.

Such an approach is valid if one adopts a principle of the primacy of domestic politics in international affairs, and if the central issue for historians of international politics and the international system as well as general historians is whether the Monarchy was still a viable great power and would prove able to carry through the internal reforms required for effective foreign policy and action before 1914, or if one privileges variants of this approach—questions of how these internal problems affected its foreign policy and military decisions or its prosecution of the war, or why it ultimately collapsed in defeat, and other related issues. All these questions and attention to them are doubtless important for the general history of Austria-Hungary, Southeastern Europe, and Europe as a whole. This kind of approach, however, is not suitable if the central questions at issue are those of the origins of the war and the general nature and course of international politics and the international system. On these issues a principle, circumscribed but clear, of the primacy of foreign policy in the formation and conduct of foreign policy must be applied. However much or little the failure of Aehrenthal's plans and hopes may say about the domestic character and ultimate fate of the Monarchy, however closely intertwined domestic and foreign policy concerns always are, especially in a state like Austria-Hungary, what counts here is how the outcome of Aehrenthal's policy in 1908–9 affected this overall story, and why. His attempt to revive the Three Emperors' League was inherently and above all a major move in foreign policy, an attempt to shift the basis of Austro-Russo-German relations back to the more sustainable and stable one of the recent past, and on that basis it must first and foremost be assessed.

The first fact to note on that score is that the attempt itself at this time indicated an important change. Aehrenthal was in instinct and sentiment the first Russophile Austrian foreign minister since Count Rechberg resigned in 1864, and was far more effective and forceful in this respect than Rechberg. All the other nineteenth-century Austrian foreign ministers from Metternich in 1809 to

Gołuchowski in 1906, like most of their predecessors in the eighteenth century, had fundamentally distrusted Russia's aims and ambitions even while working with Russia. Their Russian counterparts had mostly felt the same way about Austria even before the Crimean War and more strongly thereafter; that war undermined the original Holy Alliance well before the Italian and German wars wrecked the Vienna system as a whole. The same underlying distrust and antipathy plagued the original Three Emperors' League. A product of necessity and convenience rather than mutual attraction from the start, it broke down not merely over differences on how to deal with the anti-Turk revolts in Bosnia and Bulgaria but from a basic distrust and antipathy manifested by both sides during the crisis. In 1876 Tsar Alexander II tried hard if unsuccessfully to get Bismarck to force Austria to remain neutral in a Russian war with Turkey. In response, in January 1877 when the Russians decided they must go to war with Turkey and reluctantly negotiated the terms for Austria's pledge of neutrality, Austria extracted a heavy price in compensations and restrictions on the eventual peace terms. The Russian response in early 1878 went even further. Once it had finally defeated the Turks after a harder and longer struggle than anticipated, Russia deliberately and flagrantly violated the central conditions of its Treaty of Budapest with Austria in the peace Treaty of San Stefano it imposed on the Ottoman Empire in January 1878. The breakdown of the revived Three Emperors' Alliance in the mid-1880s came about in similar fashion. Here Austro-Russian hostility grew mainly out of the failure of heavy-handed Russian efforts to exercise full control over its newly independent client Bulgaria—a humiliating outcome actually due to shrewd, stubborn Bulgarian resistance, which Russians chose to blame on Austrian influence.

It was just this long-term scenario that Aehrenthal genuinely was trying to change.[4] As ambassador to Russia since 1900 he

---

4   I may want to draw a parallel here between his ideas and efforts and those of Gorbachev's in wanting to end the Cold War with the USA in order to draw the USSR closer to Europe. I will certainly bring in at some point how this attempt and its breakdown fits not merely into the story of the origins of war in 1914, but also into the course of the war and of various German and especially Austrian attempts to end it.

had pleaded for years with his superiors at Vienna for remaking the Austro-Russian relationship into an alliance of mutual restraint designed less for capability aggregation or joint defense than for coexistence as great powers who, though inescapably rivals in their overlapping spheres of influence and unavoidable conflicts of interest, were at the same time neighbors, similar composite monarchies and multi-national empires with shared vital needs and interests, facing similar internal and external problems and threats. His revived Three Emperors' League was intended to provide the basis for mutual recognition of each other's legitimacy and rights as great powers and a framework for managing their problems and conflicts by negotiation, avoiding a war and resultant revolution that could easily prove fatal to both.

None of these ideas, aims and insights, of course, were Aehrenthal's invention; they were historical coin of the realm. In early versions this kind of Austro-Russian relationship emerged already in the first half of the eighteenth century. On this kind of understanding the two powers had allied and gone to war against Prussia in 1756–63. Failure then had led to estrangement and serious tensions afterward, but the alliance was painfully renewed in 1781 and lasted precariously through their joint war against the Ottoman Empire up to 1792. It was successively renewed and repeatedly wrecked during the Revolutionary-Napoleonic Wars, and apparently ended decisively in 1809–12 with Austria firmly if uncomfortably in Napoleon's camp. Russia's survival and victory in 1812 revived the possibility of it; the developments of early and mid-1813 eventually convinced both powers of the vital need for it; subsequent Allied defeats and victories in 1813–14 forged, developed, and sustained it in spite of many difficulties and strains, and the ultimate Allied victory and the successful negotiations in 1814–15 preserved it from breakdown more than once and codified it in various treaties, the last being the so-called Holy Alliance pact of September 1815. It endured through the whole Vienna era, despite frequent tests, and even after being wrecked by the mid-century wars briefly resurfaced in the form of Three Emperors' League and the Three Emperors Alliance.

It is hard to overstate, moreover, how important this mutually restraining alliance was not only for the three Eastern Powers, but for Europe as a whole. Without it one cannot explain the most central, surprising, and widely overlooked fact in modern European international history before 1914: the long peace that generally reigned between the Eastern Powers from 1763 to 1914. Throughout those 150 years three great military monarchies stood face to face with each other within the same vital, closely packed, contested space. All had authoritarian governments whose polities ranged from semi-absolutist to fully autocratic, in which monarchs always made the ultimate decisions over peace and war. Each had long fortified frontiers with both of the others, with large standing armies stationed on these frontiers. Each had serious, longstanding territorial and other disagreements and differences with both of the others; each recurrently faced crises and dangers of war with one or both of the others. Yet only once in all that time did real war break out among them, between Austria and Prussia in 1866, and then it was because Prussia's leader Bismarck had decided that his goals required one.

What this shows is that Aehrenthal's idea of restoring the Three Emperors' League as an alliance of mutual restraint and management was not a quixotic, reactionary notion from a bygone absolutist era, rendered obsolete and irrelevant by the nationalist, imperialist, and populist-revolutionary currents of the time. Nor was it primarily a device to help Austria ward off its internal nationalities problems and crises. It was an up-to-date idea, embodied in the current actual policy Austria and Russia pursued with German approval especially in the Balkans, where it was sought and used by Russia to keep the volatile Macedonian Question under control so that Russia could concentrate on its quest for empire in the Far East. It paid off handsomely for Russia in that arena, until Russia's reckless Far Eastern policy got it into a war with Japan leading to a disastrous defeat and to revolution at home—making it even more invaluable. In simple, hard fact, Austrian and German assurances of benevolent neutrality in the war, which they concretely affirmed during the Tsarist regime's worst perils, saved it from collapse in 1904–5. The only way the regime could hold out in 1905 against the pressure from revolutionary parties and nationalist forces for the overthrow of autocracy was to use the Russian army to crush the revolution, and the only way the premier Count Witte could persuade its generals to abandon their prime duty of defending Russia's frontiers for the distasteful and ugly task of pacifying and policing the countryside was to assure them that they could count on German and Austrian benevolent neutrality.

This is, I emphasize, not at all an argument that a real opportunity arose in the early 1900s for a change of course that might have prevented Russia and Austria from sliding back toward confrontation and war in the Balkans, and that the unnecessary crisis over Bosnia ruined it. I contend that in reality no genuine chance to promote a durable peace was lost in 1908–9. The crisis shows instead why a useful proposal for doing something concrete in this direction had no real chance to be realized under the prevailing system. Aehrenthal's hope of reviving the Three Emperors' Alliance was without doubt unrealistic—not, however, because the idea was reactionary, obsolete and unworkable, but because there was no real room or audience for it in Russia, for that matter, elsewhere in Europe—France, Britain, Italy, even in some respects Germany.

This interpretation finds solid ground in numerous actions and attitudes of Russia and the other powers in 1908–9 and after. One can start with Izvolski's strategy and tactics. In proposing the deal, he expressly planned first to gain a payment from Austria for Russia's consent to the annexation (a consent, his subordinate Charykov reminded him, Russia had already given twice by treaty) and then after Russia's payoff had been secured through international approval of the change in the status of the Straits at an international conference, to withhold Russia's approval of the annexation and seek further Austrian concessions to Serbia. This scheme, too clever by half, quickly came apart following the meeting at Buchlau when the French and British made it clear to Izvolski that they would not agree in advance to the Straits provision. Then the Russian government itself repudiated any deal with Austria because it would offend Russian public opinion and damage Russia's reputation in the Balkan and Slavic world—a price too high to pay for improving Austro-Russian relations; the desired change in the status of the Straits could wait till later. When Tsar Nicholas, as usual, folded in the face of this pressure and left Izvolski dangling, Izvolski tried to save himself by blaming everything on Aehrenthal for deliberately deceiving him.

All this should cause no surprise; it illustrates the general character and rules of the system and, more importantly, the relative value Russia placed on a good working relationship with Austria even in its dangerously weak position in 1908. Historians regularly describe how two groups in prewar Russian politics, one pro-Western and one pro-German, contended for control of Russian foreign policy, with the former gaining ground. The virtual absence of any pro-Austrian sentiment at all gets little notice. This disdain, at this time at least, was onesided. Even after the Bosnian Crisis, almost to the eve of the assassination in 1914, the Austrian government at the top—Aehrenthal until his death in early 1911 and after him his successor Berchtold, Franz Joseph, and Franz Ferdinand—continued to try for Russian cooperation in bringing the increasingly dangerous Balkan situation under control. Russia made no similar effort even before the Bosnian Crisis, and hardened its attitude thereafter. Basically Russia did not consider Austria a great power or equal partner, and probably had not done so since the Crimean War. Though on occasion, as in 1900–6, Austria might serve as a useful tool, it was in Russian eyes a decaying corrupt state, slippery and treacherous but not formidable, a Catholic power ruling over Orthodox believers who should enjoy Russian protection, and an illegitimate competitor with Russia for influence in the Slavic world. If the Austrians wanted to survive in peace, they needed to stay out of Russia's sphere and path. If Germany wanted Russian friendship and cooperation, it needed to keep Austria in line. If Germany did so, then when the Habsburg Monarchy collapsed and dissolved, as the Tsar and many leading Russians expected it to do, Germany might join Russia in dividing the spoils, with Russia taking the lead and the larger share.

This general attitude toward the Monarchy was far from being uniquely Russian. Anti-Austrian attitudes among Serbians and Romanian and Italian nationalists can be taken for granted. Those of the other great powers in the crisis and afterwards, though not directly hostile, reveal a collective mentality of indifference—"not our problem—what's in it for us?" French opposition to the Russo-Austrian deal in 1908 was predictable— the government did not want to get involved in a Balkan question, was already encountering problems with Germany over France's creeping violations of the Treaty of Algeciras in 1906, and did not mind paying Russia back for its failure to support France in 1904–5 in the first Moroccan Crisis. Britain's opposition to the Bosnian deal, more direct and passive-aggressive in nature, is also easy to understand. The British wanted to prevent a closer Austro-Russian-German rapprochement, protecting thereby its own recent rapprochement with Russia obtained by dividing Persia with Russia into spheres of influence in 1907, to the exclusion of Germany. Italy was opposed to any Austro-Russian rapprochement for obvious strategic, political, and nationalist reasons.

One should nonetheless, without righteous indignation about it, note the measure of inconsistency, hypocrisy, and double standards involved in this, most plainly in the widespread denunciation of Austria-Hungary, above all in Britain and persisting in the historical literature, for violating the Treaty of Berlin by annexing Bosnia and thereby undermining the rule of law in international affairs. That treaty, already thirty years old, had been conceived from the outset as a provisional modus vivendi arrangement for preventing more war and as subject to revision by the powers over time. The provision authorizing Austria-Hungary to occupy and administer Bosnia-Herzegovina indefinitely militarily and administratively (a provision both supported and formally proposed by Britain's foreign secretary Lord Salisbury), was a major example of this. Austria-Hungary could have annexed the province without international resistance even by Russia at that time or various times thereafter; internal politics in the Monarchy kept it from doing so. The Sultan's sovereignty in Bosnia as in other parts of his empire (e.g., Egypt, occupied and governed by Britain with far greater international illegality from 1882 on) was a legal fiction and dead letter even before the Serbian revolt rendered genuine Ottoman rule unthinkable. Since 1878 direct rule by the Monarchy, sovereign in everything but name, had transformed the provinces politically and economically, above all by state-sponsored industrialization. The Berlin Treaty in general, moreover, had over the years repeatedly been violated, revised, and overthrown in other central provisions (e.g., the division of Bulgaria), for good reasons and bad, mainly by Britain's and Russia's doing. As noted, Russia had twice given its consent in earlier treaties with Austria and Germany to annexation—the very treaty violation Austria was now charged with. The change made no practical difference in the existing territorial order or the balance of power and was regarded in Europe as bound to happen sooner or later. The accusation of treaty violation, finally, was levelled at the height of an era of high imperialism in which every major power and a good many smaller ones, with Britain, Russia, France, Italy, the USA, and Japan in the lead, had repeatedly (including that very moment) been guilty of flagrantly, almost routinely, disregarding and breaking international treaties. Under these circumstances, one can be pardoned for noting that the judgment against Austria-Hungary for undermining the rule of international law smacks of straining at gnats and swallowing camels, of seeing the moat in others' eyes and not the beam in one's own, or of campfire-blackened pots calling a relatively shiny kettle black.

There is no point in high dudgeon about this. Hypocrisy and double standards are commonplace and to a considerable degree inevitable in international relations. At some point, however, they become significant, have implications for peace and stability in the international system. Whether the current judgment of this crisis is fair to Austria-Hungary is not very important; what its outcome did to the prospects for sustainable peace between Russia and Austria, and therefore of Europe in general, is. It quickly became clear that Austria-Hungary was the real loser, and the chances for durable peace never recovered from its failure. Russia immediately launched its diplomatic campaign to isolate and paralyze Austria in the Balkans. It was welcomed and eagerly exploited by the Balkan states for their own purposes, and quickly escaped Russia's control. From 1910 on France and Italy actively supported the Russian campaign for their particular ends, while Britain as *tertius gaudens* accepted and endorsed it. Even Germany, intent on its own separate, ultimately futile effort to court Russia, did not actively oppose Russia's anti-Austrian diplomatic campaign, but mainly tried instead to restrain Austria-Hungary and urge it to get along with Serbia, while itself competing successfully against Austrian trade in the region.

Again, as always, this can readily be explained, even defended, in terms of the prevailing rules of the game and of the reigning ideologies, national sentiments and ambitions, and particular state interests involved. It ought to be recognized, however, as an element of a major tectonic shift in a vital aspect of the European system. For centuries it had been widely assumed that the Habsburg Monarchy was an indispensable element in the European balance of power, meaning that it filled crucial European functions in its region as nothing else could do. This was at bottom not a product of feeling or sentiment, but a realistic calculation with serious implications. The history of early modern Europe up to the Napoleonic Wars and beyond gives abundant evidence of a sentiment or attitude I term "negative Austrophilia." It refers to stances, policies and actions taken by various governments and leaders at different times who, though they had no high regard for Austria, were even its rivals, and had motives and opportunities for destroying it or eliminating it as a serious opponent, nonetheless shrank from exploiting these opportunities to do so, sometimes for obvious immediate reasons but often also because they did not know what could replace it and fulfill its functions, or how the European system could work without it. This negative Austrophilia became strikingly evident in the Revolutionary-Napoleonic period. Napoleon had several chances to dispose of Austria, breaking it up or replacing the Habsburg dynasty, but never chose to exploit them, not out of carefully calculated reasons of state and certainly not out of any sympathy for the Monarchy, for which he had a certain contempt, but because he never knew what he could put in its place more useful for his aims, whatever those happened to be. This same spirit of negative Austrophilia carried over into the Vienna era. One can argue, as does F. R. Bridge, that this was carried too far in the Vienna treaties and system. Austria ended up burdened with more systemic responsibilities than it could safely bear or than its rulers really wanted, e.g., the territorial possession and defense of Lombardy and the responsibility for defending the Papal State. (The Austrians did firmly reject one responsibility that Britain and the United Provinces had imposed on it in the eighteenth century, the defense of the Low Countries against France.)

This sentiment of negative Austrophilia declined under the assaults of nationalism, to be sure, and more direct challenges from the power-political ambitions of Cavour, Napoleon III, and Bismarck. Yet negative Austrophilia in certain forms survived despite Austria's defeats, losses, and widespread unpopularity at that time. Bismarck, much as he disliked and distrusted Austria and was determined to get it out of Prussia's way, firmly opposed destroying or unnecessarily humiliating it in 1866 and always tried thereafter to preserve the Monarchy and use it for his purposes. This German attitude toward the Monarchy remained much the same after his fall. From the 1860s into the 1890s the British, the French, the Italians, and even the Russians also, all at different times in various self-interested ways, demonstrated a belief that Austria, even if it was a rival or a nuisance, remained an indispensable element in the balance of power. The Serbian government, so long as the Obrenović dynasty ruled, leaned on it for protection.

The Bosnian Crisis proves that this spirit of negative Austrophilia was dead and could not be resuscitated. The main question about Austria in European politics no longer concerned what it was actually doing in international politics or how this fit into diverging concepts of its proper role and function in the European system. It was now more a question of whether it would survive or collapse from its internal problems and external challenges and threats, as the Ottoman and Spanish empires, also once considered important elements in the European balance, had already done and/or were currently doing. In the meantime, the concern of other powers became simply how to use the Monarchy to their particular advantage in the zero-sum competitive balance-of-power game of the era. The rest was not their problem.

To repeat tiresomely: given the character of the game by that time, this attitude ought to surprise no one. It ought to strike international historians, however, how little serious European attention, recognition, and discussion at the highest diplomatic and governmental levels focused on what the potential consequences of the Monarchy's dissolution would be, what it might cause and entail, and the almost complete absence of serious proposals for controlling unanticipated and unintended consequences. That historically significant change needs attention and explanation, perhaps again by "eyes wide shut."

[Possible footnote material in the book on examples of this: Germany, eager for a rapprochement with Russia before the war, proposed that the two powers secretly agree to neutralize the

Monarchy and guarantee its territorial integrity á la Switzerland or Belgium to minimize possibly dangerous effects from its dissolution. The Russian response was one of the most decisive and insulting possible in diplomacy—one of *non avenu*, no response or formal acknowledgment at all, as if the proposal had never been made. The insulting character was probably a reply to Germany's so-called ultimatum in 1909, and the Russians, harboring important territorial ambitions vis-à-vis the Monarchy, saw no interest in preventing its dissolution. It is further striking evidence, however, of how leading Russians at the time saw no serious problem in the breakup of the Monarchy, either for Russia itself, or the region, or Europe in general.

That Pan-Slavs and Russian nationalists, to say nothing of revolutionaries, should feel this way is understandable; that a similar myopia affected even one of Russia's most intelligent and liberal leaders, Pavel Miliukov, leader of the Kadet (Constitutional Democratic) party in the Russian Duma, the only party that favored real electoral and political reform in Russia and opposed the regime's policies of repression, Russification, and force against restive nationalities. In a major speech in the Duma in 1912 dealing with the nationalities question in Russia, Austria, and the Balkans generally, Miliukov praised the Austrian government's attempts to manage the Monarchy's nationalities problems through electoral reform and cultural autonomy, holding them up as a model for Russia to follow. But he expressly reassured his fellow Duma members that any success Austria might enjoy in revitalizing itself internally by these reforms would not hinder the growth of Russia's power and influence in the region or interfere with Russia's foreign policy goals, for even if Austria succeeded in its efforts at managing its internal problems better, this would only make it less united and strong for purposes of foreign policy and defense and encourage the various Slavic nationalities to look to Russia for support for their particular interests within the Monarchy. In short, "Whether Austria wins or loses its struggle to survive through reform, we win." Such sentiments, to be found in Italy, France, and Britain as well, had the effect of encouraging the opponents of internal reform and foreign policy restraint within the Monarchy, including unsavory ones—right radicals, anti-Semites, Pan-Germans, Hungarian nationalists, and military proponents of preventive war—to push for a harder line internally and in foreign policy.]

The demise of negative Austrophilia figured not only in the origins of the war but once the war began grew into the goal of destroying it. This assertion is controversial, of course. Much of the reigning historiography, especially the Anglophone part, conventionally portrays Austria-Hungary's demise as, like those of other empires—Russia, Germany, the Ottoman Empire—simply a result of the lost war, brought on in Austria's case above all by its own weaknesses and inept performance, subservience to Germany, and reckless folly in having started it. No doubt this verdict is true enough, but not the whole story. The other side is that the war was fought to destroy Austria-Hungary. For Serbia, Romania, and Italy this was a prime, central war aim throughout—for Italy and Romania, whose military performance in it was much more ineffective than the Monarchy's, the only one pursued with conviction and skill. As for the Allied great powers, the idea that they only accepted the destruction of the Monarchy as a necessary corollary of the effort to defeat Germany and eliminate the German threat to Europe cannot be defended. In Russia's case this is obvious. Russia, in first negotiating and then renewing its alliance with France, had steadily insisted against French opposition on making the Monarchy its prime military target, and well before 1914 Russians expected and intended that the military defeat would break up the Monarchy, leaving Russia to control Eastern Europe as well as the Balkans and to annex all of Galicia as its share of the territorial spoils. As for France and Britain, every wartime treaty signed between themselves and Russia either endorsed this outcome or took it for granted and every treaty they negotiated with other powers included chunks of Austrian and Ottoman territory to pay them to enter the war. Allied military strategy was no different. Both French and British strategists had hopes and plans at various times to avoid the stalemate and carnage of the Western Front and win the war by going through the supposed soft underbelly of Austria-Hungary (the Straits expedition, for example, was intended to pave the way for this). When these efforts proved counterproductive, as Russia's finally did on the Eastern Front, and when the collapse of the Russian war effort loomed in 1916, some British, especially the premier David Lloyd-George, turned to schemes for "saving" Austria-Hungary as a useful element in a new balance of power by getting it to switch sides and join the fight against Germany— a scheme unmatched for *légèreté* even by some of the strategies the British tried on the continent against France in 1793–1807 or against Russia in the Crimean War.

All this must sound like propaganda, the product of nostalgia, casting the villain of the piece as the victim. I do not think so, or detect any historical bias for or against the Monarchy in myself or in the argument offered here, revisionist though it certainly is. My basic attitude toward the Monarchy in this era (if anyone cares, and no one needs to) is precisely that of negative Austrophilia: a mixture of praise, criticism, and wavering judgment on Austrian foreign and domestic policy before, during, and after the war, paired with conviction on one blindingly obvious point: the existing European international system could not continue to function at all, much less be useful for durable general peace, were the Monarchy to be destroyed by war or collapse internally, barring the extremely unlikely development of serious collective European action to control the inevitable unintended consequences and avert the probable dangers, chaos, and catastrophe. True, no one could predict the exact results of the disappearance of the Monarchy, but the likely main outcomes could have been foreseen: either an unstable hegemonic partnership between Russia and Germany to divide the spoils, control Central and Eastern Europe in partnership, and dominate the rest; or, more probably, an all-out struggle between Germany and Russia for mastery on the continent; or, if by some unlikely turn of events both of these powers suffered defeat, a general chaotic struggle among the surviving smaller contenders for territory and advantage in the region that could not be controlled by the remaining major powers in the West. All these ugly scenarios emerged clearly as possibilities during World War I itself; all were realized in terrible form after it, in the interwar era, and in World War II.

Even if accepted, this view might seem once again to offer proof that World War I was really a modern war rather than an eighteenth-century one—the suggestion that this allegedly critical shift in European collective mentality, the disappearance of negative Austrophilia (and coincidentally the rise of negative

Russophilia) was a natural result of late nineteenth- and early twentieth-century global and societal changes and trends—globalization, economic growth and transformation, imperialism, ideological conflicts, racism and identity politics, democratization and the beginnings of mass politics, and above all the struggle for international world power and position.

As usual, much of this is true, but such a change in outlook was not unique to the era before World War I. Analogous social, political, cultural, and economic developments in Europe and the world in the latter eighteenth century help account for analogous developments in the international system of that era, as I will try to show briefly in the book. They differed of course in dimension, were far broader and more pervasive in society in the latter; I will not suggest a neat jigsaw-puzzle fit between the two eras in societal development any more than in international politics and the international system. The central point remains, however, that the basic reasons for the origins of war, the central international issues at stake—power, position, and security in continental Europe—and the prevailing game and rules were not much different.

The same can be said about the general conduct of both great wars and the goals at which the parties aimed—but here a crucial difference emerged. As described earlier, the conduct, aims, and goals of the Allied powers engaged in the first war decisively changed after 1812. Those who fought World War I kept them essentially the same or intensified them, fighting on both sides to win decisive victory and eliminate any future threat from the enemy to the end and beyond. In that sense, and really only in that sense, was it a war to end wars. As always, there are qualifications to this generalization. Germany at certain points (late 1916 and mid-July 1917) proposed negotiated settlements on both fronts, though ones still favorable to itself; Austria-Hungary, exhausted and desperate, tried genuinely after October 1916 to end the war at almost any cost; the USA attempted to control the terms of peace itself, first as a neutral and then as a late entrant and associate on the Allied side, with only a limited political commitment to its allies; and the short-lived Revolutionary Defensist government in Russia under Tsereteli really wanted and sought a peace without annexations in 1917. But none of these efforts or any of the plans and pleas from neutrals or individuals and groups in the Allied camp stopped France, Britain, Italy, and Tsarist Russia and Russia's first post-revolutionary government from seeking final victory and all-out war goals to the end, or deterred the Bolsheviks once they were victorious in Russia's civil war from continuing to fight for their version of revolutionary victory. Nor were the new countries of Eastern and Southeastern Europe—Poland, the Baltic states and Finland, Romania, so-called Yugoslavia, Greece, and even Czechoslovakia, really different. The decisive difference between this war and the eighteenth-century great war is that the latter was deliberately brought to an end, by mutual consent, almost everywhere and at once, with the victorious side negotiating peace terms well short of final victory in the interest of a durable consensus settlement.

I do not suggest that this was possible in 1914–18 or should necessarily have been done, though one might argue it should have been more seriously considered and attempted during the war. Unquestionably the circumstances were vastly different and more unfavorable in 1914–19 than in 1787–1815—the war, though shorter in time, was far more intense and destructive and left behind a much greater tsunami tide of hatred and revenge. One can say paradoxically about World War I that for the purpose of achieving durable peace it was too short, considering that it was so long—unbearably long and terrible in the human, psychic, material, and spiritual damage caused, too short for the longer implications and consequences of these to be absorbed and the necessary consensus on remedies and action achieved. I agree with the general verdict that a peace like that of 1814–15 was impossible in 1919, and that the Versailles treaty, though far from satisfactory, was about as good as one could hope for, much better and more defensible than the other four treaties of the Peace of Paris. All this reinforces the unique character of the Vienna system.

One can apply the analogy as well to the origins and final outbreak of both wars. I earlier raised the question in the pre–World War I era, whether any important actors made serious proposals or put forward strategies for long-term durable management of the growing general European crisis rather than seeking temporary fixes and/or individual gains, and if anyone did, why these efforts failed. If one asks the same question about the period before 1792–3, one finds similar evidence for the same answer down to some striking details. Omitting some earlier ideas here that may be discussed in the book, one major example should be mentioned. This was a proposal prior to the outbreak of general war in 1792 for preventing a general conflict from breaking out as a result of the revolutionary and international crises developing concurrently in Western Europe (France, the Low Countries, Germany, and Italy), Eastern Europe, especially Poland, and in the Balkans, all of them with roots in and connections to the revolutions in France and Poland and the Russo-Austrian war against the Ottoman Empire. In short, a strategy for keeping a set of dangerous brush fires from turning into a raging forest fire. This plan also came from Austria, specifically from Emperor Leopold II (1790–2). Its central proposition was that Austria, Russia, and Prussia should join in recognizing and supporting the moderate constitutional monarchies newly established in Poland and France and under pressure there from radical revolutionary and reactionary forces at home as well as foreign threats. Leopold argued that this would inherently benefit the three Eastern Powers themselves in terms of security and foreign policy, because constitutional governments would weaken these countries internally for military purposes and therefore incline them to be more manageable, stable, and peaceful, and would promote general peace and stability because the three Eastern Powers by working together vis-à-vis France and Poland could not only help both states restrain radical forces at home and in other parts of Europe but also better enable the three Eastern Powers to manage their own differences at home and abroad. The similarities in concept and purpose between this approach to peace and style of crisis management and those of the Allies generally, especially the Holy Alliance, from 1813 to 1848, and of the Austrian peace party in the early twentieth century are unmistakeable.

So also, unfortunately, are the reasons why this plan had no serious chance of being adopted in 1790–2 and why some very good historians have judged Leopold's ideas impractical and unrealistic, as others have judged Aehrenthal's scheme was a century later. The prime reason was not that the proposals were inherently Utopian, but that no serious partners were available for them—as little in the Europe of Catherine II's Russia, Friedrich Wilhelm II's Prussia, the Britain of the younger Pitt, Dundas, and Grenville, a France already revolutionized and split between radical republicans, beleaguered monarchists and diehard emigrés as in Europe before 1914. Every one of these regimes preferred to exploit these crises for competitive advantage even at the grave risk of heightening the danger of general war, while smaller players (principalities and smaller states in Germany and Italy, the French emigrés, factions in Poland) joined in or urged them on for their own reasons. Finally Austria itself under a new, inexperienced and mediocre emperor led the plunge into war. One can almost say of 1792, "1914 *avant la lettre*."

This is as far as I have currently decided to take the main body of my argument and interpretation. Other questions and challenges with significant implications may be addressed, but only to the extent that they do not distract from its main goals and purpose.

Conclusion: So what?

This is the serious question that must be addressed: Even if my whole argument more or less holds up, why should anyone today care—historians, other scholars, leaders, policymakers, or ordinary citizens, especially Americans? What practical meaning and importance can it have, what difference would it make for leaders and people in today's world so vastly different from that of the early twentieth century, to say nothing of the early nineteenth? History books written *ars gratia artis* need not face this question, but only try to add to the general store of historical knowledge. This one claims to show that history can be a teacher of life. At my stage in life there are no other career, academic, or other purposes for trying to write it; if it does not say something worth thinking about in the current world situation, it is not worth doing.

That fact poses an additional challenge in terms of knowledge. Any attempt to answer it takes me beyond the area of historical scholarship where I can claim some authority into ones where I think I know enough to be entitled to an opinion but cannot claim expertise, and from a well-known past into an uncertain present and unknown, mostly unpredictable future. It means further showing the book's relevance to today's world of international politics in specific terms, indicating how it might contribute concretely to thinking about current situations and responding to them more appropriately.

Now to the point: the "So what? Why should it matter today?" question to each of the main propositions I have asserted in this outline and propose to develop further in the book.

1. Both World War I and the Great War of 1787–1815 arose fundamentally from similar tides of reckless international conduct spurred on by the prevalence of "eyes wide shut" attitudes and actions in foreign policy, products of an international system that penalized restraint and incentivized the exploitation of opportunities for gain and competitive advantage in a zerosum balance-of-power game.

2. The Vienna system, while recognizing an unavoidable major element of competition and conflict in international affairs, was designed to restrain, manage, and limit that conflict to preserve general peace and stability in the international community. In this it represented something new and different—a breakthrough, an advance, major progress in international politics.

3. This system, though it depended for its development to a considerable degree on favorable circumstances and individual contingent events and decisions, nonetheless grew out of collective historical learning—a recognition by various actors derived from hard experience that they were willy-nilly connected in an international community and that to survive and live tolerably in it they had to do things differently—recognize certain rules, adopt other practices, develop new and better institutions, and respect needed norms, limits, and responsibilities.

4. The gradual decline and breakdown of the Vienna system and return to an eighteenth-century-style of Realpolitik from the mid-nineteenth century on, concurrent with, and to an extent caused by, rapid deep developments and general changes in Europe and much of the rest of the world, ultimately culminated in a much greater and more destructive general war in World War I. At the same time, the fact that important elements of the Vienna system survived for a long time, along with the

efforts of certain actors at various times to sustain and revive them, helps explain the prolonged avoidance and postponement of the war.

I will not try here to give any detailed answers on how and why each of these four main theses apply to current international politics and international system questions and issues, or to explore important implications and lessons for them as examples not of blueprints or paradigms to follow, but as analogies and perspectives to learn from. There are too many, some of them complex and controversial. That discussion has to wait for the proposed book. All I will offer here is some general idea and some samples of such insights potentially useful for various groups including ordinary citizens to consider, and some indication of why I think it important especially for Americans to pay attention.

All the four points above, especially 2 and 3, could serve to widen and sharpen our sense of the real possibilities and limits of what can work in international politics. A major obstacle today to thinking seriously about forming an effective international community capable of the self-restraint and cooperation needed to limit and manage international conflict is an almost automatic assumption that the idea is inherently Utopian, naïve, and unrealistic, especially in an age of ever-changing actors of different varieties, multiple threats, means and modes of conflict and warfare, and motives and drives behind them. One reply among others to this objection is that this has happened—this project of fashioning an international security community has actually been tried and to a surprising degree accomplished at least once in a not remote past, in the face of analogous fears, doubts, and skepticism. Nor has this been a one-time effort confined to a vanished past. There are further examples in recent times of the development of a useful international security community—NATO, the European Union, and to some degree the UN. The task has always been difficult and vulnerable, but not impossible. (What George Bernard Shaw, not a believer, said about Christianity—that it had not been tried and found wanting, but found difficult and not tried—applies historically to this task, except for some notable exceptions.)

The converse also applies in regard to (1) and (4) in particular: what happens when this possibility is ignored or overturned and Realpolitik is assumed to be the only sane way of conducting international politics. There are plenty of examples of this in more recent twentieth- and twenty-first-century politics with similar results—e.g., ignoring the opportunity to expand the European Union to include Russia or form links with it after the downfall of the USSR, in favor of expanding NATO to the borders of a shrunken, chaotic, and humiliated Russia, or the decision to invade Iraq. One might argue further that the most striking examples in the last seventy years of both positive success and/or the avoidance of disaster in Western policy have come over time precisely from avoiding the sorts of policies and actions flowing too often from unalloyed Realpolitik. America's and the West's long-term successes, often unpredicted and unexpected, have instead come from recognizing limits, not trying for the impossible, accepting drawn conflicts (Korea, the Cuban missile crisis), defeat (Vietnam and the two-China policy), and coexistence (the Helsinki Accords, legitimacy of the Soviet bloc, and a nuclear stalemate with the USSR). One might predict now (I certainly would) that the current change of the USA's stance and policy toward Cuba, involving the tacit admission that the old one was not working and could not succeed, will ultimately produce good results, though not in the way and of the kind some might like.

In particular reference to theses 2 and 3, important pundits today (e.g., Fareed Zakaria and Thomas Friedman) expressly call for building just such an international system intentionally designed to limit, control, and manage competition and conflict and thereby promote cooperation and overall peace and stability. So do some highly respected political scientists (e.g., Robert Jervis and Richard Rosecrance) and plenty of historians and theorists of various schools—constructivists, liberal internationalists, the so-called English School—who do not consider this an impractical dream.

Thesis 3 emphasizes that the breakthrough achieved in the Vienna system was the fruit of collective learning based on long hard experience of war and revolution and the conviction that no other course to overcome ongoing disasters and durably avoid similar ones was viable—in short, that there was no virtue like necessity, and no necessity like the virtue of recognizing it. To see how relevant this observation is today, one need only see the obvious, an elephant in the room still widely denied or ignored in many quarters for lesser concerns—the war of climate change that the world has long been waging against nature itself. In that war, now rapidly approaching a critical stage, victory as normally defined is inconceivable. The only tolerable long-range outcome, i.e., a stable worldwide truce and coexistence with its forces or at least a slow, manageable retreat from the battle, cannot be conceived, much less achieved, without the development of a better, more comprehensive, and more durable international system expressly designed for purposes of limiting, controlling, and managing international competition and conflict in this global arena, and thereby enabling, incentivizing, promoting, and where necessary compelling the kinds of cooperation necessary to prevent the looming disasters. This danger and task trumps all others; recognizing and facing it internationally could conceivably promote the sense of necessity and the moral imperative required to develop it.

The obvious difficulties and obstacles are huge, of course—enough to make some look to Utopian solutions like extraterritorial colonization and to suggest to very many that the idea of seeing any kind of example or lesson in history from two centuries ago is absurd. That world has disappeared; too much has changed; this one and the one to come are far more complicated, diverse, and unmanageable. True enough; this is one reason for grim determination and realism in the task—but not for pessimism and surrender. My argument on this point will merely be to point out that while the task of establishing a different kind of international system for durable peace is very different from that faced by Europe in 1812, far more complex and in some ways demanding, so that no one can suggest the Vienna system as any kind of model or blueprint, this does not make the task necessarily less possible given the necessary resolve, intelligence, and reasonably favorable conditions. It will further argue (or assert at least) that some of the necessary conditions are more favorable now than in 1812–15 (e.g., that the disutility of major war as a solution to international problems is far clearer, the threat of general war between the great powers far less immediate, the

extent of concrete conditions for peace and successful management of difficult international problems and needs such as the
regulation of business and commerce worldwide far more
impressive, along with similar developments show the actuality
and possibility of real progress in international affairs). What the
example of the Vienna system provides is only some analogies
and hints of what is needed and how to get to it, and how not to,
and some reason to believe that the task is possible—but that is
worth a good deal.

This leads me to the last item in this outline: the reasons why
Americans especially need to pay attention to this whole argument of the proposed book, and especially to the current need
for a new world order. I will say very little about this here. The
overall reason in a nutshell is the exceptionalism so deeply rooted
in America's history, institutions, and popular culture, especially
in its current debased and dangerous form, and the extraordinary
provincialism, self-preoccupation, and superficiality this entails
in world affairs. The phenomenon is widely discussed and usually
decried, but still not fully understood, particularly as it affects
American thought and practice in international politics. It justifies, I believe, the verdict that the USA among all major countries
is the most in need of confronting the problems discussed above,
for its own sake and everyone else's, but least disposed and
equipped by its history, self-image, basic outlook, and current
political institutions and habits to do so. If a book such as the
one I propose would make even a slight contribution toward
changing this, it would be worth doing.

Sources

CHAPTER

1. *Journal of Modern History*, September 1972: 319–45

2. T. C. W. Blanning, ed., *The Nineteenth Century: Europe 1789–1914*, Oxford, 2000: 158–209

3. *Systems, Stability, and Statecraft*, New York, 2004: 157–91

4. Holger Afflerbach and David Stevenson, eds., *An Improbable War?*, New York, 2007: 17–42

5. *Revue Roumaine d'Histoire*, 1975: 39–53

6. James W. Davis, ed., *Psychology, Strategy and Conflict*, London, 2013: 168–80

7. *Historian*, Fall 2000: 124–7

8. *International History Review*, March 2001: 3–27

9. Unpublished ms

Index